D1242608

CCNP ROUTE
Lab Manual
Version 7

Cisco Networking Academy

Cisco Press

800 East 96th Street

Indianapolis, Indiana 46240 USA

CCNP ROUTE Lab Manual Version 7
Cisco Networking Academy

Copyright© 2015 Cisco Systems, Inc.

Published by:
Cisco Press
800 East 96th Street
Indianapolis, IN 46240 USA

All rights reserved. No part of this book may be reproduced or transmitted in any form or by any means, electronic or mechanical, including photocopying, recording, or by any information storage and retrieval system, without written permission from the publisher, except for the inclusion of brief quotations in a review.

Printed in the United States of America

Second Printing   August 2015

Library of Congress Control Number: 2015932598

ISBN-13: 978-1-58713-402-9

ISBN-10: 1-58713-402-0

Warning and Disclaimer

This book is designed to provide information about networking. Every effort has been made to make this book as complete and as accurate as possible, but no warranty or fitness is implied.

The information is provided on an "as is" basis. The authors, Cisco Press, and Cisco Systems, Inc. shall have neither liability nor responsibility to any person or entity with respect to any loss or damages arising from the information contained in this book or from the use of the discs or programs that may accompany it.

The opinions expressed in this book belong to the author and are not necessarily those of Cisco Systems, Inc.

Trademark Acknowledgments

All terms mentioned in this book that are known to be trademarks or service marks have been appropriately capitalized. Cisco Press or Cisco Systems, Inc., cannot attest to the accuracy of this information. Use of a term in this book should not be regarded as affecting the validity of any trademark or service mark.

This book is part of the Cisco Networking Academy" series from Cisco Press. The products in this series support and complement the Cisco Networking Academy curriculum. If you are using this book outside the Networking Academy, theo you are not preparing with a Cisco trained and authorized Networking Academy provider.

CISCO

For more information on the Cisco Networking Academy or to locate a Networking Academy, please visit www.cisoo.com/edu.

Feedback Information

At Cisco Press, our goal is to create in-depth technical books of the highest quality and value. Each book is crafted with care and precision, undergoing rigorous development that involves the unique expertise of members from the professional technical community.

Readers' feedback is a natural continuation of this process. If you have any comments regarding how we could improve the quality of this book, or otherwise alter it to better suit your needs, you can contact us through email at feedback@ciscopress.com. Please make sure to include the book title and ISBN in your message.

We greatly appreciate your assistance.

Publisher	Paul Boger
Associate Publisher	Dave Dusthimer
Business Operations Manager, Cisco Press	Jan Cornelssen
Executive Editor	Mary Beth Ray
Managing Editor	Sandra Schroeder
Editorial Assistant	Vanessa Evans
Cover Designer	Mark Shirar
Proofreader	Paula Lowell

Americas Headquarters	Asia Pacific Headquarters	Europe Headquarters
Cisco Systems, Inc.	Cisco Systems (USA) Pte. Ltd.	Cisco Systems International BV
San Jose, CA	Singapore	Amsterdam, The Netherlands

Cisco has more than 200 offices worldwide. Addresses, phone numbers, and fax numbers are listed on the Cisco Website at **www.cisco.com/go/offices.**

CCDE, CCENT, Cisco Eos, Cisco HealthPresence, the Cisco logo, Cisco Lumin, Cisco Nexus, Cisco StadiumVision, Cisco TelePresence, Cisco WebEx, DCE, and Welcome to the Human Network are trademarks; Changing the Way We Work, Live, Play, and Learn and Cisco Store are service marks; and Access Registrar, Aironet, AsyncOS, Bringing the Meeting To You, Catalyst, CCDA, CCDP, CCIE, CCIP, CCNA, CCNP, CCSP, CCVP, Cisco, the Cisco Certified Internetwork Expert logo, Cisco IOS, Cisco Press, Cisco Systems, Cisco Systems Capital, the Cisco Systems logo, Cisco Unity, Collaboration Without Limitation, EtherFast, EtherSwitch, Event Center, Fast Step, Follow Me Browsing, FormShare, GigaDrive, HomeLink, Internet Quotient, IOS, iPhone, iQuick Study, IronPort, the IronPort logo, LightStream, Linksys, MediaTone, MeetingPlace, MeetingPlace Chime Sound, MGX, Networkers, Networking Academy, Network Registrar, PCNow, PIX, PowerPanels, ProConnect, ScriptShare, SenderBase, SMARTnet, Spectrum Expert, StackWise, The Fastest Way to Increase Your Internet Quotient, TransPath, WebEx, and the WebEx logo are registered trademarks of Cisco Systems, Inc. and/or its affiliates in the United States and certain other countries.

All other trademarks mentioned in this document or website are the property of their respective owners. The use of the word partner does not imply a partnership relationship between Cisco and any other company. (0812R)

Contents

About This Lab Manual

This is the only authorized Lab Manual for the Cisco Networking Academy CCNP ROUTE version 7 course.

A CCNP Routing and Switching certification equips students with the knowledge and skills needed to plan, implement, secure, maintain, and troubleshoot converged enterprise networks. The CCNP Routing and Switching certification requires candidates to pass three 120-minute exams—ROUTE 300-101, SWITCH 300-115, TSHOOT 300-135—that validate the key competencies of network engineers.

The Cisco Networking CCNP Routing and Switching consists of three experience-oriented courses that employ industry-relevant instructional approaches to prepare students for professional-level jobs: CCNP ROUTE: Implementing IP Routing, CCNP SWITCH: Implementing IP Switching, and CCNP TSHOOT: Maintaining and Troubleshooting IP Networks.

CCNP ROUTE: Implementing IP Routing

This course teaches students how to implement, monitor, and maintain routing services in an enterprise network. Students will learn how to plan, configure, and verify the implementation of complex enterprise LAN and WAN routing solutions, using a range of routing protocols in IPv4 and IPv6 environments. The course also covers the configuration of secure routing solutions to support branch offices and mobile workers.

The 21 comprehensive labs in this manual emphasize hands-on learning and practice to reinforce configuration skills.

Command Syntax Conventions

The conventions used to present command syntax in this book are the same conventions used in the IOS Command Reference. The Command Reference describes these conventions as follows:

- **Boldface** indicates commands and keywords that are entered literally as shown. In actual configuration examples and output (not general command syntax), boldface indicates commands that are manually input by the user (such as a show command).
- *Italic* indicates arguments for which you supply actual values.
- Vertical bars (|) separate alternative, mutually exclusive elements.
- Square brackets ([ ]) indicate an optional element.
- Braces ({ }) indicate a required choice.
- Braces within brackets ([{ }]) indicate a required choice within an optional element.

Chapter 1: Basic Network and Routing Concepts

Lab 1-1 Basic RIPng and Default Gateway Configuration

Topology

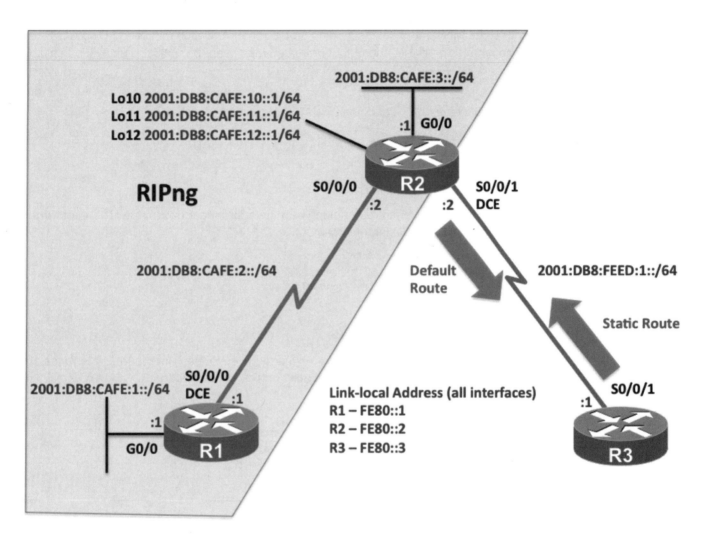

Objectives

- Configure IPv6 addressing.
- Configure and verify RIPng on R1 and R2.
- Configure IPv6 static routes between R2 and R3.
- Propagate a default route using RIPng.
- Examine the RIP process and RIP database.

Background

In this lab you will be configuring a new network to connect a company's Engineering, Marketing, and Accounting departments using IPv6 and RIPng on two routers. You will also be configuring IPv6 static routing between the company's gateway router (R2) and an ISP (R3). The gateway router will propagate the IPv6 default route via RIPng. Your task is to configure RIPng to enable full connectivity between all routers.

Note: This lab uses Cisco 1941 routers with Cisco IOS Release 15.4 with IP Base. The switches are Cisco WS-C2960-24TT-L with Fast Ethernet interfaces; therefore, the router will use routing metrics associated with a 100 Mb/s interface. Depending on the router or switch model and Cisco IOS Software version, the commands available and output produced might vary from what is shown in this lab.

Required Resources

- 3 routers (Cisco IOS Release 15.2 or comparable)
- 2 switches (LAN interfaces)
- Serial and Ethernet cables

Step 0: Suggested starting configurations.

a. Apply the following configuration to each router along with the appropriate **hostname**. The **exec-timeout 0 0** command should only be used in a lab environment.

```
Router(config)# no ip domain-lookup
Router(config)# line con 0
Router(config-line)# logging synchronous
Router(config-line)# exec-timeout 0 0
```

Step 1: Configure addressing and loopbacks.

a. Using the addressing scheme in the diagram, apply IPv6 addresses to the Fast Ethernet interfaces and serial interfaces R1, R2, and R3 . Then create Loopback1 on R1, Loopback2 on R2, and Loopback3 on R3 and address them according to the diagram.

```
R1(config)# interface GigabitEthernet 0/0
R1(config-if)# description Engineering Department
R1(config-if)# ipv6 address 2001:db8:cafe:1::1/64
R1(config-if)# ipv6 address fe80::1 link-local
R1(config-if)# no shutdown
R1(config-if)# exit
R1(config)# interface serial 0/0/0
R1(config-if)# description Serial link to R2
R1(config-if)# ipv6 address 2001:db8:cafe:2::1/64
R1(config-if)# ipv6 address fe80::1 link-local
R1(config-if)# clock rate 64000
R1(config-if)# no shutdown

R2(config)# interface GigabitEthernet 0/0
R2(config-if)# description Accounting Department
R2(config-if)# ipv6 address 2001:db8:cafe:3::1/64
R2(config-if)# ipv6 address fe80::2 link-local
R2(config-if)# no shutdown
R2(config-if)# exit
R2(config)# interface Loopback 10
R2(config-if)# description Marketing Department
```

```
R2(config-if)# ipv6 address 2001:db8:cafe:10::1/64
R2(config-if)# ipv6 address fe80::2 link-local
R2(config-if)# exit
R2(config)# interface Loopback 11
R2(config-if)# description Marketing Department
R2(config-if)# ipv6 address 2001:db8:cafe:11::1/64
R2(config-if)# ipv6 address fe80::2 link-local
R2(config-if)# exit
R2(config)# interface Loopback 12
R2(config-if)# description Marketing Department
R2(config-if)# ipv6 address 2001:db8:cafe:12::1/64
R2(config-if)# ipv6 address fe80::2 link-local
R2(config-if)# exit
R2(config)# interface Serial 0/0/0
R2(config-if)# description Serial link to R1
R2(config-if)# ipv6 address 2001:db8:cafe:2::2/64
R2(config-if)# ipv6 address fe80::2 link-local
R2(config-if)# no shutdown
R2(config-if)# exit
R2(config)# interface Serial 0/0/1
R2(config-if)# description Serial link to R3
R2(config-if)# ipv6 address 2001:db8:feed:1::2/64
R2(config-if)# ipv6 address fe80::2 link-local
R2(config-if)# clock rate 64000
R2(config-if)# no shutdown
R2(config-if)# exit

R3(config)# interface Serial 0/0/1
R3(config-if)# description Serial link to R2
R3(config-if)# ipv6 address 2001:db8:feed:1::1/64
R3(config-if)# ipv6 address fe80::3 link-local
R3(config-if)# no shutdown
```

Leave the switch in its default (blank) configuration. By default, all switch ports are in VLAN1 and are not administratively down.

Note: If the switch has been previously configured, erase the startup config, delete the vlan.dat file from flash memory, and reload the switch.

b. Verify that the line protocol of each interface is up and that you can successfully ping across each link. You should see output similar to the following on each router.

```
R2# show ipv6 interface brief
GigabitEthernet0/0      [up/up]
    FE80::2
    2001:DB8:CAFE:3::1
Serial0/0/0             [up/up]
    FE80::2
    2001:DB8:CAFE:2::2
Serial0/0/1             [up/up]
    FE80::2
    2001:DB8:FEED:1::2
Loopback10              [up/up]
    FE80::2
    2001:DB8:CAFE:10::1
Loopback11              [up/up]
    FE80::2
```

```
    2001:DB8:CAFE:11::1
Loopback12              [up/up]
    FE80::2
    2001:DB8:CAFE:12::1
R2#
```

Step 2: Configure RIPng on R1 and R2.

a. After you have implemented your addressing scheme, enable RIPng on R1 using the following
    commands in global configuration mode.

```
R1(config)# ipv6 router rip ROUTING-RIPng
% IPv6 routing not enabled
R1(config)# ipv6 unicast-routing
R1(config)# ipv6 router rip ROUTING-RIPng
R1(config-rtr)# exit
R1(config)# interface gigabitethernet 0/0
R1(config-if)# ipv6 rip ROUTING-RIPng enable
R1(config-if)# exit
R1(config)# interface serial 0/0/0
R1(config-if)# ipv6 rip ROUTING-RIPng enable
```

Notice that IPv6 routing must be enabled prior to configuring RIPng using the **ipv6 unicast-routing**
command. The network statement has been eliminated in RIPng. RIPng routing is enabled at the
interface level instead, and is identified by a locally significant process name as multiple processes can
be created with RIPng.

b. Configure RIPng on R2 using the following commands.

```
R2(config)# ipv6 unicast-routing
R2(config)# interface serial 0/0/0
R2(config-if)# ipv6 rip ROUTING-RIPng enable
R2(config-if)# exit
R2(config)# interface gigabitEthernet 0/0
R2(config-if)# ipv6 rip ROUTING-RIPng enable
R2(config-if)# exit
R2(config)# interface loopback 10
R2(config-if)# ipv6 rip ROUTING-RIPng enable
R2(config-if)# exit
R2(config)# interface loopback 11
R2(config-if)# ipv6 rip ROUTING-RIPng enable
R2(config-if)# exit
R2(config)# interface loopback 12
R2(config-if)# ipv6 rip ROUTING-RIPng enable
```

As shown on R2, the RIPng process can be configured on the interface without first configuring the RIPng
process in global configuration mode. The RIPng process will automatically be created if it doesn't
already exist.

Step 3: Verify the RIPng configuration.

a. Verify that the RIPng process is running on R2.

```
R2# show ipv6 protocols
IPv6 Routing Protocol is "connected"
IPv6 Routing Protocol is "application"
IPv6 Routing Protocol is "ND"
```

```
IPv6 Routing Protocol is "rip ROUTING-RIPng"
  Interfaces:
    Loopback12
    Loopback11
    Loopback10
    GigabitEthernet0/0
    Serial0/0/0
  Redistribution:
    None
R2#
```

Which interfaces are involved in the RIPng routing process on router R2?

_____

_____

Which active interface(s) are NOT involved in the RIPng routing process on router R2?

_____

_____

b. Use the **show ipv6 route** command to view R1's IPv6 routing table.

```
R1#show ipv6 route
IPv6 Routing Table - default - 9 entries
Codes: C - Connected, L - Local, S - Static, U - Per-user Static route
       B - BGP, R - RIP, I1 - ISIS L1, I2 - ISIS L2
       IA - ISIS interarea, IS - ISIS summary, D - EIGRP, EX - EIGRP external
       ND - ND Default, NDp - ND Prefix, DCE - Destination, NDr - Redirect
       O - OSPF Intra, OI - OSPF Inter, OE1 - OSPF ext 1, OE2 - OSPF ext 2
       ON1 - OSPF NSSA ext 1, ON2 - OSPF NSSA ext 2, a - Application
C   2001:DB8:CAFE:1::/64 [0/0]
     via GigabitEthernet0/0, directly connected
L   2001:DB8:CAFE:1::1/128 [0/0]
     via GigabitEthernet0/0, receive
C   2001:DB8:CAFE:2::/64 [0/0]
     via Serial0/0/0, directly connected
L   2001:DB8:CAFE:2::1/128 [0/0]
     via Serial0/0/0, receive
R   2001:DB8:CAFE:3::/64 [120/2]
     via FE80::2, Serial0/0/0
R   2001:DB8:CAFE:10::/64 [120/2]
     via FE80::2, Serial0/0/0
R   2001:DB8:CAFE:11::/64 [120/2]
     via FE80::2, Serial0/0/0
R   2001:DB8:CAFE:12::/64 [120/2]
     via FE80::2, Serial0/0/0
L   FF00::/8 [0/0]
     via Null0, receive
R1#
```

What is the next-hop address and the type of IPv6 address for the RIPng routes on R1?

_____

c. Ping the following remote addresses: 2001:db8:cafe:3::1, 2001:db8:cafe:10::1, and 2001:db8:feed:1::1.

Which pings were successful and which were not? If there were any pings that were unsuccessful, explain the reason why.

_____

_____

Step 4: Configure IPv6 static routing between R2 and R3.

a. Configure an IPv6 static route on R3 forwarding all packets for the 2001:DB8:CAFE::/48 prefix to R2.

```
R3(config)# ipv6 unicast-routing
R3(config)# ipv6 route 2001:db8:cafe::/48 2001:db8:feed:1::2
```

Note: The **ipv6 unicast-routing** command is required for a router to forward IPv6 packets; however, IPv6 static routes can be configured without this command and forwarding IPv6 packets will be successful. However, it is suggested to use the **ipv6 unicast-routing** command.

b. Configure an IPv6 default static route on R2, forwarding packets to R3. Propagate the default route to other RIPng routers in addition to other routes in R2's routing table.

```
R2(config)# ipv6 route ::/0 2001:db8:feed:1::1
```

Step 5: Propagate the default route along with other routes via RIPng and verify.

a. Propagate the default route to other RIPng routers in addition to other routes in R2's routing table.

```
R2(config)# interface serial 0/0/0
R2(config-if)# ipv6 rip ROUTING-RIPng default-information originate
```

The **originate** keyword propagates the default route in R2's routing table.

b. Display the RIPng routes in R1's IPv6 routing table. Verify that R1 is receiving both an IPv6 default route and other routes from R2 via RIPng.

```
R1# show ipv6 route rip
IPv6 Routing Table - default - 10 entries
Codes: C - Connected, L - Local, S - Static, U - Per-user Static route
       B - BGP, R - RIP, I1 - ISIS L1, I2 - ISIS L2
       IA - ISIS interarea, IS - ISIS summary, D - EIGRP, EX - EIGRP external
       ND - ND Default, NDp - ND Prefix, DCE - Destination, NDr - Redirect
       O - OSPF Intra, OI - OSPF Inter, OE1 - OSPF ext 1, OE2 - OSPF ext 2
       ON1 - OSPF NSSA ext 1, ON2 - OSPF NSSA ext 2, a - Application
R   ::/0 [120/2]
     via FE80::2, Serial0/0/0
R   2001:DB8:CAFE:3::/64 [120/2]
     via FE80::2, Serial0/0/0
R   2001:DB8:CAFE:10::/64 [120/2]
     via FE80::2, Serial0/0/0
R   2001:DB8:CAFE:11::/64 [120/2]
     via FE80::2, Serial0/0/0
```

```
R    2001:DB8:CAFE:12::/64 [120/2]
       via FE80::2, Serial0/0/0
R1#
```

What is the RIPng hop count for the default and other routes? Explain how the hop count is determined.

_____

_____

c. To check whether you have full connectivity, from R1 ping the interfaces on R2 and R3. If you have successfully pinged all the remote interfaces, congratulations! You have configured RIPng including a default route.

Step 6: Propagate only the default route via RIPng and verify.

a. Remove the previous command that propagates the default route using the originate keyword and replace it with the same command using the **only** keyword.

```
R2(config)# interface serial 0/0/0
R2(config-if)# no ipv6 rip ROUTING-RIPng default-information originate
R2(config-if)# ipv6 rip ROUTING-RIPng default-information only
```

b. Display the RIPng routes in R1's IPv6 routing table. Verify that R1 is only receiving an IPv6 default route from R2 via RIPng. You will need to wait for the routes to expire on R1 or issue the **clear ipv6 rip ROUTING-RIPng** command to clear the RIPng databases on R1 and R2.

```
R1# clear ipv6 rip ROUTING-RIPng
R1# show ipv6 route rip
IPv6 Routing Table - default - 6 entries
Codes: C - Connected, L - Local, S - Static, U - Per-user Static route
       B - BGP, R - RIP, I1 - ISIS L1, I2 - ISIS L2
       IA - ISIS interarea, IS - ISIS summary, D - EIGRP, EX - EIGRP external
       ND - ND Default, NDp - ND Prefix, DCE - Destination, NDr - Redirect
       O - OSPF Intra, OI - OSPF Inter, OE1 - OSPF ext 1, OE2 - OSPF ext 2
       ON1 - OSPF NSSA ext 1, ON2 - OSPF NSSA ext 2, a - Application
R    ::/0 [120/2]
       via FE80::2, Serial0/0/0
R1#
```

Step 7: Examine the RIPng process on R2.

a. On R2, use the **show ipv6 rip** command to display the RIPng process.

```
R2# show ipv6 rip
RIP process "ROUTING-RIPng", port 521, multicast-group FF02::9, pid 240
     Administrative distance is 120. Maximum paths is 16
     Updates every 30 seconds, expire after 180
     Holddown lasts 0 seconds, garbage collect after 120
     Split horizon is on; poison reverse is off
     Default routes are generated
     Periodic updates 338, trigger updates 5
     Full Advertisement 0, Delayed Events 0
   Interfaces:
     Loopback12
```

```
        Loopback11
        Loopback10
        GigabitEthernet0/0
        Serial0/0/0
    Redistribution:
        None
R2#
```

How many RIPng processes are running on R2 and what are the process names?

_____

_____

What port number does RIPng use?

_____

_____

What destination address and type of address does RIPng use to send updates?

_____

_____

Step 8: Examine the RIPng database and next-hops on R2.

a. On R2, examine the RIPng database.

```
R2# show ipv6 rip database
RIP process "ROUTING-RIPng", local RIB
 2001:DB8:CAFE:1::/64, metric 2, installed
     Serial0/0/0/FE80::1, expires in 171 secs
 2001:DB8:CAFE:2::/64, metric 2
     Serial0/0/0/FE80::1, expires in 171 secs
R2#
```

How many entries are in the RIP database?

_____

_____

Which entry is installed in the IPv6 routing table and why is the other route not included?

_____

_____

What is the next-hop IPv6 address and exit-interface of both RIP database entries?

_____

_____

What happens when "expires in n seconds" reaches 0? What keeps this value from expiring?

_____

_____

b. On R2, examine the number of next-hops for the RIPng process.

```
R2# show ipv6 rip ROUTING-RIPng next-hops
 RIP process "ROUTING-RIPng", Next Hops
  FE80::1/Serial0/0/0 [2 paths]
R2#
```

Why are there two paths from the next-hop FE80::1/Serial0/0/0 but only one route in the IPv6 routing table using the next-hop FE80::1?

_____

_____

Chapter 2: EIGRP Implementation

Lab 2-1 EIGRP Load Balancing

Topology

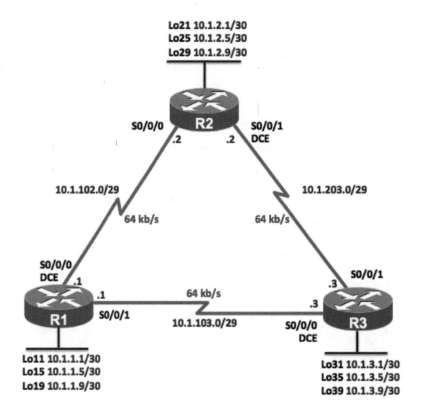

Objectives

- Review a basic EIGRP configuration.
- Explore the EIGRP topology table.
- Identify successors, feasible successors, and feasible distances.
- Use **show** and **debug** commands for the EIGRP topology table.
- Configure and verify equal-cost load balancing with EIGRP.
- Configure and verify unequal-cost load balancing with EIGRP.

Background

As a senior network engineer, you are considering deploying EIGRP in your corporation and want to evaluate its ability to converge quickly in a changing environment. You are also interested in equal-cost and unequal-cost load balancing because your network contains redundant links. These links are not often used by other link-state routing protocols because of high metrics. Because you are interested in testing the EIGRP claims that you have read about, you decide to implement and test on a set of three lab routers before deploying EIGRP throughout your corporate network.

Note: This lab uses Cisco 1941 routers with Cisco IOS Release 15.4 with IP Base. Depending on the Cisco IOS Software version, the commands available and output produced might vary from what is shown in this lab.

Required Resources

- 3 routers (Cisco IOS Release 15.2 or comparable)
- Serial and Ethernet cables

Step 0: Suggested starting configurations.

a. Apply the following configuration to each router along with the appropriate **hostname**. The **exec-timeout 0 0** command should only be used in a lab environment.

```
Router(config)# no ip domain-lookup
Router(config)# line con 0
Router(config-line)# logging synchronous
Router(config-line)# exec-timeout 0 0
```

Step 1: Configure the addressing and serial links.

a. Create three loopback interfaces on each router and address them as 10.1.X.1/30, 10.1.X.5/30, and 10.1.X.9/30, where X is the number of the router. Use the following table or the initial configurations located at the end of the lab.

Router	Interface	IP Address/Mask
R1	Loopback11	10.1.1.1/30
R1	Loopback15	10.1.1.5/30
R1	Loopback19	10.1.1.9/30
R2	Loopback21	10.1.2.1/30
R2	Loopback25	10.1.2.5/30
R2	Loopback29	10.1.2.9/30
R3	Loopback31	10.1.3.1/30
R3	Loopback35	10.1.3.5/30
R3	Loopback39	10.1.3.9/30

```
R1(config)# interface Loopback 11
R1(config-if)# ip address 10.1.1.1 255.255.255.252
R1(config-if)# exit
R1(config)# interface Loopback 15
R1(config-if)# ip address 10.1.1.5 255.255.255.252
R1(config-if)# exit
R1(config)# interface Loopback 19
R1(config-if)# ip address 10.1.1.9 255.255.255.252
R1(config-if)# exit

R2(config)# interface Loopback 21
R2(config-if)# ip address 10.1.2.1 255.255.255.252
R2(config-if)# exit
```

```
R2(config)# interface Loopback 25
R2(config-if)# ip address 10.1.2.5 255.255.255.252
R2(config-if)# exit
R2(config)# interface Loopback 29
R2(config-if)# ip address 10.1.2.9 255.255.255.252
R2(config-if)# exit

R3(config)# interface Loopback 31
R3(config-if)# ip address 10.1.3.1 255.255.255.252
R3(config-if)# exit
R3(config)# interface Loopback 35
R3(config-if)# ip address 10.1.3.5 255.255.255.252
R3(config-if)# exit
R3(config)# interface Loopback 39
R3(config-if)# ip address 10.1.3.9 255.255.255.252
R3(config-if)# exit
```

b. Specify the addresses of the serial interfaces as shown in the topology diagram. Set the clock rate to 64 kb/s, and manually configure the interface bandwidth to 64 kb/s.

Note: If you have WIC-2A/S serial interfaces, the maximum clock rate is 128 kb/s. If you have WIC-2T serial interfaces, the maximum clock rate is much higher (2.048 Mb/s or higher depending on the hardware), which is more representative of a modern network WAN link. However, this lab uses 64 kb/s and 128 kb/s settings.

```
R1(config)# interface Serial 0/0/0
R1(config-if)# description R1-->R2
R1(config-if)# clock rate 64000
R1(config-if)# bandwidth 64
R1(config-if)# ip address 10.1.102.1 255.255.255.248
R1(config-if)# no shutdown
R1(config-if)# exit
R1(config)# interface Serial 0/0/1
R1(config-if)# description R1-->R3
R1(config-if)# bandwidth 64
R1(config-if)# ip address 10.1.103.1 255.255.255.248
R1(config-if)# no shutdown
R1(config-if)# exit

R2(config)# interface Serial 0/0/0
R2(config-if)# description R2-->R1
R2(config-if)# bandwidth 64
R2(config-if)# ip address 10.1.102.2 255.255.255.248
R2(config-if)# no shutdown
R2(config-if)# exit
R2(config)# interface Serial 0/0/1
R2(config-if)# description R2-->R3
R2(config-if)# clock rate 64000
R2(config-if)# bandwidth 64
R2(config-if)# ip address 10.1.203.2 255.255.255.248
R2(config-if)# no shutdown
R2(config-if)# exit

R3(config)# interface Serial 0/0/0
R3(config-if)# description R3-->R1
R3(config-if)# clock rate 64000
```

```
R3(config-if)# bandwidth 64
R3(config-if)# ip address 10.1.103.3 255.255.255.248
R3(config-if)# no shutdown
R3(config-if)# exit
R3(config)# interface Serial 0/0/1
R3(config-if)# description R3-->R2
R3(config-if)# bandwidth 64
R3(config-if)# ip address 10.1.203.3 255.255.255.248
R3(config-if)# no shutdown
R3(config-if)# exit
```

c. Verify connectivity by pinging across each of the local networks connected to each router.

d. Issue the **show interfaces description** command on each router. This command displays a brief listing of the interfaces, their status, and a description (if a description is configured). Router R1 is shown as an example.

```
R1# show interfaces description
Interface                      Status         Protocol Description
Em0/0                          admin down     down
Gi0/0                          admin down     down
Gi0/1                          admin down     down
Se0/0/0                        up             up       R1-->R2
Se0/0/1                        up             up       R1-->R3
Lo11                           up             up
Lo15                           up             up
Lo19                           up             up
R1#
```

e. Issue the **show protocols** command on each router. This command displays a brief listing of the interfaces, their status, and the IP address and subnet mask configured (in prefix format /xx) for each interface. Router R1 is shown as an example.

```
R1# show protocols
Global values:
  Internet Protocol routing is enabled
Embedded-Service-Engine0/0 is administratively down, line protocol is down
GigabitEthernet0/0 is administratively down, line protocol is down
GigabitEthernet0/1 is administratively down, line protocol is down
Serial0/0/0 is up, line protocol is up
  Internet address is 10.1.102.1/29
Serial0/0/1 is up, line protocol is up
  Internet address is 10.1.103.1/29
Loopback11 is up, line protocol is up
  Internet address is 10.1.1.1/30
Loopback15 is up, line protocol is up
  Internet address is 10.1.1.5/30
Loopback19 is up, line protocol is up
  Internet address is 10.1.1.9/30
R1#
```

Step 2: Configure EIGRP.

· a. Enable EIGRP AS 100 for all interfaces on R1 and R2 using the commands. Do not enable EIGRP yet on R3. For your reference, these are the commands that can be used:

```
R1(config)# router eigrp 100
```

```
R1(config-router)# network 10.0.0.0

R2(config)# router eigrp 100
R2(config-router)# network 10.0.0.0
```

b. Use the **debug ip routing** and the **debug ip eigrp 100** commands to watch EIGRP install the routes in the routing table when your routers become adjacent. (Note: The type of output you receive may vary depending upon the IOS.) You get output similar to the following.

```
R3# debug ip routing
IP routing debugging is on
R3# debug ip eigrp 100
R3# conf t
Enter configuration commands, one per line.  End with CNTL/Z.
R3(config)# router eigrp 100
*Jun 22 11:06:09.315: RT: add router 2048, all protocols have local database
R3(config-router)# network 10.0.0.0
*Jun 22 11:06:18.591: %DUAL-5-NBRCHANGE: EIGRP-IPv4 100: Neighbor 10.1.103.1
(Serial0/0/0) is up: new adjacency
*Jun 22 11:06:18.591: %DUAL-5-NBRCHANGE: EIGRP-IPv4 100: Neighbor 10.1.203.2
(Serial0/0/1) is up: new adjacency
*Jun 22 11:06:19.055: RT: updating eigrp 10.1.102.0/29 (0x0)  :
     via 10.1.103.1 Se0/0/0  0 1048578

*Jun 22 11:06:19.055: RT: add 10.1.102.0/29 via 10.1.103.1, eigrp metric
[90/41024000]
*Jun 22 11:06:19.055: RT: updating eigrp 10.1.1.0/30 (0x0)  :
     via 10.1.103.1 Se0/0/0
R3(config-router)#end  0 1048578

*Jun 22 11:06:19.055: RT: add 10.1.1.0/30 via 10.1.103.1, eigrp metric
[90/40640000]
*Jun 22 11:06:19.055: RT: updating eigrp 10.1.1.4/30 (0x0)  :
     via 10.1.103.1 Se0/0/0  0 1048578

*Jun 22 11:06:19.055: RT: add 10.1.1.4/30 via 10.1.103.1, eigrp metric
[90/40640000]
*Jun 22 11:06:19.055: RT: updating eigrp 10.1.1.8/30 (0x0)  :
     via 10.1.103.1 Se0/0/0  0 1048578

*Jun 22 11:06:19.055: RT: add 10.1.1.8/30 via 10.1.103.1, eigrp metric
[90/40640000]
*Jun 22 11:06:19.059: RT: updating eigrp 10.1.2.0/30 (0x0)  :
     via 10.1.103.1 Se0/0/0  0 1048578

*Jun 22 11:06:19.059: RT: add 10.1.2.0/30 via 10.1.103.1, eigrp metric
[90/41152000]
*Jun 22 11:06:19.059: RT: updating eigrp 10.1.2.4/30 (0x0)  :
     via 10.1.103.1 Se0/0/0  0 1048578

<output omitted>
R3#
R3(config-router)# end
R3#
R3#undebug all
All possible debugging has been turned off
```

```
R3#
```

Essentially, the EIGRP DUAL state machine has just computed the topology table for these routes and installed them in the routing table.

c. Check to see that these routes exist in the routing table with the **show ip route** command.

```
R3# show ip route
Codes: L - local, C - connected, S - static, R - RIP, M - mobile, B - BGP
       D - EIGRP, EX - EIGRP external, O - OSPF, IA - OSPF inter area
       N1 - OSPF NSSA external type 1, N2 - OSPF NSSA external type 2
       E1 - OSPF external type 1, E2 - OSPF external type 2
       i - IS-IS, su - IS-IS summary, L1 - IS-IS level-1, L2 - IS-IS level-2
       ia - IS-IS inter area, * - candidate default, U - per-user static
       route
       o - ODR, P - periodic downloaded static route, H - NHRP, l - LISP
       a - application route
       + - replicated route, % - next hop override

Gateway of last resort is not set

      10.0.0.0/8 is variably subnetted, 17 subnets, 3 masks
D        10.1.1.0/30 [90/40640000] via 10.1.103.1, 00:10:54, Serial0/0/0
D        10.1.1.4/30 [90/40640000] via 10.1.103.1, 00:10:54, Serial0/0/0
D        10.1.1.8/30 [90/40640000] via 10.1.103.1, 00:10:54, Serial0/0/0
D        10.1.2.0/30 [90/40640000] via 10.1.203.2, 00:10:54, Serial0/0/1
D        10.1.2.4/30 [90/40640000] via 10.1.203.2, 00:10:54, Serial0/0/1
D        10.1.2.8/30 [90/40640000] via 10.1.203.2, 00:10:54, Serial0/0/1
C        10.1.3.0/30 is directly connected, Loopback31
L        10.1.3.1/32 is directly connected, Loopback31
C        10.1.3.4/30 is directly connected, Loopback35
L        10.1.3.5/32 is directly connected, Loopback35
C        10.1.3.8/30 is directly connected, Loopback39
L        10.1.3.9/32 is directly connected, Loopback39
D        10.1.102.0/29 [90/41024000] via 10.1.203.2, 00:10:54, Serial0/0/1
                      [90/41024000] via 10.1.103.1, 00:10:54, Serial0/0/0
C        10.1.103.0/29 is directly connected, Serial0/0/0
L        10.1.103.3/32 is directly connected, Serial0/0/0
C        10.1.203.0/29 is directly connected, Serial0/0/1
L        10.1.203.3/32 is directly connected, Serial0/0/1
R3#
```

d. After you have full adjacency between the routers, ping all the remote loopbacks to ensure full connectivity.

You should receive ICMP echo replies for each address pinged.

e. Verify the EIGRP neighbor relationships with the **show ip eigrp neighbors** command.

```
R1# show ip eigrp neighbors
EIGRP-IPv4 Neighbors for AS(100)
H    Address           Interface        Hold Uptime   SRTT   RTO  Q    Seq
                                        (sec)         (ms)        Cnt  Num
```

```
1    10.1.103.3          Se0/0/1                    13 00:14:20    49      2340 0   6
0    10.1.102.2          Se0/0/0                    10 00:29:14    37      2340 0   36
R1#


R2# show ip eigrp neighbors
EIGRP-IPv4 Neighbors for AS(100)
H    Address             Interface                  Hold Uptime    SRTT    RTO  Q  Seq
                                                    (sec)          (ms)       Cnt Num
1    10.1.203.3          Se0/0/1                    13 00:14:28    71      2340  0 7
0    10.1.102.1          Se0/0/0                    13 00:29:21    35      2340  0 36
R2#


R3# show ip eigrp neighbors
EIGRP-IPv4 Neighbors for AS(100)
H    Address             Interface                  Hold Uptime    SRTT    RTO  Q  Seq
                                                    (sec)          (ms)       Cnt Num
1    10.1.203.2          Se0/0/1                    13 00:14:07    1305    5000  0 37
0    10.1.103.1          Se0/0/0                    14 00:14:07    42      2340  0 37
R3#
```

Step 3: Examine the EIGRP topology table.

a. EIGRP builds a topology table containing all successor routes. The course content covered the vocabulary for EIGRP routes in the topology table. What is the feasible distance of route 10.1.1.0/30 in the R3 topology table in the following output?

_____

_____

```
R3# show ip eigrp topology
EIGRP-IPv4 Topology Table for AS(100)/ID(10.1.3.9)
Codes: P - Passive, A - Active, U - Update, Q - Query, R - Reply,
       r - reply Status, s - sia Status

P 10.1.102.0/29, 2 successors, FD is 41024000
        via 10.1.103.1 (41024000/40512000), Serial0/0/0
        via 10.1.203.2 (41024000/40512000), Serial0/0/1
P 10.1.1.8/30, 1 successors, FD is 40640000
        via 10.1.103.1 (40640000/128256), Serial0/0/0
P 10.1.3.0/30, 1 successors, FD is 128256
        via Connected, Loopback31
P 10.1.3.4/30, 1 successors, FD is 128256
        via Connected, Loopback35
P 10.1.3.8/30, 1 successors, FD is 128256
        via Connected, Loopback39
P 10.1.2.8/30, 1 successors, FD is 40640000
        via 10.1.203.2 (40640000/128256), Serial0/0/1
P 10.1.2.0/30, 1 successors, FD is 40640000
        via 10.1.203.2 (40640000/128256), Serial0/0/1
P 10.1.103.0/29, 1 successors, FD is 40512000
        via Connected, Serial0/0/0
P 10.1.203.0/29, 1 successors, FD is 40512000
        via Connected, Serial0/0/1
P 10.1.1.4/30, 1 successors, FD is 40640000
```

```
            via 10.1.103.1 (40640000/128256), Serial0/0/0
     P 10.1.2.4/30, 1 successors, FD is 40640000
            via 10.1.203.2 (40640000/128256), Serial0/0/1
     P 10.1.1.0/30, 1 successors, FD is 40640000
            via 10.1.103.1 (40640000/128256), Serial0/0/0

     R3#
```

b. The most important thing is the two successor routes in the passive state on R3. R1 and R2 are both advertising their connected subnet of 10.1.102.0/30. Because both routes have the same feasible distance of 41024000, both are installed in the topology table. This distance of 41024000 reflects the composite metric of more granular properties about the path to the destination network. Can you view the metrics before the composite metric is computed?

_____

_____

_____

_____

c. Use the **show ip eigrp topology 10.1.102.0/29** command to view the information that EIGRP has received about the route from R1 and R2.

```
R3# show ip eigrp topology 10.1.102.0/29
EIGRP-IPv4 Topology Entry for AS(100)/ID(10.1.3.9) for 10.1.102.0/29
  State is Passive, Query origin flag is 1, 2 Successor(s), FD is 41024000
  Descriptor Blocks:
  10.1.103.1 (Serial0/0/0), from 10.1.103.1, Send flag is 0x0
      Composite metric is (41024000/40512000), route is Internal
      Vector metric:
        Minimum bandwidth is 64 Kbit
        Total delay is 40000 microseconds
        Reliability is 255/255
        Load is 1/255
        Minimum MTU is 1500
        Hop count is 1
        Originating router is 10.1.1.9
  10.1.203.2 (Serial0/0/1), from 10.1.203.2, Send flag is 0x0
      Composite metric is (41024000/40512000), route is Internal
      Vector metric:
        Minimum bandwidth is 64 Kbit
        Total delay is 40000 microseconds
        Reliability is 255/255
        Load is 1/255
        Minimum MTU is 1500
        Hop count is 1
        Originating router is 10.1.2.9
R3#
```

The output of this command shows the following information regarding EIGRP:

*   The bandwidth metric represents the *minimum* bandwidth among all links comprising the path to the destination network.

*   The delay metric represents the *total* delay over the path.

- The minimum MTU represents the smallest MTU along the path.
- If you do not have full knowledge of your network, you can use the hop count information to check how many Layer 3 devices are between the router and the destination network.

Step 4: Observe equal-cost load balancing.

EIGRP produces equal-cost load balancing to the destination network 10.1.102.0/29 from R1. Two equal-cost paths are available to this destination per the earlier topology table output.

a. Use the **traceroute 10.1.102.1** command to view the hops from R3 to this R1 IP address. Notice that both R1 and R2 are listed as hops because there are two equal-cost paths and packets can reach this network via either link.

```
R3# traceroute 10.1.102.1
Type escape sequence to abort.
Tracing the route to 10.1.102.1
VRF info: (vrf in name/id, vrf out name/id)
  1 10.1.203.2 24 msec
    10.1.103.1 12 msec
    10.1.203.2 24 msec
R3#
```

Cisco IOS enables Cisco Express Forwarding (CEF), which, by default, performs per-destination load balancing. CEF allows for very rapid switching without the need for route processing. However, if you were to ping the destination network, you would not see load balancing occurring on a packet level because CEF treats the entire series of pings as one flow.

CEF on R3 overrides the per-packet balancing behavior of process switching with per-destination load balancing.

b. To see the full effect of EIGRP equal-cost load balancing, temporarily disable CEF and route caching so that all IP packets are processed individually and not fast-switched by CEF.

```
R3(config)# no ip cef

R3(config)# interface S0/0/0
R3(config-if)# no ip route-cache
R3(config-if)# interface S0/0/1
R3(config-if)# no ip route-cache
```

Note: Typically, you would not disable CEF in a production network. It is done here only to illustrate load balancing. Another way to demonstrate per-packet load balancing, that does not disable CEF, is to use the per-packet load balancing command **ip load-share per-packet** on outgoing interfaces S0/0/0 and S0/0/1.

c. Verify load balancing with the **debug ip packet** command, and then ping 10.1.102.1. Like any debug command, **debug ip packet** should be used with caution on a production network. Without any ACL filtering, this command will overwhelm the router's CPU processes in a production environment. Issue the **undebug all** command to stop debug processing. You see output similar to the following:

```
R3# debug ip packet
IP packet debugging is on

R3# ping 10.1.102.1
Type escape sequence to abort.
Sending 5, 100-byte ICMP Echos to 10.1.102.1, timeout is 2 seconds:
!!!!!
```

```
Success rate is 100 percent (5/5), round-trip min/avg/max = 28/36/44 ms
R3#
Success rate is 100 percent (5/5), round-trip min/avg/max = 28/36/44 ms
R3#
*Jun 22 11:39:37.043: IP: tableid=0, s=10.1.203.3 (local), d=10.1.102.1
(Serial0/0/1), routed via RIB
*Jun 22 11:39:37.043: IP: s=10.1.203.3 (local), d=10.1.102.1 (Serial0/0/1),
len 100, sending
*Jun 22 11:39:37.043: IP: s=10.1.203.3 (local), d=10.1.102.1 (Serial0/0/1),
len 100, sending full packet
*Jun 22 11:39:37.087: IP: s=10.1.102.1 (Serial0/0/0), d=10.1.203.3, len 100,
input feature, MCI Check(104), rtype 0, forus FALSE, sendself FALSE, mtu 0,
fwdchk FALSE
*Jun 22 11:39:37.087: IP: tableid=0, s=
R3#10.1.102.1 (Serial0/0/0), d=10.1.203.3 (Serial0/0/1), routed via RIB
*Jun 22 11:39:37.087: IP: s=10.1.102.1 (Serial0/0/0), d=10.1.203.3, len 100,
rcvd 4
*Jun 22 11:39:37.087: IP: s=10.1.102.1 (Serial0/0/0), d=10.1.203.3, len 100,
stop process pak for forus packet
*Jun 22 11:39:37.087: IP: tableid=0, s=10.1.103.3 (local), d=10.1.102.1
(Serial0/0/0), routed via RIB
*Jun 22 11:39:37.087: IP: s=10.1.103.3 (local), d=10.1.102.1 (Serial0/0/0),
len 100, sending
*Jun 22 11:39:37.087: IP: s=10.1.103.3 (local),
R3# d=10.1.102.1 (Serial0/0/0), len 100, sending full packet
*Jun 22 11:39:37.115: IP: s=10.1.102.1 (Serial0/0/0), d=10.1.103.3, len 100,
input feature, MCI Check(104), rtype 0, forus FALSE, sendself FALSE, mtu 0,
fwdchk FALSE

<output omitted>
R3# undebug all
```

Notice that EIGRP load-balances between Serial0/0/0 (s=10.1.103.3) and Serial0/0/1 (s=10.1.203.3). This behavior is part of EIGRP. It can help utilize underused links in a network, especially during periods of congestion.

Step 5: Analyze alternate EIGRP paths not in the topology table.

a. Issue the **show ip eigrp topology** command on R3 to see successors and feasible successors for each route that R3 has learned through EIGRP.

```
R3# show ip eigrp topology
EIGRP-IPv4 Topology Table for AS(100)/ID(10.1.3.9)
Codes: P - Passive, A - Active, U - Update, Q - Query, R - Reply,
       r - reply Status, s - sia Status

P 10.1.102.0/29, 2 successors, FD is 41024000
        via 10.1.103.1 (41024000/40512000), Serial0/0/0
        via 10.1.203.2 (41024000/40512000), Serial0/0/1
P 10.1.1.8/30, 1 successors, FD is 40640000
        via 10.1.103.1 (40640000/128256), Serial0/0/0
P 10.1.3.0/30, 1 successors, FD is 128256
        via Connected, Loopback31
P 10.1.3.4/30, 1 successors, FD is 128256
        via Connected, Loopback35
P 10.1.3.8/30, 1 successors, FD is 128256
```

```
              via Connected, Loopback39
P 10.1.2.8/30, 1 successors, FD is 40640000
              via 10.1.203.2 (40640000/128256), Serial0/0/1
P 10.1.2.0/30, 1 successors, FD is 40640000
              via 10.1.203.2 (40640000/128256), Serial0/0/1
P 10.1.103.0/29, 1 successors, FD is 40512000
              via Connected, Serial0/0/0
P 10.1.203.0/29, 1 successors, FD is 40512000
              via Connected, Serial0/0/1
P 10.1.1.4/30, 1 successors, FD is 40640000
              via 10.1.103.1 (40640000/128256), Serial0/0/0
P 10.1.2.4/30, 1 successors, FD is 40640000
              via 10.1.203.2 (40640000/128256), Serial0/0/1
P 10.1.1.0/30, 1 successors, FD is 40640000
              via 10.1.103.1 (40640000/128256), Serial0/0/0

R3#
```

Perhaps you expected to see two entries to the R1 and R2 loopback networks in the R3 topology table. Why is there only one entry shown in the topology table?

_____

_____

_____

_____

_____

_____

b. Issue the **show ip eigrp topology all-links** command to see all routes that R3 has learned through EIGRP. This command shows all entries that EIGRP holds on this router for networks in the topology, including the exit serial interface and IP address of the next hop to each destination network, and the serial number (serno) that uniquely identifies a destination network in EIGRP.

```
R3# show ip eigrp topology all-links
EIGRP-IPv4 Topology Table for AS(100)/ID(10.1.3.9)
Codes: P - Passive, A - Active, U - Update, Q - Query, R - Reply,
       r - reply Status, s - sia Status

P 10.1.102.0/29, 2 successors, FD is 41024000, serno 13
          via 10.1.103.1 (41024000/40512000), Serial0/0/0
          via 10.1.203.2 (41024000/40512000), Serial0/0/1
P 10.1.1.8/30, 1 successors, FD is 40640000, serno 9
          via 10.1.103.1 (40640000/128256), Serial0/0/0
          via 10.1.203.2 (41152000/40640000), Serial0/0/1
P 10.1.3.0/30, 1 successors, FD is 128256, serno 3
          via Connected, Loopback31
P 10.1.3.4/30, 1 successors, FD is 128256, serno 4
          via Connected, Loopback35
P 10.1.3.8/30, 1 successors, FD is 128256, serno 5
          via Connected, Loopback39
P 10.1.2.8/30, 1 successors, FD is 40640000, serno 16
```

```
             via 10.1.203.2 (40640000/128256), Serial0/0/1
             via 10.1.103.1 (41152000/40640000), Serial0/0/0
P 10.1.2.0/30, 1 successors, FD is 40640000, serno 14
             via 10.1.203.2 (40640000/128256), Serial0/0/1
             via 10.1.103.1 (41152000/40640000), Serial0/0/0
P 10.1.103.0/29, 1 successors, FD is 40512000, serno 1
             via Connected, Serial0/0/0
P 10.1.203.0/29, 1 successors, FD is 40512000, serno 2
             via Connected, Serial0/0/1
P 10.1.1.4/30, 1 successors, FD is 40640000, serno 8
             via 10.1.103.1 (40640000/128256), Serial0/0/0
             via 10.1.203.2 (41152000/40640000), Serial0/0/1
P 10.1.2.4/30, 1 successors, FD is 40640000, serno 15
             via 10.1.203.2 (40640000/128256), Serial0/0/1
             via 10.1.103.1 (41152000/40640000), Serial0/0/0
P 10.1.1.0/30, 1 successors, FD is 40640000, serno 7
             via 10.1.103.1 (40640000/128256), Serial0/0/0
             via 10.1.203.2 (41152000/40640000), Serial0/0/1

R3#
```

What is the reported distance to the R1's loopback networks using R1 and R2 as next-hop routers?

_____

_____

_____

_____

_____

c. Use the **show ip eigrp topology 10.1.2.0/30** command to see the granular view of the alternate paths to
    10.1.2.0, including ones with a higher reported distance than the feasible distance.

```
R3# show ip eigrp topology 10.1.2.0/30
IP-EIGRP (AS 100): Topology entry for 10.1.2.0/30
   State is Passive, Query origin flag is 1, 1 Successor(s), FD is 40640000
   Routing Descriptor Blocks:
   10.1.203.2 (Serial0/0/1), from 10.1.203.2, Send flag is 0x0
       Composite metric is (40640000/128256), Route is Internal
       Vector metric:
         Minimum bandwidth is 64 Kbit
         Total delay is 25000 microseconds
         Reliability is 255/255
         Load is 1/255
         Minimum MTU is 1500
         Hop count is 1
   10.1.103.1 (Serial0/0/0), from 10.1.103.1, Send flag is 0x0
       Composite metric is (41152000/40640000), Route is Internal
       Vector metric:
         Minimum bandwidth is 64 Kbit
         Total delay is 45000 microseconds
         Reliability is 255/255
         Load is 1/255
```

```
Minimum MTU is 1500
Hop count is 2
```

When using the **show ip eigrp topology** command, why is the route to 10.1.2.0/30 through R1 (via 10.1.103.1) not listed in the topology table?

_____

_____

_____

_____

What is its reported distance from R1?

What is its feasible distance?

If the R2 Serial0/0/1 interface were shut down, would EIGRP route through R1 to get to 10.1.2.0/30? Why isn't the switch to a new path as quick as it could be?

_____

_____

_____

_____

_____

_____

_____

_____

Record your answer, and then experiment by shutting down the R1 S0/0/1 interface while an extended ping is running as described next.

d. Start a ping with a high repeat count on R3 to the R1 Serial0/0/0 interface 10.1.102.1.

    R3# **ping 10.1.102.1 repeat 10000**

e. Enter interface configuration mode on R1 and shut down port Serial0/0/1, which is the direct link from R1 to R3.

    R1(config)# **interface serial 0/0/1**
    R1(config-if)# **shutdown**

f. When the adjacency between R1 and R3 goes down, some pings will be lost. After pings are again being successfully received, stop the ping using Ctrl+Shift+^.

    R3#ping 10.1.102.1 repeat 10000
    Type escape sequence to abort.

```
Sending 10000, 100-byte ICMP Echos to 10.1.102.1, timeout is 2 seconds:
!!!!!!!!!!!!!!!!!!!!!!!!!!!!!!!!!!!!!!!!!!!!!!!!!!!!!!!!!!!!!!!!!!!!!!!!!!!!
<output omitted>
!!!!!!!!!!!!!!!!!!!!!!!!!!!!!!!!!!!!!!!!!!!!!!!!!!!!!!!!!!!!!!!!!!!!!!!!!!!!
!!!!!!!!!!!!!!!!!!!!!!!!!!!!!!!!!!!!!!!!!!!!!!!!!!!!!!!!!!!!.!!!!!!!
*Jun 22 12:56:45.739: %LINK-3-UPDOWN: Interface Serial0/0/1, changed state to
down!!!!!!!!!!!!!!!!
!!!!!!!!!!!!!!!!!!!!!!
*Jun 22 12:56:45.739: %DUAL-5-NBRCHANGE: EIGRP-IPv4 100: Neighbor 10.1.203.2
(Serial0/0/1) is down: interface down
*Jun 22 12:56:46.739: %LINEPROTO-5-UPDOWN: Line protocol on Interface
Serial0/0/1, changed state to
down!!!!!!!!!!!!!!!!!!!!!!!!!!!!!!!!!!!!!!!!!!!!!!!!!!!!!!!
!!!!!!!!!!!!!!!!!!!!!!!!!!!!!!!!!!!!!!!!!!!!!!!!!!!!!!!!!!!!!!!!!!!!!!!!!!!!
<output omitted>
!!!!!!!!!!!!!!!!!!!!!!!!!!!!!!!!!!!!!!!!!!!!!!!!!!!!!!!!!!!!!!!!!!!!!!!!!!!!
!
*Jun 22 12:57:08.723: %LINK-3-UPDOWN: Interface Serial0/0/1, changed state to
up
*Jun 22 12:57:09.723: %LINEPROTO-5-UPDOWN: Line protocol on Interface
Serial0/0/1, changed state to
up!!!!!!!!!!!!!!!!!!!!!!!!!!!!!!!!!!!!!!!!!!!!!!!!!!!!!!!!!!!!!!!!!!!!!!!!!!!!
!!!
*Jun 22 12:57:10.003: %DUAL-5-NBRCHANGE: EIGRP-IPv4 100: Neighbor 10.1.203.2
(Serial0/0/1) is up: new
adjacency!!!!!!!!!!!!!!!!!!!!!!!!!!!!!!!!!!!!!!!!!!!!!!!!!!!!!!!!!!!!!!!!!!!!!!!!!
!!!!!!!!!!!!!!!!!!!!!!!!!!!!!!!!!!!!!!!!!!!!!!!!!!!!!!!!!!!!!!!!!!!!!!!!!!!!
Success rate is 99 percent (2039/2041), round-trip min/avg/max = 24/31/104 ms
R3#
```

How many packets were dropped?

_____

Note: When examining the EIGRP reconvergence speed after deactivating the serial link between R1 and R3, the focus should not be on the count of lost ping packets but rather on the duration of connectivity loss or how long it took to perform a successful cutover. The router waits for up to two seconds for each sent ICMP ECHO request to receive a reply and only then does it send another ECHO request. If the router did not wait for the reply, the count of lost packets would be much higher. Because two packets were lost, the cutover took approximately 4 seconds.

Another factor to consider is that an interface deliberately delays the information about loss of connectivity for 2 seconds to prevent transient link flaps (link going up and down) from introducing instability into the network. If the real speed of EIGRP is to be observed, this delay can be made as short as possible using the command **carrier-delay msec 0** on all serial interfaces.

g. Issue the **no shutdown** command on the R1 Serial0/0/1 interface before continuing to the next step.

Step 6: Observe unequal-cost load balancing.

Topology showing modified bandwidths as configured in step 6-b.

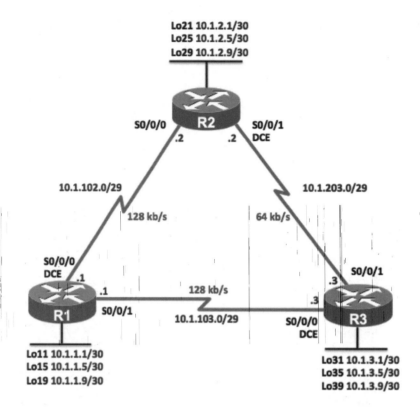

Lo21 10.1.2.1/30
Lo25 10.1.2.5/30
Lo29 10.1.2.9/30

a. Review the composite metrics advertised by EIGRP using the **show ip eigrp topology 10.1.2.0/30** command.

```
R3# show ip eigrp topology 10.1.2.0/30
IP-EIGRP (AS 100): Topology entry for 10.1.2.0/30
  State is Passive, Query origin flag is 1, 1 Successor(s), FD is 40640000
  Routing Descriptor Blocks:
  10.1.203.2 (Serial0/0/1), from 10.1.203.2, Send flag is 0x0
     Composite metric is (40640000/128256), Route is Internal
     Vector metric:
       Minimum bandwidth is 64 Kbit
       Total delay is 25000 microseconds
       Reliability is 255/255
       Load is 1/255
       Minimum MTU is 1500
       Hop count is 1
  10.1.103.1 (Serial0/0/0), from 10.1.103.1, Send flag is 0x0
     Composite metric is (41152000/40640000), Route is Internal
     Vector metric:
       Minimum bandwidth is 64 Kbit
       Total delay is 45000 microseconds
       Reliability is 255/255
       Load is 1/255
       Minimum MTU is 1500
       Hop count is 2
```

The reported distance for a loopback network is higher than the feasible distance, so DUAL does not consider it a feasible successor route.

b. To demonstrate unequal-cost load balancing in your internetwork, upgrade the path to the destination network through R1 with a higher bandwidth. Change the clock rate and bandwidth on the R1, R2, and R3 serial interfaces to 128 kb/s.

```
R1(config)# interface serial 0/0/0
R1(config-if)# bandwidth 128
R1(config-if)# clock rate 128000
R1(config-if)# interface serial 0/0/1
R1(config-if)# bandwidth 128

R2(config)# interface serial 0/0/0
R2(config-if)# bandwidth 128

R3(config)# interface serial 0/0/0
R3(config-if)# clock rate 128000
R3(config-if)# bandwidth 128
```

c. Issue the **show ip eigrp topology 10.1.2.0/30** command again on R3 to see what has changed.

```
R3# show ip eigrp topology 10.1.2.0/30
EIGRP-IPv4 Topology Entry for AS(100)/ID(10.1.3.9) for 10.1.2.0/30
  State is Passive, Query origin flag is 1, 1 Successor(s), FD is 21152000
  Descriptor Blocks:
  10.1.103.1 (Serial0/0/0), from 10.1.103.1, Send flag is 0x0
      Composite metric is (21152000/20640000), route is Internal
      Vector metric:
        Minimum bandwidth is 128 Kbit
        Total delay is 45000 microseconds
        Reliability is 255/255
        Load is 1/255
        Minimum MTU is 1500
        Hop count is 2
        Originating router is 10.1.2.9
  10.1.203.2 (Serial0/0/1), from 10.1.203.2, Send flag is 0x0
      Composite metric is (40640000/128256), route is Internal
      Vector metric:
        Minimum bandwidth is 64 Kbit
        Total delay is 25000 microseconds
        Reliability is 255/255
        Load is 3/255
        Minimum MTU is 1500
        Hop count is 1
        Originating router is 10.1.2.9
R3#
```

After manipulating the bandwidth parameter, the preferred path for R3 to the loopback interfaces of R2 is now through R1. Even though the hop count is two and the delay through R1 is nearly twice that of the R2 path, the higher bandwidth and lower FD results in this being the preferred route.

Note: Hop count is only mentioned to help you visualize the two paths. Hop count is not part of the composite EIGRP metric.

d. Issue the **show ip route** command to verify that the preferred route to network 10.1.2.0 is through R1 via Serial0/0/0 to next hop 10.1.103.1. There is only one route to this network due to the difference in bandwidth.

```
R3# show ip route eigrp
<output omitted>
        10.0.0.0/8 is variably subnetted, 17 subnets, 3 masks
D       10.1.1.0/30 [90/20640000] via 10.1.103.1, 00:05:09, Serial0/0/0
D       10.1.1.4/30 [90/20640000] via 10.1.103.1, 00:05:09, Serial0/0/0
D       10.1.1.8/30 [90/20640000] via 10.1.103.1, 00:05:09, Serial0/0/0
D       10.1.2.0/30 [90/21152000] via 10.1.103.1, 00:05:09, Serial0/0/0
D       10.1.2.4/30 [90/21152000] via 10.1.103.1, 00:05:09, Serial0/0/0
D       10.1.2.8/30 [90/21152000] via 10.1.103.1, 00:05:09, Serial0/0/0
D       10.1.102.0/29 [90/21024000] via 10.1.103.1, 00:05:09, Serial0/0/0
R3#
```

e. The **variance** command is used to enable unequal-cost load balancing. Setting the **variance** command allows you to install multiple loop-free paths with unequal costs into the routing table. EIGRP will always install the successor with the best path. Additional feasible successors are candidates for unequal-cost paths to be included in the routing table. These candidates must meet two conditions:

   - The route must be loop-free, a current feasible successor in the topology table.

   - The metric of the route must be lower than the metric of the best route (successor), multiplied by the variance configured on the router.

In the previous output, R3 shows the best path for 10.1.2.0/30 through R1 via 10.1.103.1. Examining the topology table on R3, there is also a feasible successor to this network through R2 via 10.1.203.1.

```
R3# show ip eigrp topology
EIGRP-IPv4 Topology Table for AS(100)/ID(10.1.3.9)
Codes: P - Passive, A - Active, U - Update, Q - Query, R - Reply,
       r - reply Status, s - sia Status

P 10.1.102.0/29, 1 successors, FD is 21024000
        via 10.1.103.1 (21024000/20512000), Serial0/0/0
        via 10.1.203.2 (41024000/20512000), Serial0/0/1
P 10.1.1.8/30, 1 successors, FD is 20640000
        via 10.1.103.1 (20640000/128256), Serial0/0/0
P 10.1.3.0/30, 1 successors, FD is 128256
        via Connected, Loopback31
P 10.1.3.4/30, 1 successors, FD is 128256
        via Connected, Loopback35
P 10.1.3.8/30, 1 successors, FD is 128256
        via Connected, Loopback39
P 10.1.2.8/30, 1 successors, FD is 21152000
        via 10.1.103.1 (21152000/20640000), Serial0/0/0
        via 10.1.203.2 (40640000/128256), Serial0/0/1
P 10.1.2.0/30, 1 successors, FD is 21152000
        via 10.1.103.1 (21152000/20640000), Serial0/0/0
        via 10.1.203.2 (40640000/128256), Serial0/0/1
P 10.1.103.0/29, 1 successors, FD is 20512000
        via Connected, Serial0/0/0
P 10.1.203.0/29, 1 successors, FD is 40512000
        via Connected, Serial0/0/1
P 10.1.1.4/30, 1 successors, FD is 20640000
        via 10.1.103.1 (20640000/128256), Serial0/0/0
P 10.1.2.4/30, 1 successors, FD is 21152000
        via 10.1.103.1 (21152000/20640000), Serial0/0/0
        via 10.1.203.2 (40640000/128256), Serial0/0/1
P 10.1.1.0/30, 1 successors, FD is 20640000
```

```
                    via 10.1.103.1 (20640000/128256), Serial0/0/0

R3#
```

f. Issue the **debug ip eigrp 100** command on R3 to show route events changing in real time. Then, under the EIGRP router configuration on R3, issue the **variance 2** command, which allows unequal-cost load balancing bounded by a maximum distance of (2) × (FD), where FD represents the feasible distance for each route in the routing table. Using 10.1.2.0/30 as an example, (2) x (21152000) = 42304000. The FD of the feasible successor is 40640000, which is less that the variance-modified FD of 42304000. Therefore, the feasible successor route become an additional successor and is added to the routing table.

```
R3# debug ip eigrp 100
EIGRP-IPv4 Route Event debugging is on for AS(100)
R3# conf t
Enter configuration commands, one per line.  End with CNTL/Z.
R3(config)# router eigrp 100
R3(config-router)# variance 2
R3(config-router)#
*Jun 22 13:16:19.087: EIGRP-IPv4(100): table(default): route installed for
10.1.102.0/29 (90/21024000) origin(10.1.103.1)
*Jun 22 13:16:19.087: EIGRP-IPv4(100): table(default): route installed for
10.1.102.0/29 (90/41024000) origin(10.1.203.2)
*Jun 22 13:16:19.091: EIGRP-IPv4(100): table(default): route installed for
10.1.1.8/30 (90/20640000) origin(10.1.103.1)
*Jun 22 13:16:19.091: EIGRP-IPv4(100): table(default): 10.1.1.8/30 routing
table not updated thru 10.1.203.2
*Jun 22 13:16:19.091: EIGRP-IPv4
R3(config-router)#(100): table(default): route installed for 10.1.2.8/30
(90/21152000) origin(10.1.103.1)
*Jun 22 13:16:19.091: EIGRP-IPv4(100): table(default): route installed for
10.1.2.8/30 (90/40640000) origin(10.1.203.2)
*Jun 22 13:16:19.091: EIGRP-IPv4(100): table(default): route installed for
10.1.2.0/30 (90/21152000) origin(10.1.103.1)
*Jun 22 13:16:19.091: EIGRP-IPv4(100): table(default): route installed for
10.1.2.0/30 (90/40640000) origin(10.1.203.2)
*Jun 22 13:16:19.091: EIGRP-IPv4(100): table(default): 10.1
R3(config-router)#.103.0/29 routing table not updated thru 10.1.203.2
*Jun 22 13:16:19.091: EIGRP-IPv4(100): table(default): route installed for
10.1.1.4/30 (90/20640000) origin(10.1.103.1)
*Jun 22 13:16:19.091: EIGRP-IPv4(100): table(default): 10.1.1.4/30 routing
table not updated thru 10.1.203.2
*Jun 22 13:16:19.091: EIGRP-IPv4(100): table(default): route installed for
10.1.2.4/30 (90/21152000) origin(10.1.103.1)
*Jun 22 13:16:19.091: EIGRP-IPv4(100): table(default): route installed for
10.1.2.4/30 (90/40640000) origi
R3(config-router)#n(10.1.203.2)
*Jun 22 13:16:19.091: EIGRP-IPv4(100): table(default): route installed for
10.1.1.0/30 (90/20640000) origin(10.1.103.1)
*Jun 22 13:16:19.091: EIGRP-IPv4(100): table(default): 10.1.1.0/30 routing
table not updated thru 10.1.203.2
*Jun 22 13:16:19.103: EIGRP-IPv4(100): table(default): 10.1.102.0/29 - do
advertise out Serial0/0/0
<output omitted>
```

g. Issue the **show ip route** command again to verify that there are now two routes to network 10.1.2.0. Notice that the two routes have different (unequal) metrics (feasible distances).

```
R3# show ip route eigrp

     10.0.0.0/8 is variably subnetted, 17 subnets, 3 masks
D       10.1.1.0/30 [90/20640000] via 10.1.103.1, 00:05:56, Serial0/0/0
D       10.1.1.4/30 [90/20640000] via 10.1.103.1, 00:05:56, Serial0/0/0
D       10.1.1.8/30 [90/20640000] via 10.1.103.1, 00:05:56, Serial0/0/0
D       10.1.2.0/30 [90/40640000] via 10.1.203.2, 00:05:56, Serial0/0/1
                    [90/21152000] via 10.1.103.1, 00:05:56, Serial0/0/0
D       10.1.2.4/30 [90/40640000] via 10.1.203.2, 00:05:56, Serial0/0/1
                    [90/21152000] via 10.1.103.1, 00:05:56, Serial0/0/0
D       10.1.2.8/30 [90/40640000] via 10.1.203.2, 00:05:56, Serial0/0/1
                    [90/21152000] via 10.1.103.1, 00:05:56, Serial0/0/0
D       10.1.102.0/29 [90/41024000] via 10.1.203.2, 00:05:56, Serial0/0/1
                      [90/21024000] via 10.1.103.1, 00:05:56, Serial0/0/0
R3#
```

h. These unequal-cost routes also show up in the EIGRP topology table as an additional successor. Use the **show ip eigrp topology** command to verify this. Notice there are two successor routes with different (unequal) feasible distances.

```
R3# show ip eigrp topology
EIGRP-IPv4 Topology Table for AS(100)/ID(10.1.3.9)
Codes: P - Passive, A - Active, U - Update, Q - Query, R - Reply,
       r - reply Status, s - sia Status

P 10.1.102.0/29, 2 successors, FD is 21024000
        via 10.1.103.1 (21024000/20512000), Serial0/0/0
        via 10.1.203.2 (41024000/20512000), Serial0/0/1
P 10.1.1.8/30, 1 successors, FD is 20640000
        via 10.1.103.1 (20640000/128256), Serial0/0/0
P 10.1.3.0/30, 1 successors, FD is 128256
        via Connected, Loopback31
P 10.1.3.4/30, 1 successors, FD is 128256
        via Connected, Loopback35
P 10.1.3.8/30, 1 successors, FD is 128256
        via Connected, Loopback39
P 10.1.2.8/30, 2 successors, FD is 21152000
        via 10.1.203.2 (40640000/128256), Serial0/0/1
        via 10.1.103.1 (21152000/20640000), Serial0/0/0
P 10.1.2.0/30, 2 successors, FD is 21152000
        via 10.1.203.2 (40640000/128256), Serial0/0/1
        via 10.1.103.1 (21152000/20640000), Serial0/0/0
P 10.1.103.0/29, 1 successors, FD is 20512000
        via Connected, Serial0/0/0
P 10.1.203.0/29, 1 successors, FD is 40512000
        via Connected, Serial0/0/1
P 10.1.1.4/30, 1 successors, FD is 20640000
        via 10.1.103.1 (20640000/128256), Serial0/0/0
P 10.1.2.4/30, 2 successors, FD is 21152000
        via 10.1.203.2 (40640000/128256), Serial0/0/1
        via 10.1.103.1 (21152000/20640000), Serial0/0/0
P 10.1.1.0/30, 1 successors, FD is 20640000
        via 10.1.103.1 (20640000/128256), Serial0/0/0

R3#
```

i. Load balancing over serial links occurs in blocks of packets, the number of which are recorded in the routing table's detailed routing information. Use the **show ip route 10.1.2.0** command to get a detailed view of how traffic is shared between the two links. The traffic share counters represent the ratio of traffic over the shared paths. In this case the ratio is 48:25 or about 2-to-1. The path through R1, 10.1.103.1, will be sent twice as much traffic as the path through R2, 10.1.203.2. A traffic share count of 1 on all routes indicates equal cost load balancing. If the traffic share count is 0, the path is not in use.

```
R3# show ip route 10.1.2.0
Routing entry for 10.1.2.0/30
  Known via "eigrp 100", distance 90, metric 21152000, type internal
  Redistributing via eigrp 100
  Last update from 10.1.203.2 on Serial0/0/1, 00:10:11 ago
  Routing Descriptor Blocks:
    10.1.203.2, from 10.1.203.2, 00:10:11 ago, via Serial0/0/1
      Route metric is 40640000, traffic share count is 25
      Total delay is 25000 microseconds, minimum bandwidth is 64 Kbit
      Reliability 255/255, minimum MTU 1500 bytes
      Loading 3/255, Hops 1
  * 10.1.103.1, from 10.1.103.1, 00:10:11 ago, via Serial0/0/0
      Route metric is 21152000, traffic share count is 48
      Total delay is 45000 microseconds, minimum bandwidth is 128 Kbit
      Reliability 255/255, minimum MTU 1500 bytes
      Loading 1/255, Hops 2
R3#
```

j. Check the actual load balancing using the **debug ip packet** command. Ping from R3 to 10.1.2.1 with a high enough repeat count to view the load balancing over both paths. In the case above, the traffic share is 25 packets routed to R2 to every 48 packets routed to R1.

To filter the debug output to make it more useful, use the following extended access list.

```
R3(config)# access-list 100 permit icmp any any echo
R3(config)# end

R3# debug ip packet 100
IP packet debugging is on for access list 100

R3# ping 10.1.2.1 repeat 50

Type escape sequence to abort.
Sending 50, 100-byte ICMP Echos to 10.1.2.1, timeout is 2 seconds:
!!!!!!!!!!!!!!!!!!!!!!!!!!!!!!!!!!!!!!!!!!!!!!!!!!!
*Jun 22 13:48:23.598: IP: tableid=0, s=10.1.103.3 (local), d=10.1.2.1
(Serial0/0/0), routed via RIB
*Jun 22 13:48:23.598: IP: s=10.1.103.3 (local), d=10.1.2.1 (Serial0/0/0), len
100, sending
*Jun 22 13:48:23.598: IP: s=10.1.103.3 (local), d=10.1.2.1 (Serial0/0/0), len
100, sending full packet
*Jun 22 13:48:23.626: IP: tableid=0, s=10.1.103.3 (local), d=10.1.2.1
(Serial0/0/0), routed via RIB
*Jun 22 13:48:23.626: IP: s=10.1.103.3 (local), d=10.1.2.1 (Serial0/0/0), len
100, sending
!!!!!!!!!!!!!!!!!!!!!!!!!!!!!!!!!!!!!!!!!!!!
*Jun 22 13:48:23.626: IP: s=10.1.103.3 (local), d=10.1.2.1 (Serial0/0/0), len
100, sending full packet
```

```
*Jun 22 13:48:23.654: IP: tableid=0, s=10.1.103.3 (local), d=10.1.2.1
(Serial0/0/0), routed via RIB
*Jun 22 13:48:23.654: IP: s=10.1.103.3 (local), d=10.1.2.1 (Serial0/0/0), len
100, sending
*Jun 22 13:48:23.654: IP: s=10.1.103.3 (local), d=10.1.2.1 (Serial0/0/0), len
100, sending full packet
!
```

R3 just switched to load-share the outbound ICMP packets to Serial0/0/1.

```
!
*Jun 22 13:48:24.954: IP: s=10.1.203.3 (local), d=10.1.2.1 (Serial0/0/1), len
100, sending
*Jun 22 13:48:24.954: IP: s=10.1.203.3 (local), d=10.1.2.1 (Serial0/0/1), len
100, sending full packet
*Jun 22 13:48:24.982: IP: tableid=0, s=10.1.203.3 (local), d=10.1.2.1
(Serial0/0/1), routed via RIB
*Jun 22 13:48:24.982: IP: s=10.1.203.3 (local), d=10.1.2.1 (Serial0/0/1), len
100, sending
*Jun 22 13:48:24.982: IP: s=10.1.203.3 (local), d=10.1.2.1 (Serial0/0/1,
R3#), len 100, sending full packet
R3#
<output omitted>
```

Note: If a deliberate metric manipulation is necessary on a router to force it to prefer one interface over another for EIGRP-discovered routes, it is recommended to use the interface-level command "delay" for these purposes. While the "bandwidth" command can also be used to influence the metrics of EIGRP-discovered routes through a particular interface, it is discouraged because the "bandwidth" will also influence the amount of bandwidth reserved for EIGRP packets and other IOS subsystems as well. The "delay" parameter specifies the value of the interface delay that is used exclusively by EIGRP to perform metric calculations and does not influence any other area of IOS operation.

k. Issue the **show ip protocols** command to verify the **variance** parameter and the number of maximum paths used by EIGRP. By default, EIGRP will use a maximum of 4 paths for load balancing. This value can be changed using the **maximum-path** EIGRP configuration command.

```
R3# show ip protocols
*** IP Routing is NSF aware ***

Routing Protocol is "application"
  Sending updates every 0 seconds
  Invalid after 0 seconds, hold down 0, flushed after 0
  Outgoing update filter list for all interfaces is not set
  Incoming update filter list for all interfaces is not set
  Maximum path: 32
  Routing for Networks:
  Routing Information Sources:
    Gateway         Distance      Last Update
  Distance: (default is 4)

Routing Protocol is "eigrp 100"
  Outgoing update filter list for all interfaces is not set
  Incoming update filter list for all interfaces is not set
  Default networks flagged in outgoing updates
  Default networks accepted from incoming updates
  EIGRP-IPv4 Protocol for AS(100)
    Metric weight K1=1, K2=0, K3=1, K4=0, K5=0
```

```
   NSF-aware route hold timer is 240
   Router-ID: 10.1.3.9
   Topology : 0 (base)
     Active Timer: 3 min
     Distance: internal 90 external 170
     Maximum path: 4
     Maximum hopcount 100
     Maximum metric variance 2

Automatic Summarization: disabled
Maximum path: 4
Routing for Networks:
  10.0.0.0
Routing Information Sources:
  Gateway            Distance        Last Update
  10.1.103.1              90         00:39:03
  10.1.203.2              90         00:39:03
Distance: internal 90 external 170

R3#
```

Lab 2-2 EIGRP Stub Routing

Topology

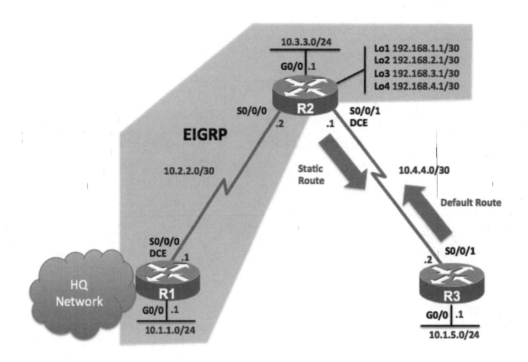

Objectives

- Configure basic EIGRP.
- Configure EIGRP stub routing options.
- Verify EIGRP stub routing options.

Background

To improve network stability and reduce resource utilization on the HQ network you have decided to configure one of the branch routers, R2 as an EIGRP stub router.

Note: This lab uses Cisco 1941 routers with Cisco IOS Release 15.4 with IP Base. The switches are Cisco WS-C2960-24TT-L with Fast Ethernet interfaces; therefore, the router will use routing metrics associated with a 100 Mb/s interface. Depending on the router or switch model and Cisco IOS Software version, the commands available and output produced might vary from what is shown in this lab.

Required Resources

- 3 routers (Cisco IOS Release 15.2 or comparable)
- 3 switches (LAN interfaces)
- Serial and Ethernet cables

Step 0: Suggested starting configurations.

a. Apply the following configuration to each router along with the appropriate **hostname**. The **exec-timeout 0 0** command should only be used in a lab environment.

```
Router(config)# no ip domain-lookup
Router(config)# line con 0
Router(config-line)# logging synchronous
Router(config-line)# exec-timeout 0 0
```

Step 1: Configure the addressing and serial links.

a. Using the addressing scheme in the diagram, configure the interfaces on each router.

```
R1(config)# interface gigabitethernet 0/0
R1(config-if)# ip address 10.1.1.1 255.255.255.0
R1(config-if)# no shutdown
R1(config-if)# exit
R1(config)# interface serial 0/0/0
R1(config-if)# ip address 10.2.2.1 255.255.255.252
R1(config-if)# clock rate 64000
R1(config-if)# no shutdown
R1(config-if)# exit


R2(config)# interface serial 0/0/0
R2(config-if)# ip address 10.2.2.2 255.255.255.252
R2(config-if)# no shutdown
R2(config-if)# exit
R2(config)# interface gigabitethernet 0/0
R2(config-if)# ip address 10.3.3.1 255.255.255.0
R2(config-if)# no shutdown
R2(config-if)# exit
R2(config)# interface serial 0/0/1
R2(config-if)# ip address 10.4.4.1 255.255.255.252
R2(config-if)# clockrate 64000
R2(config-if)# no shutdown
R2(config-if)# exit
R2(config)# interface Loopback1
R2(config-if)# ip address 192.168.1.1 255.255.255.252
R2(config-if)# exit
R2(config)# interface Loopback2
R2(config-if)# ip address 192.168.2.1 255.255.255.252
R2(config-if)# exit
R2(config)# interface Loopback3
R2(config-if)# ip address 192.168.3.1 255.255.255.252
R2(config-if)# exit
R2(config)# interface Loopback4
R2(config-if)# ip address 192.168.4.1 255.255.255.252
R2(config-if)# exit


R3(config)# interface serial 0/0/1
R3(config-if)# ip address 10.4.4.2 255.255.255.252
R3(config-if)# no shutdown
R3(config-if)# exit
R3(config)# interface gigabitethernet 0/0
R3(config-if)# ip address 10.1.5.1 255.255.255.0
```

```
R3(config-if)# no shutdown
R3(config-if)# exit
```

b. Verify connectivity by pinging across each of the local networks connected to each router.

c. Issue the **show ip interface brief** command on each router. This command displays a brief listing of the interfaces, their status, and their IP addresses. Router R2 is shown as an example.

```
R2# show ip interface brief
Interface                  IP-Address     OK? Method Status
Protocol
Embedded-Service-Engine0/0 unassigned     YES unset  administratively down down
GigabitEthernet0/0         10.3.3.1       YES manual up                      up
Serial0/0/0                10.2.2.2       YES manual up                      up
Serial0/0/1                10.4.4.1       YES manual up                      up
R2#
```

Step 2: Configure EIGRP.

a. Enable EIGRP AS 100 for all interfaces on R1 and R2. For your reference, these are the commands that can be used:

```
R1(config)# router eigrp 100
R1(config-router)# network 10.0.0.0

R2(config)# router eigrp 100
R2(config-router)# network 10.0.0.0
R2(config-router)# network 192.168.0.0 0.0.255.255
```

b. Summarize R2's loopback interfaces in its EIGRP update to R1 using manual summarization.

```
R2(config)# interface serial 0/0/0
R2(config-if)# ip summary-address eigrp 100 192.168.0.0 255.255.248.0
```

c. Configure a static route on R2 to R3's LAN. Configure a default static route on R3 forwarding all traffic to R2.

```
R2(config)# ip route 10.1.5.0 255.255.255.0 10.4.4.2

R3(config)# ip route 0.0.0.0 0.0.0.0 10.4.4.1
```

d. Verify that R2 and R3 can ping the other's LAN interfaces.

```
R2# ping 10.1.5.1
Type escape sequence to abort.
Sending 5, 100-byte ICMP Echos to 10.1.5.1, timeout is 2 seconds:
!!!!!
Success rate is 100 percent (5/5), round-trip min/avg/max = 28/28/28 ms
R2#

R3# ping 10.3.3.1
Type escape sequence to abort.
Sending 5, 100-byte ICMP Echos to 10.3.3.1, timeout is 2 seconds:
!!!!!
Success rate is 100 percent (5/5), round-trip min/avg/max = 28/28/28 ms
R3#
```

e. Verify the EIGRP neighbor relationship between R1 and R2 with the **show ip eigrp neighbors** command. Verify that R1 is receiving a summary route for R2's loopback networks. The output for R2 is as follows.

```
R2# show ip eigrp neighbors
EIGRP-IPv4 Neighbors for AS(100)
H   Address                  Interface           Hold Uptime   SRTT   RTO
Q   Seq
                                                 (sec)         (ms)
Cnt Num
0   10.2.2.1                 Se0/0/0             12 00:51:26   363    2178
0   9
R2#
```

f. Examine R1's routing table with the **show ip route eigrp** command.

```
R1# show ip route
Codes: L -  local, C - connected, S - static, R - RIP, M - mobile, B - BGP
       D - EIGRP, EX - EIGRP external, O - OSPF, IA - OSPF inter area
       N1 - OSPF NSSA external type 1, N2 - OSPF NSSA external type 2
       E1 - OSPF external type 1, E2 - OSPF external type 2
       i - IS-IS, su - IS-IS summary, L1 - IS-IS level-1, L2 - IS-IS level-2
       ia - IS-IS inter area, * - candidate default, U - per-user static
       route
       o - ODR, P - periodic downloaded static route, H - NHRP, l - LISP
       a - application route
       + - replicated route, % - next hop override

Gateway of last resort is not set

      10.0.0.0/8 is variably subnetted, 6 subnets, 3 masks
C        10.1.1.0/24 is directly connected, GigabitEthernet0/0
L        10.1.1.1/32 is directly connected, GigabitEthernet0/0
C        10.2.2.0/30 is directly connected, Serial0/0/0
L        10.2.2.1/32 is directly connected, Serial0/0/0
D        10.3.3.0/30 [90/2172416] via 10.2.2.2, 00:52:58, Serial0/0/0
D        10.4.4.0/30 [90/2681856] via 10.2.2.2, 00:52:58, Serial0/0/0
D     192.168.0.0/21 [90/2297856] via 10.2.2.2, 00:47:02, Serial0/0/0
R1#
```

Does R1 have a route to R3's LAN? Why or why not?

_____

_____

Step 3: Configure and verify EIGRP stub routing.

a. The EIGRP stub routing feature enables you to limit the EIGRP Query messages' scope in the network. Routers configured as stubs do not forward EIGRP learned routes to other neighbors.

Use the **eigrp stub** command to configure a router as a stub where the router directs all IP traffic to a distribution router.

The **eigrp stub** command can be modified with several options, and these options can be used in any combination except for the **receive-only** keyword. The **receive-only** keyword will restrict the router from sharing any of its routes with any other router in that EIGRP autonomous system, and the **receive-only** keyword will not permit any other option to be specified because it prevents any type of route from being sent. The four other optional keywords (**connected**, **static**, **summary**, and **redistributed**) can be used in any combination but cannot be used with the **receive-only** keyword.

If any of these five keywords is used with the **eigrp stub** command, only the route types specified by the particular keyword(s) will be sent. Route types specified by the remaining keywords will not be sent.

The **connected** keyword permits the EIGRP stub routing feature to send connected routes. If the connected routes are not covered by a network statement, it may be necessary to redistribute connected routes with the redistribute connected command under the EIGRP process. *This option is enabled by default*.

The **static** keyword permits the EIGRP stub routing feature to send static routes. Without the configuration of this option, EIGRP will not send any static routes, including internal static routes that normally would be automatically redistributed. It will still be necessary to redistribute static routes with the redistribute static command.

The **summary** keyword permits the EIGRP stub routing feature to send summary routes. Summary routes can be created manually with the summary address command or automatically at a major network border router with the auto-summary command enabled. *This option is enabled by default*.

The **redistributed** keyword permits the EIGRP stub routing feature to send other routing protocols and autonomous systems. Without the configuration of this option, EIGRP will not advertise redistributed routes.

Note: There is one more keyword: the **leak-map** option. The **leak-map** keyword permits the EIGRP stub routing feature to reference a leak map that identifies routes that are allowed to be advertised on an EIGRP stub router that would normally have been suppressed.

Configure R2 as a stub router using the default **eigrp stub** command.

```
R2(config)# router eigrp 100
R2(config-router)# eigrp stub ?
  connected      Do advertise connected routes
  leak-map       Allow dynamic prefixes based on the leak-map
  receive-only   Set receive only neighbor
  redistributed  Do advertise redistributed routes
  static         Do advertise static routes
  summary        Do advertise summary routes
  <cr>
 R2(config-router)# eigrp stub
*Jul 22 00:41:02.667: %DUAL-5-NBRCHANGE: EIGRP-IPv4 100: Neighbor 10.2.2.1
(Serial0/0/0) is down: peer info changed
R2(config-router)#
*Jul 22 00:41:03.899: %DUAL-5-NBRCHANGE: EIGRP-IPv4 100: Neighbor 10.2.2.1
(Serial0/0/0) is up: new adjacency
R2(config-router)
```

b. Examine the EIGRP section in R2's running-config.

```
R2# show running-config | section eigrp
 ip summary-address eigrp 100 192.168.0.0 255.255.248.0
router eigrp 100
 network 10.0.0.0
 network 192.168.0.0 0.0.255.255
 eigrp stub connected summary
R2#
```

What EIGRP stub options are implemented by default?

_____

_____

c. Examine the EIGRP routes in R1's routing table.

```
R1# show ip route eigrp

      10.0.0.0/8 is variably subnetted, 6 subnets, 3 masks
D        10.3.3.0/24 [90/2172416] via 10.2.2.2, 00:10:34, Serial0/0/0
D        10.4.4.0/30 [90/2681856] via 10.2.2.2, 00:10:34, Serial0/0/0
D     192.168.0.0/21 [90/2297856] via 10.2.2.2, 00:10:34, Serial0/0/0
R1#
```

Notice that R1 shows EIGRP routes for R2's connected networks and R2's 192.16.0.0/21 summary route.

d. Issue the **show ip eigrp neighbors detail** command to verify that R1 sees R2 as a stub router.

```
R1# show ip eigrp neighbors detail
EIGRP-IPv4 Neighbors for AS(100)
H   Address                 Interface            Hold Uptime   SRTT   RTO
Q   Seq
                                                 (sec)         (ms)
Cnt Num
0   10.2.2.2                Se0/0/0              14 00:21:37   20    120
0   15
    Version 16.0/2.0, Retrans: 0, Retries: 0, Prefixes: 3
    Topology-ids from peer - 0
    Stub Peer Advertising (CONNECTED SUMMARY ) Routes
    Suppressing queries
Max Nbrs: 0, Current Nbrs: 0
R1#
```

Step 4: Configure and verify EIGRP stub routing options static, connected, and summary.

a. Modify R2's stub routing to also include its static route in its EIGRP update to R1. It is necessary to also include the **redistribute static** command.

```
R2(config)# router eigrp 100
R2(config-router)# redistribute static
R2(config-router)# eigrp stub static
*Jul 22 01:08:39.891: %DUAL-5-NBRCHANGE: EIGRP-IPv4 100: Neighbor 10.2.2.1
(Serial0/0/0) is down: peer info changed
```

```
*Jul 22 01:08:40.919: %DUAL-5-NBRCHANGE: EIGRP-IPv4 100: Neighbor 10.2.2.1
(Serial0/0/0) is up: new adjacency
```

With each change of the EIGRP stub settings, reestablishment of the EIGRP neighbor session is required.

b. Examine R1's EIGRP routes using the **show ip route eigrp** command.

```
R1# show ip route eigrp

      10.0.0.0/8 is variably subnetted, 5 subnets, 3 masks
D EX    10.1.5.0/24 [170/2681856] via 10.2.2.2, 00:00:23, Serial0/0/0
R1#
```

Why does R1 only have R2's static route to R3's LAN? What do you need to do so R1 includes the previous EIGRP routes?

_____

_____

c. R2's stub configuration can be verified using the **show ip eigrp neighbors detail** command on R1 and **show running-config | section eigrp** on R2.

```
R1# show ip eigrp neighbors detail
EIGRP-IPv4 Neighbors for AS(100)
H   Address                   Interface           Hold Uptime   SRTT   RTO
Q   Seq
                                                  (sec)         (ms)
Cnt Num
0   10.2.2.2                  Se0/0/0             13 00:14:45   22     132
0   20
    Version 16.0/2.0, Retrans: 0, Retries: 0, Prefixes: 1
    Topology-ids from peer - 0
    Stub Peer Advertising (STATIC ) Routes
    Suppressing queries
Max Nbrs: 0, Current Nbrs: 0
R1#

R2# show running-config | section eigrp
 ip summary-address eigrp 100 192.168.0.0 255.255.248.0
router eigrp 100
 network 10.0.0.0
 network 192.168.0.0 0.0.255.255
 redistribute static
 eigrp stub static
R2#
```

d. Configure R2 EIGRP stub routing to include the connected, summary, and static options.

```
R2(config)# router eigrp 100
R2(config-router)# eigrp stub connected summary static
*Jul 22 01:29:15.411: %DUAL-5-NBRCHANGE: EIGRP-IPv4 100: Neighbor 10.2.2.1
(Serial0/0/0) is down: peer info changed
*Jul 22 01:29:17.195: %DUAL-5-NBRCHANGE: EIGRP-IPv4 100: Neighbor 10.2.2.1
(Serial0/0/0) is up: new adjacency
```

e. Examine R1's routing table and notice R1 is now sending its connected, summarized, and static routes to
    R1.

    ```
    R1# show ip route eigrp

         10.0.0.0/8 is variably subnetted, 7 subnets, 3 masks
    D EX    10.1.5.0/24 [170/2681856] via 10.2.2.2, 00:02:11, Serial0/0/0
    D       10.3.3.0/24 [90/2172416] via 10.2.2.2, 00:02:11, Serial0/0/0
    D       10.4.4.0/30 [90/2681856] via 10.2.2.2, 00:02:11, Serial0/0/0
    D    192.168.0.0/21 [90/2297856] via 10.2.2.2, 00:02:11, Serial0/0/0
    R1#
    ```

f. Verify R2's modified stub configuration using the **show ip eigrp neighbors detail** command on R1.

    ```
    R1# show ip eigrp neighbor detail
    EIGRP-IPv4 Neighbors for AS(100)
    H   Address                Interface          Hold Uptime   SRTT   RTO
    Q   Seq
                                                  (sec)         (ms)
    Cnt Num
    0   10.2.2.2               Se0/0/0            11 00:02:37 1289   5000
    0   22
        Version 16.0/2.0, Retrans: 0, Retries: 0, Prefixes: 4
        Topology-ids from peer - 0
        Stub Peer Advertising (CONNECTED STATIC SUMMARY ) Routes
        Suppressing queries
    Max Nbrs: 0, Current Nbrs: 0
    R1#
    ```

g. Examine the change to R2's running-configuration using the **show running-config | section eigrp**
    command.

    ```
    R2# show running-config | section eigrp
     ip summary-address eigrp 100 192.168.0.0 255.255.248.0
    router eigrp 100
     network 10.0.0.0
     network 192.168.0.0 0.0.255.255
     redistribute static
     eigrp stub connected static summary
    R2#
    ```

h. At this point R1 and R3 should now be able to ping the other's LAN.

    ```
    R1# ping 10.1.5.1
    Type escape sequence to abort.
    Sending 5, 100-byte ICMP Echos to 10.1.5.1, timeout is 2 seconds:
    !!!!!
    Success rate is 100 percent (5/5), round-trip min/avg/max = 56/56/56 ms
    R1#


    R3# ping 10.1.1.1
    Type escape sequence to abort.
    Sending 5, 100-byte ICMP Echos to 10.1.1.1, timeout is 2 seconds:
    !!!!!
    Success rate is 100 percent (5/5), round-trip min/avg/max = 52/55/56 ms
    R3#
    ```

Step 5: Configure and verify EIGRP stub routing option receive-only.

a. The **receive-only** option prevents the stub router from sharing any of its routes with any other router in the EIGRP AS. This option does not permit any other option to be included. The option is not as common as the previous options. Examples of the **receive-only** option include when the router has a single interface or if NAT/PAT is configured with host hidden behind the stub router.

```
R2(config)# router eigrp 100
R2(config-router)# eigrp stub receive-only
*Jul 22 01:51:37.995: %DUAL-5-NBRCHANGE: EIGRP-IPv4 100: Neighbor 10.2.2.1
(Serial0/0/0) is down: peer info changed
*Jul 22 01:51:41.115: %SYS-5-CONFIG_I: Configured from console by console
*Jul 22 01:51:41.843: %DUAL-5-NBRCHANGE: EIGRP-IPv4 100: Neighbor 10.2.2.1
(Serial0/0/0) is up: new adjacency
```

What EIGRP routes do you expect R1 to have in its routing table?

_____

_____

b. Issue the **show ip route eigrp** command to examine the EIGRP routes R1 is receiving from R2.

```
R1# show ip route eigrp
Codes: L - local, C - connected, S - static, R - RIP, M - mobile, B - BGP
       D - EIGRP, EX - EIGRP external, O - OSPF, IA - OSPF inter area
       N1 - OSPF NSSA external type 1, N2 - OSPF NSSA external type 2
       E1 - OSPF external type 1, E2 - OSPF external type 2
       i - IS-IS, su - IS-IS summary, L1 - IS-IS level-1, L2 - IS-IS level-2
       ia - IS-IS inter area, * - candidate default, U - per-user static
       route
       o - ODR, P - periodic downloaded static route, H - NHRP, l - LISP
       a - application route
       + - replicated route, % - next hop override

Gateway of last resort is not set

R1#
```

Notice that R1 does not receive any EIGRP routes from R2.

c. Issue the **show ip eigrp neighbor detail** command on R1 to verify it sees R2 as a receive-only stub router .

```
R1# show ip eigrp neighbor detail
EIGRP-IPv4 Neighbors for AS(100)
H   Address                 Interface        Hold Uptime   SRTT   RTO
Q   Seq
                                             (sec)         (ms)
Cnt Num
0   10.2.2.2                Se0/0/0          11 00:01:58   19     114
0   24
    Version 16.0/2.0, Retrans: 0, Retries: 0
    Topology-ids from peer - 0
    Receive-Only Peer Advertising (No) Routes
    Suppressing queries
Max Nbrs: 0, Current Nbrs: 0
R1#
```

Lab 2-3 EIGRP for IPv6

Topology

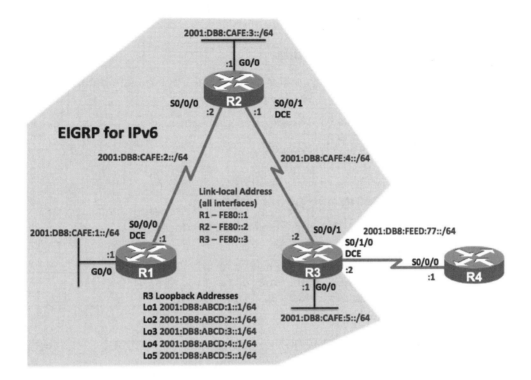

Objectives

- Configure EIGRP for IPv6.
- Verify EIGRP for IPv6.
- Configure and verify passive routes using EIGRP for IPv6.
- Configure and verify summary routes using EIGRP for IPv6.
- Configure and verify default route using EIGRP for IPv6.

Background

EIGRP for IPv6 has the same overall operation and features as EIGRP for IPv4. However, there are a few major differences between them:

- EIGRP for IPv6 is configured directly on the router interfaces.
- In the absence of the router having any IPv4 addresses, a 32-bit router ID must be configured for the routing process to start.
- IPv6 unicast routing must be enabled before the routing process can be configured.

In this lab, you will configure the network with EIGRP routing for IPv6. You will also assign router IDs, configure passive interfaces, a summary route, and verify the network is fully converged.

Note: This lab uses Cisco 1941 routers with Cisco IOS Release 15.2 with IP Base. The switches are Cisco WS-C2960-24TT-L with Fast Ethernet interfaces; therefore, the router will use routing metrics associated with a 100 Mb/s interface. Depending on the router or switch model and Cisco IOS Software version, the commands available and output produced might vary from what is shown in this lab.

Required Resources

- 4 routers (Cisco IOS Release 15.2 or comparable)
- 3 switches (LAN interfaces)
- Serial and Ethernet cables

Step 0: Suggested starting configurations.

a. Apply the following configuration to each router along with the appropriate **hostname**. The **exec-timeout 0 0** command should only be used in a lab environment.

```
Router(config)# no ip domain-lookup
Router(config)# line con 0
Router(config-line)# logging synchronous
Router(config-line)# exec-timeout 0 0
```

Step 1: Configure the addressing and serial links.

a. Using the topology, configure the IPv6 addresses on the interfaces of each router including the loopback addresses on R3.

```
R1(config)# interface gigabitethernet 0/0
R1(config-if)# ipv6 address 2001:db8:cafe:1::1/64
R1(config-if)# ipv6 address fe80::1 link-local
R1(config-if)# no shutdown
R1(config-if)# exit
R1(config)# interface serial 0/0/0
R1(config-if)# ipv6 address 2001:db8:cafe:2::1/64
R1(config-if)# ipv6 address fe80::1 link-local
R1(config-if)# clock rate 64000
R1(config-if)# no shutdown
R1(config-if)# exit


R2(config)# interface serial 0/0/0
R2(config-if)# ipv6 address 2001:db8:cafe:2::2/64
R2(config-if)# ipv6 address fe80::2 link-local
R2(config-if)# no shutdown
R2(config-if)# exit
R2(config)# interface gigabitethernet 0/0
R2(config-if)# ipv6 address 2001:db8:cafe:3::1/64
R2(config-if)# ipv6 address fe80::2 link-local
R2(config-if)# no shutdown
R2(config)# interface serial 0/0/1
R2(config-if)# ipv6 address 2001:db8:cafe:4::1/64
R2(config-if)# ipv6 address fe80::2 link-local
R2(config-if)# clock rate 64000
R2(config-if)# no shutdown
R2(config-if)# exit


R3(config)# interface serial 0/0/1
R3(config-if)# ipv6 address 2001:db8:cafe:4::2/64
R3(config-if)# ipv6 address fe80::3 link-local
R3(config-if)# no shutdown
R3(config-if)# exit
```

```
R3(config)# interface gigabitethernet 0/0
R3(config-if)# ipv6 address 2001:db8:cafe:5::1/64
R3(config-if)# ipv6 address fe80::3 link-local
R3(config-if)# no shutdown
R3(config-if)# exit
R3(config)# interface loopback 1
R3(config-if)# ipv6 address 2001:db8:abcd:1::1/64
R3(config-if)# exit
R3(config)# interface loopback 2
R3(config-if)# ipv6 address 2001:db8:abcd:2::1/64
R3(config-if)# exit
R3(config)# interface loopback 3
R3(config-if)# ipv6 address 2001:db8:abcd:3::1/64
R3(config-if)# exit
R3(config)# interface loopback 4
R3(config-if)# ipv6 address 2001:db8:abcd:4::1/64
R3(config-if)# exit
R3(config)# interface loopback 5
R3(config-if)# ipv6 address 2001:db8:abcd:5::1/64
R3(config-if)# exit
R3(config)# interface serial 0/1/0
R3(config-if)# ipv6 address 2001:db8:feed:77::2/64
R3(config-if)# ipv6 address fe80::3 link-local
R3(config-if)# clock rate 64000
R3(config-if)# no shutdown
R3(config-if)# exit
R3(config)#


R4(config)# interface serial 0/0/0
R4(config-if)# ipv6 address 2001:db8:feed:77::1/64
R4(config-if)# ipv6 address fe80::4 link-local
R4(config-if)# no shutdown
R4(config-if)# exit
R4(config)# ipv6 route 2001:db8:cafe::/48 2001:db8:feed:77::2
R4(config)# ipv6 route 2001:db8:abcd::/48 2001:db8:feed:77::2
```

b. Verify connectivity by pinging across each of the local networks connected to each router.

c. Issue the **show ipv6 interface brief** command on each router. This command displays a brief listing of the interfaces, their status, and their IPv6 addresses. Router R1 is shown as an example.

```
R1# show ipv6 interface brief
Em0/0                    [administratively down/down]
    unassigned
GigabitEthernet0/0       [up/up]
    FE80::1
    2001:DB8:CAFE:1::1
GigabitEthernet0/1       [administratively down/down]
    unassigned
Serial0/0/0              [up/up]
    FE80::1
    2001:DB8:CAFE:2::1
Serial0/0/1              [administratively down/down]
    unassigned
R1#
```

Step 2: Configure EIGRP for IPv6 routing.

a. Enable IPv6 unicast routing and EIGRP for IPv6 on each router. Since there are no active IPv4 addresses configured, EIGRP for IPv6 requires the configuration of a 32-bit router ID. Use the **router-id** command to configure the router ID in the router configuration mode.

Note: Prior to IOS 15.2 the EIGRP IPv6 routing process is shut down by default and the **no shutdown** router configuration mode command is required to enable the routing process. Although not required with the IOS used in creating this lab, an example of the **no shutdown** command is shown for router R1.

```
R1(config)# ipv6 unicast-routing
R1(config)# ipv6 router eigrp 1
R1(config-rtr)# eigrp router-id 1.1.1.1
R1(config-rtr)# no shutdown

R2(config)# ipv6 unicast-routing
R2(config)# ipv6 router eigrp 1
R2(config-rtr)# router-id 2.2.2.2

R3(config)# ipv6 unicast-routing
R3(config)# ipv6 router eigrp 1
R3(config-rtr)# eigrp router-id 3.3.3.3
```

Step 3: Configure EIGRP for IPv6 on Serial, Gigabit Ethernet, and Loopback interfaces on all routers.

a. Issue the **ipv6 eigrp 1** command on the interfaces that participate in the EIGRP routing process. EIGRP for IPv6 does not use the **network** command. IPv6 prefixes are enabled on the interface. Similar to EIGRP for IPv4, the AS number must match the neighbor's configuration for the router to form an adjacency.

```
R1(config)# interface g0/0
R1(config-if)# ipv6 eigrp 1
R1(config-if)# exit
R1(config)# interface s0/0/0
R1(config-if)# ipv6 eigrp 1

R2(config)# interface g0/0
R2(config-if)# ipv6 eigrp 1
R2(config-if)# exit
R2(config)# interface s0/0/0
R2(config-if)# ipv6 eigrp 1
R2(config-if)# exit
R2(config)# interface s0/0/1
R2(config-if)# ipv6 eigrp 1

R3(config)# interface g0/0
R3(config-if)# ipv6 eigrp 1
R3(config-if)# exit
R3(config)# interface s0/0/1
R3(config-if)# ipv6 eigrp 1
```

```
R3(config-if)# exit
R3(config)# interface loop1
R3(config-if)# ipv6 eigrp 1
R3(config-if)# exit
R3(config)# interface loop2
R3(config-if)# ipv6 eigrp 1
R3(config-if)# exit
R3(config)# interface loop3
R3(config-if)# ipv6 eigrp 1
R3(config-if)# exit
R3(config)# interface loop4
R3(config-if)# ipv6 eigrp 1
R3(config-if)# exit
R3(config)# interface loop5
R3(config-if)# ipv6 eigrp 1
```

b. When you assign EIGRP for IPv6 on R2's serial 0/0/0 interface you will see the neighbor adjacency message as the interface is added to the EIGRP routing process.

```
R1#
*Sep 24 15:28:13.911: %DUAL-5-NBRCHANGE: EIGRP-IPv6 1: Neighbor FE80::2 (Serial0/0/0)
is up: new adjacency
R1#
```

What address on R2 is used to form the neighbor adjacency with R1? What type of IPv6 address is used to establish the adjacencies?

_____

Step 4: Verify EIGRP for IPv6 routing.

a. On R2, issue the **show ipv6 eigrp neighbors** command to verify the adjacency has been established with its neighboring routers. The link-local addresses of the neighboring routers are displayed in the adjacency table.

```
R2# show ipv6 eigrp neighbors
EIGRP-IPv6 Neighbors for AS(1)
H   Address              Interface      Hold Uptime    SRTT  RTO   Q   Seq
                                        (sec)          (ms)        Cnt Num
1   Link-local address:  Se0/0/1        11 00:27:22    31    186   0   8
    FE80::3
0   Link-local address:  Se0/0/0        14 00:28:17    288   1728  0   10
    FE80::1
R2#
```

b. Verify reachability by pinging the IPv6 addresses on R3 from R1.

```
R1# ping 2001:db8:cafe:5::1
Type escape sequence to abort.
Sending 5, 100-byte ICMP Echos to 2001:DB8:CAFE:5::1, timeout is 2 seconds:
!!!!!
Success rate is 100 percent (5/5), round-trip min/avg/max = 56/56/56 ms
R1# ping 2001:db8:abcd:1::1
Type escape sequence to abort.
Sending 5, 100-byte ICMP Echos to 2001:DB8:ABCD:1::1, timeout is 2 seconds:
!!!!!
Success rate is 100 percent (5/5), round-trip min/avg/max = 52/55/56 ms
R1#
```

c. Use the **show ipv6 route eigrp** command to display IPv6-specific EIGRP routes on all the routers. The output of R1's routing table is displayed next.

```
R1# show ipv6 route eigrp
IPv6 Routing Table - default - 13 entries
Codes: C - Connected, L - Local, S - Static, U - Per-user Static route
       B - BGP, R - RIP, H - NHRP, I1 - ISIS L1
       I2 - ISIS L2, IA - ISIS interarea, IS - ISIS summary, D - EIGRP
       EX - EIGRP external, ND - ND Default, NDp - ND Prefix, DCE -
       Destination
       NDr - Redirect, O - OSPF Intra, OI - OSPF Inter, OE1 - OSPF ext 1
       OE2 - OSPF ext 2, ON1 - OSPF NSSA ext 1, ON2 - OSPF NSSA ext 2
       a - Application
D   2001:DB8:ABCD:1::/64 [90/2809856]
     via FE80::2, Serial0/0/0
D   2001:DB8:ABCD:2::/64 [90/2809856]
     via FE80::2, Serial0/0/0
D   2001:DB8:ABCD:3::/64 [90/2809856]
     via FE80::2, Serial0/0/0
D   2001:DB8:ABCD:4::/64 [90/2809856]
     via FE80::2, Serial0/0/0
D   2001:DB8:ABCD:5::/64 [90/2809856]
     via FE80::2, Serial0/0/0
D   2001:DB8:CAFE:3::/64 [90/2172416]
     via FE80::2, Serial0/0/0
D   2001:DB8:CAFE:4::/64 [90/2681856]
     via FE80::2, Serial0/0/0
D   2001:DB8:CAFE:5::/64 [90/2684416]
     via FE80::2, Serial0/0/0
R1#
```

d. Examine R1's EIGRP for IPv6 topology table using the **show ipv6 eigrp topology** command.

```
R1# show ipv6 eigrp topology
EIGRP-IPv6 Topology Table for AS(1)/ID(1.1.1.1)
Codes: P - Passive, A - Active, U - Update, Q - Query, R - Reply,
       r - reply Status, s - sia Status

P 2001:DB8:CAFE:5::/64, 1 successors, FD is 2684416
        via FE80::2 (2684416/2172416), Serial0/0/0
P 2001:DB8:ABCD:1::/64, 1 successors, FD is 2809856
        via FE80::2 (2809856/2297856), Serial0/0/0
P 2001:DB8:ABCD:2::/64, 1 successors, FD is 2809856
        via FE80::2 (2809856/2297856), Serial0/0/0
P 2001:DB8:CAFE:3::/64, 1 successors, FD is 2172416
        via FE80::2 (2172416/28160), Serial0/0/0
P 2001:DB8:CAFE:4::/64, 1 successors, FD is 2681856
        via FE80::2 (2681856/2169856), Serial0/0/0
P 2001:DB8:CAFE:2::/64, 1 successors, FD is 2169856
        via Connected, Serial0/0/0
P 2001:DB8:ABCD:3::/64, 1 successors, FD is 2809856
        via FE80::2 (2809856/2297856), Serial0/0/0
P 2001:DB8:ABCD:5::/64, 1 successors, FD is 2809856
        via FE80::2 (2809856/2297856), Serial0/0/0
P 2001:DB8:ABCD:4::/64, 1 successors, FD is 2809856
        via FE80::2 (2809856/2297856), Serial0/0/0
P 2001:DB8:CAFE:1::/64, 1 successors, FD is 28160
```

```
        via Connected, GigabitEthernet0/0
```

R1#

Why are there no feasible successors?

_____

Why are there two more entries in R1's EIGRP topology table than there are when displaying R1's EIGRP
routes with the **show ipv6 route eigrp** command?

_____

e.   Issue the **show ipv6 protocols** command to verify the configured parameters. Examining the output,
     EIGRP for IPv6 is the configured IPv6 routing protocol with 1.1.1.1 as the router ID for R1. This routing
     protocol is associated with autonomous system 1 with two active interfaces: G0/0 and S0/0/0.

```
R1# show ipv6 protocols
IPv6 Routing Protocol is "connected"
IPv6 Routing Protocol is "application"
IPv6 Routing Protocol is "ND"
IPv6 Routing Protocol is "eigrp 1"
EIGRP-IPv6 Protocol for AS(1)
  Metric weight K1=1, K2=0, K3=1, K4=0, K5=0
  NSF-aware route hold timer is 240
  Router-ID: 1.1.1.1
  Topology : 0 (base)
    Active Timer: 3 min
    Distance: internal 90 external 170
    Maximum path: 16
    Maximum hopcount 100
    Maximum metric variance 1

  Interfaces:
    GigabitEthernet0/0
    Serial0/0/0
  Redistribution:
    None
R1#
```

Step 5: Configure and verify passive interfaces.

a.   A passive interface does not allow outgoing and incoming routing updates over the configured interface.
     The **passive-interface** *interface* command causes the router to stop sending and receiving Hello packets
     over an interface but continues to advertise that network in its routing updates. Configure passive
     interfaces on each of the three routers' LAN interfaces.

```
R1(config)# ipv6 router eigrp 1
R1(config-rtr)# passive-interface g0/0

R2(config)# ipv6 router eigrp 1
R2(config-rtr)# passive-interface g0/0

R3(config)# ipv6 router eigrp 1
R3(config-rtr)# passive-interface g0/0
```

What would be the result if the **ipv6 eigrp 1** commands were removed from the G0/0 interfaces instead of using the **passive-interface** command? _____

_____

b. Issue the **show ipv6 protocols** command on R1 and verify that G0/0 has been configured as passive.

```
R1# show ipv6 protocols
IPv6 Routing Protocol is "connected"
IPv6 Routing Protocol is "application"
IPv6 Routing Protocol is "ND"
IPv6 Routing Protocol is "eigrp 1"
EIGRP-IPv6 Protocol for AS(1)
  Metric weight K1=1, K2=0, K3=1, K4=0, K5=0
  NSF-aware route hold timer is 240
  Router-ID: 1.1.1.1
  Topology : 0 (base)
    Active Timer: 3 min
    Distance: internal 90 external 170
    Maximum path: 16
    Maximum hopcount 100
    Maximum metric variance 1

  Interfaces:
    Serial0/0/0
    GigabitEthernet0/0 (passive)
  Redistribution:
    None
R1#
```

c. Issue the **show ipv6 route eigrp** command on R3 to verify it is still receiving EIGRP updates containing the IPv6 prefixes that were configured as passive-interfaces.

```
R3# show ipv6 route eigrp
IPv6 Routing Table - default - 18 entries
Codes: C - Connected, L - Local, S - Static, U - Per-user Static route
       B - BGP, R - RIP, H - NHRP, I1 - ISIS L1
       I2 - ISIS L2, IA - ISIS interarea, IS - ISIS summary, D - EIGRP
       EX - EIGRP external, ND - ND Default, NDp - ND Prefix, DCE -
       Destination
       NDr - Redirect, O - OSPF Intra, OI - OSPF Inter, OE1 - OSPF ext 1
       OE2 - OSPF ext 2, ON1 - OSPF NSSA ext 1, ON2 - OSPF NSSA ext 2
       a - Application
D   2001:DB8:CAFE:1::/64 [90/2684416]
     via FE80::2, Serial0/0/1
D   2001:DB8:CAFE:2::/64 [90/2681856]
     via FE80::2, Serial0/0/1
D   2001:DB8:CAFE:3::/64 [90/2172416]
     via FE80::2, Serial0/0/1
R3#
```

Step 6: Configure and verify a summary route.

a. Issue the **show ipv6 route eigrp** command on R1 and verify that it has all five of R3's loopback prefixes in its IPv6 routing table.

```
R1# show ipv6 route eigrp
IPv6 Routing Table - default - 13 entries
Codes: C - Connected, L - Local, S - Static, U - Per-user Static route
       B - BGP, R - RIP, H - NHRP, I1 - ISIS L1
       I2 - ISIS L2, IA - ISIS interarea, IS - ISIS summary, D - EIGRP
       EX - EIGRP external, ND - ND Default, NDp - ND Prefix, DCE -
       Destination
       NDr - Redirect, O - OSPF Intra, OI - OSPF Inter, OE1 - OSPF ext 1
       OE2 - OSPF ext 2, ON1 - OSPF NSSA ext 1, ON2 - OSPF NSSA ext 2
       a - Application
D   2001:DB8:ABCD:1::/64 [90/2809856]
     via FE80::2, Serial0/0/0
D   2001:DB8:ABCD:2::/64 [90/2809856]
     via FE80::2, Serial0/0/0
D   2001:DB8:ABCD:3::/64 [90/2809856]
     via FE80::2, Serial0/0/0
D   2001:DB8:ABCD:4::/64 [90/2809856]
     via FE80::2, Serial0/0/0
D   2001:DB8:ABCD:5::/64 [90/2809856]
     via FE80::2, Serial0/0/0
D   2001:DB8:CAFE:3::/64 [90/2172416]
     via FE80::2, Serial0/0/0
D   2001:DB8:CAFE:4::/64 [90/2681856]
     via FE80::2, Serial0/0/0
D   2001:DB8:CAFE:5::/64 [90/2684416]
     via FE80::2, Serial0/0/0
R1#
```

b. To optimize EIGRP for IPv6, on R3 summarize the loopback addresses as a single route and advertise the summary route in R3's EIGRP updates to R2. Using the same summarization method used for IPv4, the IPv6 loopback addresses can be summarized as 2001:DB8:ABCD::/61. The loopback addresses have the first 61 bits in common. After configuring the summary route on the interface, notice that the neighbor adjacency between R3 and R2 is resynchronized (restarted).

```
R3(config)# interface serial 0/0/1
R3(config-if)# ipv6 summary-address eigrp 1 2001:db8:abcd::/61
*Jun 25 08:35:05.383: %DUAL-5-NBRCHANGE: EIGRP-IPv6 1: Neighbor FE80::2
(Serial0/0/1) is resync: summary configured
```

c. Examine R1's routing table and verify that R1 is now only receiving a summary route for R3's loopback prefixes.

```
R1# show ipv6 route eigrp
IPv6 Routing Table - default - 9 entries
Codes: C - Connected, L - Local, S - Static, U - Per-user Static route
       B - BGP, R - RIP, H - NHRP, I1 - ISIS L1
       I2 - ISIS L2, IA - ISIS interarea, IS - ISIS summary, D - EIGRP
       EX - EIGRP external, ND - ND Default, NDp - ND Prefix, DCE -
       Destination
       NDr - Redirect, O - OSPF Intra, OI - OSPF Inter, OE1 - OSPF ext 1
       OE2 - OSPF ext 2, ON1 - OSPF NSSA ext 1, ON2 - OSPF NSSA ext 2
       a - Application
D   2001:DB8:ABCD::/61 [90/2809856]
     via FE80::2, Serial0/0/0
D   2001:DB8:CAFE:3::/64 [90/2172416]
     via FE80::2, Serial0/0/0
```

```
D    2001:DB8:CAFE:4::/64 [90/2681856]
        via FE80::2, Serial0/0/0
D    2001:DB8:CAFE:5::/64 [90/2684416]
        via FE80::2, Serial0/0/0
R1#
```

d. From R1, ping R3's loopback addresses to verify reachability to each address.

```
R1# ping 2001:db8:abcd:1::1
Type escape sequence to abort.
Sending 5, 100-byte ICMP Echos to 2001:DB8:ABCD:1::1, timeout is 2 seconds:
!!!!!
Success rate is 100 percent (5/5), round-trip min/avg/max = 52/55/56 ms
R1# ping 2001:db8:abcd:2::1
Type escape sequence to abort.
Sending 5, 100-byte ICMP Echos to 2001:DB8:ABCD:2::1, timeout is 2 seconds:
!!!!!
Success rate is 100 percent (5/5), round-trip min/avg/max = 52/55/56 ms
R1# ping 2001:db8:abcd:3::1
Type escape sequence to abort.
Sending 5, 100-byte ICMP Echos to 2001:DB8:ABCD:3::1, timeout is 2 seconds:
!!!!!
Success rate is 100 percent (5/5), round-trip min/avg/max = 56/56/56 ms
R1# ping 2001:db8:abcd:4::1
Type escape sequence to abort.
Sending 5, 100-byte ICMP Echos to 2001:DB8:ABCD:4::1, timeout is 2 seconds:
!!!!!
Success rate is 100 percent (5/5), round-trip min/avg/max = 56/56/56 ms
R1#R1# ping 2001:db8:abcd:5::1
Type escape sequence to abort.
Sending 5, 100-byte ICMP Echos to 2001:DB8:ABCD:5::1, timeout is 2 seconds:
!!!!!
Success rate is 100 percent (5/5), round-trip min/avg/max = 52/56/60 ms
R1#
```

e. Issue the **show ipv6 protocols** command on R3 to verify the configured summary route. From the output, EIGRP for IPv6 is still advertising the loopback addresses and that there is address summarization is in effect.

```
R3# show ipv6 protocols
IPv6 Routing Protocol is "connected"
IPv6 Routing Protocol is "application"
IPv6 Routing Protocol is "ND"
IPv6 Routing Protocol is "eigrp 1"
EIGRP-IPv6 Protocol for AS(1)
  Metric weight K1=1, K2=0, K3=1, K4=0, K5=0
  NSF-aware route hold timer is 240
  Router-ID: 3.3.3.3
  Topology : 0 (base)
    Active Timer: 3 min
    Distance: internal 90 external 170
    Maximum path: 16
    Maximum hopcount 100
    Maximum metric variance 1
```

```
Interfaces:
  Serial0/0/1
  Loopback1
  Loopback2
  Loopback3
  Loopback4
  Loopback5
  GigabitEthernet0/0 (passive)
Redistribution:
  None
Address Summarization:
  2001:DB8:ABCD::/61 for Se0/0/1
     Summarizing 5 components with metric 128256
R3#
```

Step 7: Configure and verify a default route and CEF.

a. On R3 configure an IPv6 default static route using the next-hop address of R4. Redistribute the static route in EIGRP using the **redistribute static** command.

Note: With the use of CEF (Cisco Express Forwarding) it is recommended practice that a next-hop IP address is used instead of an exit-interface. There is a bug in IOS 15.4 that prevents an IPv6 static route with only a next-hop address from being redistributed. A fully specified static route with both an exit-interface and a next-hop address is used in the example.

```
R3(config)# ipv6 route ::/0 serial0/1/0 2001:db8:feed:77::1
R3(config)# ipv6 router eigrp 1
R3(config-rtr)# redistribute static
```

b. Issue the **show ipv6 route eigrp** command on R1 to verify it has received the default route using EIGRP.

```
R1# show ipv6 route eigrp
IPv6 Routing Table - default - 10 entries
Codes: C - Connected, L - Local, S - Static, U - Per-user Static route
       B - BGP, R - RIP, H - NHRP, I1 - ISIS L1
       I2 - ISIS L2, IA - ISIS interarea, IS - ISIS summary, D - EIGRP
       EX - EIGRP external, ND - ND Default, NDp - ND Prefix, DCE -
       Destination
       NDr - Redirect, O - OSPF Intra, OI - OSPF Inter, OE1 - OSPF ext 1
       OE2 - OSPF ext 2, ON1 - OSPF NSSA ext 1, ON2 - OSPF NSSA ext 2
       a - Application
EX   ::/0 [170/3193856]
     via FE80::2, Serial0/0/0
D    2001:DB8:ABCD::/61 [90/2809856]
     via FE80::2, Serial0/0/0
D    2001:DB8:CAFE:3::/64 [90/2172416]
     via FE80::2, Serial0/0/0
D    2001:DB8:CAFE:4::/64 [90/2681856]
     via FE80::2, Serial0/0/0
D    2001:DB8:CAFE:5::/64 [90/2684416]
     via FE80::2, Serial0/0/0
R1#
```

Why does the default route have a code of "EX"?

c. Verify reachability to R4 by pinging its serial interface.

```
R1# ping 2001:db8:feed:77::1
Type escape sequence to abort.
Sending 5, 100-byte ICMP Echos to 2001:DB8:FEED:77::1, timeout is 2 seconds:
!!!!!
Success rate is 100 percent (5/5), round-trip min/avg/max = 80/83/84 ms
R1#
```

d. IPv6 Routing CEF is a forwarding mechanism to optimize the layer 3 and layer 2 lookup processes into a single process. Starting with IOS 15.4, CEF for IPv6 is enabled automatically when IPv6 unicast-routing is configured. The **show ipv6 cef** command can be used to verify the status of CEF for IPv6. If CEF is disabled, it can be enabled with the **ipv6 cef** global configuration command. The following output shows an example of CEF currently disabled and then enabled.

Note: CEF for IPv4 is enabled by default.

```
R1# show ipv6 cef summary
IPv6 CEF is disabled.
VRF Default
 1 prefix (1/0 fwd/non-fwd)
 Table id 0x1E000000
 Database epoch:        0 (1 entry at this epoch)

R1# conf t
Enter configuration commands, one per line.  End with CNTL/Z.
R1(config)# ipv6 cef
R1(config)# exit
R1# show ipv6 cef summary
IPv6 CEF is enabled and running centrally.
VRF Default
 14 prefixes (14/0 fwd/non-fwd)
 Table id 0x1E000000
 Database epoch:        0 (14 entries at this epoch)
```

Lab 2-4 Named EIGRP Configuration

Topology

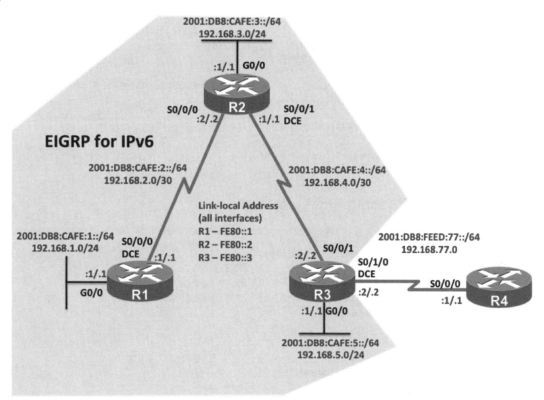

Objectives

- Configure Named EIGRP for IPv4 and IPv6.
- Verify Named EIGRP configuration.
- Configure and verify passive routes Named EIGRP configuration.
- Configure and verify default route using Named EIGRP configuration.

Background

What is known as "classic" EIGRP requires separate EIGRP configuration modes and commands for IPv4 and IPv6. Each process is configured separately: **router eigrp** *as-number* for IPv4 and **ipv6 router eigrp** *as-number* for IPv6.

Named EIGRP uses the address family (AF) feature to unify the configuration process when implementing both IPv4 and IPv6. In this lab, you will configure named EIGRP for IPv4 and IPv6.

Note: This lab uses Cisco 1941 routers with Cisco IOS Release 15.4 with IP Base. The switches are Cisco WS-C2960-24TT-L with Fast Ethernet interfaces; therefore, the router will use routing metrics associated with a 100 Mb/s interface. Depending on the router or switch model and Cisco IOS Software version, the commands available and output produced might vary from what is shown in this lab.

Required Resources

- 4 routers (Cisco IOS Release 15.2 or comparable)
- 3 switches (LAN interfaces)
- Serial and Ethernet cables

Step 0: Suggested starting configurations.

a. Apply the following configuration to each router along with the appropriate **hostname**. The **exec-timeout 0 0** command should only be used in a lab environment.

```
Router(config)# no ip domain-lookup
Router(config)# line con 0
Router(config-line)# logging synchronous
Router(config-line)# exec-timeout 0 0
```

Step 1: Configure the addressing and serial links.

a. Using the topology, configure the IPv4 and IPv6 addresses on the interfaces of each router.

```
R1(config)# interface GigabitEthernet0/0
R1(config-if)# ip address 192.168.1.1 255.255.255.0
R1(config-if)# ipv6 address FE80::1 link-local
R1(config-if)# ipv6 address 2001:DB8:CAFE:1::1/64
R1(config-if)# no shutdown
R1(config-if)# exit
R1(config)# interface Serial0/0/0
R1(config-if)# ip address 192.168.2.1 255.255.255.252
R1(config-if)# ipv6 address FE80::1 link-local
R1(config-if)# ipv6 address 2001:DB8:CAFE:2::1/64
R1(config-if)# clock rate 64000
R1(config-if)# no shutdown

R2(config)# interface GigabitEthernet0/0
R2(config-if)# ip address 192.168.3.1 255.255.255.0
R2(config-if)# ipv6 address FE80::2 link-local
R2(config-if)# ipv6 address 2001:DB8:CAFE:3::1/64
R2(config-if)# no shutdown
R2(config-if)# exit
R2(config)# interface Serial0/0/0
R2(config-if)# ip address 192.168.2.2 255.255.255.252
R2(config-if)# ipv6 address FE80::2 link-local
R2(config-if)# ipv6 address 2001:DB8:CAFE:2::2/64
R2(config-if)# no shutdown
R2(config-if)# exit
R2(config)# interface Serial0/0/1
R2(config-if)# ip address 192.168.4.1 255.255.255.252
R2(config-if)# ipv6 address FE80::2 link-local
R2(config-if)# ipv6 address 2001:DB8:CAFE:4::1/64
R2(config-if)# clock rate 64000
R2(config-if)# no shutdown

R3(config)# interface GigabitEthernet0/0
R3(config-if)# ip address 192.168.5.1 255.255.255.0
R3(config-if)# ipv6 address FE80::3 link-local
R3(config-if)# ipv6 address 2001:DB8:CAFE:5::1/64
```

```
R3(config-if)# no shutdown
R3(config-if)# exit
R3(config)# interface Serial0/0/1
R3(config-if)# ip address 192.168.4.2 255.255.255.252
R3(config-if)# ipv6 address FE80::3 link-local
R3(config-if)# ipv6 address 2001:DB8:CAFE:4::2/64
R3(config-if)# no shutdown
R3(config-if)# exit
R3(config)# interface Serial0/1/0
R3(config-if)# ip address 192.168.77.2 255.255.255.0
R3(config-if)# ipv6 address FE80::3 link-local
R3(config-if)# ipv6 address 2001:DB8:FEED:77::2/64
R3(config-if)# clock rate 64000
R3(config-if)# no shutdown
R3(config-if)#

R4(config)# interface Serial0/0/0
R4(config-if)# ip address 192.168.77.1 255.255.255.0
R4(config-if)# ipv6 address FE80::4 link-local
R4(config-if)# ipv6 address 2001:DB8:FEED:77::1/64
R4(config-if)# no shutdown
R4(config-if)# exit
R4(config)# ipv6 route 2001:DB8:CAFE::/48 2001:DB8:FEED:77::2
R4(config)# ip route 0.0.0.0 0.0.0.0 192.168.77.2
R4(config)#
```

b. Verify connectivity by pinging across each of the local networks connected to each router.

c. Issue the **show ip interface brief** and **show ipv6 interface brief** commands on each router. This command displays a brief listing of the interfaces, their status, and their IP addresses. Router R1 is shown as an example.

```
R1# show ip interface brief
Interface                  IP-Address      OK? Method Status                Protocol
Embedded-Service-Engine0/0 unassigned      YES unset  administratively down down
GigabitEthernet0/0         192.168.1.1     YES manual up                    up
GigabitEthernet0/1         unassigned      YES unset  administratively down down
Serial0/0/0                192.168.2.1     YES manual up                    up
Serial0/0/1                unassigned      YES unset  administratively down down
R1# show ipv6 interface brief
Em0/0                      [administratively down/down]
    unassigned
GigabitEthernet0/0         [up/up]
    FE80::1
    2001:DB8:CAFE:1::1
GigabitEthernet0/1         [administratively down/down]
    unassigned
Serial0/0/0                [up/up]
    FE80::1
    2001:DB8:CAFE:2::1
Serial0/0/1                [administratively down/down]
    unassigned
R1#
```

Step 2: Configure named EIGRP for IPv4 on R1.

a. Named EIGRP is organized in a hierarchical manner. Configuration for each routing protocol, EIGRP for IPv4, and EIGRP for IPv6 is done within its own address family. To configure named EIGRP configuration use the **router eigrp** *virtual-instance-name* command in global configuration mode. The virtual-instance-names do not have to match between neighbors.

Note: IPv6 unicast routing must be enabled prior to configuring the IPv6 address family.

```
R1(config)# ipv6 unicast-routing
R1(config)# router eigrp DUAL-STACK
R1(config-router)#
```

b. EIGRP doesn't start until at least one address family has been defined (IPv4 or IPv6). The address family command starts the EIGRP protocol (IPv4 or IPv6) for the defined autonomous system.

To configure the IPv4 address family and autonomous system you use the **address-family ipv4 unicast autonomous-system** command. This command puts you into the address family configuration mode. Issue the **address-family ?** command see the two address families available. After configuring the IPv4 address family for EIGRP use the **?** to see what commands are available in address family configuration mode such as the **af-interface**, **eigrp**, and **network** commands.

```
R1(config-router)# address-family ?
  ipv4  Address family IPv4
  ipv6  Address family IPv6

R1(config-router)# address-family ipv4 unicast autonomous-system 4
R1(config-router-af)# ?
Address Family configuration commands:
  af-interface         Enter Address Family interface configuration
  default              Set a command to its defaults
  eigrp                EIGRP Address Family specific commands
  exit-address-family  Exit Address Family configuration mode
  help                 Description of the interactive help system
  maximum-prefix       Maximum number of prefixes acceptable in aggregate
  metric               Modify metrics and parameters for address advertisement
  neighbor             Specify an IPv4 neighbor router
  network              Enable routing on an IP network
  no                   Negate a command or set its defaults
  shutdown             Shutdown address family
  timers               Adjust peering based timers
  topology             Topology configuration mode

R1(config-router-af)#
```

c. In address family configuration mode you can enable EIGRP for specific interfaces and define other general parameters such as the router ID and stub routing. Issue the **eigrp ?** command to see the available options configured using the **eigrp** command. Use the **eigrp router-id** command to configure the EIGRP router ID for the IPv4 address family.

```
R1(config-router-af)# eigrp ?
  default-route-tag     Default Route Tag for the Internal Routes
  log-neighbor-changes  Enable/Disable EIGRP neighbor logging
  log-neighbor-warnings Enable/Disable EIGRP neighbor warnings
```

```
router-id              router id for this EIGRP process
stub                   Set address-family in stubbed mode
```

```
R1(config-router-af)# eigrp router-id 1.1.1.1
R1(config-router-af)#
```

d. While still in the address family configuration mode for IPv4, use the **network** command to enable EIGRP on the interfaces. These are the same **network** commands used in "classic" EIGRP for IPv4.

```
R1(config-router-af)# network 192.168.1.0
R1(config-router-af)# network 192.168.2.0 0.0.0.3
R1(config-router-af)#
```

e. Exit the IPv4 address family configuration mode using the **exit-address-family** command or the shorter **exit** command. Notice that you are still in named EIGRP configuration mode.

```
R1(config-router-af)# exit-address-family
R1(config-router)#
```

Step 3: Configure named EIGRP for IPv6 on R1.

a. Configure the IPv6 address family using the autonomous system (process ID) of 6. Use the **?** the view the command options available under each mode and for some of the commands. There is no requirement for the AS numbers to match between the IPv4 and IPv6 address families, but they must match their neighbors' AS. In this example, routers R2 and R3 must use AS 4 for the IPv4 address family and AS 6 for the IPv6 address family.

```
R1(config-router)# address-family ipv6 unicast autonomous-system 6
R1(config-router-af)#
```

b. Use the **eigrp router-id** command to configure the EIGRP router ID for the IPv4 address family. The IPv6 router ID does not have to match the a router ID configured for IPv4.

```
R1(config-router-af)# eigrp router-id 1.1.1.1
R1(config-router-af)#
```

c. By default, all IPv6 interfaces are automatically enabled for EIGRP for IPv6. This will be explored further in the next step.

In this scenario, is the **eigrp router-id** command required to configure a router ID for the IPv4 AF? Is it required for the IPv6 AF? What would happen if the router ID was not configured using the **eigrp router-id** command?

_____

_____

_____

_____

Step 4: Configure named EIGRP on R2 and R3.

a. Configure named EIGRP on R2 for the IPv4 address family. The IPv6 unicast routing is enabled in preparation for configuring the IPv6 address family.

```
R2(config)# ipv6 unicast-routing

R2(config)# router eigrp DUAL-STACK

R2(config-router)# address-family ipv4 unicast autonomous-system 4

R2(config-router-af)# eigrp router-id 2.2.2.2

R2(config-router-af)# network 192.168.2.0 0.0.0.3

*Jul 25 20:11:37.643: %DUAL-5-NBRCHANGE: EIGRP-IPv4 4: Neighbor 192.168.2.1
(Serial0/0/0) is up: new adjacency

R2(config-router-af)# network 192.168.3.0

R2(config-router-af)# network 192.168.4.0 0.0.0.3

R2(config-router-af)# exit-address-family

R2(config-router)#
```

Notice that the adjacency between R1 and R2 is established after enabling EIGRP for IPv4 on the serial 0/0/0 interface.

b. Configure the IPv6 address family for EIGRP on R2.

```
R2(config-router)# address-family ipv6 unicast autonomous-system 6

*Jul 25 20:19:05.435: %DUAL-5-NBRCHANGE: EIGRP-IPv6 6: Neighbor FE80::1
(Serial0/0/0) is up: new adjacency

R2(config-router-af)# eigrp router-id 2.2.2.2

R2(config-router-af)#
```

Notice that the IPv6 adjacency with R1 comes up immediately after configuring the IPv6 AF. This is because by default, all IPv6 interfaces are enabled automatically.

c. On R3, configure named EIGRP on R3 for both the IPv4 and IPv6 address families. After the appropriate commands are configured the IPv4 and IPv6 EIGRP adjacencies are established between R2 and R3. The serial link between R3 and R4 is also automatically enabled in EIGRP for IPv6. This link is not supposed to be included and will be disabled in EIGRP for IPv6 later in step 6.

```
R3(config)# ipv6 unicast-routing

R3(config)# router eigrp DUAL-STACK

R3(config-router)# address-family ipv4 unicast autonomous-system 4

R3(config-router-af)# eigrp router-id 3.3.3.3

R3(config-router-af)# network 192.168.4.0 0.0.0.3

*Jun 26 13:11:41.343: %DUAL-5-NBRCHANGE: EIGRP-IPv4 4: Neighbor 192.168.4.1
(Serial0/0/1) is up: new adjacency

R3(config-router-af)# network 192.168.5.0

R3(config-router-af)# exit-address-family

R3(config-router)# address-family ipv6 unicast autonomous-system 6

*Jun 26 13:12:22.819: %DUAL-5-NBRCHANGE: EIGRP-IPv6 6: Neighbor FE80::2
(Serial0/0/1) is up: new adjacency

R3(config-router-af)# eigrp router-id 3.3.3.3

R3(config-router-af)#
```

Step 5: Configure passive interfaces for named EIGRP.

a. Within each IPv4 and IPv6 AF is the address family interface configuration mode. This mode is used to configure EIGRP specific parameters on an interface, such as the hello timer and summarization. From address family configuration mode, use the **af-interface** *interface-type interface-number* command to enter address family interface configuration mode. The following output shows the sequence of commands starting from global configuration mode.

```
R1(config)# router eigrp DUAL-STACK
R1(config-router)# address-family ipv4 unicast autonomous-system 4
R1(config-router-af)# af-interface gigabitethernet 0/0
R1(config-router-af-interface)#
```

b. Issue the **?** to see the commands available in address family interface configuration mode. Notice various commands to configure interface specific parameters such as the hello interval, hold timer, passive interfaces, and summarization.

```
R1(config-router-af-interface)# ?
Address Family Interfaces configuration commands:
    add-paths            Advertise add paths
    authentication       authentication subcommands
    bandwidth-percent    Set percentage of bandwidth percentage limit
    bfd                  Enable Bidirectional Forwarding Detection
    dampening-change     Percent interface metric must change to cause update
    dampening-interval   Time in seconds to check interface metrics
    default              Set a command to its defaults
    exit-af-interface    Exit from Address Family Interface configuration mode
    hello-interval       Configures hello interval
    hold-time            Configures hold time
    next-hop-self        Configures EIGRP next-hop-self
    no                   Negate a command or set its defaults
    passive-interface    Suppress address updates on an interface
    shutdown             Disable Address-Family on interface
    split-horizon        Perform split horizon
    summary-address      Perform address summarization

R1(config-router-af-interface)#
```

The interface configuration mode commands are similar for both the IPv4 and IPv6 address families. Commands issued are specific for an interface within the address family, IPv4 or IPv6.

c. Using the **passive-interface** command, configure G0/0 interface as passive for both the IPv4 and IPv6 EIGRP address families.

```
R1(config-router-af-interface)# passive-interface
R1(config-router-af-interface)# exit-af-interface
R1(config-router-af)# exit-address-family
R1(config-router)# address-family ipv6 unicast autonomous-system 6
R1(config-router-af)# af-interface gigabitethernet 0/0
R1(config-router-af-interface)# passive-interface
R1(config-router-af-interface)# exit-af-interface
```

```
R1(config-router-af)# exit-address-family
R1(config-router)#
```

d. Configure R2's G0/0 interface as passive for both the IPv4 and IPv6 address families.

```
R2(config)# router eigrp DUAL-STACK
R2(config-router)# address-family ipv4 unicast autonomous-system 4
R2(config-router-af)# af-interface gigabitethernet 0/0
R2(config-router-af-interface)# passive-interface
R2(config-router-af-interface)# exit-af-interface
R2(config-router-af)# exit-address-family
R2(config-router)# address-family ipv6 unicast autonomous-system 6
R2(config-router-af)# af-interface gigabitethernet 0/0
R2(config-router-af-interface)# passive-interface
R2(config-router-af-interface)# exit
R2(config-router-af)# exit
R2(config-router)#
```

e. Configure R3's G0/0 interface as passive for both the IPv4 and IPv6 address families.

```
R3(config)# router eigrp DUAL-STACK
R3(config-router)# address-family ipv4 unicast autonomous-system 4
R3(config-router-af)# af-interface gigabitethernet 0/0
R3(config-router-af-interface)# passive-interface
R3(config-router-af-interface)# exit-af-interface
R3(config-router-af)# exit-address-family
R3(config-router)# address-family ipv6 unicast autonomous-system 6
R3(config-router-af)# af-interface gigabitethernet 0/0
R3(config-router-af-interface)# passive-interface
R3(config-router-af-interface)# exit
R3(config-router-af)# exit
R3(config-router)#
```

Notice the **exit** command was used as the shorter method for the **exit-af-interface** and **exit-address-family** commands.

Step 6: Disable named EIGRP on a specific IPv6 interface.

a. By default, all IPv6 interfaces are enabled for EIGRP for IPv6. This happens when enabling the IPv6 address family with the **address-family ipv6 unicast autonomous-system** command. Issue the **show ipv6 protocols** command on R3 to verify that all three of its IPv6 interfaces are enabled for EIGRP for IPv6. Notice that the Serial 0/1/0 interface is also included.

```
R3# show ipv6 protocols
IPv6 Routing Protocol is "connected"
IPv6 Routing Protocol is "application"
IPv6 Routing Protocol is "ND"
IPv6 Routing Protocol is "eigrp 6"
EIGRP-IPv6 VR(DUAL-STACK) Address-Family Protocol for AS(6)
```

```
Metric weight K1=1, K2=0, K3=1, K4=0, K5=0 K6=0
Metric rib-scale 128
Metric version 64bit
NSF-aware route hold timer is 240
Router-ID: 3.3.3.3
Topology : 0 (base)
  Active Timer: 3 min
  Distance: internal 90 external 170
  Maximum path: 16
  Maximum hopcount 100
  Maximum metric variance 1
  Total Prefix Count: 6
  Total Redist Count: 0

Interfaces:
  Serial0/0/1
  Serial0/1/0
  GigabitEthernet0/0 (passive)
Redistribution:
  None
R3#
```

b. As shown in the topology, R3's S0/1/0 interface does not need to be included in the EIGRP updates. A default route will be configured later in this lab for reachability beyond the EIGRP routing domain. When we configured the IPv4 AF we excluded the **network** command for this interface. However, the same interface is automatically included when configuring the IPv6 AF. The **shutdown** address family interface command is used to disable EIGRP on a specific interface. This does not disable the physical interface, but only removes it from participating in EIGRP.

```
R3(config)# router eigrp DUAL-STACK
R3(config-router)# address-family ipv6 unicast autonomous-system 6
R3(config-router-af)# af-interface serial 0/1/0
R3(config-router-af-interface)# shutdown
R3(config-router-af-interface)# end
R3#
```

How can you verify that the IPv6 interface is still active, in the "up and up" state?

_____

c. Using the **show ipv6 protocols** command, verify that R3 is no longer including S0/1/0 in EIGRP for IPv6.

```
R3# show ipv6 protocols
IPv6 Routing Protocol is "connected"
IPv6 Routing Protocol is "application"
IPv6 Routing Protocol is "ND"
IPv6 Routing Protocol is "eigrp 6"
EIGRP-IPv6 VR(DUAL-STACK) Address-Family Protocol for AS(6)
```

```
Metric weight K1=1, K2=0, K3=1, K4=0, K5=0 K6=0
Metric rib-scale 128
Metric version 64bit
NSF-aware route hold timer is 240
Router-ID: 3.3.3.3
Topology : 0 (base)
  Active Timer: 3 min
  Distance: internal 90 external 170
  Maximum path: 16
  Maximum hopcount 100
  Maximum metric variance 1
  Total Prefix Count: 5
  Total Redist Count: 0

Interfaces:
  Serial0/0/1
  GigabitEthernet0/0 (passive)
Redistribution:
  None
R3#
```

Does the **shutdown** command used on S0/1/0 within the IPv6 AF also have the same effect for that interface within the IPv4 AF?

Step 7: Configure and distribute a default static route in named EIGRP.

a. On R3 configure IPv4 and IPv6 default static routes using an R4 as the next-hop router.

   Note: With the use of CEF (Cisco Express Forwarding) it is recommended practice that a next-hop IP address is used instead of an exit-interface. There is a bug in IOS 15.4 that prevents an IPv6 static route with only a next-hop address from being redistributed. A fully specified static route with both an exit-interface and a next-hop address is used in the example.

   ```
   R3(config)# ip route 0.0.0.0 0.0.0.0 192.168.77.1
   R3(config)# ipv6 route ::/0 serial0/1/0 2001:db8:feed:77::1
   R3(config)#
   ```

b. Redistribution of static routes in named EIGRP is done in topology configuration mode. Topology configuration mode is a subset of an address family. By default, EIGRP has a base topology for each address family. Additional topologies can be configured for Multitopology Routing (MTR), which is used to enable an EIGRP process for a specified topology. MTR is beyond the scope of CCNP.

   For each address family, issue the **topology base** command to enter the base EIGRP topology. In topology configuration mode use the **redistribute static** command to redistribute the default static route into EIGRP.

   ```
   R3(config)# router eigrp DUAL-STACK
   R3(config-router)# address-family ipv4 unicast autonomous-system 4
   ```

```
R3(config-router-af)# topology base
R3(config-router-af-topology)# ?
Address Family Topology configuration commands:
   auto-summary        Enable automatic network number summarization
   default             Set a command to its defaults
   default-information Control distribution of default information
   default-metric      Set metric of redistributed routes
   distance            Define an administrative distance
   distribute-list     Filter entries in eigrp updates
   eigrp               EIGRP specific commands
   exit-af-topology    Exit from Address Family Topology configuration mode
   maximum-paths       Forward packets over multiple paths
   metric              Modify metrics and parameters for advertisement
   no                  Negate a command or set its defaults
   offset-list         Add or subtract offset from EIGRP metrics
   redistribute        Redistribute IPv4 routes from another routing protocol
   snmp                Modify snmp parameters
   summary-metric      Specify summary to apply metric/filtering
   timers              Adjust topology specific timers
   traffic-share       How to compute traffic share over alternate paths
   variance            Control load balancing variance

R3(config-router-af-topology)# redistribute static
R3(config-router-af-topology)# exit-af-topology
R3(config-router-af)# exit-address-family
R3(config-router)# address-family ipv6 unicast autonomous-system 6
R3(config-router-af)# topology base
R3(config-router-af-topology)# redistribute static
R3(config-router-af-topology)# exit-af-topology
R3(config-router-af)# exit-address-family
R3(config-router)#
```

c. Issue the **show ip protocols** and **show ipv6 protocols** commands to verify that EIGRP is redistributing the static route.

```
R3# show ip protocols
*** IP Routing is NSF aware ***

Routing Protocol is "application"
  Sending updates every 0 seconds
  Invalid after 0 seconds, hold down 0, flushed after 0
  Outgoing update filter list for all interfaces is not set
  Incoming update filter list for all interfaces is not set
  Maximum path: 32
  Routing for Networks:
  Routing Information Sources:
```

```
      Gateway          Distance       Last Update
   Distance: (default is 4)


Routing Protocol is "eigrp 4"
   Outgoing update filter list for all interfaces is not set
   Incoming update filter list for all interfaces is not set
   Default networks not flagged in outgoing updates
   Default networks not accepted from incoming updates
   Redistributing: static
   EIGRP-IPv4 VR(DUAL-STACK) Address-Family Protocol for AS(4)
     Metric weight K1=1, K2=0, K3=1, K4=0, K5=0 K6=0
     Metric rib-scale 128
     Metric version 64bit
     NSF-aware route hold timer is 240
     Router-ID: 3.3.3.3
     Topology : 0 (base)
       Active Timer: 3 min
       Distance: internal 90 external 170
       Maximum path: 4
       Maximum hopcount 100
       Maximum metric variance 1
       Total Prefix Count: 5
       Total Redist Count: 1


   Automatic Summarization: disabled
   Maximum path: 4
   Routing for Networks:
     192.168.4.0/30
     192.168.5.0
   Passive Interface(s):
     GigabitEthernet0/0
   Routing Information Sources:
     Gateway          Distance       Last Update
     192.168.4.1            90        02:07:02
   Distance: internal 90 external 170


R3# show ipv6 protocols
IPv6 Routing Protocol is "connected"
IPv6 Routing Protocol is "application"
IPv6 Routing Protocol is "ND"
IPv6 Routing Protocol is "eigrp 6"
EIGRP-IPv6 VR(DUAL-STACK) Address-Family Protocol for AS(6)
   Metric weight K1=1, K2=0, K3=1, K4=0, K5=0 K6=0
   Metric rib-scale 128
```

```
    Metric version 64bit
    NSF-aware route hold timer is 240
    Router-ID: 3.3.3.3
    Topology : 0 (base)
      Active Timer: 3 min
      Distance: internal 90 external 170
      Maximum path: 16
      Maximum hopcount 100
      Maximum metric variance 1
      Total Prefix Count: 6
      Total Redist Count: 1

    Interfaces:
      Serial0/0/1
      GigabitEthernet0/0 (passive)
    Redistribution:
      Redistributing protocol static
IPv6 Routing Protocol is "static"
R3#
```

Why does the **show ip protocols** command indicate that automatic summarization is disabled?

_____

_____

d. Examine the IPv4 and IPv6 routing tables on R1 to verify that it is receiving the default static route using EIGRP.

```
R1# show ip route eigrp
Codes: L - local, C - connected, S - static, R - RIP, M - mobile, B - BGP
       D - EIGRP, EX - EIGRP external, O - OSPF, IA - OSPF inter area
       N1 - OSPF NSSA external type 1, N2 - OSPF NSSA external type 2
       E1 - OSPF external type 1, E2 - OSPF external type 2
       i - IS-IS, su - IS-IS summary, L1 - IS-IS level-1, L2 - IS-IS level-2
       ia - IS-IS inter area, * - candidate default, U - per-user static
       route
       o - ODR, P - periodic downloaded static route, H - NHRP, l - LISP
       a - application route
       + - replicated route, % - next hop override

Gateway of last resort is 192.168.2.2 to network 0.0.0.0

D*EX  0.0.0.0/0 [170/34036062] via 192.168.2.2, 00:03:23, Serial0/0/0
       192.168.4.0/30 is subnetted, 1 subnets
D         192.168.4.0 [90/23796062] via 192.168.2.2, 01:28:22, Serial0/0/0
```

```
D       192.168.5.0/24 [90/23847262] via 192.168.2.2, 01:28:15, Serial0/0/0
R1# show ipv6 route eigrp
IPv6 Routing Table - default - 9 entries
Codes: C - Connected, L - Local, S - Static, U - Per-user Static route
       B - BGP, R - RIP, H - NHRP, I1 - ISIS L1
       I2 - ISIS L2, IA - ISIS interarea, IS - ISIS summary, D - EIGRP
       EX - EIGRP external, ND - ND Default, NDp - ND Prefix, DCE -
       Destination
       NDr - Redirect, O - OSPF Intra, OI - OSPF Inter, OE1 - OSPF ext 1
       OE2 - OSPF ext 2, ON1 - OSPF NSSA ext 1, ON2 - OSPF NSSA ext 2
       a - Application
EX   ::/0 [170/34036062]
     via FE80::2, Serial0/0/0
D    2001:DB8:CAFE:4::/64 [90/23796062]
     via FE80::2, Serial0/0/0
D    2001:DB8:CAFE:5::/64 [90/23847262]
     via FE80::2, Serial0/0/0
D    2001:DB8:CAFE:99::/64 [90/23796702]
     via FE80::2, Serial0/0/0
R1#
```

Step 8: Verify named EIGRP.

a. Although named EIGRP unifies configuration for EIGRP for IPv4 and IPv6, the neighbor tables, topology tables, and EIGRP routing processes are still separate. Use the **show ip protocols** and **show ipv6 protocols** command to verify both EIGRP for IPv4 and IPv6 processes. The following is the output displayed for R2.

```
R2# show ip protocols
*** IP Routing is NSF aware ***

Routing Protocol is "application"
  Sending updates every 0 seconds
  Invalid after 0 seconds, hold down 0, flushed after 0
  Outgoing update filter list for all interfaces is not set
  Incoming update filter list for all interfaces is not set
  Maximum path: 32
  Routing for Networks:
  Routing Information Sources:
    Gateway         Distance      Last Update
  Distance: (default is 4)


Routing Protocol is "eigrp 4"
  Outgoing update filter list for all interfaces is not set
  Incoming update filter list for all interfaces is not set
  Default networks flagged in outgoing updates
```

```
   Default networks accepted from incoming updates
 EIGRP-IPv4 VR(DUAL-STACK) Address-Family Protocol for AS(4)
    Metric weight K1=1, K2=0, K3=1, K4=0, K5=0 K6=0
    Metric rib-scale 128
    Metric version 64bit
    NSF-aware route hold timer is 240
    Router-ID: 2.2.2.2
    Topology : 0 (base)
      Active Timer: 3 min
      Distance: internal 90 external 170
      Maximum path: 4
      Maximum hopcount 100
      Maximum metric variance 1
      Total Prefix Count: 6
      Total Redist Count: 0

  Automatic Summarization: disabled
  Maximum path: 4
  Routing for Networks:
    192.168.2.0/30
    192.168.3.0
    192.168.4.0/30
  Passive Interface(s):
    GigabitEthernet0/0
  Routing Information Sources:
    Gateway          Distance        Last Update
    192.168.2.1           90         00:04:54
    192.168.4.2           90         00:04:54
  Distance: internal 90 external 170

R2#
R2# show ipv6 protocols
IPv6 Routing Protocol is "connected"
IPv6 Routing Protocol is "application"
IPv6 Routing Protocol is "ND"
IPv6 Routing Protocol is "eigrp 6"
EIGRP-IPv6 VR(DUAL-STACK) Address-Family Protocol for AS(6)
  Metric weight K1=1, K2=0, K3=1, K4=0, K5=0 K6=0
  Metric rib-scale 128
  Metric version 64bit
  NSF-aware route hold timer is 240
  Router-ID: 2.2.2.2
  Topology : 0 (base)
    Active Timer: 3 min
```

```
    Distance: internal 90 external 170
    Maximum path: 16
    Maximum hopcount 100
    Maximum metric variance 1
    Total Prefix Count: 6
    Total Redist Count: 0

Interfaces:
  Serial0/0/0
  Serial0/0/1
  GigabitEthernet0/0 (passive)
Redistribution:
  None
R2#
```

b. Issue the **show ip eigrp neighbors** and **show ipv6 eigrp neighbors** commands on R1 to verify the neighbor adjacencies with R2.

```
R1# show ip eigrp neighbors
EIGRP-IPv4 VR(DUAL-STACK) Address-Family Neighbors for AS(4)
H    Address              Interface        Hold Uptime     SRTT   RTO Q  Seq
                                           (sec)           (ms)       Cnt Num
0    192.168.2.2          Se0/0/0          13 03:56:20     31     186 0  8
R1# show ipv6 eigrp neighbors
EIGRP-IPv6 VR(DUAL-STACK) Address-Family Neighbors for AS(6)
H    Address              Interface        Hold Uptime     SRTT   RTO  Q  Seq
                                           (sec)           (ms)        Cnt Num
0    Link-local address:  Se0/0/0          13 00:09:14     669    4014 0  21
     FE80::2
R1#
```

c. Examine R1's EIGRP topology tables for IPv4 and IPv6 using the **show ip eigrp topology** and **show ipv6 eigrp topology** commands.

```
R1# show ip eigrp topology
EIGRP-IPv4 VR(DUAL-STACK) Topology Table for AS(4)/ID(1.1.1.1)
Codes: P - Passive, A - Active, U - Update, Q - Query, R - Reply,
       r - reply Status, s - sia Status

P 192.168.2.0/30, 1 successors, FD is 1735175958
        via Connected, Serial0/0/0
P 192.168.1.0/24, 1 successors, FD is 13107200
        via Connected, GigabitEthernet0/0
P 0.0.0.0/0, 1 successors, FD is 4356615958
        via 192.168.2.2 (4356615958/3045895958), Serial0/0/0
P 192.168.4.0/30, 1 successors, FD is 3045895958
        via 192.168.2.2 (3045895958/1735175958), Serial0/0/0
```

```
P 192.168.5.0/24, 1 successors, FD is 3052449558
        via 192.168.2.2 (3052449558/1741729558), Serial0/0/0


R1# show ipv6 eigrp topology
EIGRP-IPv6 VR(DUAL-STACK) Topology Table for AS(6)/ID(1.1.1.1)
Codes: P - Passive, A - Active, U - Update, Q - Query, R - Reply,
       r - reply Status, s - sia Status


P 2001:DB8:CAFE:5::/64, 1 successors, FD is 3052449558
        via FE80::2 (3052449558/1741729558), Serial0/0/0
P 2001:DB8:CAFE:4::/64, 1 successors, FD is 3045895958
        via FE80::2 (3045895958/1735175958), Serial0/0/0
P 2001:DB8:CAFE:99::/64, 1 successors, FD is 3045977878
        via FE80::2 (3045977878/1735257878), Serial0/0/0
P 2001:DB8:CAFE:2::/64, 1 successors, FD is 1735175958
        via Connected, Serial0/0/0
P ::/0, 1 successors, FD is 4356615958
        via FE80::2 (4356615958/3045895958), Serial0/0/0
P 2001:DB8:CAFE:1::/64, 1 successors, FD is 13107200
        via Connected, GigabitEthernet0/0


R1#
```

d. Verify that R1 has all the IPv4 and IPv6 routes shown in the topology with the exclusion of R2's LAN by using the **show ip route eigrp** and **show ipv6 route eigrp** commands.

```
R1# show ip route eigrp
Codes: L - local, C - connected, S - static, R - RIP, M - mobile, B - BGP
        D - EIGRP, EX - EIGRP external, O - OSPF, IA - OSPF inter area
        N1 - OSPF NSSA external type 1, N2 - OSPF NSSA external type 2
        E1 - OSPF external type 1, E2 - OSPF external type 2
        i - IS-IS, su - IS-IS summary, L1 - IS-IS level-1, L2 - IS-IS level-2
        ia - IS-IS inter area, * - candidate default, U - per-user static
        route
        o - ODR, P - periodic downloaded static route, H - NHRP, l - LISP
        a - application route
        + - replicated route, % - next hop override

Gateway of last resort is 192.168.2.2 to network 0.0.0.0

D*EX  0.0.0.0/0 [170/34036062] via 192.168.2.2, 00:10:25, Serial0/0/0
D       192.168.3.0/24 [90/13607262] via 192.168.2.2, 00:48:46, Serial0/0/0
        192.168.4.0/30 is subnetted, 1 subnets
D         192.168.4.0 [90/23796062] via 192.168.2.2, 00:48:33, Serial0/0/0
D       192.168.5.0/24 [90/23847262] via 192.168.2.2, 00:38:12, Serial0/0/0
R1# show ipv6 route eigrp
```

```
IPv6 Routing Table - default - 9 entries
Codes: C - Connected, L - Local, S - Static, U - Per-user Static route
       B - BGP, R - RIP, H - NHRP, I1 - ISIS L1
       I2 - ISIS L2, IA - ISIS interarea, IS - ISIS summary, D - EIGRP
       EX - EIGRP external, ND - ND Default, NDp - ND Prefix, DCE -
       Destination
       NDr - Redirect, O - OSPF Intra, OI - OSPF Inter, OE1 - OSPF ext 1
       OE2 - OSPF ext 2, ON1 - OSPF NSSA ext 1, ON2 - OSPF NSSA ext 2
       a - Application
EX  ::/0 [170/34036062]
     via FE80::2, Serial0/0/0
D    2001:DB8:CAFE:3::/64 [90/13607262]
     via FE80::2, Serial0/0/0
D    2001:DB8:CAFE:4::/64 [90/23796062]
     via FE80::2, Serial0/0/0
D    2001:DB8:CAFE:5::/64 [90/23847262]
     via FE80::2, Serial0/0/0
R1#
```

e. As a final verification of end-to-end reachability, from R1 ping the IPv4 and IPv6 addresses on R5's LAN.

```
R1# ping 192.168.5.1
Type escape sequence to abort.
Sending 5, 100-byte ICMP Echos to 192.168.5.1, timeout is 2 seconds:
!!!!!
Success rate is 100 percent (5/5), round-trip min/avg/max = 56/56/56 ms
R1# ping 2001:db8:cafe:5::1
Type escape sequence to abort.
Sending 5, 100-byte ICMP Echos to 2001:DB8:CAFE:5::1, timeout is 2 seconds:
!!!!!
Success rate is 100 percent (5/5), round-trip min/avg/max = 52/55/56 ms
R1#
```

f. Examine the named EIGRP configuration showing both the IPv4 and IPv6 address families with the **show running-config | section router eigrp** command. Here is the output for R3:

```
R3# show running-config | section router eigrp
router eigrp DUAL-STACK
 !
 address-family ipv4 unicast autonomous-system 4
  !
  af-interface GigabitEthernet0/0
   passive-interface
  exit-af-interface
  !
  topology base
   redistribute static
  exit-af-topology
```

```
  network 192.168.4.0 0.0.0.3
  network 192.168.5.0
  eigrp router-id 3.3.3.3
 exit-address-family
 !
 address-family ipv6 unicast autonomous-system 6
  !
  af-interface GigabitEthernet0/0
   passive-interface
  exit-af-interface
  !
  af-interface Serial0/1/0
   shutdown
  exit-af-interface
  !
  topology base
   redistribute static
  exit-af-topology
  eigrp router-id 3.3.3.3
 exit-address-family
R3#
```

Chapter 3: OSPF Implementation

Lab 3-1 OSPF Virtual Links

Topology

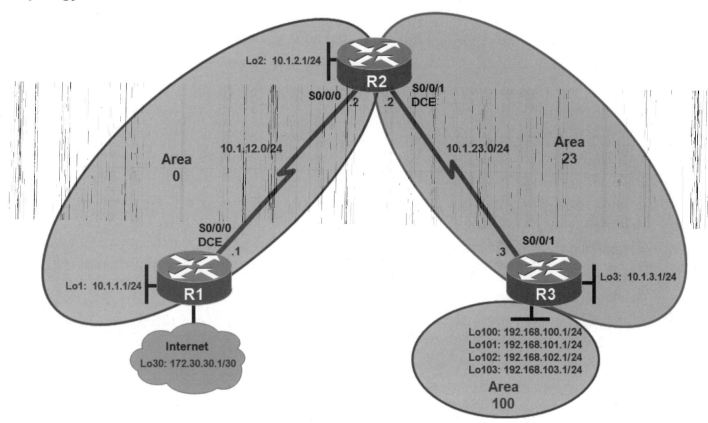

Objectives

- Configure multi-area OSPF on a router.
- Verify multi-area behavior.
- Create an OSPF virtual link.
- Summarize an area.
- Generate a default route into OSPF.

Background

You are responsible for configuring the new network to connect your company's engineering, marketing, and accounting departments, represented by loopback interfaces on each of the three routers. The physical devices have just been installed and connected by serial cables. Configure multiple-area OSPFv2 to allow full connectivity between all departments.

In addition, R1 has a loopback interface representing a connection to the Internet. This connection will not be added into OSPFv2. R3 will have four additional loopback interfaces representing connections to branch offices.

Note: This lab uses Cisco 1941 routers with Cisco IOS Release 15.4 with IP Base. The switches are Cisco WS-C2960-24TT-L with Fast Ethernet interfaces; therefore, the router will use routing metrics associated with a 100 Mb/s interface. Depending on the router or switch model and Cisco IOS Software version, the commands available and output produced might vary from what is shown in this lab.

Required Resources

- 3 routers (Cisco IOS Release 15.2 or comparable)
- Serial and Ethernet cables

Step 0: Suggested starting configurations.

a. Apply the following configuration to each router along with the appropriate **hostname**. The **exec-timeout 0 0** command should only be used in a lab environment.

```
Router(config)# no ip domain-lookup
Router(config)# line con 0
Router(config-line)# logging synchronous
Router(config-line)# exec-timeout 0 0
```

Step 1: Configure addressing and loopbacks.

a. Using the addressing scheme in the diagram, apply IP addresses to the serial interfaces on R1, R2, and R3. Create loopbacks on R1, R2, and R3, and address them according to the diagram.

```
R1# configure terminal
Enter configuration commands, one per line.  End with CNTL/Z.
R1(config)# interface loopback 1
R1(config-if)# description Engineering Department
R1(config-if)# ip address 10.1.1.1 255.255.255.0
R1(config-if)# interface loopback 30
R1(config-if)# ip address 172.30.30.1 255.255.255.252
R1(config-if)# interface serial 0/0/0
R1(config-if)# ip address 10.1.12.1 255.255.255.0
R1(config-if)# clockrate 64000
R1(config-if)# no shutdown

R2# configure terminal
Enter configuration commands, one per line.  End with CNTL/Z.
R2(config)# interface loopback 2
R2(config-if)# description Marketing Department
R2(config-if)# ip address 10.1.2.1 255.255.255.0
R2(config-if)# interface serial 0/0/0
R2(config-if)# ip address 10.1.12.2 255.255.255.0
R2(config-if)# no shutdown
R2(config-if)# interface serial 0/0/1
R2(config-if)# ip address 10.1.23.2 255.255.255.0
R2(config-if)# clockrate 64000
R2(config-if)# no shutdown

R3# configure terminal
Enter configuration commands, one per line.  End with CNTL/Z.
R3(config)# interface loopback 3
R3(config-if)# description Accounting Department
R3(config-if)# ip address 10.1.3.1 255.255.255.0
R3(config-if)# interface loopback 100
R3(config-if)# ip address 192.168.100.1 255.255.255.0
```

```
R3(config-if)# interface loopback 101
R3(config-if)# ip address 192.168.101.1 255.255.255.0
R3(config-if)# interface loopback 102
R3(config-if)# ip address 192.168.102.1 255.255.255.0
R3(config-if)# interface loopback 103
R3(config-if)# ip address 192.168.103.1 255.255.255.0
R3(config-if)# interface serial 0/0/1
R3(config-if)# ip address 10.1.23.3 255.255.255.0
R3(config-if)# no shutdown
```

Step 2: Add interfaces into OSPF.

a. Create OSPF process 1 and OSPF router ID on all three routers. Using the **network** command, configure the subnet of the serial link between R1 and R2 to be in OSPF area 0. Add loopback 1 on R1 and loopback 2 on R2 into OSPF area 0.

Note: The default behavior of OSPF for loopback interfaces is to advertise a 32-bit host route. To ensure that the full /24 network is advertised, use the **ip ospf network point-to-point** command. Change the network type on the loopback interfaces so that they are advertised with the correct subnet.

```
R1(config)# router ospf 1
R1(config-router)# router-id 1.1.1.1
R1(config-router)# network 10.1.12.0 0.0.0.255 area 0
R1(config-router)# network 10.1.1.0 0.0.0.255 area 0
R1(config-router)# exit
R1(config)# interface loopback 1
R1(config-if)# ip ospf network point-to-point
R1(config-if)# end
```

The **show ip ospf** command should be used to verify the OSPF router ID. If the OSPF router ID is using a 32-bit value other than the one specified by the **router-id** command, you can reset the router ID by using the **clear ip ospf** *pid* **process** command and re-verify using the command **show ip ospf**.

```
R1# show ip ospf
 Routing Process "ospf 1" with ID 172.30.30.1
 Start time: 04:19:23.024, Time elapsed: 00:31:01.416
 Supports only single TOS(TOS0) routes
 Supports opaque LSA
 Supports Link-local Signaling (LLS)
 Supports area transit capability
 Supports NSSA (compatible with RFC 3101)
 Event-log enabled, Maximum number of events: 1000, Mode: cyclic
 Router is not originating router-LSAs with maximum metric
 Initial SPF schedule delay 5000 msecs
 Minimum hold time between two consecutive SPFs 10000 msecs
 Maximum wait time between two consecutive SPFs 10000 msecs
 Incremental-SPF disabled
 Minimum LSA interval 5 secs
 Minimum LSA arrival 1000 msecs
 LSA group pacing timer 240 secs
 Interface flood pacing timer 33 msecs
 Retransmission pacing timer 66 msecs
 Number of external LSA 0. Checksum Sum 0x000000
 Number of opaque AS LSA 0. Checksum Sum 0x000000
 Number of DCbitless external and opaque AS LSA 0
 Number of DoNotAge external and opaque AS LSA 0
 Number of areas in this router is 1. 1 normal 0 stub 0 nssa
```

```
R1# clear ip ospf 1 process
Reset OSPF process 1? [no]: yes
R1# show ip ospf
 Routing Process "ospf 1" with ID 1.1.1.1
 Start time: 04:19:23.024, Time elapsed: 00:31:01.416
 Supports only single TOS(TOS0) routes
 Supports opaque LSA
 Supports Link-local Signaling (LLS)
 Supports area transit capability
 Supports NSSA (compatible with RFC 3101)
 Event-log enabled, Maximum number of events: 1000, Mode: cyclic
 Router is not originating router-LSAs with maximum metric
 Initial SPF schedule delay 5000 msecs
 Minimum hold time between two consecutive SPFs 10000 msecs
 Maximum wait time between two consecutive SPFs 10000 msecs
 Incremental-SPF disabled
 Minimum LSA interval 5 secs
 Minimum LSA arrival 1000 msecs
 LSA group pacing timer 240 secs
 Interface flood pacing timer 33 msecs
 Retransmission pacing timer 66 msecs
 Number of external LSA 0. Checksum Sum 0x000000
 Number of opaque AS LSA 0. Checksum Sum 0x000000
 Number of DCbitless external and opaque AS LSA 0
 Number of DoNotAge external and opaque AS LSA 0
 Number of areas in this router is 1. 1 normal 0 stub 0 nssa

R1#

R2(config)# router ospf 1
R2(config-router)# router-id 2.2.2.2
R2(config-router)# network 10.1.12.0 0.0.0.255 area 0
R2(config-router)# network 10.1.2.0 0.0.0.255 area 0
R2(config-router)# exit
R2(config)# interface loopback 2
R2(config-if)# ip ospf network point-to-point
R2(config-if)# end
```

Again, the **show ip ospf** command should be used to verify the OSPF router ID. If the OSPF router ID is using a 32-bit value other than the one specified by the **router-id** command, you can reset the router ID by using the **clear ip ospf** *pid* **process** command and re-verify using the command **show ip ospf**.

b. Verify that you can see OSPF neighbors in the **show ip ospf neighbors** output on both routers. Verify that the routers can see each other's loopback with the **show ip route** command.

```
R1# show ip ospf neighbor

Neighbor ID     Pri   State           Dead Time   Address         Interface
2.2.2.2           0   FULL/  -        00:00:30    10.1.12.2       Serial0/0/0

R1# show ip route
Codes: L - local, C - connected, S - static, R - RIP, M - mobile, B - BGP
       D - EIGRP, EX - EIGRP external, O - OSPF, IA - OSPF inter area
       N1 - OSPF NSSA external type 1, N2 - OSPF NSSA external type 2
       E1 - OSPF external type 1, E2 - OSPF external type 2
```

```
          i - IS-IS, su - IS-IS summary, L1 - IS-IS level-1, L2 - IS-IS level-2
          ia - IS-IS inter area, * - candidate default, U - per-user static
          route
          o - ODR, P - periodic downloaded static route, H - NHRP, l - LISP
          a - application route
          + - replicated route, % - next hop override

Gateway of last resort is not set

       10.0.0.0/8 is variably subnetted, 5 subnets, 2 masks
C         10.1.1.0/24 is directly connected, Loopback1
L         10.1.1.1/32 is directly connected, Loopback1
O         10.1.2.0/24 [110/65] via 10.1.12.2, 00:05:04, Serial0/0/0
C         10.1.12.0/24 is directly connected, Serial0/0/0
L         10.1.12.1/32 is directly connected, Serial0/0/0
       172.30.0.0/16 is variably subnetted, 2 subnets, 2 masks
C         172.30.30.0/30 is directly connected, Loopback30
L         172.30.30.1/32 is directly connected, Loopback30
R1#

R2# show ip ospf neighbor

Neighbor ID     Pri    State        Dead Time    Address       Interface
1.1.1.1          0     FULL/  -     00:00:30     10.1.12.1     Serial0/0/0

R2# show ip route
Codes: L - local, C - connected, S - static, R - RIP, M - mobile, B - BGP
       D - EIGRP, EX - EIGRP external, O - OSPF, IA - OSPF inter area
       N1 - OSPF NSSA external type 1, N2 - OSPF NSSA external type 2
       E1 - OSPF external type 1, E2 - OSPF external type 2
       i - IS-IS, su - IS-IS summary, L1 - IS-IS level-1, L2 - IS-IS level-2
       ia - IS-IS inter area, * - candidate default, U - per-user static
       route
       o - ODR, P - periodic downloaded static route, H - NHRP, l - LISP
       a - application route
       + - replicated route, % - next hop override

Gateway of last resort is not set

       10.0.0.0/8 is variably subnetted, 7 subnets, 2 masks
O         10.1.1.0/24 [110/65] via 10.1.12.1, 00:06:33, Serial0/0/0
C         10.1.2.0/24 is directly connected, Loopback2
L         10.1.2.1/32 is directly connected, Loopback2
C         10.1.12.0/24 is directly connected, Serial0/0/0
L         10.1.12.2/32 is directly connected, Serial0/0/0
C         10.1.23.0/24 is directly connected, Serial0/0/1
L         10.1.23.2/32 is directly connected, Serial0/0/1
R2#
```

c. Add the subnet between R2 and R3 into OSPF area 23 using the **network** command. Add loopback 3 on R3 into area 23.

```
R2(config)# router ospf 1
R2(config-router)# network 10.1.23.0 0.0.0.255 area 23

R3(config)# router ospf 1
R3(config-router)# router-id 3.3.3.3
R3(config-router)# network 10.1.23.0 0.0.0.255 area 23
```

```
R3(config-router)# network 10.1.3.0 0.0.0.255 area 23
R3(config-router)# exit
R3(config)# interface loopback 3
R3(config-if)# ip ospf network point-to-point
```

Again, the **show ip ospf** command should used to verify the OSPF router ID. If the OSPF router ID is using a 32-bit value other than the one specified by the **router-id** command, you can reset the router ID by using the **clear ip ospf** *pid* **process** command and re-verify using the command **show ip ospf**.

d. Verify that this neighbor relationship comes up with the **show ip ospf neighbors** command.

```
R2# show ip ospf neighbor

Neighbor ID     Pri    State          Dead Time   Address       Interface
1.1.1.1          0    FULL/   -       00:00:35    10.1.12.1     Serial0/0/0
3.3.3.3          0    FULL/   -       00:00:33    10.1.23.3     Serial0/0/1
R2#
```

Step 3: Create a virtual link.

a. Add loopbacks 100 through 103 on R3 to R3's OSPF process in area 100 using the **network** command. Change the network type to advertise the correct subnet mask.

```
R3(config)# router ospf 1
R3(config-router)# network 192.168.100.0 0.0.3.255 area 100
R3(config-router)# exit
R3(config)# interface loopback 100
R3(config-if)# ip ospf network point-to-point
R3(config-if)# interface loopback 101
R3(config-if)# ip ospf network point-to-point
R3(config-if)# interface loopback 102
R3(config-if)# ip ospf network point-to-point
R3(config-if)# interface loopback 103
R3(config-if)# ip ospf network point-to-point
```

b. Look at the output of the **show ip route** command on R2. Notice that the routes to those networks do not appear. The reason for this behavior is that area 100 on R3 is not connected to the backbone. It is only connected to area 23. If an area is not connected to the backbone, its routes are not advertised outside of its area.

```
R2#show ip route
Codes: L - local, C - connected, S - static, R - RIP, M - mobile, B - BGP
       D - EIGRP, EX - EIGRP external, O - OSPF, IA - OSPF inter area
       N1 - OSPF NSSA external type 1, N2 - OSPF NSSA external type 2
       E1 - OSPF external type 1, E2 - OSPF external type 2
       i - IS-IS, su - IS-IS summary, L1 - IS-IS level-1, L2 - IS-IS level-2
       ia - IS-IS inter area, * - candidate default, U - per-user static
       route
       o - ODR, P - periodic downloaded static route, H - NHRP, l - LISP
       a - application route
       + - replicated route, % - next hop override

Gateway of last resort is not set

      10.0.0.0/8 is variably subnetted, 8 subnets, 2 masks
O        10.1.1.0/24 [110/65] via 10.1.12.1, 00:09:22, Serial0/0/0
C        10.1.2.0/24 is directly connected, Loopback2
```

```
L           10.1.2.1/32 is directly connected, Loopback2
O           10.1.3.0/24 [110/65] via 10.1.23.3, 00:08:03, Serial0/0/1
C           10.1.12.0/24 is directly connected, Serial0/0/0
L           10.1.12.2/32 is directly connected, Serial0/0/0
C           10.1.23.0/24 is directly connected, Serial0/0/1
L           10.1.23.2/32 is directly connected, Serial0/0/1
R2#
```

What would happen if routes could pass between areas without going through the backbone?

_____

_____

You can get around this situation by creating a virtual link. A virtual link is an OSPF feature that creates a logical extension of the backbone area across a regular area, without actually adding any physical interfaces into area 0.

Note: Prior to creating a virtual link you need to identify the OSPF router ID for the routers involved (R2 and R3), using a command such as **show ip ospf**, **show ip protocols**, or **show ip ospf interface**. The output for the **show ip ospf** command on R2 and R3 is shown here:

```
R2# show ip ospf
 Routing Process "ospf 1" with ID 2.2.2.2
<output omitted>

R3# show ip ospf
 Routing Process "ospf 1" with ID 3.3.3.3
<output omitted>
```

c. Create a virtual link using the **area** *transit_area* **virtual-link** *router-id* OSPF configuration command on both R2 and R3.

```
R2(config)# router ospf 1
R2(config-router)# area 23 virtual-link 3.3.3.3
R2(config-router)#

R3(config)# router ospf 1
R3(config-router)# area 23 virtual-link 2.2.2.2
*Aug  9 12:47:46.110: %OSPF-5-ADJCHG: Process 1, Nbr 2.2.2.2 on OSPF_VL0 from
LOADING to FULL, Loading Done
R3(config-router)#
```

Notice after virtual links are established IOS will report full adjacency between both routers.

d. After you see the adjacency over the virtual interface come up, issue the **show ip route** command on R2 and see the routes from area 100. You can verify the virtual link with the **show ip ospf neighbor** and **show ip ospf interface** commands.

```
R2# show ip route
Codes: L - local, C - connected, S - static, R - RIP, M - mobile, B - BGP
       D - EIGRP, EX - EIGRP external, O - OSPF, IA - OSPF inter area
       N1 - OSPF NSSA external type 1, N2 - OSPF NSSA external type 2
       E1 - OSPF external type 1, E2 - OSPF external type 2
       i - IS-IS, su - IS-IS summary, L1 - IS-IS level-1, L2 - IS-IS level-2
       ia - IS-IS inter area, * - candidate default, U - per-user static
       route
```

```
        o - ODR, P - periodic downloaded static route, H - NHRP, l - LISP
        a - application route
        + - replicated route, % - next hop override

Gateway of last resort is not set

      10.0.0.0/8 is variably subnetted, 8 subnets, 2 masks
O        10.1.1.0/24 [110/65] via 10.1.12.1, 00:18:16, Serial0/0/0
C        10.1.2.0/24 is directly connected, Loopback2
L        10.1.2.1/32 is directly connected, Loopback2
O        10.1.3.0/24 [110/65] via 10.1.23.3, 00:16:57, Serial0/0/1
C        10.1.12.0/24 is directly connected, Serial0/0/0
L        10.1.12.2/32 is directly connected, Serial0/0/0
C        10.1.23.0/24 is directly connected, Serial0/0/1
L        10.1.23.2/32 is directly connected, Serial0/0/1
O IA  192.168.100.0/24 [110/65] via 10.1.23.3, 00:03:28, Serial0/0/1
O IA  192.168.101.0/24 [110/65] via 10.1.23.3, 00:03:28, Serial0/0/1
O IA  192.168.102.0/24 [110/65] via 10.1.23.3, 00:03:28, Serial0/0/1
O IA  192.168.103.0/24 [110/65] via 10.1.23.3, 00:03:28, Serial0/0/1
R2#


R2# show ip ospf neighbor
Neighbor ID     Pri   State          Dead Time   Address         Interface
3.3.3.3           0   FULL/  -          -         10.1.23.3       OSPF_VL0
1.1.1.1           0   FULL/  -       00:00:38     10.1.12.1       Serial0/0/0
3.3.3.3           0   FULL/  -       00:00:35     10.1.23.3       Serial0/0/1

R2# show ip ospf interface
OSPF_VL0 is up, line protocol is up
  Internet Address 10.1.23.2/24, Area 0, Attached via Not Attached
  Process ID 1, Router ID 2.2.2.2, Network Type VIRTUAL_LINK, Cost: 64
  Topology-MTID    Cost    Disabled    Shutdown    Topology Name
       0            64        no          no           Base
  Configured as demand circuit
  Run as demand circuit
  DoNotAge LSA allowed
  Transmit Delay is 1 sec, State POINT_TO_POINT
  Timer intervals configured, Hello 10, Dead 40, Wait 40, Retransmit 5
    oob-resync timeout 40
    Hello due in 00:00:02
  Supports Link-local Signaling (LLS)
  Cisco NSF helper support enabled
  IETF NSF helper support enabled
  Index 3/4, flood queue length 0
  Next 0x0(0)/0x0(0)
  Last flood scan length is 1, maximum is 1
  Last flood scan time is 0 msec, maximum is 0 msec
  Neighbor Count is 1, Adjacent neighbor count is 1
    Adjacent with neighbor 3.3.3.3   (Hello suppressed)
  Suppress hello for 1 neighbor(s)
<output omitted>
```

When are virtual links useful?

_____

_____

_____

Why are virtual links a poor long-term solution?

_____

_____

_____

Step 4: Summarize an area.

Loopbacks 100 through 103 can be summarized into one supernet of 192.168.100.0 /22. You can configure area 100 to be represented by this single summary route.

a. Configure R3 (the ABR) to summarize this area using the **area** *area* **range** *network mask* command.

```
R3(config)# router ospf 1
R3(config-router)# area 100 range 192.168.100.0 255.255.252.0
```

b. You can see the summary route on R2 with the **show ip route** and **show ip ospf database** commands.

```
R2#show ip route
Codes: L - local, C - connected, S - static, R - RIP, M - mobile, B - BGP
       D - EIGRP, EX - EIGRP external, O - OSPF, IA - OSPF inter area
       N1 - OSPF NSSA external type 1, N2 - OSPF NSSA external type 2
       E1 - OSPF external type 1, E2 - OSPF external type 2
       i - IS-IS, su - IS-IS summary, L1 - IS-IS level-1, L2 - IS-IS level-2
       ia - IS-IS inter area, * - candidate default, U - per-user static
       route
       o - ODR, P - periodic downloaded static route, H - NHRP, l - LISP
       a - application route
       + - replicated route, % - next hop override

Gateway of last resort is not set

      10.0.0.0/8 is variably subnetted, 8 subnets, 2 masks
O        10.1.1.0/24 [110/65] via 10.1.12.1, 00:24:14, Serial0/0/0
C        10.1.2.0/24 is directly connected, Loopback2
L        10.1.2.1/32 is directly connected, Loopback2
O        10.1.3.0/24 [110/65] via 10.1.23.3, 00:22:55, Serial0/0/1
C        10.1.12.0/24 is directly connected, Serial0/0/0
L        10.1.12.2/32 is directly connected, Serial0/0/0
C        10.1.23.0/24 is directly connected, Serial0/0/1
L        10.1.23.2/32 is directly connected, Serial0/0/1
O IA  192.168.100.0/22 [110/65] via 10.1.23.3, 00:00:04, Serial0/0/1
R2#
```

```
R2# show ip ospf database

            OSPF Router with ID (2.2.2.2) (Process ID 1)

                Router Link States (Area 0)

Link ID         ADV Router      Age         Seq#       Checksum Link count
1.1.1.1         1.1.1.1         98          0x80000006 0x00AA98 3
2.2.2.2         2.2.2.2         608         0x80000006 0x00AF0B 4
3.3.3.3         3.3.3.3         1    (DNA)  0x80000002 0x00ADFC 1

                Summary Net Link States (Area 0)
```

```
Link ID          ADV Router       Age          Seq#        Checksum
10.1.3.0         2.2.2.2          1408         0x80000001 0x002ABB
10.1.3.0         3.3.3.3          1     (DNA)  0x80000002 0x008799
10.1.23.0        2.2.2.2          1482         0x80000001 0x00438F
10.1.23.0        3.3.3.3          1     (DNA)  0x80000002 0x0023AA
192.168.100.0    3.3.3.3          1     (DNA)  0x80000003 0x00243F

                 Router Link States (Area 23)

Link ID          ADV Router       Age          Seq#        Checksum Link count
2.2.2.2          2.2.2.2          608          0x80000003 0x0099A1 2
3.3.3.3          3.3.3.3          609          0x80000005 0x00E92B 3

                 Summary Net Link States (Area 23)

Link ID          ADV Router       Age          Seq#        Checksum
10.1.1.0         2.2.2.2          1482         0x80000002 0x003EA8
10.1.2.0         2.2.2.2          1482         0x80000002 0x00B075
10.1.12.0        2.2.2.2          1482         0x80000002 0x00BA22
192.168.100.0    3.3.3.3          43           0x80000002 0x00263E
R2#
```

c. Notice on R3 that OSPF has generated a summary route pointing toward Null0.

```
R3#show ip route
Codes: L - local, C - connected, S - static, R - RIP, M - mobile, B - BGP
       D - EIGRP, EX - EIGRP external, O - OSPF, IA - OSPF inter area
       N1 - OSPF NSSA external type 1, N2 - OSPF NSSA external type 2
       E1 - OSPF external type 1, E2 - OSPF external type 2
       i - IS-IS, su - IS-IS summary, L1 - IS-IS level-1, L2 - IS-IS level-2
       ia - IS-IS inter area, * - candidate default, U - per-user static
       route
       o - ODR, P - periodic downloaded static route, H - NHRP, l - LISP
       a - application route
       + - replicated route, % - next hop override

Gateway of last resort is not set

      10.0.0.0/8 is variably subnetted, 7 subnets, 2 masks
O        10.1.1.0/24 [110/129] via 10.1.23.2, 00:02:17, Serial0/0/1
O        10.1.2.0/24 [110/65] via 10.1.23.2, 00:02:17, Serial0/0/1
C        10.1.3.0/24 is directly connected, Loopback3
L        10.1.3.1/32 is directly connected, Loopback3
O        10.1.12.0/24 [110/128] via 10.1.23.2, 00:02:17, Serial0/0/1
C        10.1.23.0/24 is directly connected, Serial0/0/1
L        10.1.23.3/32 is directly connected, Serial0/0/1
O     192.168.100.0/22 is a summary, 00:02:17, Null0
      192.168.100.0/24 is variably subnetted, 2 subnets, 2 masks
C        192.168.100.0/24 is directly connected, Loopback100
L        192.168.100.1/32 is directly connected, Loopback100
      192.168.101.0/24 is variably subnetted, 2 subnets, 2 masks
C        192.168.101.0/24 is directly connected, Loopback101
L        192.168.101.1/32 is directly connected, Loopback101
      192.168.102.0/24 is variably subnetted, 2 subnets, 2 masks
C        192.168.102.0/24 is directly connected, Loopback102
L        192.168.102.1/32 is directly connected, Loopback102
      192.168.103.0/24 is variably subnetted, 2 subnets, 2 masks
```

```
C         192.168.103.0/24 is directly connected, Loopback103
L         192.168.103.1/32 is directly connected, Loopback103
R3#
```

This behavior is known as sending unknown traffic to the "bit bucket." This means that if the router advertising the summary route receives a packet destined for something covered by that summary but not in the routing table, it drops it.

What is the reasoning behind this behavior?

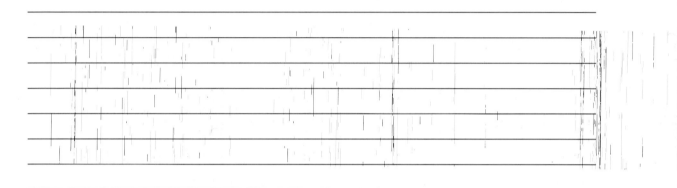

Step 5: Generate a default route into OSPF.

You can simulate loopback 30 on R1 to be a connection to the Internet. You do not need to advertise this specific network to the rest of the network. Instead, you can just have a default route for all unknown traffic to go to R1.

a. To have R1 generate a default route, use the OSPF configuration command **default-information originate always**. The **always** keyword is necessary for generating a default route in this scenario. Without this keyword, a default route is generated only into OSPF if one exists in the routing table.

```
R1(config)# router ospf 1
R1(config-router)# default-information originate always
```

b. Verify that the default route appears on R2 and R3 with the **show ip route** command.

```
R2#show ip route
Codes: L - local, C - connected, S - static, R - RIP, M - mobile, B - BGP
       D - EIGRP, EX - EIGRP external, O - OSPF, IA - OSPF inter area
       N1 - OSPF NSSA external type 1, N2 - OSPF NSSA external type 2
       E1 - OSPF external type 1, E2 - OSPF external type 2
       i - IS-IS, su - IS-IS summary, L1 - IS-IS level-1, L2 - IS-IS level-2
       ia - IS-IS inter area, * - candidate default, U - per-user static
       route
       o - ODR, P - periodic downloaded static route, H - NHRP, l - LISP
       a - application route
       + - replicated route, % - next hop override

Gateway of last resort is 10.1.12.1 to network 0.0.0.0

O*E2  0.0.0.0/0 [110/1] via 10.1.12.1, 00:00:13, Serial0/0/0
         10.0.0.0/8 is variably subnetted, 8 subnets, 2 masks
O        10.1.1.0/24 [110/65] via 10.1.12.1, 00:28:42, Serial0/0/0
```

```
C          10.1.2.0/24 is directly connected, Loopback2
L          10.1.2.1/32 is directly connected, Loopback2
O          10.1.3.0/24 [110/65] via 10.1.23.3, 00:27:23, Serial0/0/1
C          10.1.12.0/24 is directly connected, Serial0/0/0
L          10.1.12.2/32 is directly connected, Serial0/0/0
C          10.1.23.0/24 is directly connected, Serial0/0/1
L          10.1.23.2/32 is directly connected, Serial0/0/1
O IA  192.168.100.0/22 [110/65] via 10.1.23.3, 00:04:32, Serial0/0/1
R2#


R3#show ip route
Codes: L - local, C - connected, S - static, R - RIP, M - mobile, B - BGP
       D - EIGRP, EX - EIGRP external, O - OSPF, IA - OSPF inter area
       N1 - OSPF NSSA external type 1, N2 - OSPF NSSA external type 2
       E1 - OSPF external type 1, E2 - OSPF external type 2
       i - IS-IS, su - IS-IS summary, L1 - IS-IS level-1, L2 - IS-IS level-2
       ia - IS-IS inter area, * - candidate default, U - per-user static
       route
       o - ODR, P - periodic downloaded static route, H - NHRP, l - LISP
       a - application route
       + - replicated route, % - next hop override

Gateway of last resort is 10.1.23.2 to network 0.0.0.0

O*E2  0.0.0.0/0 [110/1] via 10.1.23.2, 00:00:45, Serial0/0/1
       10.0.0.0/8 is variably subnetted, 7 subnets, 2 masks
O          10.1.1.0/24 [110/129] via 10.1.23.2, 00:05:08, Serial0/0/1
O          10.1.2.0/24 [110/65] via 10.1.23.2, 00:05:08, Serial0/0/1
C          10.1.3.0/24 is directly connected, Loopback3
L          10.1.3.1/32 is directly connected, Loopback3
O          10.1.12.0/24 [110/128] via 10.1.23.2, 00:05:08, Serial0/0/1
C          10.1.23.0/24 is directly connected, Serial0/0/1
L          10.1.23.3/32 is directly connected, Serial0/0/1
O      192.168.100.0/22 is a summary, 00:05:08, Null0
       192.168.100.0/24 is variably subnetted, 2 subnets, 2 masks
C          192.168.100.0/24 is directly connected, Loopback100
L          192.168.100.1/32 is directly connected, Loopback100
       192.168.101.0/24 is variably subnetted, 2 subnets, 2 masks
C          192.168.101.0/24 is directly connected, Loopback101
L          192.168.101.1/32 is directly connected, Loopback101
       192.168.102.0/24 is variably subnetted, 2 subnets, 2 masks
C          192.168.102.0/24 is directly connected, Loopback102
L          192.168.102.1/32 is directly connected, Loopback102
       192.168.103.0/24 is variably subnetted, 2 subnets, 2 masks
C          192.168.103.0/24 is directly connected, Loopback103
L          192.168.103.1/32 is directly connected, Loopback103
R3#
```

c. You should be able to ping the interface connecting to the Internet from R2 or R3, despite never being advertised into OSPF.

```
R3# ping 172.30.30.1

Type escape sequence to abort.
Sending 5, 100-byte ICMP Echos to 172.30.30.1, timeout is 2 seconds:
!!!!!
Success rate is 100 percent (5/5), round-trip min/avg/max = 28/30/32 ms
```

Lab 3-2 Multi-Area OSPFv2 and OSPFv3 with Stub Area

Topology

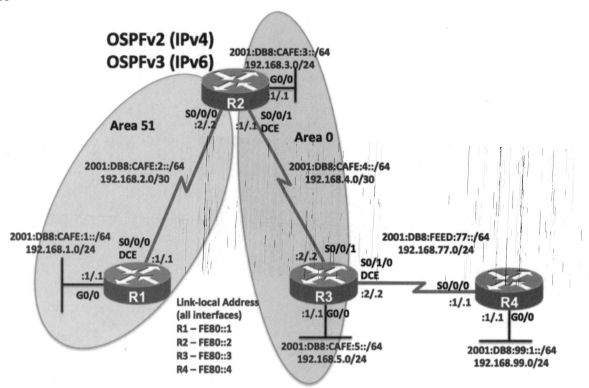

Objectives

- Configure multi-area OSPFv2 for IPv4.
- Configure multi-area OSPFv3 for IPv6.
- Verify multi-area behavior.
- Configure stub and totally stubby areas for OSPFv2.
- Configure stub and totally stubby areas for OSPFv3.

Background

In this lab, you will configure the network with multi-area OSPFv2 routing for IPv4 and multi-area OSPFv3 routing for IPv6. For both OSPFv2 and OSPFv3, area 51 will be configured as a normal OSPF area, a stub area and then a totally stubby area.

Note: This lab uses Cisco 1941 routers with Cisco IOS Release 15.4 with IP Base. The switches are Cisco WS-C2960-24TT-L with Fast Ethernet interfaces; therefore, the router will use routing metrics associated with a 100 Mb/s interface. Depending on the router or switch model and Cisco IOS Software version, the commands available and output produced might vary from what is shown in this lab.

Required Resources

- 4 routers (Cisco IOS Release 15.2 or comparable)
- 4 switches (LAN interfaces)
- Serial and Ethernet cables

Step 0: Suggested starting configurations.

a. Apply the following configuration to each router along with the appropriate **hostname**. The **exec-timeout 0 0** command should only be used in a lab environment.

```
Router(config)# no ip domain-lookup
Router(config)# line con 0
Router(config-line)# logging synchronous
Router(config-line)# exec-timeout 0 0
```

Step 1: Configure the addressing and serial links.

a. Using the topology, configure the IPv4 and IPv6 addresses on the interfaces of each router.

```
R1(config)# interface GigabitEthernet0/0
R1(config-if)# ip address 192.168.1.1 255.255.255.0
R1(config-if)# ipv6 address FE80::1 link-local
R1(config-if)# ipv6 address 2001:DB8:CAFE:1::1/64
R1(config-if)# no shutdown
R1(config-if)# exit
R1(config)# interface Serial0/0/0
R1(config-if)# ip address 192.168.2.1 255.255.255.252
R1(config-if)# ipv6 address FE80::1 link-local
R1(config-if)# ipv6 address 2001:DB8:CAFE:2::1/64
R1(config-if)# clock rate 64000
R1(config-if)# no shutdown

R2(config)# interface GigabitEthernet0/0
R2(config-if)# ip address 192.168.3.1 255.255.255.0
R2(config-if)# ipv6 address FE80::2 link-local
R2(config-if)# ipv6 address 2001:DB8:CAFE:3::1/64
R2(config-if)# no shutdown
R2(config-if)# exit
R2(config)# interface Serial0/0/0
R2(config-if)# ip address 192.168.2.2 255.255.255.252
R2(config-if)# ipv6 address FE80::2 link-local
R2(config-if)# ipv6 address 2001:DB8:CAFE:2::2/64
R2(config-if)# no shutdown
R2(config-if)# exit
R2(config)# interface Serial0/0/1
R2(config-if)# ip address 192.168.4.1 255.255.255.252
R2(config-if)# ipv6 address FE80::2 link-local
R2(config-if)# ipv6 address 2001:DB8:CAFE:4::1/64
R2(config-if)# clock rate 64000
R2(config-if)# no shutdown

R3(config)# interface GigabitEthernet0/0
R3(config-if)# ip address 192.168.5.1 255.255.255.0
R3(config-if)# ipv6 address FE80::3 link-local
R3(config-if)# ipv6 address 2001:DB8:CAFE:5::1/64
R3(config-if)# no shutdown
R3(config-if)# exit
R3(config)# interface Serial0/0/1
R3(config-if)# ip address 192.168.4.2 255.255.255.252
R3(config-if)# ipv6 address FE80::3 link-local
R3(config-if)# ipv6 address 2001:DB8:CAFE:4::2/64
R3(config-if)# no shutdown
R3(config-if)# exit
R3(config)# interface Serial0/1/0
```

```
R3(config-if)# ip address 192.168.77.2 255.255.255.0
R3(config-if)# ipv6 address FE80::3 link-local
R3(config-if)# ipv6 address 2001:DB8:FEED:77::2/64
R3(config-if)# clock rate 64000
R3(config-if)# no shutdown
R3(config-if)#

R4(config)# interface Serial0/0/0
R4(config-if)# ip address 192.168.77.1 255.255.255.0
R4(config-if)# ipv6 address FE80::4 link-local
R4(config-if)# ipv6 address 2001:DB8:FEED:77::1/64
R4(config-if)# no shutdown
R4(config-if)# exit
R4(config)# interface gigabitethernet 0/0
R4(config-if)# ip address 192.168.99.1 255.255.255.0
R4(config-if)# ipv6 address 2001:db8:99:1::1/64
R4(config-if)# no shutdown
R4(config-if)# exit
R4(config)# ipv6 unicast-routing
R4(config)# ipv6 route 2001:DB8:CAFE::/48 2001:DB8:FEED:77::2
R4(config)# ip route 0.0.0.0 0.0.0.0 192.168.77.2
R4(config)#
```

b. Verify connectivity by pinging across each of the local networks connected to each router.

c. Issue the **show ip interface brief** and the **show ipv6 interface brief** command on each router. These commands display a brief listing of the interfaces, their status, and their IP addresses. Router R1 is shown as an example.

```
R1# show ip interface brief
Interface                  IP-Address      OK? Method Status                Protocol
Embedded-Service-Engine0/0 unassigned      YES unset  administratively down down
GigabitEthernet0/0         192.168.1.1     YES manual up                    up
GigabitEthernet0/1         unassigned      YES unset  administratively down down
Serial0/0/0                192.168.2.1     YES manual up                    up
Serial0/0/1                unassigned      YES unset  administratively down down
R1# show ipv6 interface brief
Em0/0                      [administratively down/down]
    unassigned
GigabitEthernet0/0         [up/up]
    FE80::1
    2001:DB8:CAFE:1::1
GigabitEthernet0/1         [administratively down/down]
    unassigned
Serial0/0/0                [up/up]
    FE80::1
    2001:DB8:CAFE:2::1
Serial0/0/1                [administratively down/down]
    unassigned
R1#
```

Step 2: Configure multi-area OSPFv2.

Create OSPFv2 process 1 on routers R1, R2, and R3. Configure the OSPF router ID on each router. Enable directly connected networks into the OSPF process using the **ip ospf** *process-id* **area** *area-id* interface command that is available with Cisco IOS version 12.3(11)T and later.

Note: The **show ip ospf** command should used to verify the OSPF router ID. If the OSPF router ID is using a 32-bit value other than the one specified by the **router-id** command, you can reset the router ID by using the **clear ip ospf** *pid* **process** command and re-verify using the command **show ip ospf**.

a. Configure R3 as an OSPFv2 router in area 0.

```
R3(config)# router ospf 1
R3(config-router)# router-id 3.3.3.3
R3(config-router)# exit
R3(config)# interface gigabitethernet 0/0
R3(config-if)# ip ospf 1 area 0
R3(config-if)# exit
R3(config)# interface serial 0/0/1
R3(config-if)# ip ospf 1 area 0
R3(config-if)#
```

Note: Another option is to use the OSPF **network** command in router configuration mode.

b. Configure R2 as an ABR router for area 0 and area 51. Interfaces S0/0/1 and G0/0 are in area 0, while interface S0/0/0 is in area 51.

```
R2(config)# router ospf 1
R2(config-router)# router-id 2.2.2.2
R2(config-router)# exit
R2(config)# interface serial 0/0/1
R2(config-if)# ip ospf 1 area 0
R2(config-if)# exit
R2(config)# interface gigabitethernet 0/0
R2(config-if)# ip ospf 1 area 0
R2(config-if)# exit
R2(config)# interface serial 0/0/0
R2(config-if)# ip ospf 1 area 51
R2(config-if)#
```

c. Configure R1 as an internal OSPFv2 router in area 51.

```
R1(config)# router ospf 1
R1(config-router)# router-id 1.1.1.1
R1(config-router)# exit
R1(config)# interface serial 0/0/0
R1(config-if)# ip ospf 1 area 51
R1(config-if)# exit
R1(config)# interface gigabitethernet 0/0
R1(config-if)# ip ospf 1 area 51
R1(config-if)#
```

d. Verify that the routers have OSPFv2 neighbors using the **show ip ospf neighbors** command. The output for R2 is displayed.

```
R2# show ip ospf neighbor


Neighbor ID     Pri   State          Dead Time   Address        Interface
3.3.3.3           0   FULL/  -       00:00:36    192.168.4.2    Serial0/0/1
```

```
1.1.1.1         0   FULL/ -        00:00:32    192.168.2.1    Serial0/0/0
R2#
```

e. Verify that router R3 can see all the IPv4 networks in the OSPFv2 routing domain using the **show ip route** command.

```
R3# show ip route
Codes: L - local, C - connected, S - static, R - RIP, M - mobile, B - BGP
       D - EIGRP, EX - EIGRP external, O - OSPF, IA - OSPF inter area
       N1 - OSPF NSSA external type 1, N2 - OSPF NSSA external type 2
       E1 - OSPF external type 1, E2 - OSPF external type 2
       i - IS-IS, su - IS-IS summary, L1 - IS-IS level-1, L2 - IS-IS level-2
       ia - IS-IS inter area, * - candidate default, U - per-user static
       route
       o - ODR, P - periodic downloaded static route, H - NHRP, l - LISP
       a - application route
       + - replicated route, % - next hop override

Gateway of last resort is not set

O IA    192.168.1.0/24 [110/129] via 192.168.4.1, 00:14:43, Serial0/0/1
        192.168.2.0/30 is subnetted, 1 subnets
O IA    192.168.2.0 [110/128] via 192.168.4.1, 00:20:16, Serial0/0/1
O       192.168.3.0/24 [110/65] via 192.168.4.1, 00:26:25, Serial0/0/1
        192.168.4.0/24 is variably subnetted, 2 subnets, 2 masks
C          192.168.4.0/30 is directly connected, Serial0/0/1
L          192.168.4.2/32 is directly connected, Serial0/0/1
        192.168.5.0/24 is variably subnetted, 2 subnets, 2 masks
C          192.168.5.0/24 is directly connected, GigabitEthernet0/0
L          192.168.5.1/32 is directly connected, GigabitEthernet0/0
        192.168.77.0/24 is variably subnetted, 2 subnets, 2 masks
C          192.168.77.0/24 is directly connected, Serial0/1/0
L          192.168.77.2/32 is directly connected, Serial0/1/0
R3#
```

How many OSPFv2 intra-area routes area routes are in R3's IPv4 routing table? How many inter-area routes are in R3's IPv4 routing table?

_____

_____

f. Issue the **show ip route** command on R2.

```
R2# show ip route
Codes: L - local, C - connected, S - static, R - RIP, M - mobile, B - BGP
       D - EIGRP, EX - EIGRP external, O - OSPF, IA - OSPF inter area
       N1 - OSPF NSSA external type 1, N2 - OSPF NSSA external type 2
       E1 - OSPF external type 1, E2 - OSPF external type 2
       i - IS-IS, su - IS-IS summary, L1 - IS-IS level-1, L2 - IS-IS level-2
       ia - IS-IS inter area, * - candidate default, U - per-user static
       route
       o - ODR, P - periodic downloaded static route, H - NHRP, l - LISP
       a - application route
       + - replicated route, % - next hop override

Gateway of last resort is not set

O       192.168.1.0/24 [110/65] via 192.168.2.1, 00:22:38, Serial0/0/0
```

```
        192.168.2.0/24 is variably subnetted, 2 subnets, 2 masks
C          192.168.2.0/30 is directly connected, Serial0/0/0
L          192.168.2.2/32 is directly connected, Serial0/0/0
        192.168.3.0/24 is variably subnetted, 2 subnets, 2 masks
C          192.168.3.0/24 is directly connected, GigabitEthernet0/0
L          192.168.3.1/32 is directly connected, GigabitEthernet0/0
        192.168.4.0/24 is variably subnetted, 2 subnets, 2 masks
C          192.168.4.0/30 is directly connected, Serial0/0/1
L          192.168.4.1/32 is directly connected, Serial0/0/1
O       192.168.5.0/24 [110/65] via 192.168.4.2, 00:28:17, Serial0/0/1
R2#
```

Why doesn't R2 have any inter-area OSPFv2 routes in its routing table?

_____

_____

g. Configure an IPv4 default route on the ASBR, R3 forwarding traffic to R4. Propagate the default routing into OSPFv2.

```
R3(config)# ip route 0.0.0.0 0.0.0.0 192.168.77.1
R3(config)# router ospf 1
R3(config-router)# default-information originate
R3(config-router)#
```

h. Issue the **show ip route static** command on R3 to verify the static route is in the IPv4 routing table.

```
R3# show ip route static
Codes: L - local, C - connected, S - static, R - RIP, M - mobile, B - BGP
       D - EIGRP, EX - EIGRP external, O - OSPF, IA - OSPF inter area
       N1 - OSPF NSSA external type 1, N2 - OSPF NSSA external type 2
       E1 - OSPF external type 1, E2 - OSPF external type 2
       i - IS-IS, su - IS-IS summary, L1 - IS-IS level-1, L2 - IS-IS level-2
       ia - IS-IS inter area, * - candidate default, U - per-user static
       route
       o - ODR, P - periodic downloaded static route, H - NHRP, l - LISP
       a - application route
       + - replicated route, % - next hop override

Gateway of last resort is 192.168.77.1 to network 0.0.0.0

S*     0.0.0.0/0 [1/0] via 192.168.77.1
R3#
```

i. Configure an IPv4 static route on the ASBR, R3 for the 192.168.99.0/24 network on R4. Redistribute the static route into OSPFv2 using the **redistribute static subnets** command. The subnets parameter is used to include subnets and not just classful network addresses. The **redistribute** command is discussed in more detail in later chapters.

```
R3(config)# ip route 192.168.99.0 255.255.255.0 192.168.77.1
R3(config)# router ospf 1
R3(config-router)# redistribute static subnets
```

j. Issue the **show ip route ospf** command on R1 to verify that the default route and the redistributed static route are being advertised into the OSPFv2 domain.

```
R1# show ip route ospf
Codes: L - local, C - connected, S - static, R - RIP, M - mobile, B - BGP
       D - EIGRP, EX - EIGRP external, O - OSPF, IA - OSPF inter area
       N1 - OSPF NSSA external type 1, N2 - OSPF NSSA external type 2
       E1 - OSPF external type 1, E2 - OSPF external type 2
       i - IS-IS, su - IS-IS summary, L1 - IS-IS level-1, L2 - IS-IS level-2
       ia - IS-IS inter area, * - candidate default, U - per-user static
       route
       o - ODR, P - periodic downloaded static route, H - NHRP, l - LISP
       a - application route
       + - replicated route, % - next hop override

Gateway of last resort is 192.168.2.2 to network 0.0.0.0

O*E2  0.0.0.0/0 [110/1] via 192.168.2.2, 00:01:53, Serial0/0/0
O IA  192.168.3.0/24 [110/65] via 192.168.2.2, 00:06:09, Serial0/0/0
      192.168.4.0/30 is subnetted, 1 subnets
O IA     192.168.4.0 [110/128] via 192.168.2.2, 00:06:09, Serial0/0/0
O IA  192.168.5.0/24 [110/129] via 192.168.2.2, 00:06:09, Serial0/0/0
O E2  192.168.99.0/24 [110/20] via 192.168.2.2, 00:01:53, Serial0/0/0
R1#
```

What does the "E2" for the default route and the redistributed external route signify?

_____

_____

Step 3: Configure an OSPFv2 stub area.

a. Under the OSPFv2 process on R1 and R2, make area 51 a stub area using the **area** *area* **stub** command. The adjacency between the two routers might go down during the transition period, but it should come back up afterwards.

```
R1(config)# router ospf 1
R1(config-router)# area 51 stub

R2(config)# router ospf 1
R2(config-router)# area 51 stub
```

b. Confirm that both R1 and R2 are neighbors using the **show ip ospf neighbors** command.

```
R1# show ip ospf neighbor

Neighbor ID     Pri   State           Dead Time   Address         Interface
2.2.2.2           0   FULL/  -        00:00:36    192.168.2.2     Serial0/0/0
R1#


R2# show ip ospf neighbor

Neighbor ID     Pri   State           Dead Time   Address         Interface
3.3.3.3           0   FULL/  -        00:00:37    192.168.4.2     Serial0/0/1
1.1.1.1           0   FULL/  -        00:00:38    192.168.2.1     Serial0/0/0
R2#
```

c. Issue the **show ip route ospf** command on R1. Notice that R1 still has a default route pointing toward R2 but with a different cost than it had prior to being configured in a stub area. This is not the default route propagated by the ASBR R3, but the default route injected by the ABR of the stub area. Also, R1 does not receive any external routes, so it no longer has the external network 192.168.99.0/24 in its routing table. Stub routers continue to receive inter-area routes from area 0.

```
R1# show ip route ospf
Codes: L - local, C - connected, S - static, R - RIP, M - mobile, B - BGP
       D - EIGRP, EX - EIGRP external, O - OSPF, IA - OSPF inter area
       N1 - OSPF NSSA external type 1, N2 - OSPF NSSA external type 2
       E1 - OSPF external type 1, E2 - OSPF external type 2
       i - IS-IS, su - IS-IS summary, L1 - IS-IS level-1, L2 - IS-IS level-2
       ia - IS-IS inter area, * - candidate default, U - per-user static
       route
       o - ODR, P - periodic downloaded static route, H - NHRP, l - LISP
       a - application route
       + - replicated route, % - next hop override

Gateway of last resort is 192.168.2.2 to network 0.0.0.0

O*IA  0.0.0.0/0 [110/65] via 192.168.2.2, 00:06:09, Serial0/0/0
O IA  192.168.3.0/24 [110/65] via 192.168.2.2, 00:06:09, Serial0/0/0
      192.168.4.0/30 is subnetted, 1 subnets
O IA     192.168.4.0 [110/128] via 192.168.2.2, 00:06:09, Serial0/0/0
O IA  192.168.5.0/24 [110/129] via 192.168.2.2, 00:06:09, Serial0/0/0
R1#
```

d. View the output of the **show ip ospf** command on ABR R2 to see what type each area is and the number of interfaces in each area.

```
R2# show ip ospf
 Routing Process "ospf 1" with ID 2.2.2.2
 Start time: 01:49:34.272, Time elapsed: 02:04:19.324
 Supports only single TOS(TOS0) routes
 Supports opaque LSA
 Supports Link-local Signaling (LLS)
 Supports area transit capability
 Supports NSSA (compatible with RFC 3101)
 Event-log enabled, Maximum number of events: 1000, Mode: cyclic
 It is an area border router
 Router is not originating router-LSAs with maximum metric
 Initial SPF schedule delay 5000 msecs
 Minimum hold time between two consecutive SPFs 10000 msecs
 Maximum wait time between two consecutive SPFs 10000 msecs
 Incremental-SPF disabled
 Minimum LSA interval 5 secs
 Minimum LSA arrival 1000 msecs
 LSA group pacing timer 240 secs
 Interface flood pacing timer 33 msecs
 Retransmission pacing timer 66 msecs
 Number of external LSA 2. Checksum Sum 0x0174F7
 Number of opaque AS LSA 0. Checksum Sum 0x000000
 Number of DCbitless external and opaque AS LSA 0
 Number of DoNotAge external and opaque AS LSA 0
 Number of areas in this router is 2. 1 normal 1 stub 0 nssa
 Number of areas transit capable is 0
 External flood list length 0
 IETF NSF helper support enabled
 Cisco NSF helper support enabled
```

```
    Reference bandwidth unit is 100 mbps
        Area BACKBONE(0)
            Number of interfaces in this area is 2
            Area has no authentication
            SPF algorithm last executed 00:23:27.416 ago
            SPF algorithm executed 20 times
            Area ranges are
            Number of LSA 6. Checksum Sum 0x0413D3
            Number of opaque link LSA 0. Checksum Sum 0x000000
            Number of DCbitless LSA 0
            Number of indication LSA 0
            Number of DoNotAge LSA 0
            Flood list length 0
        Area 51
            Number of interfaces in this area is 1
            It is a stub area
            Generates stub default route with cost 1
            Area has no authentication
            SPF algorithm last executed 00:23:17.416 ago
            SPF algorithm executed 4 times
            Area ranges are
            Number of LSA 6. Checksum Sum 0x02E70A
            Number of opaque link LSA 0. Checksum Sum 0x000000
            Number of DCbitless LSA 0
            Number of indication LSA 0
            Number of DoNotAge LSA 0
            Flood list length 0

R2#
```

What are the advantages of having a router receive a default route rather than a more specific route?

_____

_____

Why do all routers in a stub area need to know that the area is a stub?

_____

_____

_____

Step 4: Configure a totally stubby area.

A modified version of a stubby area is a totally stubby area. A totally stubby area ABR only allows in a single, default route from the backbone, injected by the ABR. To configure a totally stubby area, you only need to change a command at the ABR: R2 in this scenario. Under the router OSPFv2 process, you will enter the **area 51 stub no-summary** command to replace the existing stub command for area 51. The **no-summary** option tells the router that this area will not receive summary (inter-area) routes.

a. To see how this works, issue the **show ip route ospf** command on R1. Notice the inter-area routes, in addition to the default route generated by R2.

```
R1# show ip route ospf
Codes: L - local, C - connected, S - static, R - RIP, M - mobile, B - BGP
       D - EIGRP, EX - EIGRP external, O - OSPF, IA - OSPF inter area
       N1 - OSPF NSSA external type 1, N2 - OSPF NSSA external type 2
```

```
        E1 - OSPF external type 1, E2 - OSPF external type 2
        i - IS-IS, su - IS-IS summary, L1 - IS-IS level-1, L2 - IS-IS level-2
        ia - IS-IS inter area, * - candidate default, U - per-user static
        route
        o - ODR, P - periodic downloaded static route, H - NHRP, l - LISP
        a - application route
        + - replicated route, % - next hop override

Gateway of last resort is 192.168.2.2 to network 0.0.0.0

O*IA  0.0.0.0/0 [110/65] via 192.168.2.2, 00:28:13, Serial0/0/0
O IA  192.168.3.0/24 [110/65] via 192.168.2.2, 00:28:13, Serial0/0/0
        192.168.4.0/30 is subnetted, 1 subnets
O IA      192.168.4.0 [110/128] via 192.168.2.2, 00:28:13, Serial0/0/0
O IA  192.168.5.0/24 [110/129] via 192.168.2.2, 00:28:13, Serial0/0/0
R1#
```

b. Look at the output of the **show ip ospf database** command on R2 to see which LSAs are in its OSPFv2 database.

```
R2# show ip ospf database

            OSPF Router with ID (2.2.2.2) (Process ID 1)

            Router Link States (Area 0)

Link ID         ADV Router      Age       Seq#        Checksum Link count
1.1.1.1         1.1.1.1         2231      0x80000002 0x00EECE 2
2.2.2.2         2.2.2.2         41        0x8000000D 0x00E63E 3
3.3.3.3         3.3.3.3         385       0x80000007 0x0071B1 3

            Summary Net Link States (Area 0)

Link ID         ADV Router      Age       Seq#        Checksum
192.168.1.0     1.1.1.1         2241      0x80000002 0x00B616
192.168.1.0     2.2.2.2         1838      0x80000001 0x001D6C
192.168.2.0     2.2.2.2         41        0x80000002 0x00F397

            Router Link States (Area 51)

Link ID         ADV Router      Age       Seq#        Checksum Link count
1.1.1.1         1.1.1.1         1847      0x8000000B 0x0043F8 3
2.2.2.2         2.2.2.2         1841      0x8000000A 0x009C16 2

            Summary Net Link States (Area 51)

Link ID         ADV Router      Age       Seq#        Checksum
0.0.0.0         2.2.2.2         41        0x80000002 0x0073C1
192.168.3.0     2.2.2.2         41        0x80000007 0x00962D
192.168.4.0     2.2.2.2         41        0x80000007 0x00F194
192.168.5.0     2.2.2.2         41        0x80000007 0x00037E

            Type-5 AS External Link States

Link ID         ADV Router      Age       Seq#        Checksum Tag
0.0.0.0         3.3.3.3         385       0x80000003 0x00DCC7 1
192.168.99.0    3.3.3.3         385       0x80000002 0x009432 0
R2#
```

c. Enter the **area 51 stub no-summary** command on R2 (the ABR) under the OSPF process.

```
R2(config)# router ospf 1
R2(config-router)# area 51 stub no-summary
```

d. Go back to R1 and issue the **show ip route ospf** command. Notice that it shows only one incoming route from the ABR R2. The default route is injected by the ABR R2. There are no inter-area OSPFv2 routes and no external OSPFv2 routes.

```
R1# show ip route ospf
Codes: L - local, C - connected, S - static, R - RIP, M - mobile, B - BGP
       D - EIGRP, EX - EIGRP external, O - OSPF, IA - OSPF inter area
       N1 - OSPF NSSA external type 1, N2 - OSPF NSSA external type 2
       E1 - OSPF external type 1, E2 - OSPF external type 2
       i - IS-IS, su - IS-IS summary, L1 - IS-IS level-1, L2 - IS-IS level-2
       ia - IS-IS inter area, * - candidate default, U - per-user static
       route
       o - ODR, P - periodic downloaded static route, H - NHRP, l - LISP
       a - application route
       + - replicated route, % - next hop override

Gateway of last resort is 192.168.2.2 to network 0.0.0.0

O*IA  0.0.0.0/0 [110/65] via 192.168.2.2, 00:01:14, Serial0/0/0
R1#
```

e. Examine the output of the **show ip ospf database** command to see which routes are in area 51. You may need to clear the OSPFv2 process to reset the entries in the OSPF LSDB.

```
R1# clear ip ospf process
Reset ALL OSPF processes? [no]: yes
*Oct  8 03:56:06.802: %OSPF-5-ADJCHG: Process 1, Nbr 2.2.2.2 on Serial0/0/0
from FULL to DOWN, Neighbor Down: Interface down or detached
*Oct  8 03:56:06.894: %OSPF-5-ADJCHG: Process 1, Nbr 2.2.2.2 on Serial0/0/0
from LOADING to FULL, Loading Done
R1#
R1# show ip ospf database

            OSPF Router with ID (1.1.1.1) (Process ID 1)

                Router Link States (Area 51)

Link ID         ADV Router      Age       Seq#        Checksum Link count
1.1.1.1         1.1.1.1         7         0x8000000D 0x003FFA 3
2.2.2.2         2.2.2.2         284       0x8000000B 0x009A17 2

                Summary Net Link States (Area 51)

Link ID         ADV Router      Age       Seq#        Checksum
0.0.0.0         2.2.2.2         330       0x80000004 0x006FC3
R1#
```

What are the advantages of making an area totally stubby instead of a regular stub area? What are the disadvantages?

_____

_____

_____

Why did only the ABR need to know that the area was totally stubby rather than all routers in the area?

_____

_____

_____

Step 5: Configure multi-area OSPFv3.

Traditional OSPFv3 implements OSPF routing for IPv6. In our dual-stack (IPv4/IPv6) environment we have previously configured OSPFv2 for routing IPv4 and now we will configure OSPFv3 for routing IPv6.

a. OSPFv3 messages are sourced from the router's IPv6 link-local address. Earlier in this lab, IPv6 GUA and link-local addresses were statically configured on each router's interface. The link-local addresses were configured to make these addresses more recognizable than being automatically created using EUI-64. Issue the **show ipv6 interface brief** command to verify the GUA and link-local addresses on the router's interfaces.

```
R1# show ipv6 interface brief
Em0/0                      [administratively down/down]
    unassigned
GigabitEthernet0/0         [up/up]
    FE80::1
    2001:DB8:CAFE:1::1
GigabitEthernet0/1         [administratively down/down]
    unassigned
Serial0/0/0                [up/up]
    FE80::1
    2001:DB8:CAFE:2::1
Serial0/0/1                [administratively down/down]
    unassigned
R1#
```

b. IPv6 routing is disabled by default. The Cisco IOS version used with the routers in this lab has IPv6 CEF enabled by default once IPv6 routing is enabled. To enable IPv6 routing, use the **ipv6 unicast-routing** command in global configuration mode. Use the **show ipv6 cef** command to verify whether IPv6 CEF is enabled. If you need to enable IPv6 CEF, use the **ipv6 cef** command. If IPv6 CEF is disabled you will see an IOS message similar to "%IPv6 CEF not running:" Enter these commands on routers R1, R2, and R3. IPv6 routing on R4 has been enabled in Step 1.

```
R1(config)# ipv6 unicast-routing
R1(config)# end
R1# show ipv6 cef
::/0
  no route
::/127
  discard
2001:DB8:CAFE:1::/64
  attached to GigabitEthernet0/0
2001:DB8:CAFE:1::1/128
  receive for GigabitEthernet0/0
```

```
2001:DB8:CAFE:2::/64
  attached to Serial0/0/0
2001:DB8:CAFE:2::1/128
  receive for Serial0/0/0
FE80::/10
  receive for Null0
FF00::/8
  multicast
R1#


R2(config)# ipv6 unicast-routing


R3(config)# ipv6 unicast-routing
```

c. Configure the OSPFv3 process on each router. Similar to OSPFv2, the process ID does not have to
    match other routers to form neighbor adjacencies. Configure the 32-bit OSPFv3 router ID on each router.
    The OSPFv3 router ID uses the same process as OSPFv2 and is required if there are no IPv4 addresses
    configured on the router.

    Note: The **show ipv6 ospf** command should used to verify the OSPF router ID. If the OSPFv3 router ID
    uses a 32-bit value other than the one specified by the **router-id** command, you can reset the router ID
    by using the **clear ipv6 ospf** *pid* **process** command and re-verify using the command **show ipv6 ospf**.

```
R1(config)# ipv6 router ospf 2
R1(config-rtr)# router-id 1.1.1.1
R1(config-rtr)# exit
R1(config)# interface gigabitethernet 0/0
R1(config-if)# ipv6 ospf 2 area 51
R1(config-if)# exit
R1(config)# interface serial 0/0/0
R1(config-if)# ipv6 ospf 2 area 51
R1(config-if)#



R2(config)# ipv6 router ospf 2
R2(config-rtr)# router-id 2.2.2.2
R2(config-rtr)# exit
R2(config)# interface serial 0/0/1
R2(config-if)# ipv6 ospf 2 area 0
R2(config-if)# exit
R2(config)# interface gigabitethernet 0/0
R2(config-if)# ipv6 ospf 2 area 0
R2(config-if)# exit
R2(config)# interface serial 0/0/0
R2(config-if)# ipv6 ospf 2 area 51
R2(config-if)#


R3(config)# ipv6 router ospf 2
R3(config-rtr)# router-id 3.3.3.3
R3(config-rtr)# exit
```

```
R3(config)# interface gigabitethernet 0/0
R3(config-if)# ipv6 ospf 2 area 0
R3(config-if)# exit
R3(config)# interface serial 0/0/1
R3(config-if)# ipv6 ospf 2 area 0
R3(config-if)#
```

d. Verify that you have OSPFv3 neighbors with the **show ipv6 ospf neighbor** command. The output for R2 is displayed.

```
R2# show ipv6 ospf neighbor

           OSPFv3 Router with ID (2.2.2.2) (Process ID 2)

Neighbor ID     Pri   State           Dead Time   Interface ID   Interface
3.3.3.3          0    FULL/ -         00:00:36    6              Serial0/0/1
1.1.1.1          0    FULL/ -         00:00:34    6              Serial0/0/0
R2#
```

e. View the OSPF routes in the IPv6 routing table on all three routers with the **show ipv6 route ospf** command.

```
R1# show ipv6 route ospf
IPv6 Routing Table - default - 8 entries
Codes: C - Connected, L - Local, S - Static, U - Per-user Static route
       B - BGP, R - RIP, H - NHRP, I1 - ISIS L1
       I2 - ISIS L2, IA - ISIS interarea, IS - ISIS summary, D - EIGRP
       EX - EIGRP external, ND - ND Default, NDp - ND Prefix, DCE -
       Destination
       NDr - Redirect, O - OSPF Intra, OI - OSPF Inter, OE1 - OSPF ext 1
       OE2 - OSPF ext 2, ON1 - OSPF NSSA ext 1, ON2 - OSPF NSSA ext 2
       a - Application
OI  2001:DB8:CAFE:3::/64 [110/65]
     via FE80::2, Serial0/0/0
OI  2001:DB8:CAFE:4::/64 [110/128]
     via FE80::2, Serial0/0/0
OI  2001:DB8:CAFE:5::/64 [110/129]
     via FE80::2, Serial0/0/0
R1#


R2# show ipv6 route ospf
IPv6 Routing Table - default - 9 entries
Codes: C - Connected, L - Local, S - Static, U - Per-user Static route
       B - BGP, R - RIP, H - NHRP, I1 - ISIS L1
       I2 - ISIS L2, IA - ISIS interarea, IS - ISIS summary, D - EIGRP
       EX - EIGRP external, ND - ND Default, NDp - ND Prefix, DCE -
       Destination
       NDr - Redirect, O - OSPF Intra, OI - OSPF Inter, OE1 - OSPF ext 1
       OE2 - OSPF ext 2, ON1 - OSPF NSSA ext 1, ON2 - OSPF NSSA ext 2
       a - Application
```

```
O    2001:DB8:CAFE:1::/64 [110/65]
       via FE80::1, Serial0/0/0
O    2001:DB8:CAFE:5::/64 [110/65]
       via FE80::3, Serial0/0/1
R2#


R3# show ipv6 route ospf
IPv6 Routing Table - default - 10 entries
Codes: C - Connected, L - Local, S - Static, U - Per-user Static route
       B - BGP, R - RIP, H - NHRP, I1 - ISIS L1
       I2 - ISIS L2, IA - ISIS interarea, IS - ISIS summary, D - EIGRP
       EX - EIGRP external, ND - ND Default, NDp - ND Prefix, DCE -
       Destination
       NDr - Redirect, O - OSPF Intra, OI - OSPF Inter, OE1 - OSPF ext 1
       OE2 - OSPF ext 2, ON1 - OSPF NSSA ext 1, ON2 - OSPF NSSA ext 2
       a - Application
OI   2001:DB8:CAFE:1::/64 [110/129]
       via FE80::2, Serial0/0/1
OI   2001:DB8:CAFE:2::/64 [110/128]
       via FE80::2, Serial0/0/1
O    2001:DB8:CAFE:3::/64 [110/65]
       via FE80::2, Serial0/0/1
R3#
```

f. Configure an IPv6 default route on the ASBR R3 forwarding traffic to R4. Propagate the default routing into OSPFv3.

```
R3(config)# ipv6 route ::/0 2001:db8:feed:77::1
R3(config)# ipv6 router ospf 2
R3(config-rtr)# default-information originate
R3(config-rtr)#
```

g. Configure an IPv6 static route on the ASBR R3 for the 2001:DB8:99:1::/64 prefix on R4. Redistribute the static route into OSPFv3.

```
R3(config)# ipv6 route 2001:db8:99:1::/64 2001:db8:feed:77::1
R3(config)# ipv6 router ospf 2
R3(config-rtr)# redistribute static
R3(config-rtr)#
```

h. Issue the show ipv6 route static command on R3 to verify both static routes are in the IPv6 routing table.

```
R3# show ipv6 route static
IPv6 Routing Table - default - 12 entries
Codes: C - Connected, L - Local, S - Static, U - Per-user Static route
       B - BGP, R - RIP, H - NHRP, I1 - ISIS L1
       I2 - ISIS L2, IA - ISIS interarea, IS - ISIS summary, D - EIGRP
       EX - EIGRP external, ND - ND Default, NDp - ND Prefix, DCE -
       Destination
       NDr - Redirect, O - OSPF Intra, OI - OSPF Inter, OE1 - OSPF ext 1
```

```
            OE2 - OSPF ext 2, ON1 - OSPF NSSA ext 1, ON2 - OSPF NSSA ext 2
            a - Application
S     ::/0 [1/0]
        via 2001:DB8:FEED:77::1
S     2001:DB8:99:1::/64 [1/0]
        via 2001:DB8:FEED:77::1
R3#
```

i. Issue the **show ipv6 route ospf** command on R1 to verify that the default route and the redistributed static route are now being advertised into the OSPFv3 domain.

```
R1# show ipv6 route ospf
IPv6 Routing Table - default - 10 entries
Codes: C - Connected, L - Local, S - Static, U - Per-user Static route
        B - BGP, R - RIP, H - NHRP, I1 - ISIS L1
        I2 - ISIS L2, IA - ISIS interarea, IS - ISIS summary, D - EIGRP
        EX - EIGRP external, ND - ND Default, NDp - ND Prefix, DCE -
        Destination
        NDr - Redirect, O - OSPF Intra, OI - OSPF Inter, OE1 - OSPF ext 1
        OE2 - OSPF ext 2, ON1 - OSPF NSSA ext 1, ON2 - OSPF NSSA ext 2
        a - Application
OE2 ::/0 [110/1], tag 2
    via FE80::2, Serial0/0/0
OE2 2001:DB8:99:1::/64 [110/20]
    via FE80::2, Serial0/0/0
OI  2001:DB8:CAFE:3::/64 [110/65]
    via FE80::2, Serial0/0/0
OI  2001:DB8:CAFE:4::/64 [110/128]
    via FE80::2, Serial0/0/0
OI  2001:DB8:CAFE:5::/64 [110/129]
    via FE80::2, Serial0/0/0
R1#
```

Step 6: Configure an OSPFv3 stub area.

a. Configuring stub areas for OSPFv3 is similar to that for OSPFv2. The stub area functionality is the same for OSPFv2 and OSPFv3. Under the OSPFv3 process on R1 and R2, make area 51 a stub area using the **area** *area* **stub** command. The adjacency between the two routers might go down during the transition period, but it should come back up afterwards.

```
R1(config)# ipv6 router ospf 2
R1(config-rtr)# area 51 stub

R2(config)# ipv6 router ospf 2
R2(config-rtr)# area 51 stub
```

b. Confirm that both R1 and R2 are neighbors using the **show ipv6 ospf neighbors** command.

```
R1# show ipv6 ospf neighbor

            OSPFv3 Router with ID (1.1.1.1) (Process ID 2)

Neighbor ID     Pri   State          Dead Time   Interface ID   Interface
2.2.2.2           0   FULL/  -       00:00:36    5              Serial0/0/0
R1#
```

```
R2# show ipv6 ospf neighbor

            OSPFv3 Router with ID (2.2.2.2) (Process ID 2)

Neighbor ID     Pri   State          Dead Time   Interface ID   Interface
3.3.3.3           0   FULL/  -       00:00:35    6              Serial0/0/1
1.1.1.1           0   FULL/  -       00:00:34    6              Serial0/0/0
R2#
```

c. To verify that the stub area functionality is the same in OSPFv3 as in OSPFv2 issue the **show ipv6 route ospf** command on R1. Similar to OSPFv2, notice that R1 still has a default route pointing toward R2 but with a different cost than it had prior to being configured in a stub area. Again, this is not the default route propagated by the ASBR R3, but the default route injected by the ABR of the stub area. R1 also does not receive any external routes, so it no longer has the 2001:DB8:99:1::/64 prefix in its routing table. Stub routers continue to receive inter-area routes.

```
R1# show ipv6 route ospf
IPv6 Routing Table - default - 9 entries
Codes: C - Connected, L - Local, S - Static, U - Per-user Static route
       B - BGP, R - RIP, H - NHRP, I1 - ISIS L1
       I2 - ISIS L2, IA - ISIS interarea, IS - ISIS summary, D - EIGRP
       EX - EIGRP external, ND - ND Default, NDp - ND Prefix, DCE -
       Destination
       NDr - Redirect, O - OSPF Intra, OI - OSPF Inter, OE1 - OSPF ext 1
       OE2 - OSPF ext 2, ON1 - OSPF NSSA ext 1, ON2 - OSPF NSSA ext 2
       a - Application
OI  ::/0 [110/65]
     via FE80::2, Serial0/0/0
OI  2001:DB8:CAFE:3::/64 [110/65]
     via FE80::2, Serial0/0/0
OI  2001:DB8:CAFE:4::/64 [110/128]
     via FE80::2, Serial0/0/0
OI  2001:DB8:CAFE:5::/64 [110/129]
     via FE80::2, Serial0/0/0
R1#
```

Step 7: Configure a totally stubby area.

As mentioned earlier in the lab, a totally stubby area ABR only allows in a single, default route from the backbone, injected by the ABR. Configuring a totally stubby area, you only need to change a command at the ABR, R2 in this scenario. Similar commands used to configure a totally stubby area for the OSPFv2 process are used for OSPFv3.

a. First, issue the **show ipv6 route ospf** command on R1 to verify that inter-area routes, in addition to the default route, are being sent by R2.

```
R1#show ipv6 route ospf
IPv6 Routing Table - default - 9 entries
Codes: C - Connected, L - Local, S - Static, U - Per-user Static route
       B - BGP, R - RIP, H - NHRP, I1 - ISIS L1
       I2 - ISIS L2, IA - ISIS interarea, IS - ISIS summary, D - EIGRP
       EX - EIGRP external, ND - ND Default, NDp - ND Prefix, DCE -
       Destination
       NDr - Redirect, O - OSPF Intra, OI - OSPF Inter, OE1 - OSPF ext 1
       OE2 - OSPF ext 2, ON1 - OSPF NSSA ext 1, ON2 - OSPF NSSA ext 2
       a - Application
```

```
OI  ::/0 [110/65]
      via FE80::2, Serial0/0/0
OI  2001:DB8:CAFE:3::/64 [110/65]
      via FE80::2, Serial0/0/0
OI  2001:DB8:CAFE:4::/64 [110/128]
      via FE80::2, Serial0/0/0
OI  2001:DB8:CAFE:5::/64 [110/129]
      via FE80::2, Serial0/0/0
R1#
```

b. Enter the **area 51 stub no-summary** command on R2 (the ABR) under the OSPFv3 process.

```
R2(config)# ipv6 router ospf 2
R2(config-rtr)# area 51 stub no-summary
```

c. On R1 issue the **show ipv6 route ospf** command. Similarly to OSPFv2, there is only one incoming route from the ABR R2. The default route is injected by the ABR R2. There are no inter-area OSPFv3 routes and no external OSPFv3 routes.

```
R1# show ipv6 route ospf
IPv6 Routing Table - default - 6 entries
Codes: C - Connected, L - Local, S - Static, U - Per-user Static route
       B - BGP, R - RIP, H - NHRP, I1 - ISIS L1
       I2 - ISIS L2, IA - ISIS interarea, IS - ISIS summary, D - EIGRP
       EX - EIGRP external, ND - ND Default, NDp - ND Prefix, DCE -
       Destination
       NDr - Redirect, O - OSPF Intra, OI - OSPF Inter, OE1 - OSPF ext 1
       OE2 - OSPF ext 2, ON1 - OSPF NSSA ext 1, ON2 - OSPF NSSA ext 2
       a - Application
OI  ::/0 [110/65]
      via FE80::2, Serial0/0/0
R1#
```

d. View the output of the **show ipv6 ospf** command on ABR R2 to see what type each area is and the number of interfaces in each area.

```
R2# show ipv6 ospf
 Routing Process "ospfv3 2" with ID 2.2.2.2
 Supports NSSA (compatible with RFC 3101)
 Event-log enabled, Maximum number of events: 1000, Mode: cyclic
 It is an area border router
 Router is not originating router-LSAs with maximum metric
 Initial SPF schedule delay 5000 msecs
 Minimum hold time between two consecutive SPFs 10000 msecs
 Maximum wait time between two consecutive SPFs 10000 msecs
 Minimum LSA interval 5 secs
 Minimum LSA arrival 1000 msecs
 LSA group pacing timer 240 secs
 Interface flood pacing timer 33 msecs
 Retransmission pacing timer 66 msecs
 Retransmission limit dc 24 non-dc 24
 Number of external LSA 2. Checksum Sum 0x00FD33
 Number of areas in this router is 2. 1 normal 1 stub 0 nssa
 Graceful restart helper support enabled
 Reference bandwidth unit is 100 mbps
 RFC1583 compatibility enabled
    Area BACKBONE(0)
```

```
        Number of interfaces in this area is 2
        SPF algorithm executed 7 times
        Number of LSA 9. Checksum Sum 0x0539E9
        Number of DCbitless LSA 0
        Number of indication LSA 0
        Number of DoNotAge LSA 0
        Flood list length 0
    Area 51
        Number of interfaces in this area is 1
        It is a stub area, no summary LSA in this area
        Generates stub default route with cost 1
        SPF algorithm executed 5 times
        Number of LSA 7. Checksum Sum 0x028798
        Number of DCbitless LSA 0
        Number of indication LSA 0
        Number of DoNotAge LSA 0
        Flood list length 0

    R2#
```

What is meant by the highlighted output for Area 51?

_____

_____

_____

_____

Lab 3-3 OSPFv3 Address Families

Topology

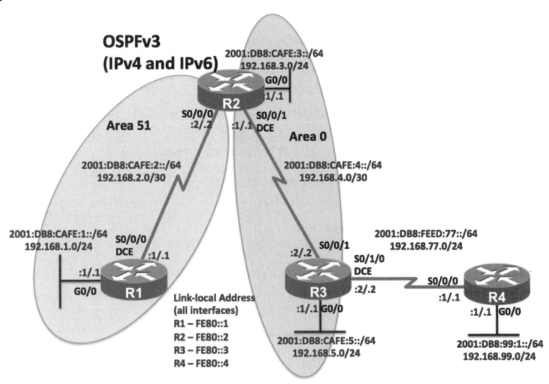

Objectives

- Configure multi-area OSPFv3 for IPv4 AF.
- Configure multi-area OSPFv3 for IPv6 AF.
- Verify multi-area behavior.
- Configure stub and totally stubby areas for both IPv4 and IPv6 AFs.

Background

In this lab, you will configure the network with multi-area OSPFv3 routing using the address family feature for both IPv4 and IPv6. For both OSPFv2 and OSPFv3, area 51 will be configured as a normal OSPF area, a stub area, and then a totally stubby area.

Note: This lab uses Cisco 1941 routers with Cisco IOS Release 15.4 with IP Base. The switches are Cisco WS-C2960-24TT-L with Fast Ethernet interfaces; therefore, the router will use routing metrics associated with a 100 Mb/s interface. Depending on the router or switch model and Cisco IOS Software version, the commands available and output produced might vary from what is shown in this lab.

Required Resources

- 4 routers (Cisco IOS Release 15.2 or comparable)
- 4 switches (LAN interfaces)
- Serial and Ethernet cables

Step 0: Suggested starting configurations.

a. Apply the following configuration to each router along with the appropriate **hostname**. The **exec-timeout 0 0** command should only be used in a lab environment.

```
Router(config)# no ip domain-lookup
Router(config)# line con 0
Router(config-line)# logging synchronous
Router(config-line)# exec-timeout 0 0
```

Step 1: Configure the addressing and serial links.

a. Using the topology, configure the IPv4 and IPv6 addresses on the interfaces of each router.

```
R1(config)# interface GigabitEthernet0/0
R1(config-if)# ip address 192.168.1.1 255.255.255.0
R1(config-if)# ipv6 address FE80::1 link-local
R1(config-if)# ipv6 address 2001:DB8:CAFE:1::1/64
R1(config-if)# no shutdown
R1(config-if)# exit
R1(config)# interface Serial0/0/0
R1(config-if)# ip address 192.168.2.1 255.255.255.252
R1(config-if)# ipv6 address FE80::1 link-local
R1(config-if)# ipv6 address 2001:DB8:CAFE:2::1/64
R1(config-if)# clock rate 64000
R1(config-if)# no shutdown

R2(config)# interface GigabitEthernet0/0
R2(config-if)# ip address 192.168.3.1 255.255.255.0
R2(config-if)# ipv6 address FE80::2 link-local
R2(config-if)# ipv6 address 2001:DB8:CAFE:3::1/64
R2(config-if)# no shutdown
R2(config-if)# exit
R2(config)# interface Serial0/0/0
R2(config-if)# ip address 192.168.2.2 255.255.255.252
R2(config-if)# ipv6 address FE80::2 link-local
R2(config-if)# ipv6 address 2001:DB8:CAFE:2::2/64
R2(config-if)# no shutdown
R2(config-if)# exit
R2(config)# interface Serial0/0/1
R2(config-if)# ip address 192.168.4.1 255.255.255.252
R2(config-if)# ipv6 address FE80::2 link-local
R2(config-if)# ipv6 address 2001:DB8:CAFE:4::1/64
R2(config-if)# clock rate 64000
R2(config-if)# no shutdown

R3(config)# interface GigabitEthernet0/0
R3(config-if)# ip address 192.168.5.1 255.255.255.0
R3(config-if)# ipv6 address FE80::3 link-local
R3(config-if)# ipv6 address 2001:DB8:CAFE:5::1/64
R3(config-if)# no shutdown
R3(config-if)# exit
R3(config)# interface Serial0/0/1
R3(config-if)# ip address 192.168.4.2 255.255.255.252
R3(config-if)# ipv6 address FE80::3 link-local
R3(config-if)# ipv6 address 2001:DB8:CAFE:4::2/64
R3(config-if)# no shutdown
R3(config-if)# exit
```

```
R3(config)# interface Serial0/1/0
R3(config-if)# ip address 192.168.77.2 255.255.255.0
R3(config-if)# ipv6 address FE80::3 link-local
R3(config-if)# ipv6 address 2001:DB8:FEED:77::2/64
R3(config-if)# clock rate 64000
R3(config-if)# no shutdown
R3(config-if)#

R4(config)# interface Serial0/0/0
R4(config-if)# ip address 192.168.77.1 255.255.255.0
R4(config-if)# ipv6 address FE80::4 link-local
R4(config-if)# ipv6 address 2001:DB8:FEED:77::1/64
R4(config-if)# no shutdown
R4(config-if)# exit
R4(config)# interface gigabitethernet 0/0
R4(config-if)# ip address 192.168.99.1 255.255.255.0
R4(config-if)# ipv6 address 2001:db8:99:1::1/64
R4(config-if)# no shutdown
R4(config-if)# exit
R4(config)# ipv6 unicast-routing
R4(config)# ipv6 route 2001:DB8:CAFE::/48 2001:DB8:FEED:77::2
R4(config)# ip route 0.0.0.0 0.0.0.0 192.168.77.2
R4(config)#
```

b. Verify connectivity by pinging across each of the local networks connected to each router.

c. Issue the **show ip interface brief** and the **show ipv6 interface brief** command on each router. These commands display a brief listing of the interfaces, their status, and their IP addresses. Router R1 is shown as an example.

```
R1# show ip interface brief
Interface                  IP-Address   OK? Method Status                Protocol
Embedded-Service-Engine0/0 unassigned   YES unset  administratively down down
GigabitEthernet0/0         192.168.1.1  YES manual up                         up
GigabitEthernet0/1         unassigned   YES unset  administratively down down
Serial0/0/0                192.168.2.1  YES manual up                         up
Serial0/0/1                unassigned   YES unset  administratively down down
R1# show ipv6 interface brief
Em0/0                   [administratively down/down]
    unassigned
GigabitEthernet0/0      [up/up]
    FE80::1
    2001:DB8:CAFE:1::1
GigabitEthernet0/1      [administratively down/down]
    unassigned
Serial0/0/0             [up/up]
    FE80::1
    2001:DB8:CAFE:2::1
Serial0/0/1             [administratively down/down]
    unassigned
R1#
```

Step 2: Configure and verify OSPFv3 address families for IPv4 and IPv6.

OSPFv3 with the address family (AF) unifies OSPF configuration for both IPv4 and IPv6. OSPFv3 with address families also combines neighbor tables and the LSDB under a single OSPF process. OSPFv3 messages are sent over IPv6 and therefore require that IPv6 routing is enabled and that the interface has a link-local IPv6 address. This is the requirement even if only the IPv4 AF is configured.

Note: After you configure the OSPFv3 address families, the **show ospfv3** command should used to verify the OSPF router ID for both the IPv4 and IPv6 AF. If the OSPF router ID is using a 32-bit value other than the one specified by the **router-id** command, you can reset the router ID by using the **clear ospfv3** *pid* **process** command and re-verify using the command **show ospfv3**.

a. After enabling IPv6 unicast routing, configure the OSPFv4 IPv4 AF on R3 using the **router ospf** *pid* command. The **?** is used to see the two address families available.

```
R3(config)# ipv6 unicast-routing
R3(config)# router ospfv3 1
R3(config-router)# address-family ?
  ipv4  Address family
  ipv6  Address family
R3(config-router)#
```

b. Enter the IPv4 address family configuration mode using the command **address-family ipv4 unicast**. The **?** is used to examine the options in the address-family configuration mode. Some of the more common configuration commands are highlighted. Use the **router-id** command to configure the router ID for the IPv4 AF.

```
R3(config-router)# address-family ipv4 unicast
R3(config-router-af)# ?
Router Address Family configuration commands:
  area                 OSPF area parameters
  authentication       Authentication parameters
  auto-cost            Calculate OSPF interface cost according to bandwidth
  bfd                  BFD configuration commands
  compatible           Compatibility list
  default              Set a command to its defaults
  default-information  Control distribution of default information
  default-metric       Set metric of redistributed routes
  discard-route        Enable or disable discard-route installation
  distance             Define an administrative distance
  distribute-list      Filter networks in routing updates
  event-log            Event Logging
  exit-address-family  Exit from Address Family configuration mode
  graceful-restart     Graceful-restart options
  help                 Description of the interactive help system
  interface-id         Source of the interface ID
  limit                Limit a specific OSPF feature
  local-rib-criteria   Enable or disable usage of local RIB as route criteria
  log-adjacency-changes Log changes in adjacency state
  max-lsa              Maximum number of non self-generated LSAs to accept
  max-metric           Set maximum metric
  maximum-paths        Forward packets over multiple paths
  no                   Negate a command or set its defaults
```

```
passive-interface    Suppress routing updates on an interface
prefix-suppression   Enable prefix suppression
queue-depth          Hello/Router process queue depth
redistribute         Redistribute information from another routing protocol
router-id            router-id for this OSPF process
shutdown             Shutdown the router process
snmp                 Modify snmp parameters
summary-prefix       Configure IP address summaries
timers               Adjust routing timers

R3(config-router-af)# router-id 3.3.3.3
R3(config-router-af)#
```

c. Use the **passive-interface** command to configure the G0/0 interface as passive for the IPv4 AF.

```
R3(config-router-af)# passive-interface gigabitethernet 0/0
```

d. Exit the IPv4 address family configuration mode and enter the IPv6 address configuration mode. The **exit-address-family** (or a shorter version of **exit**) command is used to exit address family configuration mode. Issue the **address-family ipv6 unicast** command to enter the IPv6 AF. For the IPv6 AF, use the **router-id** command to configure the router ID and the **passive-interface** command to configure G0/0 as a passive interface. Although it isn't necessary, a different router ID is being used for the IPv6 AF. The **exit** command is used to return to global configuration mode.

```
R3(config-router-af)# exit-address-family
R3(config-router)# address-family ipv6 unicast
R3(config-router-af)# router-id 3.3.3.6
R3(config-router-af)# passive-interface gigabitethernet 0/0
R3(config-router-af)# exit-address-family
R3(config-router)# exit
R3(config)#
```

e. OSPFv3 is enabled directly on the interfaces for both IPv4 and IPv6 AFs using the **ospfv3** *pid* [**ipv4** | **ipv6**] **area** *area-id* interface command. Use this command to enable OSPFv3 on both of R3's interfaces in area 0.

```
R3(config)# interface gigabitethernet 0/0
R3(config-if)# ospfv3 1 ipv4 area 0
R3(config-it)# ospfv3 1 ipv6 area 0
R3(config-if)# exit
R3(config)# interface serial 0/0/1
R3(config-if)# ospfv3 1 ipv4 area 0
R3(config-if)# ospfv3 1 ipv6 area 0
R3(config-if)#
```

f. Apply commands similar to those used on R3 to configure OSPFv3 IPv4 and IPv6 AFs on R2. Router R2 is an ABR so be sure to configure the proper area ID to each interface. The OSPF process ID does not need to match other routers.

```
R2(config)# ipv6 unicast-routing
R2(config-router)# address-family ipv4 unicast
R2(config-router-af)# router-id 2.2.2.2
```

```
R2(config-router-af)# passive-interface gigabitethernet 0/0
R2(config-router-af)# exit-address-family
R2(config-router)# address-family ipv6 unicast
R2(config-router-af)# router-id 2.2.2.6
R2(config-router-af)# passive-interface gigabitethernet 0/0
R2(config-router-af)# exit-address-family
R2(config-router)# interface serial 0/0/1
R2(config-if)# ospfv3 1 ipv4 area 0
R2(config-if)# ospfv3 1 ipv6 area 0
R2(config-if)# exit
R2(config)# interface gigabitethernet 0/0
R2(config-if)# ospfv3 1 ipv4 area 0
R2(config-if)# ospfv3 1 ipv6 area 0
R2(config-if)# exit
R2(config)# interface serial 0/0/0
R2(config-if)# ospfv3 1 ipv4 area 51
R2(config-if)# ospfv3 1 ipv6 area 51
R2(config-if)#
```

g. Finally, issue these same type of commands to configure OSPFv3 for the IPv4 and IPv6 AFs on R1, an internal router in area 51.

```
R1(config)# ipv6 unicast-routing
R1(config)# router ospfv3 1
R1(config-router)# address-family ipv4 unicast
R1(config-router-af)# router-id 1.1.1.1
R1(config-router-af)# passive-interface gigabitethernet 0/0
R1(config-router-af)# exit-address-family
R1(config-router)# address-family ipv6 unicast
R1(config-router-af)# router-id 1.1.1.6
R1(config-router-af)# passive-interface gigabitethernet 0/0
R1(config-router-af)# exit-address-family
R1(config-router)# exit
R1(config)# interface gigabitethernet 0/0
R1(config-if)# ospfv3 1 ipv4 area 51
R1(config-if)# ospfv3 1 ipv6 area 51
R1(config-if)# exit
R1(config)# interface serial 0/0/0
R1(config-if)# ospfv3 1 ipv4 area 51
R1(config-if)# ospfv3 1 ipv6 area 51
R1(config-if)#
```

h. Verify that the routers have OSPFv3 neighbors. First, issue both the **show ip ospf neighbors** and **show ipv6 ospf neighbors** command on R2. Notice which router IDs are displayed in the **show ipv6 ospf neighbor** output.

```
R2# show ip ospf neighbor
R2#
R2# show ipv6 ospf neighbor
```

```
        OSPFv3 Router with ID (2.2.2.6) (Process ID 1)


Neighbor ID     Pri   State          Dead Time   Interface ID    Interface
3.3.3.6           0   FULL/  -       00:00:39    6               Serial0/0/1
1.1.1.6           0   FULL/  -       00:00:36    6               Serial0/0/0
R2#
```

Why doesn't the **show ip ospf neighbor** command display any output?

_____

Why does the **show ipv6 ospf neighbor** command only display OSPFv3 neighbors in the IPv6 AF?

_____

_____

i. Issue the **show ospfv3 neighbor** command to verify OSPFv3 neighbor adjacencies for both the IPv4 and IPv6 AFs. The output for R2 is displayed.

```
R2# show ospfv3 neighbor


        OSPFv3 1 address-family ipv4 (router-id 2.2.2.2)


Neighbor ID     Pri   State          Dead Time   Interface ID    Interface
3.3.3.3           0   FULL/  -       00:00:30    6               Serial0/0/1
1.1.1.1           0   FULL/  -       00:00:34    6               Serial0/0/0


        OSPFv3 1 address-family ipv6 (router-id 2.2.2.6)


Neighbor ID     Pri   State          Dead Time   Interface ID    Interface
3.3.3.6           0   FULL/  -       00:00:30    6               Serial0/0/1
1.1.1.6           0   FULL/  -       00:00:35    6               Serial0/0/0
R2#
```

j. The IPv4 and IPv6 routing tables can be verified by using the **show ip route** and **show ipv6 route** commands. Each router should see all IPv4 networks and IPv6 prefixes in the OSPFv3 routing domain including those with passive interfaces. The output for R3 is shown here.

```
R3# show ip route
Codes: L - local, C - connected, S - static, R - RIP, M - mobile, B - BGP
       D - EIGRP, EX - EIGRP external, O - OSPF, IA - OSPF inter area
       N1 - OSPF NSSA external type 1, N2 - OSPF NSSA external type 2
       E1 - OSPF external type 1, E2 - OSPF external type 2
       i - IS-IS, su - IS-IS summary, L1 - IS-IS level-1, L2 - IS-IS level-2
       ia - IS-IS inter area, * - candidate default, U - per-user static
       route
       o - ODR, P - periodic downloaded static route, H - NHRP, l - LISP
       a - application route
       + - replicated route, % - next hop override
```

```
Gateway of last resort is not set

O IA   192.168.1.0/24 [110/129] via 192.168.4.1, 00:07:37, Serial0/0/1
          192.168.2.0/30 is subnetted, 1 subnets
O IA      192.168.2.0 [110/128] via 192.168.4.1, 00:07:37, Serial0/0/1
O      192.168.3.0/24 [110/65] via 192.168.4.1, 00:07:47, Serial0/0/1
          192.168.4.0/24 is variably subnetted, 2 subnets, 2 masks
C         192.168.4.0/30 is directly connected, Serial0/0/1
L         192.168.4.2/32 is directly connected, Serial0/0/1
          192.168.5.0/24 is variably subnetted, 2 subnets, 2 masks
C         192.168.5.0/24 is directly connected, GigabitEthernet0/0
L         192.168.5.1/32 is directly connected, GigabitEthernet0/0
          192.168.77.0/24 is variably subnetted, 2 subnets, 2 masks
C         192.168.77.0/24 is directly connected, Serial0/1/0
L         192.168.77.2/32 is directly connected, Serial0/1/0
R3#

R3# show ipv6 route
IPv6 Routing Table - default - 10 entries
Codes: C - Connected, L - Local, S - Static, U - Per-user Static route
       B - BGP, R - RIP, H - NHRP, I1 - ISIS L1
       I2 - ISIS L2, IA - ISIS interarea, IS - ISIS summary, D - EIGRP
       EX - EIGRP external, ND - ND Default, NDp - ND Prefix, DCE -
       Destination
       NDr - Redirect, O - OSPF Intra, OI - OSPF Inter, OE1 - OSPF ext 1
       OE2 - OSPF ext 2, ON1 - OSPF NSSA ext 1, ON2 - OSPF NSSA ext 2
       a - Application
OI  2001:DB8:CAFE:1::/64 [110/129]
       via FE80::2, Serial0/0/1
OI  2001:DB8:CAFE:2::/64 [110/128]
       via FE80::2, Serial0/0/1
O   2001:DB8:CAFE:3::/64 [110/65]
       via FE80::2, Serial0/0/1
C   2001:DB8:CAFE:4::/64 [0/0]
       via Serial0/0/1, directly connected
L   2001:DB8:CAFE:4::2/128 [0/0]
       via Serial0/0/1, receive
C   2001:DB8:CAFE:5::/64 [0/0]
       via GigabitEthernet0/0, directly connected
L   2001:DB8:CAFE:5::1/128 [0/0]
       via GigabitEthernet0/0, receive
C   2001:DB8:FEED:77::/64 [0/0]
       via Serial0/1/0, directly connected
L   2001:DB8:FEED:77::2/128 [0/0]
       via Serial0/1/0, receive
L   FF00::/8 [0/0]
       via Null0, receive
R3#
```

k. Understanding the difference between commands associated with OSPFv2 and OSPFv3 can seem challenging at times. The **show ip route ospfv3** command is used to view OSPFv3 routes in the IPv4 routing table. The **show ipv6 route ospf** command is used to view OSPFv3 routes in the IPv6 routing table. The **show ipv6 route ospf** command is the same command used with traditional OSPFv3 for IPv6.

```
R3# show ip route ospf
R3#
R3# show ip route ospfv3
```

```
Codes: L - local, C - connected, S - static, R - RIP, M - mobile, B - BGP
       D - EIGRP, EX - EIGRP external, O - OSPF, IA - OSPF inter area
       N1 - OSPF NSSA external type 1, N2 - OSPF NSSA external type 2
       E1 - OSPF external type 1, E2 - OSPF external type 2
       i - IS-IS, su - IS-IS summary, L1 - IS-IS level-1, L2 - IS-IS level-2
       ia - IS-IS inter area, * - candidate default, U - per-user static
       route
       o - ODR, P - periodic downloaded static route, H - NHRP, l - LISP
       a - application route
       + - replicated route, % - next hop override

Gateway of last resort is not set

O IA  192.168.1.0/24 [110/129] via 192.168.4.1, 00:17:13, Serial0/0/1
       192.168.2.0/30 is subnetted, 1 subnets
O IA     192.168.2.0 [110/128] via 192.168.4.1, 00:17:13, Serial0/0/1
O        192.168.3.0/24 [110/65] via 192.168.4.1, 00:17:23, Serial0/0/1
R3#
R3# show ipv6 route ospf
IPv6 Routing Table - default - 10 entries
Codes: C - Connected, L - Local, S - Static, U - Per-user Static route
       B - BGP, R - RIP, H - NHRP, I1 - ISIS L1
       I2 - ISIS L2, IA - ISIS interarea, IS - ISIS summary, D - EIGRP
       EX - EIGRP external, ND - ND Default, NDp - ND Prefix, DCE -
       Destination
       NDr - Redirect, O - OSPF Intra, OI - OSPF Inter, OE1 - OSPF ext 1
       OE2 - OSPF ext 2, ON1 - OSPF NSSA ext 1, ON2 - OSPF NSSA ext 2
       a - Application
OI  2001:DB8:CAFE:1::/64 [110/129]
     via FE80::2, Serial0/0/1
OI  2001:DB8:CAFE:2::/64 [110/128]
     via FE80::2, Serial0/0/1
O   2001:DB8:CAFE:3::/64 [110/65]
     via FE80::2, Serial0/0/1
R3#
```

Why doesn't the **show ip route ospf** command display any routes?

_____

l. Configure IPv4 and IPv6 default routes on the ASBR R3 forwarding traffic to R4. Propagate both default routes into OSPFv3 within the appropriate address family.

```
R3(config)# ip route 0.0.0.0 0.0.0.0 192.168.77.1
R3(config)# ipv6 route ::/0 2001:db8:feed:77::1
R3(config)# router ospfv3 1
R3(config-router)# address-family ipv4 unicast
R3(config-router-af)# default-information originate
R3(config-router-af)# exit-address-family
R3(config-router)# address-family ipv6 unicast
R3(config-router-af)# default-information originate
R3(config-router-af)# exit-address-family
R3(config-router)# end
R3#
```

m. Issue the **show ip route static** and **show ipv6 route static** commands on R3 to verify the static route is in the IPv4 and IPv6 routing tables.

```
R3# show ip route static
Codes: L - local, C - connected, S - static, R - RIP, M - mobile, B - BGP
       D - EIGRP, EX - EIGRP external, O - OSPF, IA - OSPF inter area
       N1 - OSPF NSSA external type 1, N2 - OSPF NSSA external type 2
       E1 - OSPF external type 1, E2 - OSPF external type 2
       i - IS-IS, su - IS-IS summary, L1 - IS-IS level-1, L2 - IS-IS level-2
       ia - IS-IS inter area, * - candidate default, U - per-user static
       route
       o - ODR, P - periodic downloaded static route, H - NHRP, l - LISP
       a - application route
       + - replicated route, % - next hop override

Gateway of last resort is 192.168.77.1 to network 0.0.0.0

S*     0.0.0.0/0 [1/0] via 192.168.77.1
R3# show ipv6 route static
IPv6 Routing Table - default - 11 entries
Codes: C - Connected, L - Local, S - Static, U - Per-user Static route
       B - BGP, R - RIP, H - NHRP, I1 - ISIS L1
       I2 - ISIS L2, IA - ISIS interarea, IS - ISIS summary, D - EIGRP
       EX - EIGRP external, ND - ND Default, NDp - ND Prefix, DCE -
       Destination
       NDr - Redirect, O - OSPF Intra, OI - OSPF Inter, OE1 - OSPF ext 1
       OE2 - OSPF ext 2, ON1 - OSPF NSSA ext 1, ON2 - OSPF NSSA ext 2
       a - Application
S   ::/0 [1/0]
     via 2001:DB8:FEED:77::1
R3#
```

n. Configure IPv4 and IPv6 static routes on the ASBR: R3 for the 192.168.99.0/24 and 2001:db8:99:1::/64 network on R4. Redistribute the static route into OSPFv3 IPv4 and IPv6 AFs using the **redistribute static** command in each address family configuration mode. The **redistribute** command is discussed in more detail in later chapters.

```
R3(config)# ip route 192.168.99.0 255.255.255.0 192.168.77.1
R3(config)# ipv6 route 2001:db8:99:1::/64 2001:db8:feed:77::1
R3(config)# router ospfv3 1
R3(config-router)# address-family ipv4 unicast
R3(config-router-af)# redistribute static
R3(config-router-af)# exit-address-family
R3(config-router)# address-family ipv6 unicast
R3(config-router-af)# redistribute static
R3(config-router-af)# end
R3#
```

o. Issue the **show ip route ospfv3** and **show ipv6 route ospf** commands on R1 to verify that the default route and the redistributed static route are being advertised into the OSPFv3 domain.

```
R1# show ip route ospfv3
Codes: L - local, C - connected, S - static, R - RIP, M - mobile, B - BGP
       D - EIGRP, EX - EIGRP external, O - OSPF, IA - OSPF inter area
       N1 - OSPF NSSA external type 1, N2 - OSPF NSSA external type 2
       E1 - OSPF external type 1, E2 - OSPF external type 2
       i - IS-IS, su - IS-IS summary, L1 - IS-IS level-1, L2 - IS-IS level-2
       ia - IS-IS inter area, * - candidate default, U - per-user static
       route
       o - ODR, P - periodic downloaded static route, H - NHRP, l - LISP
```

```
                 a - application route
                 + - replicated route, % - next hop override

Gateway of last resort is 192.168.2.2 to network 0.0.0.0

O*E2  0.0.0.0/0 [110/1] via 192.168.2.2, 00:13:18, Serial0/0/0
O IA  192.168.3.0/24 [110/65] via 192.168.2.2, 00:54:00, Serial0/0/0
        192.168.4.0/30 is subnetted, 1 subnets
O IA      192.168.4.0 [110/128] via 192.168.2.2, 00:54:00, Serial0/0/0
O IA  192.168.5.0/24 [110/129] via 192.168.2.2, 00:54:00, Serial0/0/0
O E2  192.168.99.0/24 [110/20] via 192.168.2.2, 00:03:40, Serial0/0/0
R1#
R1# show ipv6 route ospf
IPv6 Routing Table - default - 10 entries
Codes: C - Connected, L - Local, S - Static, U - Per-user Static route
       B - BGP, R - RIP, H - NHRP, I1 - ISIS L1
       I2 - ISIS L2, IA - ISIS interarea, IS - ISIS summary, D - EIGRP
       EX - EIGRP external, ND - ND Default, NDp - ND Prefix, DCE -
       Destination
       NDr - Redirect, O - OSPF Intra, OI - OSPF Inter, OE1 - OSPF ext 1
       OE2 - OSPF ext 2, ON1 - OSPF NSSA ext 1, ON2 - OSPF NSSA ext 2
       a - Application
OE2 ::/0 [110/1], tag 1
      via FE80::2, Serial0/0/0
OE2 2001:DB8:99:1::/64 [110/20]
      via FE80::2, Serial0/0/0
OI  2001:DB8:CAFE:3::/64 [110/65]
      via FE80::2, Serial0/0/0
OI  2001:DB8:CAFE:4::/64 [110/128]
      via FE80::2, Serial0/0/0
OI  2001:DB8:CAFE:5::/64 [110/129]
      via FE80::2, Serial0/0/0
R1#
```

Step 3: Configure an OSPFv2 stub area.

a. Under the OSPFv3 process for R1 and R2, for both the IPv4 and IPv6 AFs, configure area 51 as a stub area using the **area** *area* **stub** command. The adjacency between the two routers might go down during the transition period, but it should come back up afterwards.

```
R1(config)# router ospfv3 1
R1(config-router)# address-family ipv4 unicast
R1(config-router-af)# area 51 stub
R1(config-router-af)# exit-address-family
R1(config-router)# address-family ipv6 unicast
R1(config-router-af)# area 51 stub

R2(config)# router ospfv3 1
R2(config-router)# address-family ipv4 unicast
R2(config-router-af)# area 51 stub
R2(config-router-af)# exit-address-family
R2(config-router)# address-family ipv6 unicast
R2(config-router-af)# area 51 stub
```

b. Confirm that both R1 and R2 are neighbors for both IPv4 and IPv6 AFs using the **show ospfv3 neighbors** command on R2.

    R2# **show ospfv3 neighbor**

                OSPFv3 1 address-family ipv4 (router-id 2.2.2.2)

    Neighbor ID   Pri   State   Dead Time   Interface ID   Interface
    3.3.3.3   0   FULL/ -   00:00:34   6   Serial0/0/1
    1.1.1.1   0   FULL/ -   00:00:32   6   Serial0/0/0

                OSPFv3 1 address-family ipv6 (router-id 2.2.2.6)

    Neighbor ID   Pri   State   Dead Time   Interface ID   Interface
    3.3.3.6   0   FULL/ -   00:00:36   6   Serial0/0/1
    1.1.1.6   0   FULL/ -   00:00:32   6   Serial0/0/0
    R2#

c. Issue the **show ip route ospfv3** and **show ipv6 route ospf** commands on R1. Notice that R1 still has a default route pointing toward R2 but with a different cost than it had prior to being configured in a stub area. This is not the default route propagated by the ASBR R1, but the default route injected by the ABR of the stub area. R1 also does not receive any external routes, so it no longer has the 192.168.99.0/24 or the 2001:DB8:99:1::/64 networks in its IPv4 and IPv6 routing tables. Stub routers continue to receive inter-area routes.

    R1# **show ip route ospfv3**
    Codes: L - local, C - connected, S - static, R - RIP, M - mobile, B - BGP
           D - EIGRP, EX - EIGRP external, O - OSPF, IA - OSPF inter area
           N1 - OSPF NSSA external type 1, N2 - OSPF NSSA external type 2
           E1 - OSPF external type 1, E2 - OSPF external type 2
           i - IS-IS, su - IS-IS summary, L1 - IS-IS level-1, L2 - IS-IS level-2
           ia - IS-IS inter area, * - candidate default, U - per-user static
           route
           o - ODR, P - periodic downloaded static route, H - NHRP, l - LISP
           a - application route
           + - replicated route, % - next hop override

    Gateway of last resort is 192.168.2.2 to network 0.0.0.0

    O*IA 0.0.0.0/0 [110/65] via 192.168.2.2, 00:07:17, Serial0/0/0
    O IA 192.168.3.0/24 [110/65] via 192.168.2.2, 00:07:17, Serial0/0/0
             192.168.4.0/30 is subnetted, 1 subnets
    O IA   192.168.4.0 [110/128] via 192.168.2.2, 00:07:17, Serial0/0/0
    O IA 192.168.5.0/24 [110/129] via 192.168.2.2, 00:07:17, Serial0/0/0
    R1#
    R1# **show ipv6 route ospf**
    IPv6 Routing Table - default - 9 entries
    Codes: C - Connected, L - Local, S - Static, U - Per-user Static route
           B - BGP, R - RIP, H - NHRP, I1 - ISIS L1
           I2 - ISIS L2, IA - ISIS interarea, IS - ISIS summary, D - EIGRP
           EX - EIGRP external, ND - ND Default, NDp - ND Prefix, DCE -
           Destination
           NDr - Redirect, O - OSPF Intra, OI - OSPF Inter, OE1 - OSPF ext 1
           OE2 - OSPF ext 2, ON1 - OSPF NSSA ext 1, ON2 - OSPF NSSA ext 2
           a - Application
    OI ::/0 [110/65]
           via FE80::2, Serial0/0/0

```
OI  2001:DB8:CAFE:3::/64 [110/65]
      via FE80::2, Serial0/0/0
OI  2001:DB8:CAFE:4::/64 [110/128]
      via FE80::2, Serial0/0/0
OI  2001:DB8:CAFE:5::/64 [110/129]
      via FE80::2, Serial0/0/0
R1#
```

d. View the output of the **show ospfv3** command on ABR R2 to see what type each area is and the number of interfaces in each area. Prior to issuing this command notice the **show ip ospf** command displays no output. Once again, this command is for OSPFv2; we are using OSPFv3. The **show ip ospfv3** command might seem like a logical alternative; however, it is not a legitimate option. OSPFv3 is a single process for both IPv4 and IPv6 address families, so the correct command is **show ospfv3**. This will display OSPFv3 information for both AFs.

```
R2# show ip ospf
R2#
R2# show ip ospfv3
                     ^
% Invalid input detected at '^' marker.

R2# show ospfv3
 OSPFv3 1 address-family ipv4
 Router ID 2.2.2.2
 Supports NSSA (compatible with RFC 3101)
 Event-log enabled, Maximum number of events: 1000, Mode: cyclic
 It is an area border router
 Router is not originating router-LSAs with maximum metric
 Initial SPF schedule delay 5000 msecs
 Minimum hold time between two consecutive SPFs 10000 msecs
 Maximum wait time between two consecutive SPFs 10000 msecs
 Minimum LSA interval 5 secs
 Minimum LSA arrival 1000 msecs
 LSA group pacing timer 240 secs
 Interface flood pacing timer 33 msecs
 Retransmission pacing timer 66 msecs
 Retransmission limit dc 24 non-dc 24
 Number of external LSA 2. Checksum Sum 0x012EE4
 Number of areas in this router is 2. 1 normal 1 stub 0 nssa
 Graceful restart helper support enabled
 Reference bandwidth unit is 100 mbps
 RFC1583 compatibility enabled
     Area BACKBONE(0)
         Number of interfaces in this area is 2
         SPF algorithm executed 4 times
         Number of LSA 9. Checksum Sum 0x03231F
         Number of DCbitless LSA 0
         Number of indication LSA 0
         Number of DoNotAge LSA 0
         Flood list length 0
     Area 51
         Number of interfaces in this area is 1
         It is a stub area
         Generates stub default route with cost 1
         SPF algorithm executed 5 times
         Number of LSA 10. Checksum Sum 0x03F9E0
         Number of DCbitless LSA 0
         Number of indication LSA 0
```

```
            Number of DoNotAge LSA 0
            Flood list length 0


    OSPFv3 1 address-family ipv6
    Router ID 2.2.2.6
    Supports NSSA (compatible with RFC 3101)
    Event-log enabled, Maximum number of events: 1000, Mode: cyclic
    It is an area border router
    Router is not originating router-LSAs with maximum metric
    Initial SPF schedule delay 5000 msecs
    Minimum hold time between two consecutive SPFs 10000 msecs
    Maximum wait time between two consecutive SPFs 10000 msecs
    Minimum LSA interval 5 secs
    Minimum LSA arrival 1000 msecs
    LSA group pacing timer 240 secs
    Interface flood pacing timer 33 msecs
    Retransmission pacing timer 66 msecs
    Retransmission limit dc 24 non-dc 24
    Number of external LSA 2. Checksum Sum 0x00CD5F
    Number of areas in this router is 2. 1 normal 1 stub 0 nssa
    Graceful restart helper support enabled
    Reference bandwidth unit is 100 mbps
    RFC1583 compatibility enabled
        Area BACKBONE(0)
            Number of interfaces in this area is 2
            SPF algorithm executed 6 times
            Number of LSA 9. Checksum Sum 0x05479C
            Number of DCbitless LSA 0
            Number of indication LSA 0
            Number of DoNotAge LSA 0
            Flood list length 0
        Area 51
            Number of interfaces in this area is 1
            It is a stub area
            Generates stub default route with cost 1
            SPF algorithm executed 6 times
            Number of LSA 10. Checksum Sum 0x052FC7
            Number of DCbitless LSA 0
            Number of indication LSA 0
            Number of DoNotAge LSA 0
            Flood list length 0

    R2#
```

Step 4: Configure a totally stubby area.

Remember that a totally stubby area is a modified version of a stubby area. A totally stubby area ABR only allows in a single, default route from the backbone, injected by the ABR. To configure a totally stubby area, you only need to change a command at the ABR, R2 in this scenario. Under the router OSPFv3 process, you will enter the **area 51 stub no-summary** command for both the IPv4 and IPv6 AFs to replace the existing stub command for area 51. The **no-summary** option tells the router that this area will not receive summary (inter-area) routes.

a. To see how this works, issue the **show ip route ospfv3** and **show ipv6 route ospf** commands on R1. Notice the inter-area routes, in addition to the default route generated by R2.

```
R1# show ip route ospfv3
Codes: L - local, C - connected, S - static, R - RIP, M - mobile, B - BGP
       D - EIGRP, EX - EIGRP external, O - OSPF, IA - OSPF inter area
       N1 - OSPF NSSA external type 1, N2 - OSPF NSSA external type 2
       E1 - OSPF external type 1, E2 - OSPF external type 2
       i - IS-IS, su - IS-IS summary, L1 - IS-IS level-1, L2 - IS-IS level-2
       ia - IS-IS inter area, * - candidate default, U - per-user static
       route
       o - ODR, P - periodic downloaded static route, H - NHRP, l - LISP
       a - application route
       + - replicated route, % - next hop override

Gateway of last resort is 192.168.2.2 to network 0.0.0.0

O*IA  0.0.0.0/0 [110/65] via 192.168.2.2, 00:07:17, Serial0/0/0
O IA   192.168.3.0/24 [110/65] via 192.168.2.2, 00:07:17, Serial0/0/0
       192.168.4.0/30 is subnetted, 1 subnets
O IA      192.168.4.0 [110/128] via 192.168.2.2, 00:07:17, Serial0/0/0
O IA   192.168.5.0/24 [110/129] via 192.168.2.2, 00:07:17, Serial0/0/0
R1#
R1# show ipv6 route ospf
IPv6 Routing Table - default - 9 entries
Codes: C - Connected, L - Local, S - Static, U - Per-user Static route
       B - BGP, R - RIP, H - NHRP, I1 - ISIS L1
       I2 - ISIS L2, IA - ISIS interarea, IS - ISIS summary, D - EIGRP
       EX - EIGRP external, ND - ND Default, NDp - ND Prefix, DCE -
       Destination
       NDr - Redirect, O - OSPF Intra, OI - OSPF Inter, OE1 - OSPF ext 1
       OE2 - OSPF ext 2, ON1 - OSPF NSSA ext 1, ON2 - OSPF NSSA ext 2
       a - Application
OI  ::/0 [110/65]
     via FE80::2, Serial0/0/0
OI  2001:DB8:CAFE:3::/64 [110/65]
     via FE80::2, Serial0/0/0
OI  2001:DB8:CAFE:4::/64 [110/128]
     via FE80::2, Serial0/0/0
OI  2001:DB8:CAFE:5::/64 [110/129]
     via FE80::2, Serial0/0/0
R1#
```

b. Look at the output of the **show ospfv3 database** command on R2 to see which LSAs are in its OSPFv3 database. Notice that both the IPv4 and IPv6 AF LSAs are in the same LSDB. You will also notice OSPFv3 changed the names of two types of LSAs and added two others. For a comparison of OSPFv2 and OSPFv3 LSAs go to: https://supportforums.cisco.com/document/97766/comparing-ospfv3-ospfv2-routing-protocol.

```
R2# show ospfv3 database

        OSPFv3 1 address-family ipv4 (router-id 2.2.2.2)

           Router Link States (Area 0)

ADV Router       Age        Seq#        Fragment ID  Link count  Bits
  2.2.2.2        1251       0x80000007  0            1           B
  3.3.3.3        764        0x80000009  0            1           E


        Inter Area Prefix Link States (Area 0)
```

```
ADV Router          Age         Seq#          Prefix
2.2.2.2             1251        0x80000003    192.168.2.0/30
2.2.2.2             1245        0x80000001    192.168.1.0/24

        Link (Type-8) Link States (Area 0)

ADV Router          Age         Seq#          Link ID     Interface
2.2.2.2             1251        0x80000003    3           Gi0/0
2.2.2.2             1251        0x80000003    6           Se0/0/1
3.3.3.3             1275        0x80000004    6           Se0/0/1

        Intra Area Prefix Link States (Area 0)

ADV Router          Age         Seq#          Link ID     Ref-lstype    Ref-LSID
2.2.2.2             1251        0x80000003    0           0x2001        0
3.3.3.3             1275        0x80000004    0           0x2001        0

        Router Link States (Area 51)

ADV Router          Age         Seq#          Fragment ID  Link count   Bits
1.1.1.1             1248        0x80000007    0            1            None
2.2.2.2             1247        0x80000008    0            1            B

        Inter Area Prefix Link States (Area 51)

ADV Router          Age         Seq#          Prefix
2.2.2.2             1251        0x80000003    192.168.5.0/24
2.2.2.2             1251        0x80000003    192.168.4.0/30
2.2.2.2             1251        0x80000003    192.168.3.0/24
2.2.2.2             1255        0x80000001    0.0.0.0/0

        Link (Type-8) Link States (Area 51)

ADV Router          Age         Seq#          Link ID     Interface
1.1.1.1             1250        0x80000004    6           Se0/0/0
2.2.2.2             1250        0x80000006    5           Se0/0/0

        Intra Area Prefix Link States (Area 51)

ADV Router          Age         Seq#          Link ID     Ref-lstype    Ref-LSID
1.1.1.1             1250        0x80000003    0           0x2001        0
2.2.2.2             1251        0x80000005    0           0x2001        0

        Type-5 AS External Link States

ADV Router          Age         Seq#          Prefix
3.3.3.3             764         0x80000002    0.0.0.0/0
3.3.3.3             259         0x80000002    192.168.99.0/24

OSPFv3 1 address-family ipv6 (router-id 2.2.2.6)

        Router Link States (Area 0)

ADV Router          Age         Seq#          Fragment ID  Link count   Bits
2.2.2.6             1287        0x80000008    0            1            B
3.3.3.6             752         0x8000000C    0            1            E
```

```
                    Inter Area Prefix Link States (Area 0)

ADV Router          Age          Seq#         Prefix
  2.2.2.6           1287         0x80000003   2001:DB8:CAFE:2::/64
  2.2.2.6           1228         0x80000001   2001:DB8:CAFE:1::/64

                    Link (Type-8) Link States (Area 0)

ADV Router          Age          Seq#         Link ID    Interface
  2.2.2.6           1287         0x80000003   3          Gi0/0
  2.2.2.6           1287         0x80000003   6          Se0/0/1
  3.3.3.6           1268         0x80000003   6          Se0/0/1

                    Intra Area Prefix Link States (Area 0)

ADV Router          Age          Seq#         Link ID    Ref-lstype   Ref-LSID
  2.2.2.6           1287         0x80000003   0          0x2001       0
  3.3.3.6           1268         0x80000003   0          0x2001       0

                    Router Link States (Area 51)

ADV Router          Age          Seq#         Fragment ID  Link count  Bits
  1.1.1.6           1233         0x80000008   0            1           None
  2.2.2.6           1232         0x8000000A   0            1           B

                    Inter Area Prefix Link States (Area 51)

ADV Router          Age          Seq#         Prefix
  2.2.2.6           1287         0x80000003   2001:DB8:CAFE:4::/64
  2.2.2.6           1287         0x80000003   2001:DB8:CAFE:3::/64
  2.2.2.6           1287         0x80000003   2001:DB8:CAFE:5::/64
  2.2.2.6           1240         0x80000001   ::/0

                    Link (Type-8) Link States (Area 51)

ADV Router          Age          Seq#         Link ID    Interface
  1.1.1.6           1304         0x80000004   6          Se0/0/0
  2.2.2.6           1240         0x80000004   5          Se0/0/0

                    Intra Area Prefix Link States (Area 51)

ADV Router          Age          Seq#         Link ID    Ref-lstype   Ref-LSID
  1.1.1.6           1390         0x80000003   0          0x2001       0
  2.2.2.6           1287         0x80000003   0          0x2001       0

                    Type-5 AS External Link States

ADV Router          Age          Seq#         Prefix
  3.3.3.6           752          0x80000002   ::/0
  3.3.3.6           243          0x80000002   2001:DB8:99:1::/64
R2#
```

c. Enter the **area 51 stub no-summary** command on R2 (the ABR) for both IPv4 and IPv6 AFs in the OSPFv3 process.

```
R2(config)# router ospfv3 1
R2(config-router)# address-family ipv4 unicast
R2(config-router-af)# area 51 stub no-summary
```

```
R2(config-router-af)# exit-address-family
R2(config-router)# address-family ipv6 unicast
R2(config-router-af)# area 51 stub no-summary
R2(config-router-af)#
```

d. Go back to R1 and issue the **show ip route ospfv3** and **show ipv6 route ospf** commands. Notice that both routing tables only show a single incoming route from the ABR R2, the default route. The default route is injected by the ABR R2. There are no inter-area OSPFv3 routes and no external OSPFv3 routes.

```
R1# show ip route ospfv3
Codes: L - local, C - connected, S - static, R - RIP, M - mobile, B - BGP
       D - EIGRP, EX - EIGRP external, O - OSPF, IA - OSPF inter area
       N1 - OSPF NSSA external type 1, N2 - OSPF NSSA external type 2
       E1 - OSPF external type 1, E2 - OSPF external type 2
       i - IS-IS, su - IS-IS summary, L1 - IS-IS level-1, L2 - IS-IS level-2
       ia - IS-IS inter area, * - candidate default, U - per-user static
       route
       o - ODR, P - periodic downloaded static route, H - NHRP, l - LISP
       a - application route
       + - replicated route, % - next hop override

Gateway of last resort is 192.168.2.2 to network 0.0.0.0

O*IA  0.0.0.0/0 [110/65] via 192.168.2.2, 00:30:38, Serial0/0/0
R1#
R1# show ipv6 route ospf
IPv6 Routing Table - default - 6 entries
Codes: C - Connected, L - Local, S - Static, U - Per-user Static route
       B - BGP, R - RIP, H - NHRP, I1 - ISIS L1
       I2 - ISIS L2, IA - ISIS interarea, IS - ISIS summary, D - EIGRP
       EX - EIGRP external, ND - ND Default, NDp - ND Prefix, DCE -
       Destination
       NDr - Redirect, O - OSPF Intra, OI - OSPF Inter, OE1 - OSPF ext 1
       OE2 - OSPF ext 2, ON1 - OSPF NSSA ext 1, ON2 - OSPF NSSA ext 2
       a - Application
OI  ::/0 [110/65]
     via FE80::2, Serial0/0/0
R1#
```

e. View the output of the **show ospfv3** command on ABR R2 to see what type each area is and the number of interfaces in each area.

```
R2# show ospfv3
 OSPFv3 1 address-family ipv4
 Router ID 2.2.2.2
 Supports NSSA (compatible with RFC 3101)
 Event-log enabled, Maximum number of events: 1000, Mode: cyclic
 It is an area border router
 Router is not originating router-LSAs with maximum metric
 Initial SPF schedule delay 5000 msecs
 Minimum hold time between two consecutive SPFs 10000 msecs
 Maximum wait time between two consecutive SPFs 10000 msecs
 Minimum LSA interval 5 secs
 Minimum LSA arrival 1000 msecs
 LSA group pacing timer 240 secs
 Interface flood pacing timer 33 msecs
```

```
Retransmission pacing timer 66 msecs
Retransmission limit dc 24 non-dc 24
Number of external LSA 2. Checksum Sum 0x012CE5
Number of areas in this router is 2. 1 normal 1 stub 0 nssa
Graceful restart helper support enabled
Reference bandwidth unit is 100 mbps
RFC1583 compatibility enabled
    Area BACKBONE(0)
        Number of interfaces in this area is 2
        SPF algorithm executed 5 times
        Number of LSA 9. Checksum Sum 0x031327
        Number of DCbitless LSA 0
        Number of indication LSA 0
        Number of DoNotAge LSA 0
        Flood list length 0
    Area 51
        Number of interfaces in this area is 1
        It is a stub area, no summary LSA in this area
        Generates stub default route with cost 1
        SPF algorithm executed 6 times
        Number of LSA 7. Checksum Sum 0x035902
        Number of DCbitless LSA 0
        Number of indication LSA 0
        Number of DoNotAge LSA 0
        Flood list length 0

OSPFv3 1 address-family ipv6
Router ID 2.2.2.6
Supports NSSA (compatible with RFC 3101)
Event-log enabled, Maximum number of events: 1000, Mode: cyclic
It is an area border router
Router is not originating router-LSAs with maximum metric
Initial SPF schedule delay 5000 msecs
Minimum hold time between two consecutive SPFs 10000 msecs
Maximum wait time between two consecutive SPFs 10000 msecs
Minimum LSA interval 5 secs
Minimum LSA arrival 1000 msecs
LSA group pacing timer 240 secs
Interface flood pacing timer 33 msecs
Retransmission pacing timer 66 msecs
Retransmission limit dc 24 non-dc 24
Number of external LSA 2. Checksum Sum 0x00CB60
Number of areas in this router is 2. 1 normal 1 stub 0 nssa
Graceful restart helper support enabled
Reference bandwidth unit is 100 mbps
RFC1583 compatibility enabled
    Area BACKBONE(0)
        Number of interfaces in this area is 2
        SPF algorithm executed 7 times
        Number of LSA 9. Checksum Sum 0x0537A4
        Number of DCbitless LSA 0
        Number of indication LSA 0
        Number of DoNotAge LSA 0
        Flood list length 0
    Area 51
        Number of interfaces in this area is 1
        It is a stub area, no summary LSA in this area
        Generates stub default route with cost 1
```

```
            SPF algorithm executed 7 times
            Number of LSA 7. Checksum Sum 0x02E9F0
            Number of DCbitless LSA 0
            Number of indication LSA 0
            Number of DoNotAge LSA 0
            Flood list length 0
```

R2#

Why does R2 generate a stub default route into area 51? Is this the default route advertised by the ASBR?

_____

_____

f. View the output of the **show ip protocols** and **show ipv6 protocols** commands on R2.

```
R2# show ip protocols
*** IP Routing is NSF aware ***

Routing Protocol is "application"
  Sending updates every 0 seconds
  Invalid after 0 seconds, hold down 0, flushed after 0
  Outgoing update filter list for all interfaces is not set
  Incoming update filter list for all interfaces is not set
  Maximum path: 32
  Routing for Networks:
  Routing Information Sources:
    Gateway          Distance      Last Update
  Distance: (default is 4)

Routing Protocol is "ospfv3 1"
  Outgoing update filter list for all interfaces is not set
  Incoming update filter list for all interfaces is not set
  Router ID 2.2.2.2
  Area border router
  Number of areas: 1 normal, 1 stub, 0 nssa
  Interfaces (Area 0):
    Serial0/0/1
    GigabitEthernet0/0
  Interfaces (Area 51):
    Serial0/0/0
  Maximum path: 4
  Routing Information Sources:
    Gateway          Distance      Last Update
    3.3.3.3              110        00:02:26
    1.1.1.1              110        00:02:26
  Distance: (default is 110)

R2# show ipv6 protocols
IPv6 Routing Protocol is "connected"
IPv6 Routing Protocol is "application"
IPv6 Routing Protocol is "ND"
IPv6 Routing Protocol is "ospf 1"
  Router ID 2.2.2.6
  Area border router
  Number of areas: 1 normal, 1 stub, 0 nssa
  Interfaces (Area 0):
```

```
      Serial0/0/1
      GigabitEthernet0/0
    Interfaces (Area 51):
      Serial0/0/0
    Redistribution:
      None
  R2#
```

Is there any information in the output of these commands that indicate G0/0 is a passive interface?

_____

g. View the output of the **show ospfv3 interface gigabitethernet 0/0** command on R2.

```
  R2# show ospfv3 interface gigabitethernet 0/0
  GigabitEthernet0/0 is up, line protocol is up
    Link Local Address FE80::2, Interface ID 3
    Internet Address 192.168.3.1/24
    Area 0, Process ID 1, Instance ID 64, Router ID 2.2.2.2
    Network Type BROADCAST, Cost: 1
    Transmit Delay is 1 sec, State DR, Priority 1
    Designated Router (ID) 2.2.2.2, local address FE80::2
    No backup designated router on this network
    Timer intervals configured, Hello 10, Dead 40, Wait 40, Retransmit 5
      No Hellos (Passive interface)
    Graceful restart helper support enabled
    Index 1/1/1, flood queue length 0
    Next 0x0(0)/0x0(0)/0x0(0)
    Last flood scan length is 0, maximum is 0
    Last flood scan time is 0 msec, maximum is 0 msec
    Neighbor Count is 0, Adjacent neighbor count is 0
    Suppress hello for 0 neighbor(s)
  GigabitEthernet0/0 is up, line protocol is up
    Link Local Address FE80::2, Interface ID 3
    Area 0, Process ID 1, Instance ID 0, Router ID 2.2.2.6
    Network Type BROADCAST, Cost: 1
    Transmit Delay is 1 sec, State DR, Priority 1
    Designated Router (ID) 2.2.2.6, local address FE80::2
    No backup designated router on this network
    Timer intervals configured, Hello 10, Dead 40, Wait 40, Retransmit 5
      No Hellos (Passive interface)
    Graceful restart helper support enabled
    Index 1/1/1, flood queue length 0
    Next 0x0(0)/0x0(0)/0x0(0)
    Last flood scan length is 0, maximum is 0
    Last flood scan time is 0 msec, maximum is 0 msec
    Neighbor Count is 0, Adjacent neighbor count is 0
    Suppress hello for 0 neighbor(s)
  R2#
```

Is there any information in the output of this command that indicate G0/0 is a passive interface?

_____

Why are there two sets of output for the G0/0 interface?

_____

Chapter 4: Manipulating Routing Updates

Lab 4-1 Redistribution Between EIGRP and OSPF

Topology

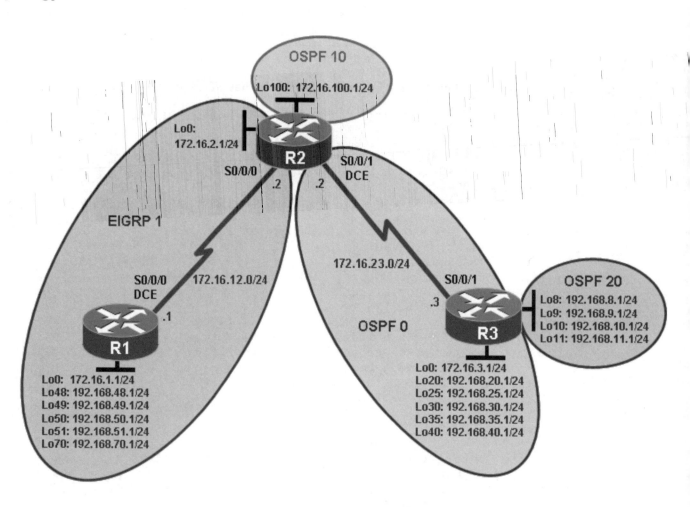

Objectives

- Review EIGRP and OSPF configuration.
- Summarize routes in EIGRP.
- Summarize in OSPF at an ABR.
- Redistribute into EIGRP.
- Redistribute into OSPF.
- Summarize in OSPF at an ASBR.

Background

Two online booksellers, Example.com and Example.net, have merged and now need a short-term solution to inter-domain routing. Since these companies provide client services to Internet users, it is essential to have minimal downtime during the transition.

Example.com is running EIGRP while Example.net is running a multi-area OSPF. Because it is imperative that the two booksellers continuously deliver Internet services, you should bridge these two routing domains without interfering with each router's path through its own routing domain to the Internet.

The CIO determines that it is preferable to keep the two protocol domains shown in the diagram during the transition period, because the network engineers on each side need to understand the other's network before deploying a long-term solution. Redistribution will be a short-term solution.

In this scenario, R1 and R2 are running EIGRP while R2 is the OSPF autonomous system border router (ASBR) consisting of areas 0, 10, and 20. You need to configure R2 to enable these two routing protocols to interact to allow full connectivity between all networks.

In this lab, R1 is running EIGRP and R3 is running multi-area OSPF. Your task is to configure redistribution on R2 to enable these two routing protocols to interact, allowing full connectivity between all networks.

Note: This lab uses Cisco 1941 routers with Cisco IOS Release 15.2 with IP Base. Depending on the router or switch model and Cisco IOS Software version, the commands available and output produced might vary from what is shown in this lab.

Required Resources

- 3 routers (Cisco IOS Release 15.2 or comparable)
- Serial and Ethernet cables

Step 1: Configure loopbacks and assign addresses.

a. Configure all loopback interfaces on the three routers in the diagram. Configure the serial interfaces with the IP addresses, bring them up, and set a DCE clock rate where appropriate.

```
R1(config)# interface Loopback0
R1(config-if)# ip address 172.16.1.1 255.255.255.0
R1(config-if)# exit
R1(config)# interface Loopback48
R1(config-if)# ip address 192.168.48.1 255.255.255.0
R1(config-if)# exit
R1(config)# interface Loopback49
R1(config-if)# ip address 192.168.49.1 255.255.255.0
R1(config-if)# exit
R1(config)# interface Loopback50
R1(config-if)# ip address 192.168.50.1 255.255.255.0
R1(config-if)# exit
R1(config)# interface Loopback51
R1(config-if)# ip address 192.168.51.1 255.255.255.0
R1(config-if)# exit
R1(config)# interface Loopback70
R1(config-if)# ip address 192.168.70.1 255.255.255.0
R1(config-if)# exit
R1(config)# interface Serial0/0/0
R1(config-if)# ip address 172.16.12.1 255.255.255.0
R1(config-if)# clock rate 64000
R1(config-if)# bandwidth 64
R1(config-if)# no shutdown
```

```
R2(config)# interface Loopback0
R2(config-if)# ip address 172.16.2.1 255.255.255.0
R2(config-if)# exit
R2(config)# interface loopback 100
R2(config-if)# ip address 172.16.100.1 255.255.255.0
R2(config-if)# exit
R2(config)# interface Serial0/0/0
R2(config-if)# ip address 172.16.12.2 255.255.255.0
R2(config-if)# bandwidth 64
R2(config-if)# no shutdown
R2(config-if)# exit
R2(config)# interface Serial0/0/1
R2(config-if)# ip address 172.16.23.2 255.255.255.0
R2(config-if)# clock rate 64000
R2(config-if)# bandwidth 64
R2(config-if)# no shutdown


R3(config)# interface Loopback0
R3(config-if)# ip address 172.16.3.1 255.255.255.0
R3(config-if)# exit
R3(config)# interface loopback 8
R3(config-if)# ip address 192.168.8.1 255.255.255.0
R3(config-if)# exit
R3(config)# interface loopback 9
R3(config-if)# ip address 192.168.9.1 255.255.255.0
R3(config-if)# exit
R3(config)# interface loopback 10
R3(config-if)# ip address 192.168.10.1 255.255.255.0
R3(config-if)# exit
R3(config)# interface loopback 11
R3(config-if)# ip address 192.168.11.1 255.255.255.0
R3(config-if)# exit
R3(config)# interface Loopback20
R3(config-if)# ip address 192.168.20.1 255.255.255.0
R3(config-if)# exit
R3(config)# interface Loopback25
R3(config-if)# ip address 192.168.25.1 255.255.255.0
R3(config-if)# exit
R3(config)# interface Loopback30
R3(config-if)# ip address 192.168.30.1 255.255.255.0
R3(config-if)# exit
R3(config)# interface Loopback35
R3(config-if)# ip address 192.168.35.1 255.255.255.0
R3(config-if)# exit
R3(config)# interface Loopback40
R3(config-if)# ip address 192.168.40.1 255.255.255.0
R3(config-if)# exit
R3(config)# interface Serial0/0/1
R3(config-if)# ip address 172.16.23.3 255.255.255.0
R3(config-if)# bandwidth 64
R3(config-if)# no shutdown
```

b. Verify that you can ping across the serial links when you are finished. Use the following Tcl script to check full and partial connectivity throughout this lab.

```
R1# tclsh
```

```
foreach address {
172.16.1.1
192.168.48.1
192.168.49.1
192.168.50.1
192.168.51.1
192.168.70.1
172.16.12.1
172.16.12.2
172.16.2.1
172.16.100.1
172.16.23.2
172.16.23.3
172.16.3.1
192.168.8.1
192.168.9.1
192.168.10.1
192.168.11.1
192.168.20.1
192.168.25.1
192.168.30.1
192.168.35.1
192.168.40.1
} { ping $address }
```

Which pings are successful and why?

_____

_____

_____

_____

Step 2: Configure EIGRP.

a. Configure R1 and R2 to run EIGRP in autonomous system 1. On R1, add in all connected interfaces either with classful **network** commands or with wildcard masks. Use a classful **network** statement on R2 and disable automatic summarization.

```
R1(config)# router eigrp 1
R1(config-router)# no auto-summary
R1(config-router)# network 172.16.0.0
R1(config-router)# network 192.168.48.0
R1(config-router)# network 192.168.49.0
R1(config-router)# network 192.168.50.0
R1(config-router)# network 192.168.51.0
R1(config-router)# network 192.168.70.0
```

or

```
R1(config)# router eigrp 1
R1(config-router)# no auto-summary
R1(config-router)# network 172.16.0.0
R1(config-router)# network 192.168.0.0 0.0.255.255

R2(config)# router eigrp 1
```

```
R2(config-router)# no auto-summary
R2(config-router)# network 172.16.0.0
```

b. Verify the EIGRP configuration using the **show ip eigrp neighbors** and **show ip route eigrp** commands on R1.

```
R1# show ip eigrp neighbors
EIGRP-IPv4 Neighbors for AS(1)
H   Address                 Interface        Hold Uptime    SRTT   RTO  Q   Seq
                                             (sec)          (ms)        Cnt Num
0   172.16.12.2             Se0/0/0            10 00:00:22    42   2340  0   3
R1#
R1# show ip route eigrp

<Output omitted>

      172.16.0.0/16 is variably subnetted, 7 subnets, 2 masks
D        172.16.2.0/24 [90/40640000] via 172.16.12.2, 00:00:31, Serial0/0/0
D        172.16.23.0/24 [90/41024000] via 172.16.12.2, 00:00:31, Serial0/0/0
D        172.16.100.0/24 [90/40640000] via 172.16.12.2, 00:00:31, Serial0/0/0
R1#
```

c. Verify the EIGRP configuration on R2.

```
R2# show ip eigrp neighbors
EIGRP-IPv4 Neighbors for AS(1)
H   Address                 Interface        Hold Uptime    SRTT   RTO  Q   Seq
                                             (sec)          (ms)        Cnt Num
0   172.16.12.1             Se0/0/0            11 00:04:14    35   2340  0   3
R2#
R2# show ip route eigrp

<Output omitted>

      172.16.0.0/16 is variably subnetted, 9 subnets, 2 masks
D        172.16.1.0/24 [90/40640000] via 172.16.12.1, 00:01:40, Serial0/0/0
D      192.168.48.0/24 [90/40640000] via 172.16.12.1, 00:01:40, Serial0/0/0
D      192.168.49.0/24 [90/40640000] via 172.16.12.1, 00:01:40, Serial0/0/0
D      192.168.50.0/24 [90/40640000] via 172.16.12.1, 00:01:40, Serial0/0/0
D      192.168.51.0/24 [90/40640000] via 172.16.12.1, 00:01:40, Serial0/0/0
D      192.168.70.0/24 [90/40640000] via 172.16.12.1, 00:01:40, Serial0/0/0
R2#
```

d. Verify that R2 can reach all of the networks in the EIGRP routing domain using the following Tcl script.

```
R1# tclsh

foreach address {
172.16.1.1
192.168.48.1
192.168.49.1
192.168.50.1
192.168.51.1
192.168.70.1
172.16.12.1
172.16.12.2
172.16.2.1
} { ping $address }
```

All pings should be successful. Troubleshoot if necessary.

Step 3: Manually summarize with EIGRP.

To make routing updates more efficient and ultimately reduce the size of routing tables, contiguous EIGRP routes can be summarized out an interface by using the **ip summary-address eigrp** *as network mask* interface configuration command.

a. On R1, advertise one supernet route summarizing the networks of loopback 48 and 49 to R2.

```
R1(config)# interface Serial0/0/0
R1(config-if)# ip summary-address eigrp 1 192.168.48.0 255.255.254.0
R1(config-if)#
*Oct 26 15:46:36.839: %DUAL-5-NBRCHANGE: EIGRP-IPv4 1: Neighbor 172.16.12.2
(Serial0/0/0) is resync: summary configured
R1(config-if)# exit
R1#
```

b. Verify the routing table of R1 using the **show ip route eigrp** command.

```
R1# show ip route eigrp

<Output omitted>

     172.16.0.0/24 is subnetted, 6 subnets
D       172.16.23.0 [90/41024000] via 172.16.12.2, 00:45:21, Serial0/0/0
D       172.16.2.0 [90/40640000] via 172.16.12.2, 00:45:21, Serial0/0/0
D       172.16.100.0 [90/40640000] via 172.16.12.2, 00:08:12, Serial0/0/0
D    192.168.48.0/23 is a summary, 04:27:07, Null0

R1#
```

Notice how EIGRP now has a route to the summarized address going to the Null 0 interface in the routing table.

c. Verify the specifics for the summarized routes using the **show ip route 192.168.48.0 255.255.254.0** command on R1.

```
R1# show ip route 192.168.48.0 255.255.254.0
Routing entry for 192.168.48.0/23, supernet
  Known via "eigrp 1", distance 5, metric 128256, type internal
  Redistributing via eigrp 1
  Routing Descriptor Blocks:
  * directly connected, via Null0
      Route metric is 128256, traffic share count is 1
      Total delay is 5000 microseconds, minimum bandwidth is 10000000 Kbit
      Reliability 255/255, minimum MTU 1514 bytes
      Loading 1/255, Hops 0
```

Notice the low administrative distance (AD) for this route. Why does EIGRP add the summarized route pointing to the Null 0 interface with a low AD?

_____

_____

_____

_____

_____

d. Verify the routing table of R2 using the **show ip route eigrp** command.

```
R2# show ip route eigrp

<Output omitted>

        172.16.0.0/16 is variably subnetted, 9 subnets, 2 masks
D          172.16.1.0/24 [90/40640000] via 172.16.12.1, 00:09:49, Serial0/0/0
D       192.168.48.0/23 [90/40640000] via 172.16.12.1, 00:09:49, Serial0/0/0
D       192.168.50.0/24 [90/40640000] via 172.16.12.1, 00:09:49, Serial0/0/0
D       192.168.51.0/24 [90/40640000] via 172.16.12.1, 00:09:49, Serial0/0/0
D       192.168.70.0/24 [90/40640000] via 172.16.12.1, 00:09:49, Serial0/0/0
R2#
```

Notice how the routing table is slightly smaller as the entry to 192.168.49.0/24 is now missing. However, 192.168.49.1 is still reachable due to the summarized route to 192.168.48.0/23. Verify by pinging the loopback 49 interface from R2.

```
R2# ping 192.168.49.1
Type escape sequence to abort.
Sending 5, 100-byte ICMP Echos to 192.168.49.1, timeout is 2 seconds:
!!!!!
Success rate is 100 percent (5/5), round-trip min/avg/max = 28/28/28 ms
R2#
```

Step 4: Configure OSPF.

By default, loopback interfaces are advertised as a host route with a /32 mask. To advertise them as network routes, the loopback interface network type must be changed point-to-point. In this step, you will advertise the loopback interfaces as point-to-point and configure multi-area OSPF between R2 and R3.

a. On R2, configure the loopback 100 interface as a point-to-point network.

```
R2(config)# interface Loopback100
R2(config-if)# ip ospf network point-to-point
R2(config-if)# exit
R2(config)#
```

b. Next, advertise serial link connecting to R3 in area 0 and the loopback 100 network is area 10.

```
R2(config)# router ospf 1
R2(config-router)# network 172.16.23.0 0.0.0.255 area 0
R2(config-router)# network 172.16.100.0 0.0.0.255 area 10
```

c. On R3, change the network type for the 10 loopback interfaces to point-to-point so that they are advertised with the correct subnet mask (/24 instead of /32). Start with loopback 0.

```
R3(config)# interface Loopback0
R3(config-if)# ip ospf network point-to-point
R3(config-if)# exit
```

d. Although we could manually configure all 9 other interface individually, we can also use the **interface range** command to simultaneously configure several interfaces. Loopback interfaces are contiguous and therefore configured by using a hyphen. The remainder of the interfaces are separated using a comma.

```
R3(config)# interface range lo 8 - 11
R3(config-if-range)# ip ospf network point-to-point
R3(config-if-range)# exit
R3(config)#
```

```
R3(config)# interface range lo 20, lo 25, lo 30, lo 35, lo 40
R3(config-if-range)# ip ospf network point-to-point
R3(config-if-range)# exit
R3(config)#
```

e.   On R3, include the serial link and all loopback interfaces in area 0 and the loopbacks in area 20.

```
R3(config)# router ospf 1
R3(config-router)# network 172.16.0.0 0.0.255.255 area 0
R3(config-router)# network 192.168.0.0 0.0.255.255 area 0
R3(config-router)# network 192.168.8.0 0.0.3.255 area 20
R3(config-router)#
*Jul 27 08:22:05.503: %OSPF-5-ADJCHG: Process 1, Nbr 172.16.100.1 on
Serial0/0/1 from LOADING to FULL, Loading Done
R3(config-router)#
```

f.   Verify that your adjacencies come up with the **show ip ospf neighbor** command, and make sure that you have routes from OSPF populating the R2 routing table using the **show ip route ospf** command.

```
R2# show ip ospf neighbor

Neighbor ID     Pri   State          Dead Time   Address         Interface
192.168.40.1      0   FULL/  -       00:00:39    172.16.23.3     Serial0/0/1
R2#
R2# show ip route ospf

<Output omitted>

      172.16.0.0/16 is variably subnetted, 10 subnets, 2 masks
O        172.16.3.0/24 [110/1563] via 172.16.23.3, 00:04:24, Serial0/0/1
O IA  192.168.8.0/24 [110/1563] via 172.16.23.3, 00:04:24, Serial0/0/1
O IA  192.168.9.0/24 [110/1563] via 172.16.23.3, 00:04:24, Serial0/0/1
O IA  192.168.10.0/24 [110/1563] via 172.16.23.3, 00:04:24, Serial0/0/1
O IA  192.168.11.0/24 [110/1563] via 172.16.23.3, 00:04:24, Serial0/0/1
O     192.168.20.0/24 [110/1563] via 172.16.23.3, 00:04:24, Serial0/0/1
O     192.168.25.0/24 [110/1563] via 172.16.23.3, 00:04:24, Serial0/0/1
O     192.168.30.0/24 [110/1563] via 172.16.23.3, 00:04:24, Serial0/0/1
O     192.168.35.0/24 [110/1563] via 172.16.23.3, 00:04:24, Serial0/0/1
O     192.168.40.0/24 [110/1563] via 172.16.23.3, 00:04:24, Serial0/0/1
R2#
```

g.   Verify your adjacencies and routing table of R3.

```
R3# show ip ospf neighbor

Neighbor ID     Pri   State          Dead Time   Address         Interface
172.16.100.1      0   FULL/  -       00:00:39    172.16.23.2     Serial0/0/1
R3#
R3# show ip route ospf

<Output omitted>

      172.16.0.0/16 is variably subnetted, 5 subnets, 2 masks
O IA    172.16.100.0/24 [110/1563] via 172.16.23.2, 00:07:02, Serial0/0/1
R3#
```

h. Verify that R1 and R2 can reach all of the networks in the OSPF routing domain using the following Tcl script.

```
R1# tclsh

foreach address {
172.16.100.1
172.16.23.2
172.16.23.3
172.16.3.1
192.168.8.1
192.168.9.1
192.168.10.1
192.168.11.1
192.168.20.1
192.168.25.1
192.168.30.1
192.168.35.1
192.168.40.1
} { ping $address }
```

All pings should be successful. Troubleshoot if necessary.

Step 5: Summarize OSPF areas at the ABR.

Review the R2 routing table. Notice the inter-area routes (O IA) for the R3 loopbacks in area 20.

Where can you summarize in OSPF?

_____

_____

_____

a. These four routes can be summarized into a single inter-area route using the **area** *area* **range** *network mask* command on the ABR, R3.

```
R3(config)# router ospf 1
R3(config-router)# area 20 range 192.168.8.0 255.255.252.0
```

b. On R2, verify the summarization with the **show ip route ospf** command on R2.

```
R2#show ip route ospf

<Output omitted>

      172.16.0.0/16 is variably subnetted, 10 subnets, 2 masks
O        172.16.3.0/24 [110/1563] via 172.16.23.3, 00:37:42, Serial0/0/1
O IA  192.168.8.0/22 [110/1563] via 172.16.23.3, 00:01:26, Serial0/0/1
O        192.168.20.0/24 [110/1563] via 172.16.23.3, 00:37:42, Serial0/0/1
O        192.168.25.0/24 [110/1563] via 172.16.23.3, 00:37:42, Serial0/0/1
O        192.168.30.0/24 [110/1563] via 172.16.23.3, 00:37:42, Serial0/0/1
O        192.168.35.0/24 [110/1563] via 172.16.23.3, 00:37:42, Serial0/0/1
O        192.168.40.0/24 [110/1563] via 172.16.23.3, 00:37:42, Serial0/0/1
R2#
```

Compare and contrast OSPF and EIGRP in terms of where summarization takes place.

_____

Step 6: Configure mutual redistribution between OSPF and EIGRP.

Notice that R2 is the only router with knowledge of all routes (EIGRP and OSPF) in the topology at this point, because it is involved with both routing protocols. Next you will redistribute the EIGRP routes into OSPF and the OSPF routes into EIGRP.

a. To redistribute the EIGRP routes into OSPF, on R2 issue the **redistribute eigrp 1 subnets** command. The **subnets** command is necessary because, by default, OSPF only redistributes classful networks and supernets.

```
R2(config)# router ospf 1
R2(config-router)# redistribute eigrp 1 subnets
R2(config-router)# exit
```

A default seed metric is not required for OSPF. Redistributed routes are assigned a metric of 20 by default.

b. To redistribute the OSPF routes into EIGRP, on R2 issue the **redistribute ospf 1 metric 10000 100 255 1 1500** command. Unlike OSPF, EIGRP must specify the metric associated to the redistributed routes. The command tells EIGRP to redistribute OSPF process 1 with these metrics: bandwidth of 10000, delay of 100, reliability of 255/255, load of 1/255, and an MTU of 1500. EIGRP requires a seed metric.

```
R2(config)# router eigrp 1
R2(config-router)# redistribute ospf 1 metric 10000 100 255 1 1500
R2(config-router)# exit
```

Alternatively, you can also set a default seed metric with the **default-metric** command.

```
R2(config-router)# default-metric 10000 100 255 1 1500
R2(config-router)# redistribute ospf 1
R2(config-router)# end
```

c. Issue the **show ip protocols** command on the redistributing router, R2. Compare your output with the following output.

```
R2# show ip protocols
*** IP Routing is NSF aware ***

<Output omitted>

Routing Protocol is "eigrp 1"
  Outgoing update filter list for all interfaces is not set
  Incoming update filter list for all interfaces is not set
  Default networks flagged in outgoing updates
  Default networks accepted from incoming updates
  Redistributing: ospf 1
  EIGRP-IPv4 Protocol for AS(1)
    Metric weight K1=1, K2=0, K3=1, K4=0, K5=0
    NSF-aware route hold timer is 240
    Router-ID: 172.16.100.1
    Topology : 0 (base)
      Active Timer: 3 min
      Distance: internal 90 external 170
      Maximum path: 4
      Maximum hopcount 100
      Maximum metric variance 1
```

```
     Automatic Summarization: disabled
     Maximum path: 4
     Routing for Networks:
       172.16.0.0
     Routing Information Sources:
       Gateway           Distance       Last Update
       172.16.12.1              90       02:00:24
     Distance: internal 90 external 170

  Routing Protocol is "ospf 1"
     Outgoing update filter list for all interfaces is not set
     Incoming update filter list for all interfaces is not set
     Router ID 172.16.100.1
     It is an area border and autonomous system boundary router
     Redistributing External Routes from,
       eigrp 1, includes subnets in redistribution
     Number of areas in this router is 2. 2 normal 0 stub 0 nssa
     Maximum path: 4
     Routing for Networks:
       172.16.23.0 0.0.0.255 area 0
       172.16.100.0 0.0.0.255 area 10
     Routing Information Sources:
       Gateway           Distance       Last Update
       192.168.40.1            110       00:37:06
     Distance: (default is 110)

  R2#
```

d. Display the routing table on R1 to verify the redistributed routes. Redistributed OSPF routes display on R1 as D EX, which means that they are external EIGRP routes.

```
R1# show ip route

<Output omitted>

Gateway of last resort is not set

      172.16.0.0/16 is variably subnetted, 8 subnets, 2 masks
C        172.16.1.0/24 is directly connected, Loopback0
L        172.16.1.1/32 is directly connected, Loopback0
D        172.16.2.0/24 [90/40640000] via 172.16.12.2, 02:08:18, Serial0/0/0
D EX     172.16.3.0/24 [170/40537600] via 172.16.12.2, 00:04:41, Serial0/0/0
C        172.16.12.0/24 is directly connected, Serial0/0/0
L        172.16.12.1/32 is directly connected, Serial0/0/0
D        172.16.23.0/24 [90/41024000] via 172.16.12.2, 02:08:18, Serial0/0/0
D        172.16.100.0/24 [90/40640000] via 172.16.12.2, 02:08:18, Serial0/0/0
D EX  192.168.8.0/22 [170/40537600] via 172.16.12.2, 00:04:41, Serial0/0/0
D EX  192.168.20.0/24 [170/40537600] via 172.16.12.2, 00:04:41, Serial0/0/0
D EX  192.168.25.0/24 [170/40537600] via 172.16.12.2, 00:04:41, Serial0/0/0
D EX  192.168.30.0/24 [170/40537600] via 172.16.12.2, 00:04:41, Serial0/0/0
D EX  192.168.35.0/24 [170/40537600] via 172.16.12.2, 00:04:41, Serial0/0/0
D EX  192.168.40.0/24 [170/40537600] via 172.16.12.2, 00:04:41, Serial0/0/0
D     192.168.48.0/23 is a summary, 02:04:14, Null0
      192.168.48.0/24 is variably subnetted, 2 subnets, 2 masks
C        192.168.48.0/24 is directly connected, Loopback48
L        192.168.48.1/32 is directly connected, Loopback48
```

```
            192.168.49.0/24 is variably subnetted, 2 subnets, 2 masks
C              192.168.49.0/24 is directly connected, Loopback49
L              192.168.49.1/32 is directly connected, Loopback49
            192.168.50.0/24 is variably subnetted, 2 subnets, 2 masks
C              192.168.50.0/24 is directly connected, Loopback50
L              192.168.50.1/32 is directly connected, Loopback50
            192.168.51.0/24 is variably subnetted, 2 subnets, 2 masks
C              192.168.51.0/24 is directly connected, Loopback51
L              192.168.51.1/32 is directly connected, Loopback51
            192.168.70.0/24 is variably subnetted, 2 subnets, 2 masks
C              192.168.70.0/24 is directly connected, Loopback70
L              192.168.70.1/32 is directly connected, Loopback70
R1#
```

e. Display the routing table on R3 to see the redistributed routes. Redistributed EIGRP routes are tagged in the R3 routing table as O E2, which means that they are OSPF external type 2. Type 2 is the default OSPF external type.

R3# **show ip route**

```
<Output omitted>



Gateway of last resort is not set

         172.16.0.0/16 is variably subnetted, 8 subnets, 2 masks
O E2       172.16.1.0/24 [110/20] via 172.16.23.2, 00:08:18, Serial0/0/1
O E2       172.16.2.0/24 [110/20] via 172.16.23.2, 00:08:18, Serial0/0/1
C          172.16.3.0/24 is directly connected, Loopback0
L          172.16.3.1/32 is directly connected, Loopback0
O E2       172.16.12.0/24 [110/20] via 172.16.23.2, 00:08:18, Serial0/0/1
C          172.16.23.0/24 is directly connected, Serial0/0/1
L          172.16.23.3/32 is directly connected, Serial0/0/1
O IA       172.16.100.0/24 [110/1563] via 172.16.23.2, 00:43:53, Serial0/0/1
O        192.168.8.0/22 is a summary, 00:43:53, Null0
         192.168.8.0/24 is variably subnetted, 2 subnets, 2 masks
C          192.168.8.0/24 is directly connected, Loopback8
L          192.168.8.1/32 is directly connected, Loopback8
         192.168.9.0/24 is variably subnetted, 2 subnets, 2 masks
C          192.168.9.0/24 is directly connected, Loopback9
L          192.168.9.1/32 is directly connected, Loopback9
         192.168.10.0/24 is variably subnetted, 2 subnets, 2 masks
C          192.168.10.0/24 is directly connected, Loopback10
L          192.168.10.1/32 is directly connected, Loopback10
         192.168.11.0/24 is variably subnetted, 2 subnets, 2 masks
C          192.168.11.0/24 is directly connected, Loopback11
L          192.168.11.1/32 is directly connected, Loopback11
         192.168.20.0/24 is variably subnetted, 2 subnets, 2 masks
C          192.168.20.0/24 is directly connected, Loopback20
L          192.168.20.1/32 is directly connected, Loopback20
         192.168.25.0/24 is variably subnetted, 2 subnets, 2 masks
C          192.168.25.0/24 is directly connected, Loopback25
L          192.168.25.1/32 is directly connected, Loopback25
         192.168.30.0/24 is variably subnetted, 2 subnets, 2 masks
C          192.168.30.0/24 is directly connected, Loopback30
```

```
L          192.168.30.1/32 is directly connected, Loopback30
        192.168.35.0/24 is variably subnetted, 2 subnets, 2 masks
C          192.168.35.0/24 is directly connected, Loopback35
L          192.168.35.1/32 is directly connected, Loopback35
        192.168.40.0/24 is variably subnetted, 2 subnets, 2 masks
C          192.168.40.0/24 is directly connected, Loopback40
L          192.168.40.1/32 is directly connected, Loopback40
O E2   192.168.48.0/23 [110/20] via 172.16.23.2, 00:08:18, Serial0/0/1
O E2   192.168.50.0/24 [110/20] via 172.16.23.2, 00:08:18, Serial0/0/1
O E2   192.168.51.0/24 [110/20] via 172.16.23.2, 00:08:18, Serial0/0/1
O E2   192.168.70.0/24 [110/20] via 172.16.23.2, 00:08:18, Serial0/0/1
R3#
```

f. Verify full connectivity with the following Tcl script:

```
R1# tclsh

foreach address {
172.16.1.1
192.168.48.1
192.168.49.1
192.168.50.1
192.168.51.1
192.168.70.1
172.16.12.1
172.16.12.2
172.16.2.1
172.16.100.1
172.16.23.2
172.16.23.3
172.16.3.1
192.168.8.1
192.168.9.1
192.168.10.1
192.168.11.1
192.168.20.1
192.168.25.1
192.168.30.1
192.168.35.1
192.168.40.1
} { ping $address }
```

All pings should now be successful. Troubleshoot as necessary.

Step 7: Summarize external routes into OSPF at the ASBR.

You cannot summarize routes redistributed into OSPF using the **area range** command. This command is effective only on routes internal to the specified area. Instead, use the OSPF **summary-address** *network mask* command.

a. Before you make any changes, display the R3 the OSPF routes in the routing table and list only those routes that have an E2 type metric.

```
R3# show ip route ospf | include E2
       E1 - OSPF external type 1, E2 - OSPF external type 2
O E2    172.16.1.0/24 [110/20] via 172.16.23.2, 00:16:22, Serial0/0/1
O E2    172.16.2.0/24 [110/20] via 172.16.23.2, 00:16:22, Serial0/0/1
O E2    172.16.12.0/24 [110/20] via 172.16.23.2, 00:16:22, Serial0/0/1
```

```
O E2   192.168.48.0/23 [110/20] via 172.16.23.2, 00:16:22, Serial0/0/1
O E2   192.168.50.0/24 [110/20] via 172.16.23.2, 00:16:22, Serial0/0/1
O E2   192.168.51.0/24 [110/20] via 172.16.23.2, 00:16:22, Serial0/0/1
O E2   192.168.70.0/24 [110/20] via 172.16.23.2, 00:16:22, Serial0/0/1
R3#
```

Notice the external routes for the R1 loopback interfaces 48, 50, and 51. Loopbacks 48 and 49 were previously summarized in EIGRP; they will be included when redistributing the EIGRP into OSPF.

Which mask should you use to summarize all loopbacks 48, 50, and 51 to one prefix?

_____

b. You can summarize this all into one supernet on R2 using the following commands.

```
R2(config)# router ospf 1
R2(config-router)# summary-address 192.168.48.0 255.255.252.0
```

c. Verify this action in the R3 routing table.

```
R3# show ip route ospf | include E2
       E1 - OSPF external type 1, E2 - OSPF external type 2
O E2     172.16.1.0/24 [110/20] via 172.16.23.2, 00:21:44, Serial0/0/1
O E2     172.16.2.0/24 [110/20] via 172.16.23.2, 00:21:44, Serial0/0/1
O E2     172.16.12.0/24 [110/20] via 172.16.23.2, 00:21:44, Serial0/0/1
O E2   192.168.48.0/22 [110/20] via 172.16.23.2, 00:00:07, Serial0/0/1
O E2   192.168.70.0/24 [110/20] via 172.16.23.2, 00:21:44, Serial0/0/1
R3#
```

What would happen if loopback 50 on R1 were to become unreachable by R2?

_____

_____

Would data destined for 192.168.50.0/24 from R3 still be sent to R2?

_____

_____

Would data destined for 192.168.50.0/24 from R2 continue to be sent to R1?

_____

_____

d. If you are unsure of the outcome, shut down the interface on R1. Issue the ICMP **traceroute** command to 192.168.50.1 from R3 and then from R2.

Is this a desirable outcome? Explain.

_____

_____

_____

_____

The resulting configuration is required for Lab 4-2.

Lab 4-2 Controlling Routing Updates

Topology

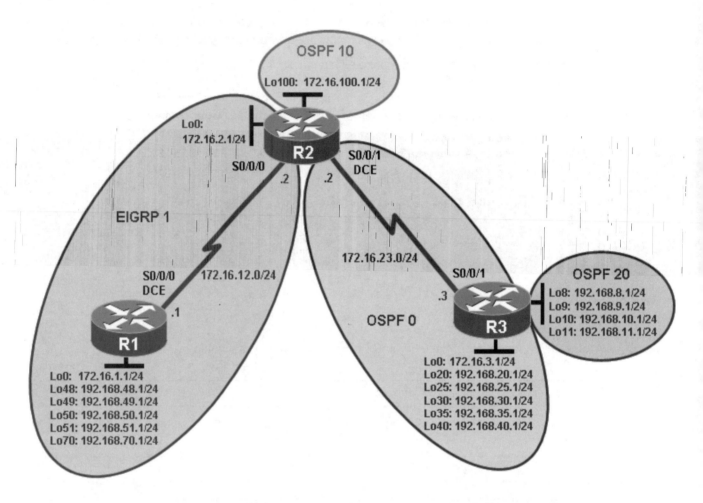

Objectives

- Filter routes using a distribute list and ACL.
- Filter routes using a distribute list and prefix list.
- Filter redistributed routes using a route map.
- Filter redistributed routes and set attributes using a route map.

Background

In this scenario, R1 and R2 are running EIGRP while R2 and R3 are running multi-area OSPF. R2 is the OSPF autonomous system border router (ASBR) consisting of areas 0, 10, and 20.

Your task is to control routing updates by using distribute lists, prefix lists, and route maps.

Note: This lab uses Cisco 1941 routers with Cisco IOS Release 15.2 with IP Base. Depending on the router or switch model and Cisco IOS Software version, the commands available and output produced might vary from what is shown in this lab.

Required Resources

- 3 routers (Cisco IOS Release 15.2 or comparable)
- Serial and Ethernet cables

Step 1: Configure loopbacks and assign addresses.

Note: The following two steps are not required if you are continuing from Lab 4-1.

a. Configure all loopback interfaces on the three routers in the diagram. Configure the serial interfaces with the IP addresses, bring them up, and set a DCE clock rate where appropriate.

```
R1(config)# interface Loopback0
R1(config-if)# ip address 172.16.1.1 255.255.255.0
R1(config-if)# exit
R1(config)#
R1(config)# interface Loopback48
R1(config-if)# ip address 192.168.48.1 255.255.255.0
R1(config-if)# exit
R1(config)#
R1(config)# interface Loopback49
R1(config-if)# ip address 192.168.49.1 255.255.255.0
R1(config-if)# exit
R1(config)#
R1(config)# interface Loopback50
R1(config-if)# ip address 192.168.50.1 255.255.255.0
R1(config-if)# exit
R1(config)#
R1(config)# interface Loopback51
R1(config-if)# ip address 192.168.51.1 255.255.255.0
R1(config-if)# exit
R1(config)#
R1(config)# interface Loopback70
R1(config-if)# ip address 192.168.70.1 255.255.255.0
R1(config-if)# exit
R1(config)#
R1(config)# interface Serial0/0/0
R1(config-if)# ip address 172.16.12.1 255.255.255.0
R1(config-if)# clock rate 64000
R1(config-if)# bandwidth 64
R1(config-if)# no shutdown

R2(config)# interface Loopback0
R2(config-if)# ip address 172.16.2.1 255.255.255.0
R2(config-if)# exit
```

```
R2(config)#
R2(config)# interface Loopback100
R2(config-if)# ip address 172.16.100.1 255.255.255.0
R2(config-if)# ip ospf network point-to-point
R2(config-if)# exit
R2(config)#
R2(config-if)# interface Serial0/0/0
R2(config-if)# bandwidth 64
R2(config-if)# ip address 172.16.12.2 255.255.255.0
R2(config-if)# no shutdown
R2(config-if)# exit
R2(config)#
R2(config)# interface Serial0/0/1
R2(config-if)# bandwidth 64
R2(config-if)# ip address 172.16.23.2 255.255.255.0
R2(config-if)# clock rate 64000
R2(config-if)# no shutdown


R3(config)# interface Loopback0
R3(config-if)# ip address 172.16.3.1 255.255.255.0
R3(config-if)# ip ospf network point-to-point
R3(config-if)# exit
R3(config)#
R3(config)# interface loopback 8
R3(config-if)# ip address 192.168.8.1 255.255.255.0
R3(config-if)# ip ospf network point-to-point
R3(config-if)# exit
R3(config)#
R3(config)# interface loopback 9
R3(config-if)# ip address 192.168.9.1 255.255.255.0
R3(config-if)# ip ospf network point-to-point
R3(config-if)# exit
R3(config)#
R3(config)# interface loopback 10
R3(config-if)# ip address 192.168.10.1 255.255.255.0
R3(config-if)# ip ospf network point-to-point
R3(config-if)# exit
R3(config)#
R3(config)# interface loopback 11
R3(config-if)# ip address 192.168.11.1 255.255.255.0
R3(config-if)# ip ospf network point-to-point
R3(config-if)# exit
R3(config)#
R3(config)# interface Loopback20
R3(config-if)# ip address 192.168.20.1 255.255.255.0
R3(config-if)# ip ospf network point-to-point
R3(config-if)# exit
R3(config)#
R3(config)# interface Loopback25
R3(config-if)# ip address 192.168.25.1 255.255.255.0
R3(config-if)# ip ospf network point-to-point
R3(config-if)# exit
R3(config)#
R3(config)# interface Loopback30
R3(config-if)# ip address 192.168.30.1 255.255.255.0
R3(config-if)# ip ospf network point-to-point
R3(config-if)# exit
```

```
R3(config)#
R3(config)# interface Loopback35
R3(config-if)# ip address 192.168.35.1 255.255.255.0
R3(config-if)# ip ospf network point-to-point
R3(config-if)# exit
R3(config)#
R3(config)# interface Loopback40
R3(config-if)# ip address 192.168.40.1 255.255.255.0
R3(config-if)# ip ospf network point-to-point
R3(config-if)# exit
R3(config)#
R3(config)# interface Serial0/0/1
R3(config-if)# ip address 172.16.23.3 255.255.255.0
R3(config-if)# bandwidth 64
R3(config-if)# no shutdown
```

Step 2: Configure routing, summarization, and redistribution.

In this step, we will configure EIGRP on R1 and R2, and OSPF on R2 and R3.

a. On R1, create a supernet route summarizing the loopback 48 and 49 networks and configure EIGRP in autonomous system 1.

```
R1(config)# interface Serial0/0/0
R1(config-if)# ip summary-address eigrp 1 192.168.48.0 255.255.254.0
R1(config-if)# exit
R1(config)# router eigrp 1
R1(config-router)# no auto-summary
R1(config-router)# network 172.16.0.0
R1(config-router)# network 192.168.0.0 0.0.255.255
R1(config-router)#
```

b. On R3, summarize area 20 routes and configure OSPF for area 0 and area 20.

```
R3(config)# router ospf 1
R3(config-router)# area 20 range 192.168.8.0 255.255.252.0
R3(config-router)# network 172.16.0.0 0.0.255.255 area 0
R3(config-router)# network 192.168.0.0 0.0.255.255 area 0
R3(config-router)# network 192.168.8.0 0.0.3.255 area 20
R3(config-router)#
```

c. On R2, configure EIGRP and redistribute the OSPF networks into EIGRP AS 1. Then configure OSPF and redistribute and summarize the EIGRP networks into OSPF.

```
R2(config)# router eigrp 1
R2(config-router)# no auto-summary
R2(config-router)# network 172.16.0.0
R2(config-router)# redistribute ospf 1 metric 10000 100 255 1 1500
R2(config-router)# exit
R2(config)#
R2(config)# router ospf 1
R2(config-router)# network 172.16.23.0 0.0.0.255 area 0
R2(config-router)# network 172.16.100.0 0.0.0.255 area 10
R2(config-router)# redistribute eigrp 1 subnets
R2(config-router)# summary-address 192.168.48.0 255.255.252.0
R2(config-router)# exit
```

```
R2(config)#
Jan 10 10:11:18.863: %DUAL-5-NBRCHANGE: EIGRP-IPv4 1: Neighbor 172.16.12.1
(Serial0/0/0) is up: new adjacency
R2(config)#
Jan 10 10:11:32.991: %OSPF-5-ADJCHG: Process 1, Nbr 192.168.40.1 on
Serial0/0/1 from LOADING to FULL, Loading Done
R2(config)#
```

d. Verify the EIGRP and OSPF routing table entries on R2.

```
R2# show ip route eigrp | begin Gateway
Gateway of last resort is not set

     172.16.0.0/16 is variably subnetted, 10 subnets, 2 masks
D        172.16.1.0/24 [90/40640000] via 172.16.12.1, 00:14:57, Serial0/0/0
D     192.168.48.0/23 [90/40640000] via 172.16.12.1, 00:14:57, Serial0/0/0
D     192.168.50.0/24 [90/40640000] via 172.16.12.1, 00:14:57, Serial0/0/0
D     192.168.51.0/24 [90/40640000] via 172.16.12.1, 00:14:57, Serial0/0/0
D     192.168.70.0/24 [90/40640000] via 172.16.12.1, 00:14:57, Serial0/0/0
R2#
R2# show ip route ospf | begin Gateway
Gateway of last resort is not set

     172.16.0.0/16 is variably subnetted, 10 subnets, 2 masks
O        172.16.3.0/24 [110/1563] via 172.16.23.3, 00:15:41, Serial0/0/1
O IA  192.168.8.0/22 [110/1563] via 172.16.23.3, 00:15:41, Serial0/0/1
O     192.168.20.0/24 [110/1563] via 172.16.23.3, 00:15:41, Serial0/0/1
O     192.168.25.0/24 [110/1563] via 172.16.23.3, 00:15:41, Serial0/0/1
O     192.168.30.0/24 [110/1563] via 172.16.23.3, 00:15:41, Serial0/0/1
O     192.168.35.0/24 [110/1563] via 172.16.23.3, 00:15:41, Serial0/0/1
O     192.168.40.0/24 [110/1563] via 172.16.23.3, 00:15:41, Serial0/0/1
O     192.168.48.0/22 is a summary, 00:15:30, Null0
R2#
```

As expected, R2 knows about the R1 routes including the summarized 192.168.48.0/22 EIGRP route. R2 also knows about the R3 OSPF area 0 routes and the summarized area 20 routes.

e. Verify the EIGRP routing table on R1.

```
R1# show ip route eigrp | begin Gateway
Gateway of last resort is not set

     172.16.0.0/16 is variably subnetted, 8 subnets, 2 masks
D        172.16.2.0/24 [90/40640000] via 172.16.12.2, 00:11:40, Serial0/0/0
D EX     172.16.3.0/24 [170/40537600] via 172.16.12.2, 00:11:40, Serial0/0/0
D        172.16.23.0/24 [90/41024000] via 172.16.12.2, 00:11:40, Serial0/0/0
D        172.16.100.0/24 [90/40640000] via 172.16.12.2, 00:11:40, Serial0/0/0
D EX  192.168.8.0/22 [170/40537600] via 172.16.12.2, 00:11:40, Serial0/0/0
D EX  192.168.20.0/24 [170/40537600] via 172.16.12.2, 00:11:40, Serial0/0/0
D EX  192.168.25.0/24 [170/40537600] via 172.16.12.2, 00:11:40, Serial0/0/0
D EX  192.168.30.0/24 [170/40537600] via 172.16.12.2, 00:11:40, Serial0/0/0
D EX  192.168.35.0/24 [170/40537600] via 172.16.12.2, 00:11:40, Serial0/0/0
D EX  192.168.40.0/24 [170/40537600] via 172.16.12.2, 00:11:40, Serial0/0/0
D EX  192.168.48.0/22 [170/40537600] via 172.16.12.2, 00:11:38, Serial0/0/0
D     192.168.48.0/23 is a summary, 00:11:40, Null0
R1#
```

R1 knows about the internal EIGRP routes and the external routes redistributed from the OSPF routing domain by R2. The highlighted entry identifies the OSPF 20 routes, which will be filtered using a distribute list and ACL in the next step.

f. Verify the EIGRP routing table on R3.

```
R3# show ip route ospf | begin Gateway
Gateway of last resort is not set

      172.16.0.0/16 is variably subnetted, 8 subnets, 2 masks
O E2     172.16.1.0/24 [110/20] via 172.16.23.2, 00:22:43, Serial0/0/1
O E2     172.16.2.0/24 [110/20] via 172.16.23.2, 00:22:52, Serial0/0/1
O E2     172.16.12.0/24 [110/20] via 172.16.23.2, 00:22:52, Serial0/0/1
O IA     172.16.100.0/24 [110/1563] via 172.16.23.2, 00:22:52, Serial0/0/1
O     192.168.8.0/22 is a summary, 00:23:10, Null0
O E2  192.168.48.0/22 [110/20] via 172.16.23.2, 00:22:41, Serial0/0/1
O E2  192.168.70.0/24 [110/20] via 172.16.23.2, 00:22:42, Serial0/0/1
R3#
```

R3 knows about the internal OSPF routes and the external routes redistributed by R2 from the EIGRP routing domain. The highlighted entries identify the EIGRP routes, which will be filtered using a distribute list and prefix list in another step.

g. Verify that you can ping across the serial links when you are finished. Use the following Tcl script to check connectivity.

```
R3# tclsh

foreach address {
172.16.1.1
192.168.48.1
192.168.49.1
192.168.50.1
192.168.51.1
192.168.70.1
172.16.12.1
172.16.12.2
172.16.2.1
172.16.100.1
172.16.23.2
172.16.23.3
172.16.3.1
192.168.8.1
192.168.9.1
192.168.10.1
192.168.11.1
192.168.20.1
192.168.25.1
192.168.30.1
192.168.35.1
192.168.40.1
} { ping $address }
```

All pings should be successful. Troubleshoot if necessary.

Step 3: Filter redistributed routes using a distribute list and ACL.

Routes can be filtered using a variety of techniques including:

Distribute list and ACL—A distribute list allows an access control list (ACL) to be applied to routing updates.

- **Distribute list and prefix list**— A distribute list with a prefix list is an alternative to ACLs designed to filter routes. Prefix lists are not exclusively used with distribute lists but can also be used with route maps and other commands.

- **Route maps**— Route maps are complex access lists that allow conditions to be tested against a packet or route, and then actions taken to modify attributes of the packet or route.

In this step, we will use a distribute list and ACL to filter routes being advertised from R2 to R1. Specifically, we will filter the OSPF 20 routes (that is, 192.168.8.0/22) from being advertised by R2 to R1.

a. On R1, verify the routing table entry for the 192.168.8.0/22 route.

```
R1# show ip route 192.168.8.0
Routing entry for 192.168.8.0/22, supernet
   Known via "eigrp 1", distance 170, metric 40537600, type external
   Redistributing via eigrp 1
   Last update from 172.16.12.2 on Serial0/0/0, 00:00:43 ago
   Routing Descriptor Blocks:
   * 172.16.12.2, from 172.16.12.2, 00:00:43 ago, via Serial0/0/0
       Route metric is 40537600, traffic share count is 1
       Total delay is 21000 microseconds, minimum bandwidth is 64 Kbit
       Reliability 255/255, minimum MTU 1500 bytes
       Loading 1/255, Hops 1
R1#
```

b. Although a distribute list could be implemented on the receiving router, it is usually best to filter routes from the distributing router. Therefore on R2, create an ACL called **OSPF20-FILTER** that denies the 192.168.8.0/22 route. The ACL must also permit all other routes; otherwise, no OSPF routes would be redistributed into EIGRP.

```
R2(config)# ip access-list standard OSPF20-FILTER
R2(config-std-nacl)# remark Used with DList to filter OSPF 20 routes
R2(config-std-nacl)# deny 192.168.8.0 0.0.3.255
R2(config-std-nacl)# permit any
R2(config-std-nacl)# exit
R2(config)#
```

c. Configure a distribute list under the EIGRP process to filter routes propagated to R1 using the pre-configured ACL.

```
R2(config)# router eigrp 1
R2(config-router)# distribute-list OSPF20-FILTER out ospf 1
R2(config-router)#
```

d. On R1, verify if the route is now missing from the R1 routing table.

```
R1# show ip route 192.168.8.0
% Network not in table
R1#
R1# show ip route eigrp | begin Gateway
Gateway of last resort is not set

     172.16.0.0/16 is variably subnetted, 8 subnets, 2 masks
D        172.16.2.0/24 [90/40640000] via 172.16.12.2, 00:00:03, Serial0/0/0
```

```
D EX    172.16.3.0/24 [170/40537600] via 172.16.12.2, 00:00:03, Serial0/0/0
D       172.16.23.0/24 [90/41024000] via 172.16.12.2, 00:00:03, Serial0/0/0
D       172.16.100.0/24 [90/40640000] via 172.16.12.2, 00:00:03, Serial0/0/0
D EX  192.168.20.0/24 [170/40537600] via 172.16.12.2, 00:00:03, Serial0/0/0
D EX  192.168.25.0/24 [170/40537600] via 172.16.12.2, 00:00:03, Serial0/0/0
D EX  192.168.30.0/24 [170/40537600] via 172.16.12.2, 00:00:03, Serial0/0/0
D EX  192.168.35.0/24 [170/40537600] via 172.16.12.2, 00:00:03, Serial0/0/0
D EX  192.168.40.0/24 [170/40537600] via 172.16.12.2, 00:00:03, Serial0/0/0
D EX  192.168.48.0/22 [170/40537600] via 172.16.12.2, 00:00:03, Serial0/0/0
D     192.168.48.0/23 is a summary, 00:00:03, Null0
R1#
```

The output confirms that the 192.168.8.0/22 route is no longer in the routing table of R1.

Note that if additional router filtering was required, only the ACL on R2 would need to be altered.

Step 4: Filter redistributed routes using a distribute list and prefix list.

In this step, a prefix list will be configured with a distribute list to filter R1 routes being advertised from R2 to R3.

a. On R3, verify the routing table entry for the routes learned externally identified with the O E2 source entry.

```
R3# show ip route ospf | include O E2
O E2    172.16.1.0/24 [110/20] via 172.16.23.2, 00:10:12, Serial0/0/1
O E2    172.16.2.0/24 [110/20] via 172.16.23.2, 00:10:12, Serial0/0/1
O E2    172.16.12.0/24 [110/20] via 172.16.23.2, 00:10:12, Serial0/0/1
O E2  192.168.48.0/22 [110/20] via 172.16.23.2, 00:02:05, Serial0/0/1
O E2  192.168.70.0/24 [110/20] via 172.16.23.2, 00:02:05, Serial0/0/1
R3#
```

Specifically, the highlighted routes will be omitted from being advertised using a prefix list.

b. R2 will be configured with a prefix list identifying which networks to advertise to advertise to R3. Specifically, only the 172.16.0.0 networks are permitted.

```
R2(config)# ip prefix-list EIGRP-FILTER description Used with DList to filter
EIGRP routes
R2(config)# ip prefix-list EIGRP-FILTER permit 172.16.0.0/16 le 24
R2(config)#
```

c. Configure a distribute list under the OSPF process to filter routes propagated to R3 using the pre-configured prefix list.

```
R2(config)# router ospf 1
R2(config-router)# distribute-list prefix EIGRP-FILTER out eigrp 1
R2(config-router)#
```

d. On R3, verify if the route is now missing from the R1 routing table.

```
R3# show ip route ospf | include O E2
O E2    172.16.1.0/24 [110/20] via 172.16.23.2, 00:13:55, Serial0/0/1
O E2    172.16.2.0/24 [110/20] via 172.16.23.2, 00:13:55, Serial0/0/1
O E2    172.16.12.0/24 [110/20] via 172.16.23.2, 00:13:55, Serial0/0/1
R3#
```

The output confirms that only the 172.16.0.0/16 networks are being advertised to R3.

Step 5: Filter redistributed routes using a route map.

The preceding two steps were simple examples of using a distribute list with an ACL and a prefix list. Both methods basically achieved the same result of filtering routes.

However, in large enterprise networks, route filtering can be quite complex. The ACLs can be very extensive and therefore taxing on router resources. For this reason, prefix lists should be used instead of ACLs since they are more efficient and less taxing on router resources than ACLs.

Route maps can also be used to filter redistributed routes. A route map works like an access list because it has multiple deny and permit statements that are read in a sequential order. However, route maps can match and set specific attributes and therefore provide additional options and more flexibility when redistributing routes.

Route maps are not just for redistribution. They are also commonly used for:

- **Policy-based routing (PBR)**—PBR allows an administrator to define routing policy other than basic destination-based routing using the routing table. The route map is applied to an interface using the **ip policy route-map** interface configuration command.

- **BGP**—Route maps are the primary tools for implementing BGP policy and allows an administrator to do path control and provide sophisticated manipulation of BGP path attributes. The route map is applied using the BGP **neighbor** router configuration command.

In this step, we will filter the R3 loopback 25 and 30 networks from being redistributed into EIGRP on R2.

a. Display the R1 routing table and verify that those two routes currently appear there.

```
R1# show ip route eigrp | begin Gateway
Gateway of last resort is not set

      172.16.0.0/16 is variably subnetted, 8 subnets, 2 masks
D        172.16.2.0/24 [90/40640000] via 172.16.12.2, 01:39:20, Serial0/0/0
D EX     172.16.3.0/24 [170/40537600] via 172.16.12.2, 01:30:13, Serial0/0/0
D        172.16.23.0/24 [90/41024000] via 172.16.12.2, 01:39:20, Serial0/0/0
D        172.16.100.0/24 [90/40640000] via 172.16.12.2, 01:39:20, Serial0/0/0
D EX  192.168.20.0/24 [170/40537600] via 172.16.12.2, 01:30:13, Serial0/0/0
D EX  192.168.25.0/24 [170/40537600] via 172.16.12.2, 01:30:13, Serial0/0/0
D EX  192.168.30.0/24 [170/40537600] via 172.16.12.2, 01:30:13, Serial0/0/0
D EX  192.168.35.0/24 [170/40537600] via 172.16.12.2, 01:30:13, Serial0/0/0
D EX  192.168.40.0/24 [170/40537600] via 172.16.12.2, 01:30:13, Serial0/0/0
D     192.168.48.0/23 is a summary, 01:39:20, Null0
R1#
```

b. There are multiple ways to configure this filtering. In this step, we will configure an ACL that matches these two network. Configure the following named access list to identify the two routes to be filtered.

```
R2(config)# ip access-list standard R3-ACL
R2(config-std-nacl)# remark ACL used with the R3-FILTER route map
R2(config-std-nacl)# permit 192.168.25.0 0.0.0.255
R2(config-std-nacl)# permit 192.168.30.0 0.0.0.255
R2(config-std-nacl)# exit
R2(config)#
```

c. Configure a route map with a statement that denies based on a match with the named ACL. Then add a **permit** statement without a **match** statement. This acts as an explicit "*permit all.*"

```
R2(config)# route-map R3-FILTER deny 10
R2(config-route-map)# description RM filters R3 OSPF routes
R2(config-route-map)# match ip address R3-ACL
```

```
R2(config-route-map)# exit
R2(config)# route-map R3-FILTER permit 20
R2(config-route-map)# description RM permits all other R3 OSPF routes
R2(config-route-map)# exit
R2(config)#
```

d. Apply this route map to EIGRP by reentering the **redistribute** command using the **route-map** keyword.

```
R2(config)# router eigrp 1
R2(config-router)# redistribute ospf 1 route-map R3-FILTER metric 64 100 255
1 1500
R2(config-router)#
```

e. Verify that the two R3 networks are filtered out in the R1 routing table.

```
R1# show ip route eigrp | begin Gateway
Gateway of last resort is not set

        172.16.0.0/16 is variably subnetted, 8 subnets, 2 masks
D         172.16.2.0/24 [90/40640000] via 172.16.12.2, 00:02:20, Serial0/0/0
D EX      172.16.3.0/24 [170/40537600] via 172.16.12.2, 00:02:04, Serial0/0/0
D         172.16.23.0/24 [90/41024000] via 172.16.12.2, 00:02:20, Serial0/0/0
D         172.16.100.0/24 [90/40640000] via 172.16.12.2, 00:02:20, Serial0/0/0
D EX    192.168.20.0/24 [170/40537600] via 172.16.12.2, 00:02:04, Serial0/0/0
D EX    192.168.35.0/24 [170/40537600] via 172.16.12.2, 00:02:04, Serial0/0/0
D EX    192.168.40.0/24 [170/40537600] via 172.16.12.2, 00:02:04, Serial0/0/0
D       192.168.48.0/23 is a summary, 00:02:31, Null0
R1#
```

Notice that the192.168.25.0/24 and 192.168.30.0/24 networks are no longer in the routing table.

Step 6: Filter redistributed routes and set attributes using a route map.

The preceding step was a simple example of using a route map to filter redistributed routes.

In this step, we will filter a route from R1 to change its metric and metric type.

a. On R3, verify the routing table entry for the routes learned externally identified with the 0 E2 source entry.

```
R3# show ip route ospf | include O E2
O E2     172.16.1.0/24 [110/20] via 172.16.23.2, 00:13:55, Serial0/0/1
O E2     172.16.2.0/24 [110/20] via 172.16.23.2, 00:13:55, Serial0/0/1
O E2     172.16.12.0/24 [110/20] via 172.16.23.2, 00:13:55, Serial0/0/1
R3#
```

The 172.16.12.0 route will be configured with additional attributes.

b. Configure a prefix list identifying the route to be filtered.

```
R2(config)# ip prefix-list R1-PL permit 172.16.12.0/24
R2(config)#
```

c. Configure a route map matching the identified route in the prefix list and assign the metric cost of 25 and change the metric type to External Type 1. Then add a **permit** statement without a **match** statement acting as an explicit "*permit all.*"

```
R2(config)# route-map R1-FILTER permit 10
R2(config-route-map)# description RM filters 172.16.12.0/24
R2(config-route-map)# match ip address prefix-list R1-PL
R2(config-route-map)# set metric 25
R2(config-route-map)# set metric-type type-1
R2(config-route-map)# exit
```

```
R2(config)# route-map R1-FILTER permit 20
R2(config-route-map)# description RM permits all other R1 OSPF routes
R2(config-route-map)# exit
R2(config)#
```

d. Apply this route map to OSPF by reentering the **redistribute** command using the **route-map** keyword.

```
R2(config)# router ospf 1
R2(config-router)# redistribute eigrp 1 subnets route-map R1-FILTER
R2(config-router)# exit
R2(config)#
```

e. Verify that the two R3 networks are filtered out in the R1 routing table.

```
R3# show ip route ospf | begin Gateway
Gateway of last resort is not set

      172.16.0.0/16 is variably subnetted, 8 subnets, 2 masks
O E2    172.16.1.0/24 [110/20] via 172.16.23.2, 00:02:57, Serial0/0/1
O E2    172.16.2.0/24 [110/20] via 172.16.23.2, 00:02:57, Serial0/0/1
O E1    172.16.12.0/24 [110/1587] via 172.16.23.2, 00:02:57, Serial0/0/1
O IA    172.16.100.0/24 [110/1563] via 172.16.23.2, 00:02:57, Serial0/0/1
O       192.168.8.0/22 is a summary, 00:02:57, Null0
R3#
```

Notice that the 172.16.12.0/24 route is now a type 1 route and calculates the actual metric.

Lab 4-3 Redistribution Between EIGRP for IPv6 and OSPFv3

Topology

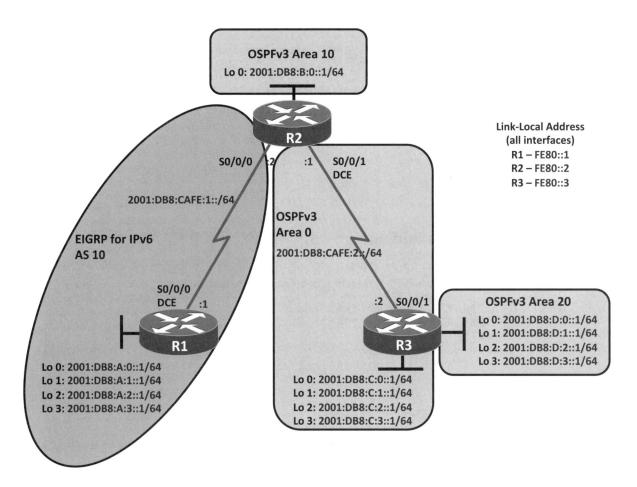

Objectives

- Review EIGRP and OSPF configuration.
- Summarize routes in EIGRP.
- Summarize in OSPF at an ABR and an ASBR.
- Redistribute into EIGRP.
- Redistribute into OSPF.

Background

Two online booksellers, Example.com and Example.net, have merged and now need a short-term solution to inter-domain routing. Since these companies provide client services to Internet users, it is essential to have minimal downtime during the transition.

Example.com is running EIGRP while Example.net is running a multi-area OSPF. Because it is imperative that the two booksellers continuously deliver Internet services, you should bridge these two routing domains without interfering with each router's path through its own routing domain to the Internet.

The CIO determines that it is preferable to keep the two protocol domains shown in the diagram during the transition period, because the network engineers on each side need to understand the other's network before deploying a long-term solution. Redistribution will be a short-term solution.

In this scenario, R1 and R2 are running EIGRP while R2 is the OSPF autonomous system border router (ASBR) consisting of areas 0, 10, and 20. You need to configure R2 to enable these two routing protocols to interact to allow full connectivity between all networks.

In this lab, R1 is running EIGRP and R3 is running multi-area OSPF. Your task is to configure redistribution on R2 to enable these two routing protocols to interact, allowing full connectivity between all networks.

Note: This lab uses Cisco 1941 routers with Cisco IOS Release 15.2 with IP Base. Depending on the router or switch model and Cisco IOS Software version, the commands available and output produced might vary from what is shown in this lab.

Required Resources

- 3 routers (Cisco IOS Release 15.2 or comparable)
- Serial and Ethernet cables

Step 1: Configure loopbacks and assign addresses.

a. Configure all loopback interfaces on the three routers in the diagram. Configure the serial interfaces with the IP addresses, bring them up, and set a DCE clock rate where appropriate.

```
R1(config-line)# interface Loopback0
R1(config-if)# ipv6 address 2001:db8:A:0::1/64
R1(config-if)# exit
R1(config)# interface Loopback1
R1(config-if)# ipv6 address 2001:db8:A:1::1/64
R1(config-if)# exit
R1(config)# interface Loopback2
R1(config-if)# ipv6 address 2001:db8:A:2::1/64
R1(config-if)# exit
R1(config)# interface Loopback3
R1(config-if)# ipv6 address 2001:db8:A:3::1/64
R1(config-if)# exit
R1(config)# interface serial 0/0/0
R1(config-if)# ipv6 address 2001:db8:cafe:1::1/64
R1(config-if)# ipv6 address fe80::1 link-local
R1(config-if)# clock rate 64000
R1(config-if)# no shutdown
R1(config-if)# exit
R1(config)#
*Oct 27 10:01:40.307: %LINEPROTO-5-UPDOWN: Line protocol on Interface
Loopback0, changed state to up
*Oct 27 10:01:40.711: %LINEPROTO-5-UPDOWN: Line protocol on Interface
Loopback1, changed state to up
*Oct 27 10:01:41.123: %LINEPROTO-5-UPDOWN: Line protocol on Interface
Loopback2, changed state to up
R1(config)#
*Oct 27 10:01:41.435: %LINEPROTO-5-UPDOWN: Line protocol on Interface
Loopback3, changed state to up
R1(config)#
*Oct 27 10:01:43.439: %LINK-3-UPDOWN: Interface Serial0/0/0, changed state to
down
R1(config)#
```

```
R1(config)#
*Oct 27 10:02:05.419: %LINK-3-UPDOWN: Interface Serial0/0/0, changed state to
up
*Oct 27 10:02:06.419: %LINEPROTO-5-UPDOWN: Line protocol on Interface
Serial0/0/0, changed state to up
R1(config)# exit
R1#


R2(config)# interface Loopback0
R2(config-if)# ipv6 address 2001:db8:B:0::1/64
R2(config-if)# exit
R2(config)#
R2(config)# interface serial 0/0/0
R2(config-if)# ipv6 address 2001:db8:cafe:1::2/64
R2(config-if)# ipv6 address fe80::2 link-local
R2(config-if)# no shutdown
R2(config-if)# exit
R2(config)#
R2(config)# interface serial 0/0/1
R2(config-if)# ipv6 address 2001:db8:cafe:2::1/64
R2(config-if)# ipv6 address fe80::2 link-local
R2(config-if)# clock rate 64000
R2(config-if)# no shutdown
R2(config-if)# exit
R2(config)#


R3(config)# interface Loopback0
R3(config-if)# ipv6 address 2001:db8:C:0::1/64
R3(config-if)# exit
R3(config)# interface Loopback1
R3(config-if)# ipv6 address 2001:db8:C:1::1/64
R3(config-if)# exit
R3(config)# interface Loopback2
R3(config-if)# ipv6 address 2001:db8:C:2::1/64
R3(config-if)# exit
R3(config)# interface Loopback3
R3(config-if)# ipv6 address 2001:db8:C:3::1/64
R3(config-if)# exit
R3(config)# interface Loopback4
R3(config-if)# ipv6 address 2001:db8:D:0::1/64
R3(config-if)# ipv6 address fe80::3 link-local
R3(config-if)# exit
R3(config)# interface Loopback5
R3(config-if)# ipv6 address 2001:db8:D:1::1/64
R3(config-if)# ipv6 address fe80::3 link-local
R3(config-if)# exit
R3(config)# interface Loopback6
R3(config-if)# ipv6 address 2001:db8:D:2::1/64
R3(config-if)# ipv6 address fe80::3 link-local
R3(config-if)# exit
R3(config)# interface Loopback7
R3(config-if)# ipv6 address 2001:db8:D:3::1/64
R3(config-if)# ipv6 address fe80::3 link-local
R3(config-if)#
R3(config)# interface serial 0/0/1
R3(config-if)# ipv6 address 2001:db8:cafe:2::2/64
```

```
R3(config-if)# ipv6 address fe80::3 link-local
R3(config-if)# clock rate 64000
R3(config-if)# no shutdown
R3(config-if)# exit
R3(config)#
```

b. Issue the **show ipv6 interface brief** command on each router and filter to include only the interface in an "up" status. Router R1 is shown as an example.

```
R1# show ipv6 interface brief | include up
Serial0/0/0              [up/up]
Loopback0                [up/up]
Loopback1                [up/up]
Loopback2                [up/up]
Loopback3                [up/up]
R1#
```

c. Verify that you can ping across the serial links when you are finished. Use the following Tcl script to check full and partial connectivity throughout this lab.

```
R1# tclsh

foreach address {
2001:db8:cafe:1::1
2001:db8:cafe:1::2
2001:db8:A:0::1
2001:db8:A:1::1
2001:db8:A:2::1
2001:db8:A:3::1
2001:db8:B:0::1
2001:db8:cafe:2::1
2001:db8:cafe:2::2
2001:db8:B:0::1
2001:db8:C:0::1
2001:db8:C:1::1
2001:db8:C:2::1
2001:db8:C:3::1
2001:db8:D:0::1
2001:db8:D:1::1
2001:db8:D:2::1
2001:db8:D:3::1
} { ping $address }
```

Which pings are successful and why?

_____

_____

_____

_____

Step 2: Configure EIGRP for IPv6.

a. Enable IPv6 unicast routing and EIGRP for IPv6 on each router. Since there are no active IPv4 addresses configured, EIGRP for IPv6 requires the configuration of a 32-bit router ID. Use the **router-id** command to configure the router ID in the router configuration mode.

Note: Prior to IOS 15.2 the EIGRP IPv6 routing process is shut down by default and the no shutdown router configuration mode command is required to enable the routing process. Although not required with the IOS used in creating this lab, an example of the **no shutdown** command is shown for router R1.

Issue the **ipv6 eigrp 1** command on the interfaces that participate in the EIGRP routing process. EIGRP for IPv6 does not use the **network** command. IPv6 prefixes are enabled on the interface. Similar to EIGRP for IPv4, the AS number must match the neighbor's configuration for the router to form an adjacency.

```
R1(config)# ipv6 unicast-routing
R1(config)# ipv6 router eigrp 1
R1(config-rtr)# eigrp router-id 1.1.1.1
R1(config-rtr)# no shutdown
R1(config-rtr)# exit
R1(config)# interface range lo 0 - 3
R1(config-if-range)# ipv6 eigrp 1
R1(config-if-range)# exit
R1(config)# interface s0/0/0
R1(config-if)# ipv6 eigrp 1
R1(config-if)#


R2(config)# ipv6 unicast-routing
R2(config)# ipv6 router eigrp 1
R2(config-rtr)# eigrp router-id 2.2.2.2
R2(config-rtr)# no shutdown
R2(config-rtr)# exit
R2(config)#
R2(config)# interface lo 0
R2(config-if)# ipv6 eigrp 1
R2(config-if)# exit
R2(config)#
R2(config)# interface s0/0/0
R2(config-if)# ipv6 eigrp 1
R2(config-if)# exit
R2(config)#
*Aug 26 09:45:14.347: %DUAL-5-NBRCHANGE: EIGRP-IPv6 1: Neighbor FE80::1
(Serial0/0/0) is up: new adjacency
R2(config)#
```

b. Verify the EIGRP configuration using the **show ipv6 eigrp neighbors** and **show ipv6 route eigrp** commands on R2.

```
R2# show ipv6 eigrp neighbors
EIGRP-IPv6 Neighbors for AS(1)
H   Address                 Interface       Hold Uptime   SRTT   RTO  Q   Seq
                                            (sec)         (ms)        Cnt Num
0   Link-local address:     Se0/0/0           12 00:32:18 1297   5000  0   3
    FE80::1
R2#
R2# show ipv6 route eigrp

<Output omitted>

D   2001:DB8:A::/64 [90/2297856]
     via FE80::1, Serial0/0/0
D   2001:DB8:A:1::/64 [90/2297856]
     via FE80::1, Serial0/0/0
```

```
D    2001:DB8:A:2::/64 [90/2297856]
        via FE80::1, Serial0/0/0
D    2001:DB8:A:3::/64 [90/2297856]
        via FE80::1, Serial0/0/0
R2#
```

c. Verify that R2 can reach all of the networks in the EIGRP for the IPv6 routing domain using the following Tcl script.

```
R1# tclsh

foreach address {
2001:db8:cafe:1::1
2001:db8:cafe:1::2
2001:db8:A:0::1
2001:db8:A:1::1
2001:db8:A:2::1
2001:db8:A:3::1
} { ping $address }
```

All pings should be successful. Troubleshoot if necessary.

Step 3: Manually summarize with EIGRP for IPv6.

To make routing updates more efficient and ultimately reduce the size of routing tables, contiguous EIGRP routes can be summarized out an interface by using the **ipv6 summary-address eigrp** *as network mask* interface configuration command.

a. On R1, summarize the loopback interface networks.

```
R1(config)# interface s0/0/0
R1(config-if)# ipv6 summary-address eigrp 1 2001:db8:A::/62
R1(config-if)#
*Oct 27 11:05:33.019: %DUAL-5-NBRCHANGE: EIGRP-IPv6 1: Neighbor FE80::2
(Serial0/0/0) is resync: summary configured
R1(config-if)#
```

b. Verify the routing table of R2 using the **show ipv6 route eigrp** command.

```
R2# show ipv6 route eigrp

<Output omitted>

D    2001:DB8:A::/62 [90/2297856]
        via FE80::1, Serial0/0/0
R2#
```

c. Verify that R2 can still reach all of the networks in the EIGRP for IPv6 routing domain using the following Tcl script.

```
R1# tclsh

foreach address {
2001:db8:cafe:1::1
2001:db8:cafe:1::2
2001:db8:A:0::1
2001:db8:A:1::1
2001:db8:A:2::1
```

```
2001:db8:A:3::1
} { ping $address }
```

All pings should be successful. Troubleshoot if necessary.

Step 4: Configure OSPFv3 address family.

OSPFv3 with the address family (AF) unifies OSPF configuration for both IPv4 and IPv6. OSPFv3 with address families also combines neighbor tables and the LSDB under a single OSPF process. OSPFv3 messages are sent over IPv6 and therefore require that IPv6 routing is enabled and that the interface has a link-local IPv6 address. This is the requirement even if only the IPv4 AF is configured.

a. On R2, configure OSPFv3 address family and router ID, and enable the OSPFv3 on the interface using the **ospfv3 1 ipv6 area** command.

```
R2(config)# ipv6 unicast-routing
R2(config)#
R2(config)# router ospfv3 1
R2(config-router)# address-family ipv6 unicast
*Aug 26 10:40:35.203: %OSPFv3-4-NORTRID: Process OSPFv3-1-IPv6 could not pick
a router-id, please configure manually
R2(config-router-af)# router-id 2.2.2.2
R2(config-router-af)# exit-address-family
R2(config-router)# exit
R2(config)#
R2(config)# interface Loopback0
R2(config-if)# ospfv3 1 ipv6 area 10
R2(config-if)# exit
R2(config)#
R2(config)# interface serial 0/0/1
R2(config-if)# ospfv3 1 ipv6 area 0
R2(config-if)# exit
R2(config)#
```

b. On R3, configure OSPFv3 address family and router ID, and enable the OSPFv3 on the interface using the **ospfv3 1 ipv6 area** command.

```
R3(config)# router ospfv3 1
R3(config-router)# address-family ipv6 unicast
R3(config-router-af)#
*Jul 28 03:10:48.395: %OSPFv3-4-NORTRID: Process OSPFv3-1-IPv6 could not pick
a router-id, please configure manually
R3(config-router-af)# router-id 3.3.3.3
R3(config-router-af)# exit-address-family
R3(config-router)# exit
R3(config)#
R3(config)# interface range lo 0 - 3
R3(config-if-range)# ospfv3 1 ipv6 area 0
R3(config-if-range)# exit
R3(config)#
R3(config)# interface range lo 4 - 7
R3(config-if-range)# ospfv3 1 ipv6 area 20
R3(config-if-range)# exit
R3(config)#
R3(config-if)# interface serial 0/0/1
R3(config-if)# ospfv3 1 ipv6 area 0
```

```
R3(config-if)# exit
R3(config)#
*Jul 28 03:20:29.267: %OSPFv3-5-ADJCHG: Process 1, IPv6, Nbr 2.2.2.2 on
Serial0/0/1 from LOADING to FULL, Loading Done
R3(config)#
R3(config)#
```

c. Verify that your adjacencies come up with the **show ipv6 ospf neighbor** command, and make sure that you have routes from OSPF populating the R2 routing table using the **show ipv6 route ospf** command.

```
R2# show ipv6 ospf neighbor

            OSPFv3 Router with ID (2.2.2.2) (Process ID 1)

Neighbor ID     Pri   State          Dead Time   Interface ID   Interface
3.3.3.3           0   FULL/  -       00:00:31    6              Serial0/0/1
R2#
R2# show ipv6 route ospf

<Output omitted>

O   2001:DB8:C::1/128 [110/64]
      via FE80::3, Serial0/0/1
O   2001:DB8:C:1::1/128 [110/64]
      via FE80::3, Serial0/0/1
O   2001:DB8:C:2::1/128 [110/64]
      via FE80::3, Serial0/0/1
O   2001:DB8:C:3::1/128 [110/64]
      via FE80::3, Serial0/0/1
OI  2001:DB8:D::1/128 [110/64]
      via FE80::3, Serial0/0/1
OI  2001:DB8:D:1::1/128 [110/64]
      via FE80::3, Serial0/0/1
OI  2001:DB8:D:2::1/128 [110/64]
      via FE80::3, Serial0/0/1
OI  2001:DB8:D:3::1/128 [110/64]
      via FE80::3, Serial0/0/1
R2#
```

d. Verify the OSPF IPv6 routing table of R3.

```
R3# sho ipv6 route ospf

<Output omitted>

OI  2001:DB8:B::1/128 [110/64]
      via FE80::2, Serial0/0/1
R3#
```

e. Verify that R2 and R3 can reach all of the networks in the OSPFv3 routing domain using the following Tcl script.

```
R3# tclsh

foreach address {
2001:db8:B:0::1
2001:db8:cafe:2::1
```

```
2001:db8:cafe:2::2
2001:db8:B:0::1
2001:db8:C:0::1
2001:db8:C:1::1
2001:db8:C:2::1
2001:db8:C:3::1
2001:db8:D:0::1
2001:db8:D:1::1
2001:db8:D:2::1
2001:db8:D:3::1
} { ping $address }
```

All pings should be successful. Troubleshoot if necessary.

Step 5: Configure mutual redistribution between OSPFv3 and EIGRP for IPv6.

Notice that R2 is the only router with knowledge of all routes (EIGRP for IPv6 and OSPFv3) in the topology at this point, because it is involved with both routing protocols. Next you will redistribute the EIGRP for IPv6 routes into OSPFv3 and the OSPFv3 routes into EIGRP for IPv6.

a. To redistribute the EIGRP for IPv6 routes into OSPFv3, on R2 issue the **redistribute eigrp 1 include-connected** command.

```
R2(config)# router ospfv3 1
R2(config-router)# address-family ipv6 unicast
R2(config-router-af)# redistribute eigrp 1 include-connected
R2(config-router-af)# exit
R2(config-router)# exit
```

A default seed metric is not required for OSPFv3. Redistributed routes are assigned a metric of 20 by default.

b. To redistribute the OSPFv3 routes into EIGRP for IPv6, on R2 issue the **redistribute ospf 1 metric 10000 100 255 1 1500** command. Unlike OSPFv3, EIGRP for IPv6 must specify the metric associated to the redistributed routes. The command tells EIGRP to redistribute OSPF process 1 with these metrics: bandwidth of 10000, delay of 100, reliability of 255/255, load of 1/255, and an MTU of 1500.

```
R2(config)# ipv6 router eigrp 1
R2(config-rtr)# redistribute ospf 1 metric 1500 100 255 1 1500 include-connected
R2(config-rtr)# exit
R2(config)#
```

c. Issue the **show ipv6 protocols** command on the redistributing router, R2. Compare your output with the following output.

```
R2# show ipv6 protocols
IPv6 Routing Protocol is "connected"
IPv6 Routing Protocol is "application"
IPv6 Routing Protocol is "ND"
IPv6 Routing Protocol is "eigrp 1"
EIGRP-IPv6 Protocol for AS(1)
  Metric weight K1=1, K2=0, K3=1, K4=0, K5=0
  NSF-aware route hold timer is 240
  Router-ID: 2.2.2.2
  Topology : 0 (base)
    Active Timer: 3 min
```

```
        Distance: internal 90 external 170
        Maximum path: 16
        Maximum hopcount 100
        Maximum metric variance 1

    Interfaces:
      Loopback0
      Serial0/0/0
    Redistribution:
      Redistributing protocol ospf 1 with metric 1500 100 255 1 1500 (internal,
external 1 & 2, nssa-external 1 & 2) include-connected
IPv6 Routing Protocol is "ospf 1"
    Router ID 2.2.2.2
    Area border and autonomous system boundary router
    Number of areas: 2 normal, 0 stub, 0 nssa
    Interfaces (Area 0):
      Serial0/0/1
    Interfaces (Area 10):
      Loopback0
    Redistribution:
      Redistributing protocol eigrp 1 include-connected
R2#
```

d. Display the routing table on R1 to verify the redistributed routes. Redistributed OSPFv3 routes display on R1 as EX, which means that they are external EIGRP for IPv6 routes.

```
R1# show ipv6 route eigrp

<Output omitted>

D    2001:DB8:A::/61 [5/128256]
     via Null0, directly connected
D    2001:DB8:B::/64 [90/2297856]
     via FE80::2, Serial0/0/0
EX   2001:DB8:C::1/128 [170/2244096]
     via FE80::2, Serial0/0/0
EX   2001:DB8:C:1::1/128 [170/2244096]
     via FE80::2, Serial0/0/0
EX   2001:DB8:C:2::1/128 [170/2244096]
     via FE80::2, Serial0/0/0
EX   2001:DB8:C:3::1/128 [170/2244096]
     via FE80::2, Serial0/0/0
EX   2001:DB8:D::1/128 [170/2244096]
     via FE80::2, Serial0/0/0
EX   2001:DB8:D:1::1/128 [170/2244096]
     via FE80::2, Serial0/0/0
EX   2001:DB8:D:2::1/128 [170/2244096]
     via FE80::2, Serial0/0/0
EX   2001:DB8:D:3::1/128 [170/2244096]
     via FE80::2, Serial0/0/0
EX   2001:DB8:CAFE:2::/64 [170/2244096]
     via FE80::2, Serial0/0/0
R1#
```

e. Display the routing table on R3 to see the redistributed routes. Redistributed EIGRP routes are tagged in the R3 routing table as O E2, which means that they are OSPF external type 2. Type 2 is the default OSPF external type.

```
R3# show ipv6 route ospf

<Output omitted>

OE2 2001:DB8:A::/61 [110/20]
     via FE80::2, Serial0/0/1
OI  2001:DB8:B::1/128 [110/64]
     via FE80::2, Serial0/0/1
OE2 2001:DB8:CAFE:1::/64 [110/20]
     via FE80::2, Serial0/0/1
R3#
```

f. Verify full connectivity with the following Tcl script:

```
R1# tclsh


foreach address {
2001:db8:cafe:1::1
2001:db8:cafe:1::2
2001:db8:A:0::1
2001:db8:A:1::1
2001:db8:A:2::1
2001:db8:A:3::1
2001:db8:B:0::1
2001:db8:cafe:2::1
2001:db8:cafe:2::2
2001:db8:B:0::1
2001:db8:C:0::1
2001:db8:C:1::1
2001:db8:C:2::1
2001:db8:C:3::1
2001:db8:D:0::1
2001:db8:D:1::1
2001:db8:D:2::1
2001:db8:D:3::1
} { ping $address }
```

All pings should now be successful. Troubleshoot as necessary.

Chapter 5: Path Control Implementation

Lab 5-1 Configure and Verify Path Control Using PBR

Topology

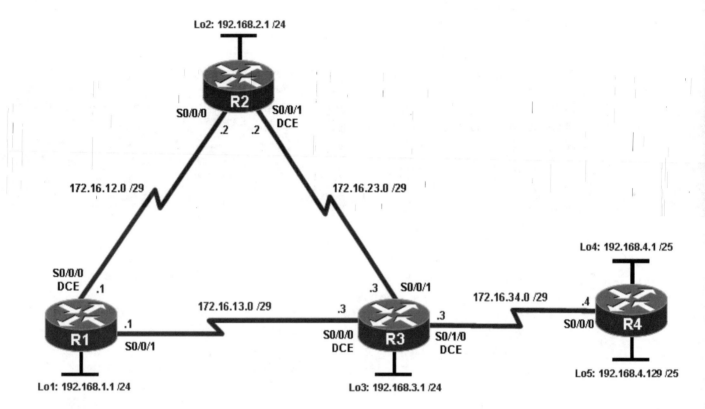

Objectives

- Configure and verify policy-based routing.
- Select the required tools and commands to configure policy-based routing operations.
- Verify the configuration and operation by using the proper show and debug commands.

Background

You want to experiment with policy-based routing (PBR) to see how it is implemented and to study how it could be of value to your organization. To this end, you have interconnected and configured a test network with four routers. All routers are exchanging routing information using EIGRP.

Note: This lab uses Cisco 1941 routers with Cisco IOS Release 15.2 with IP Base. Depending on the router or switch model and Cisco IOS Software version, the commands available and output produced might vary from what is shown in this lab.

Required Resources

- 4 routers (Cisco IOS Release 15.2 or comparable)
- Serial and Ethernet cables

Step 1: Configure loopbacks and assign addresses.

a. Cable the network as shown in the topology diagram. Erase the startup configuration, and reload each router to clear previous configurations.

b. Using the addressing scheme in the diagram, create the loopback interfaces and apply IP addresses to these and the serial interfaces on R1, R2, R3, and R4. On the serial interfaces connecting R1 to R3 and R3 to R4, specify the bandwidth as 64 Kb/s and set a clock rate on the DCE using the **clock rate 64000** command. On the serial interfaces connecting R1 to R2 and R2 to R3, specify the bandwidth as 128 Kb/s and set a clock rate on the DCE using the **clock rate 128000** command.

You can copy and paste the following configurations into your routers to begin.

Note: Depending on the router model, interfaces might be numbered differently than those listed. You might need to alter them accordingly.

Router R1

```
hostname R1
!
interface Lo1
 description R1 LAN
 ip address 192.168.1.1 255.255.255.0
!
interface Serial0/0/0
 description R1 --> R2
 ip address 172.16.12.1 255.255.255.248
 clock rate 128000
 bandwidth 128
 no shutdown
!
interface Serial0/0/1
 description R1 --> R3
 ip address 172.16.13.1 255.255.255.248
 bandwidth 64
 no shutdown
!
end
```

Router R2

```
hostname R2
!
interface Lo2
 description R2 LAN
 ip address 192.168.2.1 255.255.255.0
!
interface Serial0/0/0
 description R2 --> R1
 ip address 172.16.12.2 255.255.255.248
 bandwidth 128
 no shutdown

interface Serial0/0/1
 description R2 --> R3
 ip address 172.16.23.2 255.255.255.248
 clock rate 128000
 bandwidth 128
 no shutdown
```

```
!
end
```

Router R3

```
hostname R3
!
interface Lo3
 description R3 LAN
 ip address 192.168.3.1 255.255.255.0
!
interface Serial0/0/0
 description R3 --> R1
 ip address 172.16.13.3 255.255.255.248
 clock rate 64000
 bandwidth 64
 no shutdown
!
interface Serial0/0/1
 description R3 --> R2
 ip address 172.16.23.3 255.255.255.248
 bandwidth 128
 no shutdown
!
interface Serial0/1/0
 description R3 --> R4
 ip address 172.16.34.3 255.255.255.248
 clock rate 64000
 bandwidth 64
 no shutdown
!
end
```

Router R4

```
hostname R4
!
interface Lo4
 description R4 LAN A
 ip address 192.168.4.1 255.255.255.128
!
interface Lo5
 description R4 LAN B
 ip address 192.168.4.129 255.255.255.128
!
interface Serial0/0/0
 description R4 --> R3
 ip address 172.16.34.4 255.255.255.248
 bandwidth 64
 no shutdown
!
end
```

c.   Verify the configuration with the **show ip interface brief**, **show protocols,** and **show interfaces description** commands. The output from router R3 is shown here as an example.

```
R3# show ip interface brief | include up
Serial0/0/0            172.16.13.3     YES manual up                   up
```

```
Serial0/0/1                     172.16.23.3     YES manual up                    up
Serial0/1/0                     172.16.34.3     YES manual up                    up
Loopback3                       192.168.3.1     YES manual up                    up
R3#
R3# show protocols
Global values:
  Internet Protocol routing is enabled
Embedded-Service-Engine0/0 is administratively down, line protocol is down
GigabitEthernet0/0 is administratively down, line protocol is down
GigabitEthernet0/1 is administratively down, line protocol is down
Serial0/0/0 is up, line protocol is up
  Internet address is 172.16.13.3/29
Serial0/0/1 is up, line protocol is up
  Internet address is 172.16.23.3/29
Serial0/1/0 is up, line protocol is up
  Internet address is 172.16.34.3/29
Serial0/1/1 is administratively down, line protocol is down
Loopback3 is up, line protocol is up
  Internet address is 192.168.3.1/24
R3#
R3# show interfaces description | include up
Se0/0/0                         up              up      R3 --> R1
Se0/0/1                         up              up      R3 --> R2
Se0/1/0                         up              up      R3 --> R4
Lo3                             up              up      R3 LAN
R3#
```

Step 2: Configure basic EIGRP.

a. Implement EIGRP AS 1 over the serial and loopback interfaces as you have configured it for the other EIGRP labs.

b. Advertise networks 172.16.12.0/29, 172.16.13.0/29, 172.16.23.0/29, 172.16.34.0/29, 192.168.1.0/24, 192.168.2.0/24, 192.168.3.0/24, and 192.168.4.0/24 from their respective routers.

You can copy and paste the following configurations into your routers.

Router R1

```
router eigrp 1
 network 192.168.1.0
 network 172.16.12.0 0.0.0.7
 network 172.16.13.0 0.0.0.7
 no auto-summary
```

Router R2

```
router eigrp 1
 network 192.168.2.0
 network 172.16.12.0 0.0.0.7
 network 172.16.23.0 0.0.0.7
 no auto-summary
```

Router R3

```
router eigrp 1
 network 192.168.3.0
 network 172.16.13.0 0.0.0.7
 network 172.16.23.0 0.0.0.7
```

```
network 172.16.34.0 0.0.0.7
no auto-summary
```

Router R4

```
router eigrp 1
network 192.168.4.0
network 172.16.34.0 0.0.0.7
no auto-summary
```

You should see EIGRP neighbor relationship messages being generated.

Step 3: Verify EIGRP connectivity.

a. Verify the configuration by using the **show ip eigrp neighbors** command to check which routers have EIGRP adjacencies.

```
R1# show ip eigrp neighbors
EIGRP-IPv4 Neighbors for AS(1)
H   Address              Interface        Hold Uptime   SRTT   RTO  Q   Seq
                                          (sec)         (ms)        Cnt Num
1   172.16.13.3          Se0/0/1           10 00:01:55   27   2340  0   9
0   172.16.12.2          Se0/0/0           13 00:02:07    8   1170  0   11
R1#
```

```
R2# show ip eigrp neighbors
EIGRP-IPv4 Neighbors for AS(1)
H   Address              Interface        Hold Uptime   SRTT   RTO  Q   Seq
                                          (sec)         (ms)        Cnt Num
1   172.16.23.3          Se0/0/1           12 00:02:15   12   1170  0   10
0   172.16.12.1          Se0/0/0           11 00:02:27    9   1170  0   13
R2#
```

```
R3# show ip eigrp neighbors
EIGRP-IPv4 Neighbors for AS(1)
H   Address              Interface        Hold Uptime   SRTT   RTO  Q   Seq
                                          (sec)         (ms)        Cnt Num
2   172.16.34.4          Se0/1/0           12 00:02:14   44   2340  0   3
1   172.16.23.2          Se0/0/1           11 00:02:23   10   1170  0   10
0   172.16.13.1          Se0/0/0           10 00:02:23 1031   5000  0   12
R3#
R4# show ip eigrp neighbors
EIGRP-IPv4 Neighbors for AS(1)
H   Address              Interface        Hold Uptime   SRTT   RTO  Q   Seq
                                          (sec)         (ms)        Cnt Num
0   172.16.34.3          Se0/0/0           10 00:02:22   37   2340  0   11

R4#
```

Did you receive the output you expected?

---

b. Run the following Tcl script on all routers to verify full connectivity.

```
R1# tclsh

foreach address {
172.16.12.1
172.16.12.2
```

```
172.16.13.1
172.16.13.3
172.16.23.2
172.16.23.3
172.16.34.3
172.16.34.4
192.168.1.1
192.168.2.1
192.168.3.1
192.168.4.1
192.168.4.129
} { ping $address }
```

You should get ICMP echo replies for every address pinged. Make sure to run the Tcl script on each router.

Step 4: Verify the current path.

Before you configure PBR, verify the routing table on R1.

a. On R1, use the **show ip route** command. Notice the next-hop IP address for all networks discovered by EIGRP.

```
R1# show ip route | begin Gateway
Gateway of last resort is not set

      172.16.0.0/16 is variably subnetted, 6 subnets, 2 masks
C        172.16.12.0/29 is directly connected, Serial0/0/0
L        172.16.12.1/32 is directly connected, Serial0/0/0
C        172.16.13.0/29 is directly connected, Serial0/0/1
L        172.16.13.1/32 is directly connected, Serial0/0/1
D        172.16.23.0/29 [90/21024000] via 172.16.12.2, 00:07:22, Serial0/0/0
D        172.16.34.0/29 [90/41024000] via 172.16.13.3, 00:07:22, Serial0/0/1
      192.168.1.0/24 is variably subnetted, 2 subnets, 2 masks
C        192.168.1.0/24 is directly connected, Loopback1
L        192.168.1.1/32 is directly connected, Loopback1
D     192.168.2.0/24 [90/20640000] via 172.16.12.2, 00:07:22, Serial0/0/0
D     192.168.3.0/24 [90/21152000] via 172.16.12.2, 00:07:22, Serial0/0/0
      192.168.4.0/25 is subnetted, 2 subnets
D        192.168.4.0 [90/41152000] via 172.16.13.3, 00:07:14, Serial0/0/1
D        192.168.4.128 [90/41152000] via 172.16.13.3, 00:07:14, Serial0/0/1
R1#
```

b. On R4, use the **traceroute** command to the R1 LAN address and source the ICMP packet from R4 LAN A and LAN B.

Note: You can specify the source as the interface address (for example 192.168.4.1) or the interface designator (for example, Fa0/0).

```
R4# traceroute 192.168.1.1 source 192.168.4.1
Type escape sequence to abort.
Tracing the route to 192.168.1.1
VRF info: (vrf in name/id, vrf out name/id)
  1 172.16.34.3 12 msec 12 msec 16 msec
  2 172.16.23.2 20 msec 20 msec 20 msec
  3 172.16.12.1 24 msec *  24 msec
R4#
R4# traceroute 192.168.1.1 source 192.168.4.129
Type escape sequence to abort.
```

```
Tracing the route to 192.168.1.1
VRF info: (vrf in name/id, vrf out name/id)
  1 172.16.34.3 12 msec 16 msec 12 msec
  2 172.16.23.2 28 msec 20 msec 16 msec
  3 172.16.12.1 24 msec *  24 msec
R4#
```

Notice that the path taken for the packets sourced from the R4 LANs are going through R3 --> R2 --> R1.

Why are the R4 interfaces not using the R3 --> R1 path?

_____

_____

_____

c. On R3, use the **show ip route** command and note that the preferred route from R3 to R1 LAN 192.168.1.0/24 is via R2 using the R3 exit interface S0/0/1.

```
R3# show ip route | begin Gateway
Gateway of last resort is not set

      172.16.0.0/16 is variably subnetted, 7 subnets, 2 masks
D        172.16.12.0/29 [90/21024000] via 172.16.23.2, 00:10:54, Serial0/0/1
C        172.16.13.0/29 is directly connected, Serial0/0/0
L        172.16.13.3/32 is directly connected, Serial0/0/0
C        172.16.23.0/29 is directly connected, Serial0/0/1
L        172.16.23.3/32 is directly connected, Serial0/0/1
C        172.16.34.0/29 is directly connected, Serial0/1/0
L        172.16.34.3/32 is directly connected, Serial0/1/0
D     192.168.1.0/24 [90/21152000] via 172.16.23.2, 00:10:54, Serial0/0/1
D        192.168.2.0/24 [90/20640000] via 172.16.23.2, 00:10:54, Serial0/0/1
      192.168.3.0/24 is variably subnetted, 2 subnets, 2 masks
C        192.168.3.0/24 is directly connected, Loopback3
L        192.168.3.1/32 is directly connected, Loopback3
      192.168.4.0/25 is subnetted, 2 subnets
D        192.168.4.0 [90/40640000] via 172.16.34.4, 00:10:47, Serial0/1/0
D        192.168.4.128 [90/40640000] via 172.16.34.4, 00:10:47, Serial0/1/0
R3#
```

d. On R3, use the **show interfaces serial 0/0/0** and **show interfaces s0/0/1** commands.

```
R3# show interfaces serial0/0/0
Serial0/0/0 is up, line protocol is up
  Hardware is WIC MBRD Serial
  Description: R3 --> R1
  Internet address is 172.16.13.3/29
  MTU 1500 bytes, BW 64 Kbit/sec, DLY 20000 usec,
     reliability 255/255, txload 1/255, rxload 1/255
  Encapsulation HDLC, loopback not set
  Keepalive set (10 sec)
  Last input 00:00:01, output 00:00:00, output hang never
  Last clearing of "show interface" counters never
  Input queue: 0/75/0/0 (size/max/drops/flushes); Total output drops: 0
  Queueing strategy: fifo
  Output queue: 0/40 (size/max)
  5 minute input rate 0 bits/sec, 0 packets/sec
  5 minute output rate 0 bits/sec, 0 packets/sec
     399 packets input, 29561 bytes, 0 no buffer
```

```
      Received 186 broadcasts (0 IP multicasts)
      0 runts, 0 giants, 0 throttles
      0 input errors, 0 CRC, 0 frame, 0 overrun, 0 ignored, 0 abort
      393 packets output, 29567 bytes, 0 underruns
      0 output errors, 0 collisions, 3 interface resets
      0 unknown protocol drops
      0 output buffer failures, 0 output buffers swapped out
      0 carrier transitions
      DCD=up  DSR=up  DTR=up  RTS=up  CTS=up

R3# show interfaces serial0/0/0 | include BW
  MTU 1500 bytes, BW 64 Kbit/sec, DLY 20000 usec,
R3# show interfaces serial0/0/1 | include BW
  MTU 1500 bytes, BW 128 Kbit/sec, DLY 20000 usec,
R3#
```

Notice that the bandwidth of the serial link between R3 and R1 (S0/0/0) is set to 64 Kb/s, while the bandwidth of the serial link between R3 and R2 (S0/0/1) is set to 128 Kb/s.

e. Confirm that R3 has a valid route to reach R1 from its serial 0/0/0 interface using the **show ip eigrp topology 192.168.1.0** command.

```
R3# show ip eigrp topology 192.168.1.0
EIGRP-IPv4 Topology Entry for AS(1)/ID(192.168.3.1) for 192.168.1.0/24
   State is Passive, Query origin flag is 1, 1 Successor(s), FD is 21152000
   Descriptor Blocks:
   172.16.23.2 (Serial0/0/1), from 172.16.23.2, Send flag is 0x0
      Composite metric is (21152000/20640000), route is Internal
      Vector metric:
        Minimum bandwidth is 128 Kbit
        Total delay is 45000 microseconds
        Reliability is 255/255
        Load is 1/255
        Minimum MTU is 1500
        Hop count is 2
        Originating router is 192.168.1.1
   172.16.13.1 (Serial0/0/0), from 172.16.13.1, Send flag is 0x0
      Composite metric is (40640000/128256), route is Internal
      Vector metric:
        Minimum bandwidth is 64 Kbit
        Total delay is 25000 microseconds
        Reliability is 255/255
        Load is 1/255
        Minimum MTU is 1500
        Hop count is 1
        Originating router is 192.168.1.1
R3#
```

As indicated, R4 has two routes to reach 192.168.1.0. However, the metric for the route to R1 (172.16.13.1) is much higher (40640000) than the metric of the route to R2 (21152000), making the route through R2 the successor route.

Step 5: Configure PBR to provide path control.

Now you will deploy source-based IP routing by using PBR. You will change a default IP routing decision based on the EIGRP-acquired routing information for selected IP source-to-destination flows and apply a different next-hop router.

Recall that routers normally forward packets to destination addresses based on information in their routing table. By using PBR, you can implement policies that selectively cause packets to take different paths based on source address, protocol type, or application type. Therefore, PBR overrides the router's normal routing behavior.

Configuring PBR involves configuring a route map with **match** and **set** commands and then applying the route map to the interface.

The steps required to implement path control include the following:

- Choose the path control tool to use. Path control tools manipulate or bypass the IP routing table. For PBR, **route-map** commands are used.
- Implement the traffic-matching configuration, specifying which traffic will be manipulated. The **match** commands are used within route maps.
- Define the action for the matched traffic using **set** commands within route maps.
- Apply the route map to incoming traffic.

As a test, you will configure the following policy on router R3:

- All traffic sourced from R4 LAN A must take the R3 --> R2 --> R1 path.
- All traffic sourced from R4 LAN B must take the R3 --> R1 path.

a. On router R3, create a standard access list called **PBR-ACL** to identify the R4 LAN B network.

```
R3(config)# ip access-list standard PBR-ACL
R3(config-std-nacl)# remark ACL matches R4 LAN B traffic
R3(config-std-nacl)# permit 192.168.4.128 0.0.0.127
R3(config-std-nacl)# exit
R3(config)#
```

b. Create a route map called **R3-to-R1** that matches PBR-ACL and sets the next-hop interface to the R1 serial 0/0/1 interface.

```
R3(config)# route-map R3-to-R1 permit
R3(config-route-map)# description RM to forward LAN B traffic to R1
R3(config-route-map)# match ip address PBR-ACL
R3(config-route-map)# set ip next-hop 172.16.13.1
R3(config-route-map)# exit
R3(config)#
```

c. Apply the R3-to-R1 route map to the serial interface on R3 that receives the traffic from R4. Use the **ip policy route-map** command on interface S0/1/0.

```
R3(config)# interface s0/1/0
R3(config-if)# ip policy route-map R3-to-R1
R3(config-if)# end
R3#
```

d. On R3, display the policy and matches using the **show route-map** command.

```
R3# show route-map
route-map R3-to-R1, permit, sequence 10
  Match clauses:
    ip address (access-lists): PBR-ACL
  Set clauses:
    ip next-hop 172.16.13.1
  Policy routing matches: 0 packets, 0 bytes
R3#
```

Note: There are currently no matches because no packets matching the ACL have passed through R3 S0/1/0.

Step 6: Test the policy.

Now you are ready to test the policy configured on R3. Enable the **debug ip policy** command on R3 so that you can observe the policy decision-making in action. To help filter the traffic, first create a standard ACL that identifies all traffic from the R4 LANs.

a. On R3, create a standard ACL that identifies all of the R4 LANs.

```
R3# conf t
Enter configuration commands, one per line.  End with CNTL/Z.
R3(config)# access-list 1 permit 192.168.4.0 0.0.0.255
R3(config)# exit
```

b. Enable PBR debugging only for traffic that matches the R4 LANs.

```
R3# debug ip policy ?
  <1-199>  Access list
  dynamic  dynamic PBR
  <cr>

R3# debug ip policy 1
Policy routing debugging is on for access list 1
```

c. Test the policy from R4 with the **traceroute** command, using R4 LAN A as the source network.

```
R4# traceroute 192.168.1.1 source 192.168.4.1

Type escape sequence to abort.
Tracing the route to 192.168.1.1

  1 172.16.34.3 0 msec 0 msec 4 msec
  2 172.16.23.2 0 msec 0 msec 4 msec
  3 172.16.12.1 4 msec 0 msec *
```

Notice the path taken for the packet sourced from R4 LAN A is still going through R3 --> R2 --> R1.

As the traceroute was being executed, router R3 should be generating the following debug output.

```
R3#
Jan 10 10:49:48.411: IP: s=192.168.4.1 (Serial0/1/0), d=192.168.1.1, len 28,
policy rejected -- normal forwarding
Jan 10 10:49:48.427: IP: s=192.168.4.1 (Serial0/1/0), d=192.168.1.1, len 28,
policy rejected -- normal forwarding
Jan 10 10:49:48.439: IP: s=192.168.4.1 (Serial0/1/0), d=192.168.1.1, len 28,
policy rejected -- normal forwarding
```

```
Jan 10 10:49:48.451: IP: s=192.168.4.1 (Serial0/1/0), d=192.168.1.1, len 28,
FIB policy rejected(no match) - normal forwarding
Jan 10 10:49:48.471: IP: s=192.168.4.1 (Serial0/1/0), d=192.168.1.1, len 28,
FIB policy rejected(no match) - normal forwarding
Jan 10 10:49:48.491: IP: s=192.168.4.1 (Serial0/1/0), d=192.168.1.1, len 28,
FIB policy rejected(no match) - normal forwarding
Jan 10 10:49:48.511: IP: s=192.168.4.1 (Serial0/1/0), d=192.168.1.1, len 28,
FIB policy rejected(no match) - normal forwarding
Jan 10 10:49:48.539: IP: s=192.168.4.1 (Serial0/1/0), d=192.168.1.1, len 28,
FIB policy rejected(no match) - normal forwarding
Jan 10 10:49:51.539: IP: s=192.168.4.1 (Serial0/1/0), d=192.168.1.1, len 28,
FIB policy rejected(no match) - normal forwarding
R3#
```

Why is the traceroute traffic not using the R3 --> R1 path as specified in the R3-to-R1 policy?

_____

_____

d. Test the policy from R4 with the **traceroute** command, using R4 LAN B as the source network.

```
R4# traceroute 192.168.1.1 source 192.168.4.129

Type escape sequence to abort.
Tracing the route to 192.168.1.1

  1 172.16.34.3 12 msec 12 msec 16 msec
  2 172.16.13.1 28 msec 28 msec *
```

Now the path taken for the packet sourced from R4 LAN B is R3 --> R1, as expected.

The debug output on R3 also confirms that the traffic meets the criteria of the R3-to-R1 policy.

```
R3#
R3#
Jan 10 10:50:04.283: IP: s=192.168.4.129 (Serial0/1/0), d=192.168.1.1, len
28, policy match
Jan 10 10:50:04.283: IP: route map R3-to-R1, item 10, permit
Jan 10 10:50:04.283: IP: s=192.168.4.129 (Serial0/1/0), d=192.168.1.1
(Serial0/0/0), len 28, policy routed
Jan 10 10:50:04.283: IP: Serial0/1/0 to Serial0/0/0 172.16.13.1
Jan 10 10:50:04.295: IP: s=192.168.4.129 (Serial0/1/0), d=192.168.1.1, len
28, policy match
Jan 10 10:50:04.295: IP: route map R3-to-R1, item 10, permit
Jan 10 10:50:04.295: IP: s=192.168.4.129 (Serial0/1/0), d=192.168.1.1
(Serial0/0/0), len 28, policy routed
Jan 10 10:50:04.295: IP: Serial0/1/0 to Serial0/0/0 172.16.13.1
Jan 10 10:50:04.311: IP: s=192.168.4.129 (Serial0/1/0), d=192.168.1.1, len
28, policy match
Jan 10 10:50:04.311: IP: route map R3-to-R1, item 10, permit
Jan 10 10:50:04.311: IP: s=192.168.4.129 (Serial0/1/0), d=192.168.1.1
(Serial0/0/0), len 28, policy routed
Jan 10 10:50:04.311: IP: Serial0/1/0 to Serial0/0/0 172.16.13.1
Jan 10 10:50:04.323: IP: s=192.168.4.129 (Serial0/1/0), d=192.168.1.1, len
28, FIB policy match
Jan 10 10:50:04.323: IP: s=192.168.4.129 (Serial0/1/0), d=192.168.1.1, len
28, PBR Counted
```

```
Jan 10 10:50:04.323: IP: s=192.168.4.129 (Serial0/1/0), d=192.168.1.1,
g=172.16.13.1, len 28, FIB policy routed
Jan 10 10:50:04.351: IP: s=192.168.4.129 (Serial0/1/0), d=192.168.1.1, len
28, FIB policy match
Jan 10 10:50:04.351: IP: s=192.168.4.129 (Serial0/1/0), d=192.168.1.1, len
28, PBR Counted
Jan 10 10:50:04.351: IP: s=192.168.4.129 (Serial0/1/0), d=192.168.1.1,
g=172.16.13.1, len 28, FIB policy routed
Jan 10 10:50:07.347: IP: s=192.168.4.129 (Serial0/1/0), d=192.168.1.1, len
28, FIB policy match
Jan 10 10:50:07.347: IP: s=192.168.4.129 (Serial0/1/0), d=192.168.1.1, len
28, PBR Counted
Jan 10 10:50:07.347: IP: s=192.168.4.129 (Serial0/1/0), d=192.168.1.1,
g=172.16.13.1, len 28, FIB policy routed
R3#
```

e. On R3, display the policy and matches using the **show route-map** command.

```
R3# show route-map
route-map R3-to-R1, permit, sequence 10
  Match clauses:
    ip address (access-lists): PBR-ACL
  Set clauses:
    ip next-hop 172.16.13.1
Nexthop tracking current: 0.0.0.0
172.16.13.1, fib_nh:0,oce:0,status:0

  Policy routing matches: 12 packets, 384 bytes
R3#
```

Note: There are now matches to the policy because packets matching the ACL have passed through R3 S0/1/0.

Lab 5-2 Configure IP SLA Tracking and Path Control

Topology

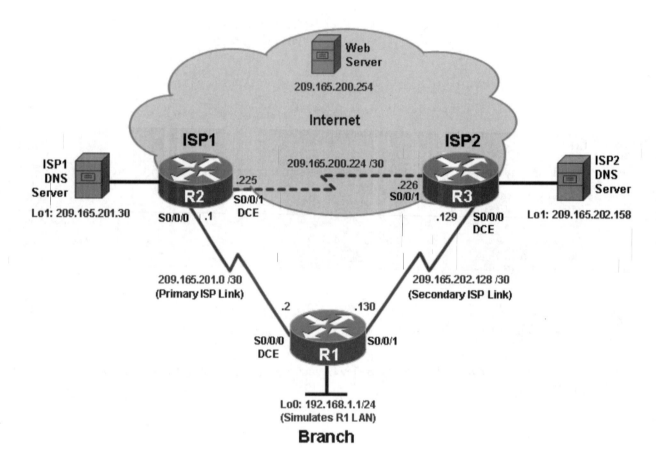

Objectives

- Configure and verify the IP SLA feature.
- Test the IP SLA tracking feature.
- Verify the configuration and operation using **show** and **debug** commands.

Background

You want to experiment with the Cisco IP Service Level Agreement (SLA) feature to study how it could be of value to your organization.

At times, a link to an ISP could be operational, yet users cannot connect to any other outside Internet resources. The problem might be with the ISP or downstream from them. Although policy-based routing (PBR) can be implemented to alter path control, you will implement the Cisco IOS SLA feature to monitor this behavior and intervene by injecting another default route to a backup ISP.

To test this, you will set up a three-router topology in a lab environment. Router R1 represents a branch office connected to two different ISPs. ISP1 is the preferred connection to the Internet, while ISP2 provides a backup link. ISP1 and ISP2 can also interconnect, and both can reach the web server. To monitor ISP1 for failure, you will configure IP SLA probes to track the reachability to the ISP1 DNS server. If connectivity to the ISP1 server fails, the SLA probes detect the failure and alter the default static route to point to the ISP2 server.

Note: This lab uses Cisco 1941 routers with Cisco IOS Release 15.2 with IP Base. Depending on the router or switch model and Cisco IOS Software version, the commands available and output produced might vary from what is shown in this lab.

Required Resources

- 3 routers (Cisco IOS Release 15.2 or comparable)
- Serial and Ethernet cables

Step 1: Configure loopbacks and assign addresses.

a. Cable the network as shown in the topology diagram. Erase the startup configuration and reload each router to clear the previous configurations. Using the addressing scheme in the diagram, create the loopback interfaces and apply IP addresses to them as well as the serial interfaces on R1, ISP1, and ISP2.

You can copy and paste the following configurations into your routers to begin.

Note: Depending on the router model, interfaces might be numbered differently than those listed. You might need to alter them accordingly.

Router R1

```
hostname R1

interface Loopback 0
 description R1 LAN
 ip address 192.168.1.1 255.255.255.0

interface Serial0/0/0
 description R1 --> ISP1
 ip address 209.165.201.2 255.255.255.252
 clock rate 128000
 bandwidth 128
 no shutdown

interface Serial0/0/1
 description R1 --> ISP2
 ip address 209.165.202.130 255.255.255.252
 bandwidth 128
 no shutdown
```

Router ISP1 (R2)

```
hostname ISP1

interface Loopback0
 description Simulated Internet Web Server
 ip address 209.165.200.254 255.255.255.255

interface Loopback1
 description ISP1 DNS Server
 ip address 209.165.201.30 255.255.255.255
```

```
interface Serial0/0/0
 description ISP1 --> R1
 ip address 209.165.201.1 255.255.255.252
 bandwidth 128
 no shutdown

interface Serial0/0/1
 description ISP1 --> ISP2
 ip address 209.165.200.225 255.255.255.252
 clock rate 128000
 bandwidth 128
 no shutdown
```

Router ISP2 (R3)

```
hostname ISP2

interface Loopback0
 description Simulated Internet Web Server
 ip address 209.165.200.254 255.255.255.255

interface Loopback1
 description ISP2 DNS Server
 ip address 209.165.202.158 255.255.255.255

interface Serial0/0/0
 description ISP2 --> R1
 ip address 209.165.202.129 255.255.255.252
 clock rate 128000
 bandwidth 128
 no shutdown

interface Serial0/0/1
 description ISP2 --> ISP1
 ip address 209.165.200.226 255.255.255.252
 bandwidth 128
 no shutdown
```

b. Verify the configuration by using the **show interfaces description** command. The output from router R1 is shown here as an example.

```
R1# show interfaces description | include up
Se0/0/0                          up              up       R1 --> ISP1
Se0/0/1                          up              up       R1 --> ISP2
Lo0                              up              up       R1 LAN
R1#
```

All three interfaces should be active. Troubleshoot if necessary.

Step 2: Configure static routing.

The current routing policy in the topology is as follows:

- Router R1 establishes connectivity to the Internet through ISP1 using a default static route.

- ISP1 and ISP2 have dynamic routing enabled between them, advertising their respective public address pools.

- ISP1 and ISP2 both have static routes back to the ISP LAN.

Note: For the purpose of this lab, the ISPs have a static route to an RFC 1918 private network address on the branch router R1. In an actual branch implementation, Network Address Translation (NAT) would be configured for all traffic exiting the branch LAN. Therefore, the static routes on the ISP routers would be pointing to the provided public pool of the branch office.

a. Implement the routing policies on the respective routers. You can copy and paste the following configurations.

Router R1

```
R1(config)# ip route 0.0.0.0 0.0.0.0 209.165.201.1
R1(config)#
```

Router ISP1 (R2)

```
ISP1(config)# router eigrp 1
ISP1(config-router)# network 209.165.200.224 0.0.0.3
ISP1(config-router)# network 209.165.201.0 0.0.0.31
ISP1(config-router)# no auto-summary
ISP1(config-router)# exit
ISP1(config)#
ISP1(config-router)# ip route 192.168.1.0 255.255.255.0 209.165.201.2
ISP1(config)#
```

Router ISP2 (R3)

```
ISP2(config)# router eigrp 1
ISP2(config-router)# network 209.165.200.224 0.0.0.3
ISP2(config-router)# network 209.165.202.128 0.0.0.31
ISP2(config-router)# no auto-summary
ISP2(config-router)# exit
ISP2(config)#
ISP2(config)# ip route 192.168.1.0 255.255.255.0 209.165.202.130
ISP2(config)#
```

EIGRP neighbor relationship messages on ISP1 and ISP2 should be generated. Troubleshoot if necessary.

b. The Cisco IOS IP SLA feature enables an administrator to monitor network performance between Cisco devices (switches or routers) or from a Cisco device to a remote IP device. IP SLA probes continuously check the reachability of a specific destination, such as a provider edge router interface, the DNS server of the ISP, or any other specific destination, and can conditionally announce a default route only if the connectivity is verified.

Before implementing the Cisco IOS SLA feature, you must verify reachability to the Internet servers. From router R1, ping the web server, ISP1 DNS server, and ISP2 DNS server to verify connectivity. You can copy the following Tcl script and paste it into R1.

```
foreach address {
209.165.200.254
209.165.201.30
209.165.202.158
} {
ping $address source 192.168.1.1
}
```

All pings should be successful. Troubleshoot if necessary.

c. Trace the path taken to the web server, ISP1 DNS server, and ISP2 DNS server. You can copy the following Tcl script and paste it into R1.

```
foreach address {
209.165.200.254
209.165.201.30
209.165.202.158
} {
trace $address source 192.168.1.1
}
```

Through which ISP is traffic flowing?

_____

_____

Step 3: Configure IP SLA probes.

When the reachability tests are successful, you can configure the Cisco IOS IP SLAs probes. Different types of probes can be created, including FTP, HTTP, and jitter probes.

In this scenario, you will configure ICMP echo probes.

a. Create an ICMP echo probe on R1 to the primary DNS server on ISP1 using the **ip sla** command.

```
R1(config)# ip sla 11
R1(config-ip-sla)# icmp-echo 209.165.201.30
R1(config-ip-sla-echo)# frequency 10
R1(config-ip-sla-echo)# exit
R1(config)#
R1(config)# ip sla schedule 11 life forever start-time now
R1(config)#
```

The operation number of 11 is only locally significant to the router. The **frequency 10** command schedules the connectivity test to repeat every 10 seconds. The probe is scheduled to start now and to run forever.

b. Verify the IP SLA's configuration of operation 11 using the **show ip sla configuration 11** command.

```
R1# show ip sla configuration 11
IP SLAs Infrastructure Engine-III
Entry number: 11
Owner:
Tag:
Operation timeout (milliseconds): 5000
Type of operation to perform: icmp-echo
Target address/Source address: 209.165.201.30/0.0.0.0
Type Of Service parameter: 0x0
Request size (ARR data portion): 28
Verify data: No
Vrf Name:
Schedule:
    Operation frequency (seconds): 10   (not considered if randomly scheduled)
    Next Scheduled Start Time: Start Time already passed
    Group Scheduled : FALSE
    Randomly Scheduled : FALSE
    Life (seconds): Forever
    Entry Ageout (seconds): never
    Recurring (Starting Everyday): FALSE
```

```
      Status of entry (SNMP RowStatus): Active
Threshold (milliseconds): 5000
Distribution Statistics:
   Number of statistic hours kept: 2
   Number of statistic distribution buckets kept: 1
   Statistic distribution interval (milliseconds): 20
Enhanced History:
History Statistics:
   Number of history Lives kept: 0
   Number of history Buckets kept: 15
   History Filter Type: None


R1#
```

The output lists the details of the configuration of operation 11. The operation is an ICMP echo to 209.165.201.30, with a frequency of 10 seconds, and it has already started (the start time has already passed).

c. Issue the **show ip sla statistics** command to display the number of successes, failures, and results of the latest operations.

```
R1# show ip sla statistics
IPSLAs Latest Operation Statistics

IPSLA operation id: 11
        Latest RTT: 8 milliseconds
Latest operation start time: 10:33:18 UTC Sat Jan 10 2015
Latest operation return code: OK
Number of successes: 51
Number of failures: 0
Operation time to live: Forever


R1#
```

You can see that operation 11 has already succeeded five times, has had no failures, and the last operation returned an OK result.

d. Although not actually required because IP SLA session 11 alone could provide the desired fault tolerance, create a second probe, 22, to test connectivity to the second DNS server located on router ISP2.

```
R1(config)# ip sla 22
R1(config-ip-sla)# icmp-echo 209.165.202.158
R1(config-ip-sla-echo)# frequency 10
R1(config-ip-sla-echo)# exit
R1(config)#
R1(config)# ip sla schedule 22 life forever start-time now
R1(config)# end
R1#
```

e. Verify the new probe using the **show ip sla configuration** and **show ip sla statistics** commands.

```
R1# show ip sla configuration 22
IP SLAs Infrastructure Engine-III
Entry number: 22
Owner:
Tag:
Operation timeout (milliseconds): 5000
```

```
Type of operation to perform: icmp-echo
Target address/Source address: 209.165.202.158/0.0.0.0
Type Of Service parameter: 0x0
Request size (ARR data portion): 28
Verify data: No
Vrf Name:
Schedule:
   Operation frequency (seconds): 10  (not considered if randomly scheduled)
   Next Scheduled Start Time: Start Time already passed
   Group Scheduled : FALSE
   Randomly Scheduled : FALSE
   Life (seconds): Forever
   Entry Ageout (seconds): never
   Recurring (Starting Everyday): FALSE
   Status of entry (SNMP RowStatus): Active
Threshold (milliseconds): 5000
Distribution Statistics:
   Number of statistic hours kept: 2
   Number of statistic distribution buckets kept: 1
   Statistic distribution interval (milliseconds): 20
Enhanced History:
History Statistics:
   Number of history Lives kept: 0
   Number of history Buckets kept: 15
   History Filter Type: None


R1#


R1# show ip sla configuration 22
IP SLAs, Infrastructure Engine-II.
Entry number: 22
Owner:
Tag:
Type of operation to perform: icmp-echo
Target address/Source address: 209.165.201.158/0.0.0.0
Type Of Service parameter: 0x0
Request size (ARR data portion): 28
Operation timeout (milliseconds): 5000
Verify data: No
Vrf Name:
Schedule:
   Operation frequency (seconds): 10   (not considered if randomly scheduled)
   Next Scheduled Start Time: Start Time already passed
   Group Scheduled : FALSE
   Randomly Scheduled : FALSE
   Life (seconds): Forever
   Entry Ageout (seconds): never
   Recurring (Starting Everyday): FALSE
   Status of entry (SNMP RowStatus): Active
Threshold (milliseconds): 5000 (not considered if react RTT is configured)
Distribution Statistics:
   Number of statistic hours kept: 2
   Number of statistic distribution buckets kept: 1
   Statistic distribution interval (milliseconds): 20
History Statistics:
```

```
        Number of history Lives kept: 0
        Number of history Buckets kept: 15
        History Filter Type: None
Enhanced History:

R1#
R1# show ip sla statistics 22
IPSLAs Latest Operation Statistics

IPSLA operation id: 22
        Latest RTT: 16 milliseconds
Latest operation start time: 10:38:29 UTC Sat Jan 10 2015
Latest operation return code: OK
Number of successes: 82
Number of failures: 0
Operation time to live: Forever


R1#
```

The output lists the details of the configuration of operation 22. The operation is an ICMP echo to 209.165.202.158, with a frequency of 10 seconds, and it has already started (the start time has already passed). The statistics also prove that operation 22 is active.

Step 4: Configure tracking options.

Although PBR could be used, you will configure a floating static route that appears or disappears depending on the success or failure of the IP SLA.

a. On R1, remove the current default route and replace it with a floating static route having an administrative distance of 5.

```
R1(config)# no ip route 0.0.0.0 0.0.0.0 209.165.201.1
R1(config)# ip route 0.0.0.0 0.0.0.0 209.165.201.1 5
R1(config)# exit
```

b. Verify the routing table.

```
R1# show ip route | begin Gateway
Gateway of last resort is 209.165.201.1 to network 0.0.0.0

S*    0.0.0.0/0 [5/0] via 209.165.201.1
      192.168.1.0/24 is variably subnetted, 2 subnets, 2 masks
C        192.168.1.0/24 is directly connected, Loopback0
L        192.168.1.1/32 is directly connected, Loopback0
      209.165.201.0/24 is variably subnetted, 2 subnets, 2 masks
C        209.165.201.0/30 is directly connected, Serial0/0/0
L        209.165.201.2/32 is directly connected, Serial0/0/0
      209.165.202.0/24 is variably subnetted, 2 subnets, 2 masks
C        209.165.202.128/30 is directly connected, Serial0/0/1
L        209.165.202.130/32 is directly connected, Serial0/0/1
R1#
```

Notice that the default static route is now using the route with the administrative distance of 5. The first tracking object is tied to IP SLA object 11.

c. From global configuration mode on R1, use the **track 1 ip sla 11 reachability** command to enter the config-track subconfiguration mode.

```
R1(config)# track 1 ip sla 11 reachability
R1(config-track)#
```

d. Specify the level of sensitivity to changes of tracked objects to 10 seconds of down delay and 1 second of up delay using the **delay down 10 up 1** command. The delay helps to alleviate the effect of flapping objects—objects that are going down and up rapidly. In this situation, if the DNS server fails momentarily and comes back up within 10 seconds, there is no impact.

```
R1(config-track)# delay down 10 up 1
R1(config-track)# exit
R1(config)#
```

e. To view routing table changes as they happen, first enable the **debug ip routing** command.

```
R1# debug ip routing
IP routing debugging is on
R1#
```

f. Configure the floating static route that will be implemented when tracking object 1 is active. Use the **ip route 0.0.0.0 0.0.0.0 209.165.201.1 2 track 1** command to create a floating static default route via 209.165.201.1 (ISP1). Notice that this command references the tracking object number 1, which in turn references IP SLA operation number 11.

```
R1(config)# ip route 0.0.0.0 0.0.0.0 209.165.201.1 2 track 1
R1(config)#
Jan 10 10:45:39.119: RT: updating static 0.0.0.0/0 (0x0)   :
    via 209.165.201.1   0 1048578

Jan 10 10:45:39.119: RT: closer admin distance for 0.0.0.0, flushing 1 routes
Jan 10 10:45:39.119: RT: add 0.0.0.0/0 via 209.165.201.1, static metric [2/0]
Jan 10 10:45:39.119: RT: updating static 0.0.0.0/0 (0x0)   :
    via 209.165.201.1   0 1048578

Jan 10 10:45:39.119: RT: rib update return code: 17
Jan 10 10:45:39.119: RT: updating static 0.0.0.0/0 (0x0)   :
    via 209.165.201.1   0 1048578

Jan 10 10:45:39.119: RT: rib update return code: 17
R1(config)#
```

Notice that the default route with an administrative distance of 5 has been immediately flushed because of a route with a better admin distance. It then adds the new default route with the admin distance of 2.

g. Repeat the steps for operation 22, track number 2, and assign the static route an admin distance higher than track 1 and lower than 5. On R1, copy the following configuration, which sets an admin distance of 3.

```
R1(config)# track 2 ip sla 22 reachability
R1(config-track)# delay down 10 up 1
R1(config-track)# exit
R1(config)#
R1(config)# ip route 0.0.0.0 0.0.0.0 209.165.202.129 3 track 2
R1(config)#
```

h. Verify the routing table again.

```
R1#show ip route | begin Gateway
```

```
Gateway of last resort is 209.165.201.1 to network 0.0.0.0

S*    0.0.0.0/0 [2/0] via 209.165.201.1
        192.168.1.0/24 is variably subnetted, 2 subnets, 2 masks
C         192.168.1.0/24 is directly connected, Loopback0
L         192.168.1.1/32 is directly connected, Loopback0
        209.165.201.0/24 is variably subnetted, 2 subnets, 2 masks
C         209.165.201.0/30 is directly connected, Serial0/0/0
L         209.165.201.2/32 is directly connected, Serial0/0/0
        209.165.202.0/24 is variably subnetted, 2 subnets, 2 masks
C         209.165.202.128/30 is directly connected, Serial0/0/1
L         209.165.202.130/32 is directly connected, Serial0/0/1
R1#
```

Although a new default route was entered, its administrative distance is not better than 2. Therefore, it does not replace the previously entered default route.

Step 5: Verify IP SLA operation.

In this step you observe and verify the dynamic operations and routing changes when tracked objects fail. The following summarizes the process:

- Disable the DNS loopback interface on ISP1 (R2).
- Observe the output of the **debug** command on R1.
- Verify the static route entries in the routing table and the IP SLA statistics of R1.
- Re-enable the loopback interface on ISP1 (R2) and again observe the operation of the IP SLA tracking feature.

a. On ISP1, disable the loopback interface 1.

```
ISP1(config-if)# int lo1
ISP1(config-if)# shutdown
ISP1(config-if)#
Jan 10 10:53:25.091: %LINK-5-CHANGED: Interface Loopback1, changed state to
administratively down
Jan 10 10:53:26.091: %LINEPROTO-5-UPDOWN: Line protocol on Interface
Loopback1, changed state to down
ISP1(config-if)#
```

b. On R1, observe the **debug** output being generated. Recall that R1 will wait up to 10 seconds before initiating action therefore several seconds will elapse before the output is generated.

```
R1#
Jan 10 10:53:59.551: %TRACK-6-STATE: 1 ip sla 11 reachability Up -> Down
Jan 10 10:53:59.551: RT: del 0.0.0.0 via 209.165.201.1, static metric [2/0]
Jan 10 10:53:59.551: RT: delete network route to 0.0.0.0/0
Jan 10 10:53:59.551: RT: default path has been cleared
Jan 10 10:53:59.551: RT: updating static 0.0.0.0/0 (0x0)  :
    via 209.165.202.129   0 1048578

Jan 10 10:53:59.551: RT: add 0.0.0.0/0 via 209.165.202.129, static metric
[3/0]
Jan 10 10:53:59.551: RT: default path is now 0.0.0.0 via 209.165.202.129
Jan 10 10:53:59.551: RT: updating static 0.0.0.0/0 (0x0)  :
    via 209.165.201.1   0 1048578

Jan 10 10:53:59.551: RT: rib update return code: 17
```

```
Jan 10 10:53:59.551: RT: updating static 0.0.0.0/0 (0x0)   :
    via 209.165.202.129   0 1048578

Jan 10 10:53:59.551: RT: updating static 0.0.0.0/0 (0x0)   :
    via 209.165.201.1   0 1048578

Jan 10 10:53:59.551: RT: rib update return code: 17
R1#
```

The tracking state of track 1 changes from up to down. This is the object that tracked reachability for IP SLA object 11, with an ICMP echo to the ISP1 DNS server at 209.165.201.30.

R1 then proceeds to delete the default route with the administrative distance of 2 and installs the next highest default route to ISP2 with the administrative distance of 3.

c. On R1, verify the routing table.

```
R1# show ip route | begin Gateway
Gateway of last resort is 209.165.202.129 to network 0.0.0.0

S*     0.0.0.0/0 [3/0] via 209.165.202.129
       192.168.1.0/24 is variably subnetted, 2 subnets, 2 masks
C        192.168.1.0/24 is directly connected, Loopback0
L        192.168.1.1/32 is directly connected, Loopback0
       209.165.201.0/24 is variably subnetted, 2 subnets, 2 masks
C        209.165.201.0/30 is directly connected, Serial0/0/0
L        209.165.201.2/32 is directly connected, Serial0/0/0
       209.165.202.0/24 is variably subnetted, 2 subnets, 2 masks
C        209.165.202.128/30 is directly connected, Serial0/0/1
L        209.165.202.130/32 is directly connected, Serial0/0/1
R1#
```

The new static route has an administrative distance of 3 and is being forwarded to ISP2 as it should.

d. Verify the IP SLA statistics.

```
R1# show ip sla statistics
IPSLAs Latest Operation Statistics

IPSLA operation id: 11
        Latest RTT: NoConnection/Busy/Timeout
Latest operation start time: 11:01:08 UTC Sat Jan 10 2015
Latest operation return code: Timeout
Number of successes: 173
Number of failures: 45
Operation time to live: Forever




IPSLA operation id: 22
        Latest RTT: 8 milliseconds
Latest operation start time: 11:01:09 UTC Sat Jan 10 2015
Latest operation return code: OK
Number of successes: 218
Number of failures: 0
Operation time to live: Forever

R1#
```

Notice that the latest return code is **Timeout** and there have been 45 failures on IP SLA object 11.

e. On R1, initiate a trace to the web server from the internal LAN IP address.

```
R1# trace 209.165.200.254 source 192.168.1.1
Type escape sequence to abort.
Tracing the route to 209.165.200.254
VRF info: (vrf in name/id, vrf out name/id)
  1 209.165.202.129 4 msec *  *
R1#
```

This confirms that traffic is leaving router R1 and being forwarded to the ISP2 router.

f. On ISP1, re-enable the DNS address by issuing the **no shutdown** command on the loopback 1 interface to examine the routing behavior when connectivity to the ISP1 DNS is restored.

```
ISP1(config-if)# no shutdown
Jan 10 11:05:45.847: %LINK-3-UPDOWN: Interface Loopback1, changed state to up
Jan 10 11:05:46.847: %LINEPROTO-5-UPDOWN: Line protocol on Interface
Loopback1, changed state to up
ISP1(config-if)#
```

Notice the output of the **debug ip routing** command on R1.

```
R1#
Jan 10 11:06:20.551: %TRACK-6-STATE: 1 ip sla 11 reachability Down -> Up
Jan 10 11:06:20.551: RT: updating static 0.0.0.0/0 (0x0)  :
    via 209.165.201.1   0 1048578

Jan 10 11:06:20.551: RT: closer admin distance for 0.0.0.0, flushing 1 routes
Jan 10 11:06:20.551: RT: add 0.0.0.0/0 via 209.165.201.1, static metric [2/0]
Jan 10 11:06:20.551: RT: updating static 0.0.0.0/0 (0x0)  :
    via 209.165.202.129   0 1048578

Jan 10 11:06:20.551: RT: rib update return code: 17
Jan 10 11:06:20.551: RT: u
R1#pdating static 0.0.0.0/0 (0x0)  :
    via 209.165.202.129   0 1048578

Jan 10 11:06:20.551: RT: rib update return code: 17
Jan 10 11:06:20.551: RT: updating static 0.0.0.0/0 (0x0)  :
    via 209.165.201.1   0 1048578

Jan 10 11:06:20.551: RT: rib update return code: 17
R1#
```

Now the IP SLA 11 operation transitions back to an up state and reestablishes the default static route to ISP1 with an administrative distance of 2.

g. Again examine the IP SLA statistics.

```
R1# show ip sla statistics
IPSLAs Latest Operation Statistics

IPSLA operation id: 11
      Latest RTT: 8 milliseconds
Latest operation start time: 11:07:38 UTC Sat Jan 10 2015
Latest operation return code: OK
Number of successes: 182
Number of failures: 75
```

```
Operation time to live: Forever



IPSLA operation id: 22
      Latest RTT: 16 milliseconds
Latest operation start time: 11:07:39 UTC Sat Jan 10 2015
Latest operation return code: OK
Number of successes: 257
Number of failures: 0
Operation time to live: Forever



R1#
```

The IP SLA 11 operation is active again, as indicated by the OK return code, and the number of successes is incrementing.

h. Verify the routing table.

```
R1# show ip route | begin Gateway
Gateway of last resort is 209.165.201.1 to network 0.0.0.0

S*    0.0.0.0/0 [2/0] via 209.165.201.1
      192.168.1.0/24 is variably subnetted, 2 subnets, 2 masks
C        192.168.1.0/24 is directly connected, Loopback0
L        192.168.1.1/32 is directly connected, Loopback0
      209.165.201.0/24 is variably subnetted, 2 subnets, 2 masks
C        209.165.201.0/30 is directly connected, Serial0/0/0
L        209.165.201.2/32 is directly connected, Serial0/0/0
      209.165.202.0/24 is variably subnetted, 2 subnets, 2 masks
C        209.165.202.128/30 is directly connected, Serial0/0/1
L        209.165.202.130/32 is directly connected, Serial0/0/1
R1#
```

The default static through ISP1 with an administrative distance of 2 is reestablished.

There are many possibilities available with object tracking and Cisco IOS IP SLAs. As shown in this lab, a probe can be based on reachability, changing routing operations, and path control based on the ability to reach an object. However, Cisco IOS IP SLAs also allow paths to be changed based on network conditions such as delay, load, and other factors.

Before deploying a Cisco IOS IP SLA solution, the impact of the additional probe traffic being generated should be considered, including how that traffic affects bandwidth utilization, and congestion levels. Tuning the configuration (for example, with the **delay** and **frequency** commands) is critical to mitigate possible issues related to excessive transitions and route changes in the presence of flapping tracked objects.

The benefits of running IP SLAs should be carefully evaluated. The IP SLA is an additional task that must be performed by the router's CPU. A large number of intensive SLAs could be a significant burden on the CPU, possibly interfering with other router functions and having detrimental impact on the overall router performance. The CPU load should be monitored after the SLAs are deployed to verify that they do not cause excessive utilization of the router CPU.

Chapter 6: Enterprise Internet Connectivity

Lab 6-1 Configure NAT Services

Topology

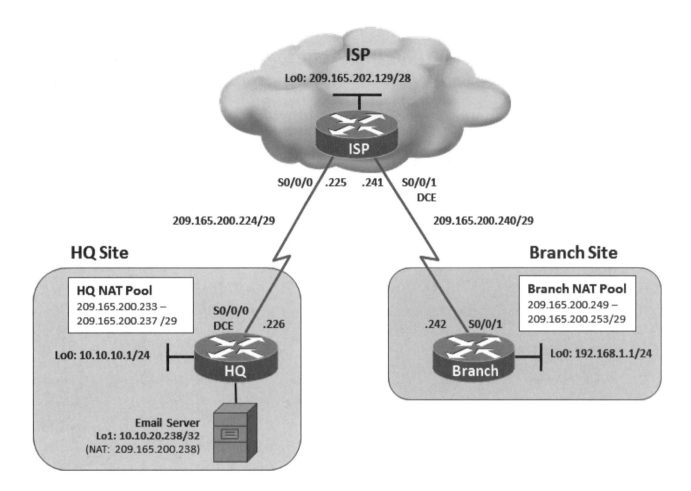

Objectives

- Configure dynamic NAT and static NAT on the HQ router.
- Configure dynamic NAT on the Branch router.
- Verify the configuration and operation using **show** commands.

Background

The HQ and Branch sites must be configured to support NAT. Specifically, the HQ and Branch routers will be configured to provide inside LAN users with outside public addresses using NAT. The HQ router will also provide static NAT to access the email server from the outside network.

Note: This lab uses Cisco 1941 routers with Cisco IOS Release 15.2 with IP Base. Depending on the router or switch model and Cisco IOS Software version, the commands available and output produced might vary from what is shown in this lab.

Required Resources

- 3 routers (Cisco IOS Release 15.2 or comparable)
- Serial and Ethernet cables

Step 1: Configure loopbacks and assign addresses.

Cable the network as shown in the topology diagram. Erase the startup configuration and reload each router to clear previous configurations. Using the addressing scheme in the diagram, apply the IP addresses to the interfaces on the HQ, ISP, and Branch routers.

You can copy and paste the following configurations into your routers to begin.

Note: Depending on the router model, interfaces might be numbered differently than those listed. You might need to alter the designations accordingly.

HQ (R1)

```
hostname HQ
!
interface Loopback0
 description Headquarters LAN
 ip address 10.10.10.1 255.255.255.0
exit
!
interface Loopback1
 description Simulates the Email Server
 ip address 10.10.20.238 255.255.255.255
exit
!
interface Serial0/0/0
 description Connection to ISP
 ip address 209.165.200.226 255.255.255.248
 clock rate 128000
 no shut
exit
!
end
```

ISP (R2)

```
hostname ISP
!
interface Loopback0
 description Simulating the Internet
 ip address 209.165.202.129 255.255.255.240
```

```
exit
!
interface Serial0/0/0
 description Connection to HQ
 ip address 209.165.200.225 255.255.255.248
 no shut
exit
!
interface Serial0/0/1
 description Connection to Branch
 ip address 209.165.200.241 255.255.255.248
 clock rate 128000
 no shut
exit
!
ip route 209.165.200.232 255.255.255.248 Serial0/0/0
ip route 209.165.200.248 255.255.255.248 Serial0/0/1
!
end
```

Branch (R3)

```
hostname Branch
!
interface Loopback0
 description Branch LAN
 ip address 192.168.1.1 255.255.255.0
exit
!
interface Serial0/0/1
 description Connection to ISP
 ip address 209.165.200.242 255.255.255.248
 no shut
exit
!
end
```

a. Verify your configuration by using the **show ip interface brief** and the **show interfaces description**
    command. The output from the Branch router is shown here as an example.

```
Branch# show ip interface brief | include up
Serial0/0/1            209.165.200.242 YES manual up                up
Loopback0             192.168.1.1     YES manual up                up
Branch#
Branch# show interfaces description | include up
Se0/0/1                         up          up       Connection to ISP
Lo0                             up          up       Branch LAN
Branch#
```

b. From the Branch router, run the following Tcl script to verify connectivity.

```
foreach address {
209.165.200.241
209.165.202.129
209.165.200.226
} { ping $address }
```

```
Branch# tclsh
Branch(tcl)# foreach address {
+>209.165.200.241
+>209.165.202.129
+>209.165.200.226
+>} { ping $address }
Type escape sequence to abort.
Sending 5, 100-byte ICMP Echos to 209.165.200.241, timeout is 2 seconds:
!!!!!
Success rate is 100 percent (5/5), round-trip min/avg/max = 12/13/16 ms
Type escape sequence to abort.
Sending 5, 100-byte ICMP Echos to 209.165.202.129, timeout is 2 seconds:
.....
Success rate is 0 percent (0/5)
Type escape sequence to abort.
Sending 5, 100-byte ICMP Echos to 209.165.200.226, timeout is 2 seconds:
......
Success rate is 0 percent (0/5)
Branch(tcl)#
```

Why do the pings to the ISP's loopback and HQ router address fail?

_____

_____

Step 2: Configure default static routes on Branch and HQ.

a. On HQ, configure a default static route to ISP.

    HQ(config)# **ip route 0.0.0.0 0.0.0.0 209.165.200.225**

b. On the Branch router, configure a default static route to ISP.

    You can copy and paste the following configurations into your routers.

    Branch(config)# **ip route 0.0.0.0 0.0.0.0 209.165.200.241**

c. From the Branch router, run the following Tcl script to verify connectivity.

    foreach address {
    209.165.200.241
    209.165.202.129
    209.165.200.226
    +>} { ping $address}

```
Branch# tclsh
Branch(tcl)# foreach address {
+>209.165.200.241
+>209.165.202.129
+>209.165.200.226
+>} { ping $address }
Type escape sequence to abort.
Sending 5, 100-byte ICMP Echos to 209.165.200.241, timeout is 2 seconds:
!!!!!
Success rate is 100 percent (5/5), round-trip min/avg/max = 12/13/16 ms
Type escape sequence to abort.
Sending 5, 100-byte ICMP Echos to 209.165.202.129, timeout is 2 seconds:
!!!!!
Success rate is 100 percent (5/5), round-trip min/avg/max = 12/13/16 ms
```

```
Type escape sequence to abort.
Sending 5, 100-byte ICMP Echos to 209.165.200.226, timeout is 2 seconds:
!!!!!
Success rate is 100 percent (5/5), round-trip min/avg/max = 28/28/28 ms
Branch(tcl)#
```

Are the pings now successful?

_____

_____

d. Connectivity from the Branch router to external addresses has been established. But could a Branch LAN user successfully reach those external addresses? To verify, initiate pings sourced from the Branch LAN interface to the ISP interface, the ISP's loopback interface, and the HQ Internet interface. Run the following Tcl script on the Branch router to verify connectivity.

```
foreach address {
209.165.200.241
209.165.202.129
209.165.200.226
} { ping $address source 192.168.1.1}

Branch# tclsh
Branch(tcl)# foreach address {
+>209.165.200.241
+>209.165.202.129
+>209.165.200.226
+>} { ping $address source 192.168.1.1}
Type escape sequence to abort.
Sending 5, 100-byte ICMP Echos to 209.165.200.241, timeout is 2 seconds:
Packet sent with a source address of 192.168.1.1
.....
Success rate is 0 percent (0/5)
Type escape sequence to abort.
Sending 5, 100-byte ICMP Echos to 209.165.202.129, timeout is 2 seconds:
Packet sent with a source address of 192.168.1.1
.....
Success rate is 0 percent (0/5)
Type escape sequence to abort.
Sending 5, 100-byte ICMP Echos to 209.165.200.226, timeout is 2 seconds:
Packet sent with a source address of 192.168.1.1
.....
Success rate is 0 percent (0/5)
Branch(tcl)#
```

Note: You can also specify the router interface designator (for example, S0/0/0, Fa0/0, or Lo1) as the source for the extended ping, as follows:

```
Branch# ping 209.165.200.226 source Lo1
```

Why are the pings unsuccessful?

_____

_____

The ISP cannot route back to the internal private address of the Branch LAN.

Step 3: Configure NAT on the HQ router.

The HQ and Branch internal LANs will be translated to global public IP addresses using NAT when exiting the corporate network.

The ISP has allocated the **209.165.200.233 – 209.165.200.238 (209.165.200.232/29)** pool of public addresses to the HQ site.

The HQ site also has an email server that must be accessible to mobile users and Branch office users. Therefore, static NAT must also be configured to use a public address to reach the email server.

a. On the HQ router, create an extended NAT ACL that matches the 10.10.10.0/24 LAN.

```
HQ(config)# ip access-list extended HQ-NAT-ACL
HQ(config-ext-nacl)# remark Permit Local LAN to use NAT
HQ(config-ext-nacl)# permit ip 10.10.10.0 0.0.0.255 any
HQ(config-ext-nacl)# exit
HQ(config)#
```

b. The NAT pool must identify addresses 209.165.200.232 /29.

```
HQ(config)# ip nat pool HQ-NAT-POOL 209.165.200.233 209.165.200.237 prefix-
length 29
HQ(config)#
```

c. The NAT pool and the ACL must be bound together.

```
HQ(config)# ip nat inside source list HQ-NAT-ACL pool HQ-NAT-POOL
HQ(config)#
```

d. The email server with private IP address 10.10.20.238 will be statically assigned the last public IP address from the NAT pool, 209.165.200.238. Interface loopback 0 on HQ simulates this server.

```
HQ(config)# ip nat inside source static 10.10.20.238 209.165.200.238
HQ(config)#
```

e. The LAN interface must be identified as an inside NAT interface, and the Internet interface must be identified as an outside NAT interface.

```
HQ(config)# interface Loopback 0
HQ(config-if)# ip nat inside
HQ(config-if)# exit
HQ(config)#
HQ(config)# interface Loopback 1
HQ(config-if)# ip nat inside
HQ(config-if)# exit
HQ(config)#
HQ(config)# interface Serial0/0/0
HQ(config-if)# ip nat outside
HQ(config-if)# exit
HQ(config)#
```

Step 4: Configure NAT on the Branch router.

The ISP has allocated the **209.165.200.249 – 209.165.200.254 (209.165.200.248/29)** pool of public addresses to the Branch site.

a. On the Branch router, create a standard NAT ACL that identifies the 192.168.1.0/24 LAN.

```
Branch(config)# ip access-list extended BRANCH-NAT-ACL
Branch(config-ext-nacl)# remark Permit Local LAN to use NAT
Branch(config-ext-nacl)# permit ip 192.168.1.0 0.0.0.255 any
```

```
Branch(config-ext-nacl)# exit
Branch(config)#
```

b. The NAT pool must identify addresses 209.165.200.232 /29.

```
Branch(config)# ip nat pool BRANCH-NAT-POOL 209.165.200.249 209.165.200.254
prefix-length 29
Branch(config)#
```

c. The NAT pool and the ACL must be bound together.

```
Branch(config)# ip nat inside source list BRANCH-NAT-ACL pool BRANCH-NAT-POOL
Branch(config)#
```

d. The LAN interface must be identified as an inside NAT interface, and the Internet interface must be
    identified as an outside NAT interface.

```
Branch(config)# interface Loopback 0
Branch(config-if)# ip nat inside
Branch(config-if)# exit
Branch(config)#
Branch(config)# interface Serial0/0/1
Branch(config-if)# ip nat outside
Branch(config-if)# exit
Branch(config)#
```

Step 5: Verify NAT Configuration.

a. Verify the NAT configuration by using the **show ip nat statistics** and **show ip nat translations**
    commands.

```
Branch# show ip nat statistics
Total active translations: 0 (0 static, 0 dynamic; 0 extended)
Peak translations: 0
Outside interfaces:
  Serial0/0/1
Inside interfaces:
  Loopback0
Hits: 0  Misses: 0
CEF Translated packets: 0, CEF Punted packets: 0
Expired translations: 0
Dynamic mappings:
-- Inside Source
[Id: 1] access-list BRANCH-NAT-ACL pool BRANCH-NAT-POOL refcount 0
 pool BRANCH-NAT-POOL: netmask 255.255.255.248
      start 209.165.200.249 end 209.165.200.254
      type generic, total addresses 6, allocated 0 (0%), misses 0

Total doors: 0
Appl doors: 0
Normal doors: 0
Queued Packets: 0
Branch#
```

As shown in the preceding, the pool has been configured and the interfaces assigned. The output of the
show ip nat translations command confirms that there are currently no active NAT translations:

```
Branch# show ip nat translations
Branch#
```

b. Initiate NAT traffic by pinging from the Branch LAN to the ISP interface, the ISP's loopback, the HQ Internet interface, and this time also include the HQ public email server address. Run the following Tcl script on the Branch router to verify connectivity.

```
foreach address {
209.165.200.241
209.165.202.129
209.165.200.226
209.165.200.238
} { ping $address source 192.168.1.1}
```

```
Branch# tclsh
Branch(tcl)# foreach address {
+>209.165.200.241
+>209.165.202.129
+>209.165.200.226
+>209.165.200.238
+>} { ping $address source 192.168.1.1}
Type escape sequence to abort.
Sending 5, 100-byte ICMP Echos to 209.165.200.241, timeout is 2 seconds:
Packet sent with a source address of 192.168.1.1
!!!!!
Success rate is 100 percent (5/5), round-trip min/avg/max = 12/13/16 ms
Type escape sequence to abort.
Sending 5, 100-byte ICMP Echos to 209.165.202.129, timeout is 2 seconds:
Packet sent with a source address of 192.168.1.1
!!!!!
Success rate is 100 percent (5/5), round-trip min/avg/max = 12/13/16 ms
Type escape sequence to abort.
Sending 5, 100-byte ICMP Echos to 209.165.200.226, timeout is 2 seconds:
Packet sent with a source address of 192.168.1.1
!!!!!
Success rate is 100 percent (5/5), round-trip min/avg/max = 28/28/28 ms
Type escape sequence to abort.
Sending 5, 100-byte ICMP Echos to 209.165.200.238, timeout is 2 seconds:
Packet sent with a source address of 192.168.1.1
!!!!!
Success rate is 100 percent (5/5), round-trip min/avg/max = 28/28/28 ms
Branch(tcl)#
```

All pings should be successful. Troubleshoot if necessary.

c. Verify that NAT is occurring by using the **show ip nat statistics** and **show ip nat translations** commands.

```
Branch# show ip nat statistics
Total active translations: 5 (0 static, 5 dynamic; 4 extended)
Peak translations: 5, occurred 00:00:13 ago
Outside interfaces:
  Serial0/0/1
Inside interfaces:
  Loopback0
Hits: 40  Misses: 0
CEF Translated packets: 20, CEF Punted packets: 0
Expired translations: 0
```

```
Dynamic mappings:
-- Inside Source
[Id: 1] access-list BRANCH-NAT-ACL pool BRANCH-NAT-POOL refcount 5
 pool BRANCH-NAT-POOL: netmask 255.255.255.248
        start 209.165.200.249 end 209.165.200.254
        type generic, total addresses 6, allocated 1 (16%), misses 0

Total doors: 0
Appl doors: 0
Normal doors: 0
Queued Packets: 0
Branch#
Branch# show ip nat translations
Pro Inside global      Inside local      Outside local      Outside global
icmp 209.165.200.249:31 192.168.1.1:31   209.165.200.241:31 209.165.200.241:31
icmp 209.165.200.249:32 192.168.1.1:32   209.165.202.129:32 209.165.202.129:32
icmp 209.165.200.249:33 192.168.1.1:33   209.165.200.226:33 209.165.200.226:33
icmp 209.165.200.249:34 192.168.1.1:34   209.165.200.238:34 209.165.200.238:34
--- 209.165.200.249      192.168.1.1      ---                ---
Branch#
```

Notice that translations are occurring. The output lists the details of the NAT translations sourced by the 192.168.1.1 Branch LAN IP address, which was translated to public IP address 209.165.200.249.

Chapter 7: BGP Implementation

Lab 7-1 Configuring BGP with Default Routing

Topology

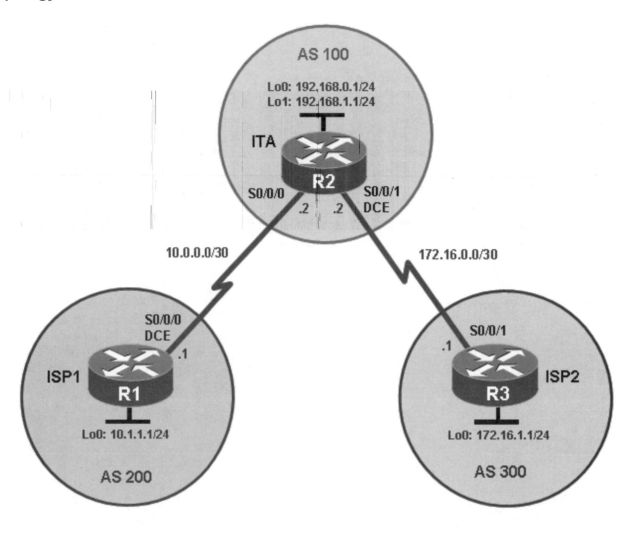

Objectives

- Configure BGP to exchange routing information with two ISPs.

Background

The International Travel Agency (ITA) relies extensively on the Internet for sales. For this reason, the ITA has decided to create a multihomed ISP connectivity solution and contracted with two ISPs for Internet connectivity with fault tolerance. Because the ITA is connecting to two different service providers, you must configure BGP, which runs between the ITA boundary router and the two ISP routers.

Note: This lab uses Cisco 1941 routers with Cisco IOS Release 15.4 with IP Base. The switches are Cisco WS-C2960-24TT-L with Fast Ethernet interfaces; therefore, the router will use routing metrics associated with a 100 Mb/s interface. Depending on the router or switch model and Cisco IOS Software version, the commands available and output produced might vary from what is shown in this lab.

Required Resources

- 3 routers (Cisco IOS Release 15.2 or comparable)
- Serial and Ethernet cables

Step 0: Suggested starting configurations.

a. Apply the following configuration to each router along with the appropriate **hostname**. The **exec-timeout 0 0** command should only be used in a lab environment.

```
Router(config)# no ip domain-lookup
Router(config)# line con 0
Router(config-line)# logging synchronous
Router(config-line)# exec-timeout 0 0
```

Step 1: Configure interface addresses.

a. Using the addressing scheme in the diagram, create the loopback interfaces and apply IPv4 addresses to these and the serial interfaces on ISP1 (R1), ISP2 (R3), and ITA (R2). The ISP loopbacks simulate real networks that can be reached through the ISP. The two loopbacks for the ITA router simulate the connections between the ITA boundary router and their core routers. Set a clock rate on the DCE serial interfaces.

```
ISP1(config)# interface Lo0
ISP1(config-if)# description ISP1 Internet Network
ISP1(config-if)# ip address 10.1.1.1 255.255.255.0
ISP1(config-if)# exit
ISP1(config)# interface Serial0/0/0
ISP1(config-if)# description ISP1 -> ITA
ISP1(config-if)# ip address 10.0.0.1 255.255.255.252
ISP1(config-if)# clock rate 128000
ISP1(config-if)# no shutdown
ISP1(config-if)# end
ISP1#


ITA(config)# interface Lo0
ITA(config-if)# description Core router network link 1
ITA(config-if)# ip address 192.168.0.1 255.255.255.0
ITA(config)# exit
ITA(config-if)# interface Lo1
ITA(config-if)# description Core router network link 2
ITA(config-if)# ip address 192.168.1.1 255.255.255.0
ITA(config-if)# exit
ITA(config)# interface Serial0/0/0
ITA(config-if)# description ITA -> ISP1
ITA(config-if)# ip address 10.0.0.2 255.255.255.252
ITA(config-if)# no shutdown
ITA(config-if)# exit
ITA(config)# interface Serial0/0/1
ITA(config-if)# description ITA -> ISP2
```

```
ITA(config-if)# ip address 172.16.0.2 255.255.255.252
ITA(config-if)# clock rate 128000
ITA(config-if)# no shutdown
ITA(config-if)# end
ITA#

ISP2(config)# interface Lo0
ISP2(config-if)# description ISP2 Internet Network
ISP2(config-if)# ip address 172.16.1.1 255.255.255.0
ISP2(config)# exit
ISP2(config-if)# interface Serial0/0/1
ISP2(config-if)# description ISP2 -> ITA
ISP2(config-if)# ip address 172.16.0.1 255.255.255.252
ISP2(config-if)# no shutdown
ISP2(config-if)# end
ISP2#
```

b. Use **ping** to test the connectivity between the directly connected routers. Note that router ISP1 cannot reach router ISP2.

Step 2: Configure BGP on the ISP routers.

On the ISP1 and ISP2 routers, configure BGP to peer with the ITA boundary router and advertise the ISP loopback networks.

```
ISP1(config)# router bgp 200
ISP1(config-router)# neighbor 10.0.0.2 remote-as 100
ISP1(config-router)# network 10.1.1.0 mask 255.255.255.0

ISP2(config)# router bgp 300
ISP2(config-router)# neighbor 172.16.0.2 remote-as 100
ISP2(config-router)# network 172.16.1.0 mask 255.255.255.0
```

Step 3: Configure BGP on the ITA boundary router.

a. Configure the ITA router to run BGP with both Internet providers.

```
ITA(config)# router bgp 100
ITA(config-router)# neighbor 10.0.0.1 remote-as 200
ITA(config-router)# neighbor 172.16.0.1 remote-as 300
ITA(config-router)# network 192.168.0.0
ITA(config-router)# network 192.168.1.0
```

You should see BGP neighbor peering messages on the console similar to the following.

```
*Sep  8 16:00:21.587: %BGP-5-ADJCHANGE: neighbor 10.0.0.1 Up
```

b. To verify the configuration, check the ITA routing table with the **show ip route** command.

```
ITA# show ip route
Codes: L - local, C - connected, S - static, R - RIP, M - mobile, B - BGP
       D - EIGRP, EX - EIGRP external, O - OSPF, IA - OSPF inter area
       N1 - OSPF NSSA external type 1, N2 - OSPF NSSA external type 2
       E1 - OSPF external type 1, E2 - OSPF external type 2
       i - IS-IS, su - IS-IS summary, L1 - IS-IS level-1, L2 - IS-IS level-2
       ia - IS-IS inter area, * - candidate default, U - per-user static
       route
```

```
            o - ODR, P - periodic downloaded static route, H - NHRP, l - LISP
            a - application route
            + - replicated route, % - next hop override

Gateway of last resort is not set

        10.0.0.0/8 is variably subnetted, 3 subnets, 3 masks
C          10.0.0.0/30 is directly connected, Serial0/0/0
L          10.0.0.2/32 is directly connected, Serial0/0/0
B          10.1.1.0/24 [20/0] via 10.0.0.1, 00:01:10
        172.16.0.0/16 is variably subnetted, 3 subnets, 3 masks
C          172.16.0.0/30 is directly connected, Serial0/0/1
L          172.16.0.2/32 is directly connected, Serial0/0/1
B          172.16.1.0/24 [20/0] via 172.16.0.1, 00:00:53
        192.168.0.0/24 is variably subnetted, 2 subnets, 2 masks
C          192.168.0.0/24 is directly connected, Loopback0
L          192.168.0.1/32 is directly connected, Loopback0
        192.168.1.0/24 is variably subnetted, 2 subnets, 2 masks
C          192.168.1.0/24 is directly connected, Loopback1
L          192.168.1.1/32 is directly connected, Loopback1
ITA#
```

ITA has BGP routes to the loopback networks at each ISP router.

c. Run the following Tcl script on all routers to verify connectivity If these pings are not successful, troubleshoot. Use **exit** to exit the Tcl script.

Note: The WAN subnets connecting ITA (R2) to the ISPs (R1 and R3) are not advertised in BGP, so the ISPs will not be able to ping each other's serial interface address.

```
ITA# tclsh

foreach address {
10.0.0.1
10.0.0.2
10.1.1.1
172.16.0.1
172.16.0.2
172.16.1.1
192.168.0.1
192.168.1.1
} {
ping $address }
```

Step 4: Verify BGP on the routers.

a. To verify the BGP operation on ITA, issue the **show ip bgp** command.

```
ITA# show ip bgp
BGP table version is 5, local router ID is 192.168.1.1
Status codes: s suppressed, d damped, h history, * valid, > best, i -
internal,
             r RIB-failure, S Stale, m multipath, b backup-path, f RT-
Filter,
             x best-external, a additional-path, c RIB-compressed,
Origin codes: i - IGP, e - EGP, ? - incomplete
RPKI validation codes: V valid, I invalid, N Not found

     Network          Next Hop            Metric LocPrf Weight Path
```

```
    *>   10.1.1.0/24        10.0.0.1                  0              0 200 i
    *>   172.16.1.0/24      172.16.0.1                0              0 300 i
    *>   192.168.0.0        0.0.0.0                   0          32768 i
    *>   192.168.1.0        0.0.0.0                   0          32768 i
ITA#
```

What is the local router ID?

_____

Which table version is displayed?

_____

An asterisk (*) next to a route indicates that it is valid. An angle bracket (>) indicates that the route has been selected as the best route.

b.   To verify the operation of ISP1, issue the **show ip bgp** command.

```
ISP1# show ip bgp
BGP table version is 5, local router ID is 10.1.1.1
Status codes: s suppressed, d damped, h history, * valid, > best, i -
internal,
              r RIB-failure, S Stale, m multipath, b backup-path, f RT-
Filter,
              x best-external, a additional-path, c RIB-compressed,
Origin codes: i - IGP, e - EGP, ? - incomplete
RPKI validation codes: V valid, I invalid, N Not found

        Network          Next Hop            Metric LocPrf Weight Path
    *>   10.1.1.0/24        0.0.0.0                  0          32768 i
    *>   172.16.1.0/24      10.0.0.2                            0 100 300 i
    *>   192.168.0.0        10.0.0.2                 0            0 100 i
    *>   192.168.1.0        10.0.0.2                 0            0 100 i
ISP1#
```

Which table version is displayed and is it the same as the BGP table version for ITA?

_____

From ISP1, what is the path to network 172.16.1.0/24?

_____

c.   On the ISP1 router, issue the **shutdown** command on Loopback0. Then on ITA, issue the **show ip bgp** command again.

```
ISP1(config)# interface loopback 0
ISP1(config-if)# shutdown
ISP1(config-if)#

ITA# show ip bgp
BGP table version is 6, local router ID is 192.168.1.1
Status codes: s suppressed, d damped, h history, * valid, > best, i -
internal,
              r RIB-failure, S Stale, m multipath, b backup-path, f RT-
Filter,
              x best-external, a additional-path, c RIB-compressed,
Origin codes: i - IGP, e - EGP, ? - incomplete
RPKI validation codes: V valid, I invalid, N Not found
```

```
      Network            Next Hop          Metric LocPrf Weight Path
  *>  172.16.1.0/24      172.16.0.1             0            0 300 i
  *>  192.168.0.0        0.0.0.0                0        32768 i
  *>  192.168.1.0        0.0.0.0                0        32768 i
ITA#
```

Which table version is displayed? Why?

_____

_____

What happened to the route for network 10.1.1.0/24?

_____

d. Bring ISP1 router Loopback0 back up by issuing the **no shutdown** command.

```
ISP1(config)# interface loopback 0
ISP1(config-if)# no shutdown
ISP1(config-if)#
```

e. On ITA, issue the **show ip bgp neighbors** command. The following is a partial sample output of the command showing neighbor 172.16.0.1.

```
ITA# show ip bgp neighbors
BGP neighbor is 10.0.0.1,  remote AS 200, external link
  BGP version 4, remote router ID 10.1.1.1
  BGP state = Established, up for 00:20:47
  Last read 00:00:49, last write 00:00:41, hold time is 180, keepalive
interval is 60 seconds
  Neighbor sessions:
    1 active, is not multisession capable (disabled)
  Neighbor capabilities:
    Route refresh: advertised and received(new)
    Four-octets ASN Capability: advertised and received
    Address family IPv4 Unicast: advertised and received
    Enhanced Refresh Capability: advertised and received
    Multisession Capability:
    Stateful switchover support enabled: NO for session 1
  Message statistics:
    InQ depth is 0
    OutQ depth is 0

                    Sent        Rcvd
    Opens:            1           1
    Notifications:    0           0
    Updates:          5           1
    Keepalives:      15          17
    Route Refresh:    0           0
    Total:           21          19
  Default minimum time between advertisement runs is 30 seconds

<output omitted>
```

Based on the output of this command, what is the BGP state between this router and ISP2?

_____

_____

How long has this connection been up?

_____

Step 5: Configure route filters.

a. Check the ISP2 routing table using the **show ip route** command. ISP2 should have a route that belongs to ISP1, network 10.1.1.0.

```
ISP2# show ip route
<output omitted>

        10.0.0.0/24 is subnetted, 1 subnets
B          10.1.1.0 [20/0] via 172.16.0.2, 00:09:26
        172.16.0.0/16 is variably subnetted, 4 subnets, 3 masks
C          172.16.0.0/30 is directly connected, Serial0/0/1
L          172.16.0.1/32 is directly connected, Serial0/0/1
C          172.16.1.0/24 is directly connected, Loopback0
L          172.16.1.1/32 is directly connected, Loopback0
B       192.168.0.0/24 [20/0] via 172.16.0.2, 00:28:05
B       192.168.1.0/24 [20/0] via 172.16.0.2, 00:28:05
ISP2#
```

If ITA advertises a route belonging to ISP1, ISP2 installs that route in its table. ISP2 might then attempt to route transit traffic through the ITA. This would make ITA a transit router. A traceroute to ISP1's Lo0 interface illustrates this issue.

```
ISP2# traceroute 10.1.1.1
Type escape sequence to abort.
Tracing the route to 10.1.1.1
VRF info: (vrf in name/id, vrf out name/id)
  1 172.16.0.2 8 msec 4 msec 8 msec
  2  *   *   *
  3  *   *   *
  4  *   *   *   <control-shift-6 to break>
ISP2#
```

The **traceroute 10.1.1.1** fails because ISP1 does not have a route to the source IPv4 address of the traceroute, 172.16.0.1. It is common in BGP networks not to advertise the links between providers in BGP. A traceroute using the source IPv4 address of ISP2's Lo0 interface is successful, showing that ITA is a transit router for this network.

```
ISP2# traceroute 10.1.1.1 source loopback0
Type escape sequence to abort.
Tracing the route to 10.1.1.1
VRF info: (vrf in name/id, vrf out name/id)
  1 172.16.0.2 8 msec 4 msec 8 msec
  2 10.0.0.1 12 msec *  12 msec
ISP2#
```

b. Configure the ITA router so that it advertises only ITA networks 192.168.0.0 and 192.168.1.0 to both providers. On the ITA router, configure the following access list.

```
ITA(config)# access-list 1 permit 192.168.0.0 0.0.1.255
```

c. Apply this access list as a route filter using the **distribute-list** keyword with the BGP **neighbor** statement.

```
ITA(config)# router bgp 100
ITA(config-router)# neighbor 10.0.0.1 distribute-list 1 out
ITA(config-router)# neighbor 172.16.0.1 distribute-list 1 out
```

d. Check the routing table for ISP2 again. The route to 10.1.1.0, ISP1, should still be in the table.

```
ISP2# show ip route
<output omitted>

      10.0.0.0/24 is subnetted, 1 subnets
B        10.1.1.0 [20/0] via 172.16.0.2, 00:25:14
      172.16.0.0/16 is variably subnetted, 4 subnets, 3 masks
C        172.16.0.0/30 is directly connected, Serial0/0/1
L        172.16.0.1/32 is directly connected, Serial0/0/1
C        172.16.1.0/24 is directly connected, Loopback0
L        172.16.1.1/32 is directly connected, Loopback0
B     192.168.0.0/24 [20/0] via 172.16.0.2, 00:43:53
B     192.168.1.0/24 [20/0] via 172.16.0.2, 00:43:53
ISP2#
```

e. Return to ITA and issue the **clear ip bgp *** command. Wait until the routers reach the established state, which might take several seconds, and then recheck the ISP2 routing table. The route to ISP1, network 10.1.1.0, should no longer be in the routing table for ISP2, and the route to ISP2, network 172.16.1.0, should not be in the routing table for ISP1.

```
ITA# clear ip bgp *
ITA#
*Sep  8 16:47:25.179: %BGP-5-ADJCHANGE: neighbor 10.0.0.1 Down User reset
*Sep  8 16:47:25.179: %BGP_SESSION-5-ADJCHANGE: neighbor 10.0.0.1 IPv4
Unicast topology base removed from session  User reset
*Sep  8 16:47:25.179: %BGP-5-ADJCHANGE: neighbor 172.16.0.1 Down User reset
*Sep  8 16:47:25.179: %BGP_SESSION-5-ADJCHANGE: neighbor 172.16.0.1 IPv4
Unicast topology base removed from session  User reset
*Sep  8 16:47:25.815: %BGP-5-ADJCHANGE: neighbor 10.0.0.1 Up
*Sep  8 16:47:25.819: %BGP-5-ADJCHANGE
ITA#: neighbor 172.16.0.1 Up
ITA#
```

Note: The **clear ip bgp *** command is disruptive because it completely resets all BGP adjacencies. This is acceptable in a lab environment but could be problematic in a production network. Instead, if only a change of inbound/outbound routing policies is to be performed, it is sufficient to issue the **clear ip bgp * in** or **clear ip bgp * out** commands. These commands perform only a new BGP database synchronization without the disruptive effects of a complete BGP adjacency reset. All current Cisco IOS versions support the route refresh capability that replaces the inbound soft reconfiguration feature that previously had to be configured on a per-neighbor basis.

```
ISP2# show ip route
<output omitted>

      172.16.0.0/16 is variably subnetted, 4 subnets, 3 masks
C        172.16.0.0/30 is directly connected, Serial0/0/1
L        172.16.0.1/32 is directly connected, Serial0/0/1
```

```
C          172.16.1.0/24 is directly connected, Loopback0
L          172.16.1.1/32 is directly connected, Loopback0
B      192.168.0.0/24 [20/0] via 172.16.0.2, 00:00:06
B      192.168.1.0/24 [20/0] via 172.16.0.2, 00:00:06
ISP2#
```

```
ISP1# show ip route
<output omitted>

       10.0.0.0/8 is variably subnetted, 4 subnets, 3 masks
C          10.0.0.0/30 is directly connected, Serial0/0/0
L          10.0.0.1/32 is directly connected, Serial0/0/0
C          10.1.1.0/24 is directly connected, Loopback0
L          10.1.1.1/32 is directly connected, Loopback0
B      192.168.0.0/24 [20/0] via 10.0.0.2, 00:00:42
B      192.168.1.0/24 [20/0] via 10.0.0.2, 00:00:42
ISP1#
```

Step 6: Configure primary and backup routes using floating static routes.

With bidirectional communication established with each ISP via BGP, configure the primary and backup routes. This can be done with floating static routes or BGP.

a.   Issue the **show ip route** command on the ITA router.

```
ITA# show ip route
<output omitted>

Gateway of last resort is not set

       10.0.0.0/8 is variably subnetted, 3 subnets, 3 masks
C          10.0.0.0/30 is directly connected, Serial0/0/0
L          10.0.0.2/32 is directly connected, Serial0/0/0
B          10.1.1.0/24 [20/0] via 10.0.0.1, 00:03:51
       172.16.0.0/16 is variably subnetted, 3 subnets, 3 masks
C          172.16.0.0/30 is directly connected, Serial0/0/1
L          172.16.0.2/32 is directly connected, Serial0/0/1
B          172.16.1.0/24 [20/0] via 172.16.0.1, 00:03:51
       192.168.0.0/24 is variably subnetted, 2 subnets, 2 masks
C          192.168.0.0/24 is directly connected, Loopback0
L          192.168.0.1/32 is directly connected, Loopback0
       192.168.1.0/24 is variably subnetted, 2 subnets, 2 masks
C          192.168.1.0/24 is directly connected, Loopback1
L          192.168.1.1/32 is directly connected, Loopback1
ITA#
```

Notice that there is no gateway of last resort defined. This is a problem because ITA is the border router for the corporate network.

b.   Configure static routes to reflect the policy that ISP1 is the primary provider and that ISP2 acts as the backup by specifying a lower distance metric for the route to ISP1 (210) as compared to the backup route to ISP2 (distance metric 220).

```
ITA(config)# ip route 0.0.0.0 0.0.0.0 10.0.0.1 210
ITA(config)# ip route 0.0.0.0 0.0.0.0 172.16.0.1 220
```

c.   Verify that a default route is defined using the **show ip route** command.

```
ITA# show ip route
<output omitted>
Gateway of last resort is 10.0.0.1 to network 0.0.0.0

S*    0.0.0.0/0 [210/0] via 10.0.0.1
         10.0.0.0/8 is variably subnetted, 3 subnets, 3 masks
C        10.0.0.0/30 is directly connected, Serial0/0/0
L        10.0.0.2/32 is directly connected, Serial0/0/0
B        10.1.1.0/24 [20/0] via 10.0.0.1, 00:05:38
         172.16.0.0/16 is variably subnetted, 3 subnets, 3 masks
C        172.16.0.0/30 is directly connected, Serial0/0/1
L        172.16.0.2/32 is directly connected, Serial0/0/1
B        172.16.1.0/24 [20/0] via 172.16.0.1, 00:05:38
         192.168.0.0/24 is variably subnetted, 2 subnets, 2 masks
C        192.168.0.0/24 is directly connected, Loopback0
L        192.168.0.1/32 is directly connected, Loopback0
         192.168.1.0/24 is variably subnetted, 2 subnets, 2 masks
C        192.168.1.0/24 is directly connected, Loopback1
L        192.168.1.1/32 is directly connected, Loopback1
ITA#
```

d.   Test this default route by creating an unadvertised loopback on the router for ISP1.

```
ISP1# config t
ISP1(config)# interface loopback 100
ISP1(config-if)# ip address 192.168.100.1 255.255.255.0
```

e.   Issue the **show ip route** command to ensure that the newly added 192.168.100.0 /24 network does not appear in the routing table.

```
ITA# show ip route
<output omitted>

Gateway of last resort is 10.0.0.1 to network 0.0.0.0

S*    0.0.0.0/0 [210/0] via 10.0.0.1
         10.0.0.0/8 is variably subnetted, 3 subnets, 3 masks
C        10.0.0.0/30 is directly connected, Serial0/0/0
L        10.0.0.2/32 is directly connected, Serial0/0/0
B        10.1.1.0/24 [20/0] via 10.0.0.1, 00:07:08
         172.16.0.0/16 is variably subnetted, 3 subnets, 3 masks
C        172.16.0.0/30 is directly connected, Serial0/0/1
L        172.16.0.2/32 is directly connected, Serial0/0/1
B        172.16.1.0/24 [20/0] via 172.16.0.1, 00:07:08
         192.168.0.0/24 is variably subnetted, 2 subnets, 2 masks
C        192.168.0.0/24 is directly connected, Loopback0
L        192.168.0.1/32 is directly connected, Loopback0
         192.168.1.0/24 is variably subnetted, 2 subnets, 2 masks
C        192.168.1.0/24 is directly connected, Loopback1
L        192.168.1.1/32 is directly connected, Loopback1
ITA#
```

f. In extended ping mode, ping the ISP1 loopback 1 interface 192.168.100.1 with the source originating from the ITA loopback 1 interface 192.168.1.1.

```
ITA# ping
Protocol [ip]:
Target IP address: 192.168.100.1
Repeat count [5]:
Datagram size [100]:
Timeout in seconds [2]:
Extended commands [n]: y
Source address or interface: 192.168.1.1
Type of service [0]:
Set DF bit in IP header? [no]:
Validate reply data? [no]:
Data pattern [0xABCD]:
Loose, Strict, Record, Timestamp, Verbose[none]:
Sweep range of sizes [n]:
Type escape sequence to abort.
Sending 5, 100-byte ICMP Echos to 192.168.100.1, timeout is 2 seconds:
Packet sent with a source address of 192.168.1.1
!!!!!
Success rate is 100 percent (5/5), round-trip min/avg/max = 12/14/16 ms
ITA#
```

Note: You can bypass extended ping prompted mode and ping while specifying a source address using one of these abbreviated commands:

```
ITA# ping 192.168.100.1 source 192.168.1.1
```

or

```
ITA# ping 192.168.100.1 source Lo1
```

Note: Testing the default route by creating an unadvertised network on ISP1 and pinging it works only because the default route also points toward ISP1. If the preferred default route pointed toward ISP2, the ping to that unadvertised network on ISP1 would not succeed. If the link to ISP1 failed, the default route to ISP2 would become active, but the pings would be successful only if ISP1 and ISP2 have another working interconnection and appropriate BGP peering between them, which is currently not the case.

Step 7: Use BGP to propagate a default route.

a. An ISP router will be used to inject a default route via BGP. First, remove the current default routes on ITA.

```
ITA(config)# no ip route 0.0.0.0 0.0.0.0 10.0.0.1 210
ITA(config)# no ip route 0.0.0.0 0.0.0.0 172.16.0.1 220
```

b. Next, configure the ISP1 router to send a default route to its neighbor, the ITA router. This command does not require the presence of 0.0.0.0 in the local ISP1 router.

```
ISP1(config)# router bgp 200
ISP1(config-router)# neighbor 10.0.0.2 default-originate
ISP1(config-router)#
```

c. Verify that the default route was received by ITA using BGP.

```
ITA# show ip route
<output omitted>
```

```
Gateway of last resort is 10.0.0.1 to network 0.0.0.0

B*      0.0.0.0/0 [20/0] via 10.0.0.1, 00:01:43
        10.0.0.0/8 is variably subnetted, 3 subnets, 3 masks
C          10.0.0.0/30 is directly connected, Serial0/0/0
L          10.0.0.2/32 is directly connected, Serial0/0/0
B          10.1.1.0/24 [20/0] via 10.0.0.1, 00:06:51
        172.16.0.0/16 is variably subnetted, 3 subnets, 3 masks
C          172.16.0.0/30 is directly connected, Serial0/0/1
L          172.16.0.2/32 is directly connected, Serial0/0/1
B          172.16.1.0/24 [20/0] via 172.16.0.1, 00:06:51
        192.168.0.0/24 is variably subnetted, 2 subnets, 2 masks
C          192.168.0.0/24 is directly connected, Loopback0
L          192.168.0.1/32 is directly connected, Loopback0
        192.168.1.0/24 is variably subnetted, 2 subnets, 2 masks
C          192.168.1.0/24 is directly connected, Loopback1
L          192.168.1.1/32 is directly connected, Loopback1
ITA#
```

Lab 7-2 Using the AS_PATH Attribute

Topology

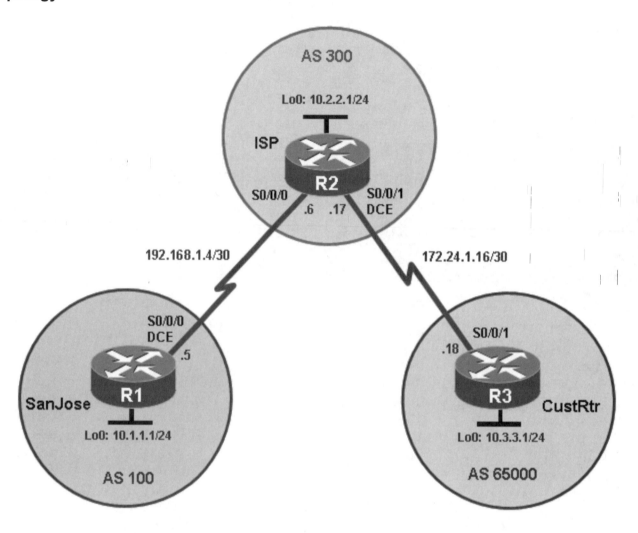

Objectives

- Use BGP commands to prevent private AS numbers from being advertised to the outside world.
- Use the AS_PATH attribute to filter BGP routes based on their source AS numbers.

Background

The International Travel Agency's ISP has been assigned an AS number of 300. This provider uses BGP to exchange routing information with several customer networks. Each customer network is assigned an AS number from the private range, such as AS 65000. Configure the ISP router to remove the private AS numbers from the AS Path information of CustRtr. In addition, the ISP would like to prevent its customer networks from receiving route information from International Travel Agency's AS 100. Use the AS_PATH attribute to implement this policy.

Note: This lab uses Cisco 1941 routers with Cisco IOS Release 15.4 with IP Base. The switches are Cisco WS-C2960-24TT-L with Fast Ethernet interfaces; therefore, the router will use routing metrics associated with a 100 Mb/s interface. Depending on the router or switch model and Cisco IOS Software version, the commands available and output produced might vary from what is shown in this lab.

Required Resources

- 3 routers (Cisco IOS Release 15.2 or comparable)
- Serial and Ethernet cables

Step 0: Suggested starting configurations.

a. Apply the following configuration to each router along with the appropriate **hostname**. The **exec-timeout 0 0** command should only be used in a lab environment.

```
Router(config)# no ip domain-lookup
Router(config)# line con 0
Router(config-line)# logging synchronous
Router(config-line)# exec-timeout 0 0
```

Step 1: Configure interface addresses.

a. Using the addressing scheme in the diagram, create the loopback interfaces and apply IPv4 addresses to these and the serial interfaces on SanJose (R1), ISP (R2), and CustRtr (R3). The ISP loopbacks simulate real networks. Set a clock rate on the DCE serial interfaces.

```
SanJose(config)# interface Loopback0
SanJose(config-if)# ip address 10.1.1.1 255.255.255.0
SanJose(config-if)# exit
SanJose(config)# interface Serial0/0/0
SanJose(config-if)# ip address 192.168.1.5 255.255.255.252
SanJose(config-if)# clock rate 128000
SanJose(config-if)# no shutdown
SanJose(config-if)# end
SanJose#

ISP(config)# interface Loopback0
ISP(config-if)# ip address 10.2.2.1 255.255.255.0
ISP(config-if)# interface Serial0/0/0
ISP(config-if)# ip address 192.168.1.6 255.255.255.252
ISP(config-if)# no shutdown
ISP(config-if)# exit
ISP(config)# interface Serial0/0/1
ISP(config-if)# ip address 172.24.1.17 255.255.255.252
ISP(config-if)# clock rate 128000
ISP(config-if)# no shutdown
ISP(config-if)# end
ISP#

CustRtr(config)# interface Loopback0
CustRtr(config-if)# ip address 10.3.3.1 255.255.255.0
CustRtr(config-if)# exit
CustRtr(config)# interface Serial0/0/1
CustRtr(config-if)# ip address 172.24.1.18 255.255.255.252
CustRtr(config-if)# no shutdown
CustRtr(config-if)# end
CustRtr#
```

b. Use **ping** to test the connectivity between the directly connected routers.

   Note: SanJose will not be able to reach either ISP's loopback (10.2.2.1) or CustRtr's loopback (10.3.3.1), nor will it be able to reach either end of the link joining ISP to CustRtr (172.24.1.17 and 172.24.1.18).

Step 2: Configure BGP.

a. Configure BGP for normal operation. Enter the appropriate BGP commands on each router so that they identify their BGP neighbors and advertise their loopback networks.

```
SanJose(config)# router bgp 100
SanJose(config-router)# neighbor 192.168.1.6 remote-as 300
SanJose(config-router)# network 10.1.1.0 mask 255.255.255.0

ISP(config)# router bgp 300
ISP(config-router)# neighbor 192.168.1.5 remote-as 100
ISP(config-router)# neighbor 172.24.1.18 remote-as 65000
ISP(config-router)# network 10.2.2.0 mask 255.255.255.0

CustRtr(config)# router bgp 65000
CustRtr(config-router)# neighbor 172.24.1.17 remote-as 300
CustRtr(config-router)# network 10.3.3.0 mask 255.255.255.0
```

b. Verify that these routers have established the appropriate neighbor relationships by issuing the **show ip bgp neighbors** command on each router.

```
ISP# show ip bgp neighbors
BGP neighbor is 172.24.1.18,  remote AS 65000, external link
  BGP version 4, remote router ID 10.3.3.1
  BGP state = Established, up for 00:00:28
  Last read 00:00:28, last write 00:00:28, hold time is 180, keepalive interval is 60
seconds
<output omitted>


BGP neighbor is 192.168.1.5,  remote AS 100, external link
  BGP version 4, remote router ID 10.1.1.1
  BGP state = Established, up for 00:01:34
  Last read 00:00:33, last write 00:00:06, hold time is 180, keepalive interval is 60
seconds
<output omitted>
```

Step 3: Remove the private AS.

a. Display the SanJose routing table using the **show ip route** command. SanJose should have a route to both 10.2.2.0 and 10.3.3.0. Troubleshoot if necessary.

```
SanJose#show ip route
Codes: L - local, C - connected, S - static, R - RIP, M - mobile, B - BGP
       D - EIGRP, EX - EIGRP external, O - OSPF, IA - OSPF inter area
       N1 - OSPF NSSA external type 1, N2 - OSPF NSSA external type 2
       E1 - OSPF external type 1, E2 - OSPF external type 2
       i - IS-IS, su - IS-IS summary, L1 - IS-IS level-1, L2 - IS-IS level-2
       ia - IS-IS inter area, * - candidate default, U - per-user static
       route
       o - ODR, P - periodic downloaded static route, H - NHRP, l - LISP
       a - application route
       + - replicated route, % - next hop override
```

```
Gateway of last resort is not set

      10.0.0.0/8 is variably subnetted, 4 subnets, 2 masks
C        10.1.1.0/24 is directly connected, Loopback0
L        10.1.1.1/32 is directly connected, Loopback0
B        10.2.2.0/24 [20/0] via 192.168.1.6, 00:04:22
B        10.3.3.0/24 [20/0] via 192.168.1.6, 00:03:14
      192.168.1.0/24 is variably subnetted, 2 subnets, 2 masks
C        192.168.1.4/30 is directly connected, Serial0/0/0
L        192.168.1.5/32 is directly connected, Serial0/0/0
SanJose#
```

b. Ping the 10.3.3.1 address from SanJose.

Why does this fail?

_____

_____

c. Ping again, this time as an extended ping, sourcing from the Loopback0 interface address.

```
SanJose# ping
Protocol [ip]:
Target IP address: 10.3.3.1
Repeat count [5]:
Datagram size [100]:
Timeout in seconds [2]:
Extended commands [n]: y
Source address or interface: 10.1.1.1
Type of service [0]:
Set DF bit in IP header? [no]:
Validate reply data? [no]:
Data pattern [0xABCD]:
Loose, Strict, Record, Timestamp, Verbose[none]:
Sweep range of sizes [n]:
Type escape sequence to abort.
Sending 5, 100-byte ICMP Echos to 10.3.3.1, timeout is 2 seconds:
Packet sent with a source address of 10.1.1.1
!!!!!
Success rate is 100 percent (5/5), round-trip min/avg/max = 28/28/28 ms
SanJose#
```

Note: You can bypass extended ping mode and specify a source address using one of these commands:

```
SanJose# ping 10.3.3.1 source 10.1.1.1
```

or

```
SanJose# ping 10.3.3.1 source Lo0
```

d. Check the BGP table from SanJose by using the **show ip bgp** command. Note the AS path for the
    10.3.3.0 network. The AS 65000 should be listed in the path to 10.3.3.0.

```
SanJose# show ip bgp
BGP table version is 5, local router ID is 10.1.1.1
Status codes: s suppressed, d damped, h history, * valid, > best, i -
internal,
            r RIB-failure, S Stale, m multipath, b backup-path, f RT-
Filter,
            x best-external, a additional-path, c RIB-compressed,
```

```
Origin codes: i - IGP, e - EGP, ? - incomplete
RPKI validation codes: V valid, I invalid, N Not found

     Network            Next Hop            Metric LocPrf Weight Path
 *>  10.1.1.0/24        0.0.0.0                  0          32768 i
 *>  10.2.2.0/24        192.168.1.6              0              0 300 i
 *>  10.3.3.0/24        192.168.1.6                             0 300 65000 i
SanJose#
```

Why is this a problem?

_____

_____

e. Configure ISP to strip the private AS numbers from BGP routes exchanged with SanJose using the following commands.

```
ISP(config)# router bgp 300
ISP(config-router)# neighbor 192.168.1.5 remove-private-as
```

f. After issuing these commands, use the **clear ip bgp *** command on ISP to reestablish the BGP relationship between the three routers. Wait several seconds and then return to SanJose to check its routing table.

Note: The **clear ip bgp * soft** command can also be used to force each router to resend its BGP table.

```
ISP# clear ip bgp *
ISP#
*Sep  8 18:40:03.551: %BGP-5-ADJCHANGE: neighbor 172.24.1.18 Down User reset
*Sep  8 18:40:03.551: %BGP_SESSION-5-ADJCHANGE: neighbor 172.24.1.18 IPv4
Unicast topology base removed from session  User reset
*Sep  8 18:40:03.551: %BGP-5-ADJCHANGE: neighbor 192.168.1.5 Down User reset
*Sep  8 18:40:03.551: %BGP_SESSION-5-ADJCHANGE: neighbor 192.168.1.5 IPv4
Unicast topology base removed from session  User reset
*Sep  8 18:40:04.515: %BGP-5-ADJCHANGE: neighbor 172.24.1.18 Up
*Sep  8 18:40:04.519: %BGP-
ISP#5-ADJCHANGE: neighbor 192.168.1.5 Up
ISP#

SanJose# show ip route
<output omitted>

      10.0.0.0/8 is variably subnetted, 4 subnets, 2 masks
C        10.1.1.0/24 is directly connected, Loopback0
L        10.1.1.1/32 is directly connected, Loopback0
B        10.2.2.0/24 [20/0] via 192.168.1.6, 00:00:20
B        10.3.3.0/24 [20/0] via 192.168.1.6, 00:01:02
      192.168.1.0/24 is variably subnetted, 2 subnets, 2 masks
C        192.168.1.4/30 is directly connected, Serial0/0/0
L        192.168.1.5/32 is directly connected, Serial0/0/0
SanJose#
```

Does SanJose still have a route to 10.3.3.0?

_____

SanJose should be able to ping 10.3.3.1 using its loopback 0 interface as the source of the ping.

```
SanJose# ping 10.3.3.1 source lo0

Type escape sequence to abort.
Sending 5, 100-byte ICMP Echos to 10.3.3.1, timeout is 2 seconds:
Packet sent with a source address of 10.1.1.1
!!!!!
Success rate is 100 percent (5/5), round-trip min/avg/max = 28/28/32 ms
```

g. Now check the BGP table on SanJose. The AS_ PATH to the 10.3.3.0 network should be AS 300. It no longer has the private AS in the path.

```
SanJose# show ip bgp
BGP table version is 9, local router ID is 10.1.1.1
Status codes: s suppressed, d damped, h history, * valid, > best, i -
internal,
              r RIB-failure, S Stale, m multipath, b backup-path, f RT-
Filter,
              x best-external, a additional-path, c RIB-compressed,
Origin codes: i - IGP, e - EGP, ? - incomplete
RPKI validation codes: V valid, I invalid, N Not found

     Network          Next Hop          Metric LocPrf Weight Path
 *>  10.1.1.0/24      0.0.0.0                0          32768 i
 *>  10.2.2.0/24      192.168.1.6            0              0 300 i
 *>  10.3.3.0/24      192.168.1.6                           0 300 i
SanJose#
```

Step 4: Use the AS_PATH attribute to filter routes.

As a final configuration, use the AS_PATH attribute to filter routes based on their origin. In a complex environment, you can use this attribute to enforce routing policy. In this case, the provider router, ISP, must be configured so that it does not propagate routes that originate from AS 100 to the customer router CustRtr.

AS-path access lists are read like regular access lists. The statements are read sequentially, and there is an implicit deny at the end. Rather than matching an address in each statement like a conventional access list, AS path access lists match on something called a regular expression. Regular expressions are a way of matching text patterns and have many uses. In this case, you will be using them in the AS path access list to match text patterns in AS paths.

a. Configure a special kind of access list to match BGP routes with an AS_PATH attribute that both begins and ends with the number 100. Enter the following commands on ISP.

```
ISP(config)# ip as-path access-list 1 deny ^100$
ISP(config)# ip as-path access-list 1 permit .*
```

The first command uses the ^ character to indicate that the AS path must begin with the given number 100. The $ character indicates that the AS_PATH attribute must also end with 100. Essentially, this statement matches only paths that are sourced from AS 100. Other paths, which might include AS 100 along the way, will not match this list.

In the second statement, the . (period) is a wildcard, and the * (asterisk) stands for a repetition of the wildcard. Together, .* matches any value of the AS_PATH attribute, which in effect permits any update that has not been denied by the previous **access-list** statement.

For more details on configuring regular expressions on Cisco routers, see:

http://www.cisco.com/c/en/us/td/docs/ios/12_2/termserv/configuration/guide/ftersv_c/tcfaapre.html

http://www.cisco.com/c/en/us/support/docs/ip/border-gateway-protocol-bgp/13754-26.html

b. Apply the configured access list using the **neighbor** command with the **filter-list** option.

```
ISP(config)# router bgp 300
ISP(config-router)# neighbor 172.24.1.18 filter-list 1 out
```

The **out** keyword specifies that the list is applied to routing information sent to this neighbor.

c. Use the **clear ip bgp *** command to reset the routing information. Wait several seconds and then check the routing table for ISP. The route to 10.1.1.0 should be in the routing table.

Note: To force the local router to resend its BGP table, a less disruptive option is to use the **clear ip bgp * out** or **clear ip bgp * soft** command (the second command performs both outgoing and incoming route resync).

```
ISP# clear ip bgp *
ISP#
*Sep  8 18:48:04.915: %BGP-5-ADJCHANGE: neighbor 172.24.1.18 Down User reset
*Sep  8 18:48:04.915: %BGP_SESSION-5-ADJCHANGE: neighbor 172.24.1.18 IPv4
Unicast topology base removed from session  User reset
*Sep  8 18:48:04.915: %BGP-5-ADJCHANGE: neighbor 192.168.1.5 Down User reset
*Sep  8 18:48:04.915: %BGP_SESSION-5-ADJCHANGE: neighbor 192.168.1.5 IPv4
Unicast topology base removed from session  User reset
*Sep  8 18:48:04.951: %BGP-5-ADJCHANGE: neighbor 172.24.1.18 Up
*Sep  8 18:48:04.955: %BGP-
ISP#5-ADJCHANGE: neighbor 192.168.1.5 Up
ISP#
```

```
ISP# show ip route
<output omitted>

      10.0.0.0/8 is variably subnetted, 4 subnets, 2 masks
B        10.1.1.0/24 [20/0] via 192.168.1.5, 00:00:29
C        10.2.2.0/24 is directly connected, Loopback0
L        10.2.2.1/32 is directly connected, Loopback0
B        10.3.3.0/24 [20/0] via 172.24.1.18, 00:00:29
      172.24.0.0/16 is variably subnetted, 2 subnets, 2 masks
C        172.24.1.16/30 is directly connected, Serial0/0/1
L        172.24.1.17/32 is directly connected, Serial0/0/1
      192.168.1.0/24 is variably subnetted, 2 subnets, 2 masks
C        192.168.1.4/30 is directly connected, Serial0/0/0
L        192.168.1.6/32 is directly connected, Serial0/0/0
ISP#
```

d. Check the routing table for CustRtr. It should not have a route to 10.1.1.0 in its routing table.

```
CustRtr# show ip route
<output omitted>

      10.0.0.0/8 is variably subnetted, 3 subnets, 2 masks
B        10.2.2.0/24 [20/0] via 172.24.1.17, 00:00:32
C        10.3.3.0/24 is directly connected, Loopback0
L        10.3.3.1/32 is directly connected, Loopback0
      172.24.0.0/16 is variably subnetted, 2 subnets, 2 masks
C        172.24.1.16/30 is directly connected, Serial0/0/1
```

```
L         172.24.1.18/32 is directly connected, Serial0/0/1
CustRtr#
```

e. Return to ISP and verify that the filter is working as intended. Issue the **show ip bgp regexp ^100$** command.

```
ISP# show ip bgp regexp ^100$
BGP table version is 4, local router ID is 10.2.2.1
Status codes: s suppressed, d damped, h history, * valid, > best, i -
internal,
              r RIB-failure, S Stale, m multipath, b backup-path, f RT-
Filter,
              x best-external, a additional-path, c RIB-compressed,
Origin codes: i - IGP, e - EGP, ? - incomplete
RPKI validation codes: V valid, I invalid, N Not found

      Network          Next Hop          Metric LocPrf Weight Path
 *>   10.1.1.0/24      192.168.1.5            0               0 100 i
ISP#
```

The output of this command shows all matches for the regular expressions that were used in the access list. The path to 10.1.1.0 matches the access list and is filtered from updates to CustRtr.

f. Run the following Tcl script on all routers to verify whether there is connectivity. All pings from ISP should be successful. SanJose should not be able to ping the CustRtr loopback 10.3.3.1 or the WAN link 172.24.1.16/30. CustRtr should not be able to ping the SanJose loopback 10.1.1.1 or the WAN link 192.168.1.4/30.

```
ISP# tclsh

foreach address {
10.1.1.1
10.2.2.1
10.3.3.1
192.168.1.5
192.168.1.6
172.24.1.17
172.24.1.18
} {
ping $address }
```

Lab 7-3 Configuring IBGP and EBGP Sessions, Local Preference, and MED

Topology

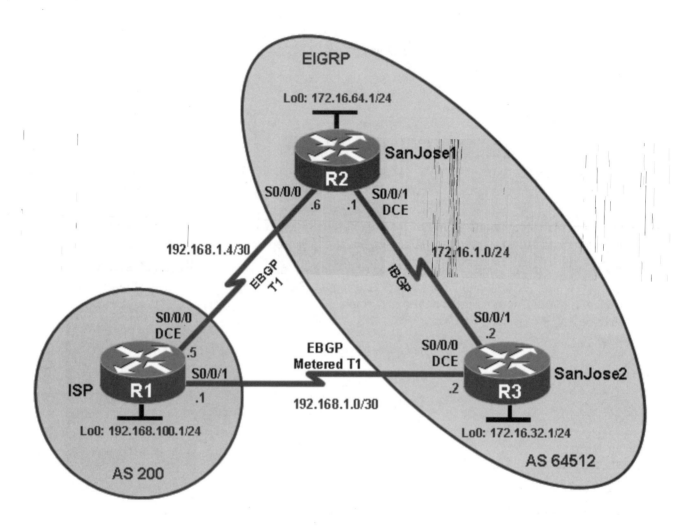

Objectives

- For IBGP peers to correctly exchange routing information, use the **next-hop-self** command with the **Local-Preference** and **MED** attributes.
- Ensure that the flat-rate, unlimited-use T1 link is used for sending and receiving data to and from the AS 200 on ISP and that the metered T1 will only be used in the event that the primary T1 link has failed.

Background

The International Travel Agency runs BGP on its SanJose1 and SanJose2 routers externally with the ISP router in AS 200. IBGP is run internally between SanJose1 and SanJose2. Your job is to configure both EBGP and IBGP for this internetwork to allow for redundancy. The metered T1 should only be used in the event that the primary T1 link has failed. Traffic sent across the metered T1 link offers the same bandwidth of the primary link but at a huge expense. Ensure that this link is not used unnecessarily.

Note: This lab uses Cisco 1941 routers with Cisco IOS Release 15.4 with IP Base. The switches are Cisco WS-C2960-24TT-L with Fast Ethernet interfaces; therefore, the router will use routing metrics associated with a 100 Mb/s interface. Depending on the router or switch model and Cisco IOS Software version, the commands available and output produced might vary from what is shown in this lab.

Required Resources

- 3 routers (Cisco IOS Release 15.2 or comparable)
- Serial and Ethernet cables

Step 0: Suggested starting configurations.

a. Apply the following configuration to each router along with the appropriate **hostname**. The **exec-timeout 0 0** command should only be used in a lab environment.

```
Router(config)# no ip domain-lookup
Router(config)# line con 0
Router(config-line)# logging synchronous
Router(config-line)# exec-timeout 0 0
```

Step 1: Configure interface addresses.

a. Using the addressing scheme in the diagram, create the loopback interfaces and apply IPv4 addresses to these and the serial interfaces on ISP (R1), SanJose1 (R2), and SanJose2 (R3).

Router R1 (hostname ISP)

```
ISP(config)# interface Loopback0
ISP(config-if)# ip address 192.168.100.1 255.255.255.0
ISP(config-if)# exit
ISP(config)# interface Serial0/0/0
ISP(config-if)# ip address 192.168.1.5 255.255.255.252
ISP(config-if)# clock rate 128000
ISP(config-if)# no shutdown
ISP(config-if)# exit
ISP(config)# interface Serial0/0/1
ISP(config-if)# ip address 192.168.1.1 255.255.255.252
ISP(config-if)# no shutdown
ISP(config-if)# end
ISP#
```

Router R2 (hostname SanJose1)

```
SanJose1(config)# interface Loopback0
SanJose1(config-if)# ip address 172.16.64.1 255.255.255.0
SanJose1(config-if)# exit
SanJose1(config)# interface Serial0/0/0
SanJose1(config-if)# ip address 192.168.1.6 255.255.255.252
SanJose1(config-if)# no shutdown
SanJose1(config-if)# exit
SanJose1(config)# interface Serial0/0/1
SanJose1(config-if)# ip address 172.16.1.1 255.255.255.0
SanJose1(config-if)# clock rate 128000
SanJose1(config-if)# no shutdown
SanJose1(config-if)# end
SanJose1#
```

Router R3 (hostname SanJose2)

```
SanJose2(config)# interface Loopback0
SanJose2(config-if)# ip address 172.16.32.1 255.255.255.0
SanJose2(config-if)# exit
SanJose2(config)# interface Serial0/0/0
SanJose2(config-if)# ip address 192.168.1.2 255.255.255.252
SanJose2(config-if)# clock rate 128000
SanJose2(config-if)# no shutdown
SanJose2(config-if)# exit
SanJose2(config)# interface Serial0/0/1
SanJose2(config-if)# ip address 172.16.1.2 255.255.255.0
SanJose2(config-if)# no shutdown
SanJose2(config-if)# end
SanJose2#
```

b. Use **ping** to test the connectivity between the directly connected routers. Both SanJose routers should be able to ping each other and their local ISP serial link IP address. The ISP router cannot reach the segment between SanJose1 and SanJose2.

Step 2: Configure EIGRP.

Configure EIGRP between the SanJose1 and SanJose2 routers. (Note: If using an IOS prior to 15.0, use the no **auto-summary router** configuration command to disable automatic summarization. This command is the default beginning with IOS 15.)

```
SanJose1(config)# router eigrp 1
SanJose1(config-router)# network 172.16.0.0

SanJose2(config)# router eigrp 1
SanJose2(config-router)# network 172.16.0.0
```

Step 3: Configure IBGP and verify BGP neighbors.

a. Configure IBGP between the SanJose1 and SanJose2 routers. On the SanJose1 router, enter the following configuration.

```
SanJose1(config)# router bgp 64512
SanJose1(config-router)# neighbor 172.16.32.1 remote-as 64512
SanJose1(config-router)# neighbor 172.16.32.1 update-source lo0
```

If multiple pathways to the BGP neighbor exist, the router can use multiple IP interfaces to communicate with the neighbor. The source IP address therefore depends on the outgoing interface. The **update-source lo0** command instructs the router to use the IP address of the interface Loopback0 as the source IP address for all BGP messages sent to that neighbor.

b. Complete the IBGP configuration on SanJose2 using the following commands.

```
SanJose2(config)# router bgp 64512
SanJose2(config-router)# neighbor 172.16.64.1 remote-as 64512
SanJose2(config-router)# neighbor 172.16.64.1 update-source lo0
```

c. Verify that SanJose1 and SanJose2 become BGP neighbors by issuing the **show ip bgp neighbors** command on SanJose1. View the following partial output. If the BGP state is not established, troubleshoot the connection.

```
SanJose2# show ip bgp neighbors
BGP neighbor is 172.16.64.1,  remote AS 64512, internal link
  BGP version 4, remote router ID 172.16.64.1
```

```
  BGP state = Established, up for 00:00:22
  Last read 00:00:22, last write 00:00:22, hold time is 180, keepalive
interval is 60 seconds
<output omitted>
```

The link between SanJose1 and SanJose2 should be identified as an internal link indicating an IBGP peering relationship, as shown in the output.

Step 4: Configure EBGP and verify BGP neighbors.

a. Configure ISP to run EBGP with SanJose1 and SanJose2. Enter the following commands on ISP.

```
ISP(config)# router bgp 200
ISP(config-router)# neighbor 192.168.1.6 remote-as 64512
ISP(config-router)# neighbor 192.168.1.2 remote-as 64512
ISP(config-router)# network 192.168.100.0
```

Because EBGP sessions are almost always established over point-to-point links, there is no reason to use the **update-source** keyword in this configuration. Only one path exists between the peers. If this path goes down, alternative paths are not available.

b. Configure a discard static route for the 172.16.0.0/16 network. Any packets that do not have a more specific match (longer match) for a 172.16.0.0 subnet will be dropped instead of sent to the ISP. Later in this lab we will configure a default route to the ISP.

```
SanJose1(config)# ip route 172.16.0.0 255.255.0.0 null0
```

c. Configure SanJose1 as an EBGP peer to ISP.

```
SanJose1(config)# router bgp 64512
SanJose1(config-router)# neighbor 192.168.1.5 remote-as 200
SanJose1(config-router)# network 172.16.0.0
```

d. Use the **show ip bgp neighbors** command to verify that SanJose1 and ISP have reached the established state. Troubleshoot if necessary.

```
SanJose1# show ip bgp neighbors
BGP neighbor is 172.16.32.1,  remote AS 64512, internal link
  BGP version 4, remote router ID 172.16.32.1
  BGP state = Established, up for 00:12:43
<output omitted>

BGP neighbor is 192.168.1.5,  remote AS 200, external link
  BGP version 4, remote router ID 192.168.100.1
  BGP state = Established, up for 00:06:49
  Last read 00:00:42, last write 00:00:45, hold time is 180, keepalive
interval is 60 seconds
<output omitted>
```

Notice that the "external link" indicates that an EBGP peering session has been established. You should also see an informational message indicating the establishment of the BGP neighbor relationship.

```
*Sep  8 21:09:59.699: %BGP-5-ADJCHANGE: neighbor 192.168.1.5 Up
```

e. Configure a discard static route for 172.16.0.0/16 on SanJose2 and as an EBGP peer to ISP.

```
SanJose2(config)# ip route 172.16.0.0 255.255.0.0 null0
SanJose2(config)# router bgp 64512
SanJose2(config-router)# neighbor 192.168.1.1 remote-as 200
SanJose2(config-router)# network 172.16.0.0
```

Step 5: View BGP summary output.

In Step 4, the **show ip bgp neighbors** command was used to verify that SanJose1 and ISP had reached the established state. A useful alternative command is **show ip bgp summary**. The output should be similar to the following.

```
SanJose2# show ip bgp summary
BGP router identifier 172.16.32.1, local AS number 64512
BGP table version is 6, main routing table version 6
2 network entries using 288 bytes of memory
4 path entries using 320 bytes of memory
4/2 BGP path/bestpath attribute entries using 640 bytes of memory
1 BGP AS-PATH entries using 24 bytes of memory
0 BGP route-map cache entries using 0 bytes of memory
0 BGP filter-list cache entries using 0 bytes of memory
BGP using 1272 total bytes of memory
BGP activity 2/0 prefixes, 4/0 paths, scan interval 60 secs

Neighbor        V    AS    MsgRcvd MsgSent  TblVer  InQ OutQ Up/Down
State/PfxRcd
172.16.64.1     4  64512       27      26       6    0    0 00:18:15        2
192.168.1.1     4    200       10       7       6    0    0 00:01:42        1
SanJose2#
```

Step 6: Verify which path the traffic takes.

a. Clear the IP BGP conversation with the **clear ip bgp *** command on ISP. Wait for the conversations to reestablish with each SanJose router.

```
ISP# clear ip bgp *
ISP#
*Nov  9 22:05:32.427: %BGP-5-ADJCHANGE: neighbor 192.168.1.2 Down User reset
*Nov  9 22:05:32.427: %BGP_SESSION-5-ADJCHANGE: neighbor 192.168.1.2 IPv4
Unicast topology base removed from session  User reset
*Nov  9 22:05:32.427: %BGP-5-ADJCHANGE: neighbor 192.168.1.6 Down User reset
*Nov  9 22:05:32.427: %BGP_SESSION-5-ADJCHANGE: neighbor 192.168.1.6 IPv4
Unicast topology base removed from session  User reset
*Nov  9 22:05:32.851: %BGP-5-ADJCHANGE: neighbor 192.168.1.2 Up
*Nov  9 22:05:32.851: %BGP-
ISP#5-ADJCHANGE: neighbor 192.168.1.6 Up
ISP#
```

b. Test whether ISP can ping the loopback 0 address of 172.16.64.1 on SanJose1 and the serial link between SanJose1 and SanJose2, 172.16.1.1.

```
ISP# ping 172.16.64.1
Type escape sequence to abort.
Sending 5, 100-byte ICMP Echos to 172.16.64.1, timeout is 2 seconds:
.....
Success rate is 0 percent (0/5)
ISP#
ISP# ping 172.16.1.1
Type escape sequence to abort.
Sending 5, 100-byte ICMP Echos to 172.16.1.1, timeout is 2 seconds:
.....
```

```
Success rate is 0 percent (0/5)
ISP#
```

c. Now ping from ISP to the loopback 0 address of 172.16.32.1 on SanJose2 and the serial link between SanJose1 and SanJose2, 172.16.1.2.

```
ISP# ping 172.16.32.1
Type escape sequence to abort.
Sending 5, 100-byte ICMP Echos to 172.16.32.1, timeout is 2 seconds:
!!!!!
Success rate is 100 percent (5/5), round-trip min/avg/max = 12/14/16 ms
ISP# ping 172.16.1.2
Type escape sequence to abort.
Sending 5, 100-byte ICMP Echos to 172.16.1.2, timeout is 2 seconds:
!!!!!
Success rate is 100 percent (5/5), round-trip min/avg/max = 12/13/16 ms
ISP#
```

You should see successful pings to each IP address on SanJose2 router. Ping attempts to 172.16.64.1 and 172.16.1.1 should fail. Why does this happen?

_____

_____

_____

_____

d. Issue the **show ip bgp** command on ISP to verify BGP routes and metrics.

```
ISP# show ip bgp
BGP table version is 3, local router ID is 192.168.100.1
Status codes: s suppressed, d damped, h history, * valid, > best, i - internal,
              r RIB-failure, S Stale, m multipath, b backup-path, f RT-Filter,
              x best-external, a additional-path, c RIB-compressed,
Origin codes: i - IGP, e - EGP, ? - incomplete
RPKI validation codes: V valid, I invalid, N Not found

     Network          Next Hop         Metric LocPrf Weight Path
 *   172.16.0.0       192.168.1.6          0               0 64512 i
 *>                   192.168.1.2          0               0 64512 i
 *>  192.168.100.0    0.0.0.0              0           32768 i
ISP#
ISP# show ip bgp
```

Notice that ISP has two valid routes to the 172.16.0.0 network, as indicated by the *. However, the link to SanJose2 has been selected as the best path, indicated by the inclusion of the ">." Why did the ISP prefer the link to SanJose2 over SanJose1?

_____

_____

_____

_____

_____

Would changing the bandwidth metric on each link help to correct this issue? Explain.

_____

_____

BGP operates differently than all other protocols. Unlike other routing protocols that use complex algorithms involving factors such as bandwidth, delay, reliability, and load to formulate a metric, BGP is policy-based. BGP determines the best path based on variables, such as AS path, weight, local preference, MED, and so on. If all things are equal, BGP prefers the route leading to the BGP speaker with the lowest BGP router ID. The SanJose2 router with BGP router ID 172.16.32.1 was preferred to the higher BGP router ID of the SanJose1 router (172.16.64.1).

e. At this point, the ISP router should be able to get to each network connected to SanJose1 and SanJose2 from the loopback address 192.168.100.1. Use the extended **ping** command and specify the source address of ISP Lo0 to test.

```
ISP# ping 172.16.1.1 source 192.168.100.1

Type escape sequence to abort.
Sending 5, 100-byte ICMP Echos to 172.16.1.1, timeout is 2 seconds:
Packet sent with a source address of 192.168.100.1
!!!!!
Success rate is 100 percent (5/5), round-trip min/avg/max = 20/21/24 ms

ISP# ping 172.16.32.1 source 192.168.100.1

Type escape sequence to abort.
Sending 5, 100-byte ICMP Echos to 172.16.32.1, timeout is 2 seconds:
Packet sent with a source address of 192.168.100.1
!!!!!
Success rate is 100 percent (5/5), round-trip min/avg/max = 12/15/16 ms

ISP# ping 172.16.1.2 source 192.168.100.1

Type escape sequence to abort.
Sending 5, 100-byte ICMP Echos to 172.16.1.2, timeout is 2 seconds:
Packet sent with a source address of 192.168.100.1
!!!!!
Success rate is 100 percent (5/5), round-trip min/avg/max = 12/15/16 ms
ISP#

ISP# ping 172.16.64.1 source 192.168.100.1

Type escape sequence to abort.
Sending 5, 100-byte ICMP Echos to 172.16.64.1, timeout is 2 seconds:
Packet sent with a source address of 192.168.100.1
!!!!!
Success rate is 100 percent (5/5), round-trip min/avg/max = 20/21/24 ms
```

You can also use the extended ping dialogue to specify the source address, as shown in this example.

```
ISP# ping
Protocol [ip]:
Target IP address: 172.16.64.1
Repeat count [5]:
Datagram size [100]:
Timeout in seconds [2]:
Extended commands [n]: y
```

```
Source address or interface: 192.168.100.1
Type of service [0]:
Set DF bit in IP header? [no]:
Validate reply data? [no]:
Data pattern [0xABCD]:
Loose, Strict, Record, Timestamp, Verbose[none]:
Sweep range of sizes [n]:
Type escape sequence to abort.
Sending 5, 100-byte ICMP Echos to 172.16.64.1, timeout is 2 seconds:
Packet sent with a source address of 192.168.100.1
!!!!!
Success rate is 100 percent (5/5), round-trip min/avg/max = 20/20/24 ms
ISP#
```

Complete reachability has been demonstrated between the ISP router and both SanJose1 and SanJose2.

Step 7: Configure the BGP next-hop-self feature.

SanJose1 is unaware of the link between ISP and SanJose2, and SanJose2 is unaware of the link between ISP and SanJose1. Before ISP can successfully ping all the internal serial interfaces of AS 64512, these serial links should be advertised via BGP on the ISP router. This can also be resolved via EIGRP on each SanJose router. One method is for ISP to advertise these links.

a. Issue the following commands on the ISP router.

```
ISP(config)# router bgp 200
ISP(config-router)# network 192.168.1.0 mask 255.255.255.252
ISP(config-router)# network 192.168.1.4 mask 255.255.255.252
```

b. Issue the **show ip bgp** command to verify that the ISP is correctly injecting its own WAN links into BGP.

```
ISP# show ip bgp
BGP table version is 5, local router ID is 192.168.100.1
Status codes: s suppressed, d damped, h history, * valid, > best, i - internal,
              r RIB-failure, S Stale, m multipath, b backup-path, f RT-Filter,
              x best-external, a additional-path, c RIB-compressed,
Origin codes: i - IGP, e - EGP, ? - incomplete
RPKI validation codes: V valid, I invalid, N Not found

     Network          Next Hop            Metric LocPrf Weight Path
 *   172.16.0.0       192.168.1.6              0             0 64512 i
 *>                   192.168.1.2              0             0 64512 i
 *>  192.168.1.0/30   0.0.0.0                  0         32768 i
 *>  192.168.1.4/30   0.0.0.0                  0         32768 i
 *>  192.168.100.0    0.0.0.0                  0         32768 i
ISP#
```

c. Verify on SanJose1 and SanJose2 that the opposite WAN link is included in the routing table. The output from SanJose2 is as follows.

```
SanJose2# show ip route
Codes: L - local, C - connected, S - static, R - RIP, M - mobile, B - BGP
       D - EIGRP, EX - EIGRP external, O - OSPF, IA - OSPF inter area
       N1 - OSPF NSSA external type 1, N2 - OSPF NSSA external type 2
       E1 - OSPF external type 1, E2 - OSPF external type 2
       i - IS-IS, su - IS-IS summary, L1 - IS-IS level-1, L2 - IS-IS level-2
       ia - IS-IS inter area, * - candidate default, U - per-user static
       route
       o - ODR, P - periodic downloaded static route, H - NHRP, l - LISP
       a - application route
       + - replicated route, % - next hop override
```

```
Gateway of last resort is not set

      172.16.0.0/16 is variably subnetted, 6 subnets, 3 masks
S         172.16.0.0/16 is directly connected, Null0
C         172.16.1.0/24 is directly connected, Serial0/0/1
L         172.16.1.2/32 is directly connected, Serial0/0/1
C         172.16.32.0/24 is directly connected, Loopback0
L         172.16.32.1/32 is directly connected, Loopback0
D         172.16.64.0/24 [90/2297856] via 172.16.1.1, 00:52:03, Serial0/0/1
      192.168.1.0/24 is variably subnetted, 3 subnets, 2 masks
C         192.168.1.0/30 is directly connected, Serial0/0/0
L         192.168.1.2/32 is directly connected, Serial0/0/0
B         192.168.1.4/30 [20/0] via 192.168.1.1, 00:01:03
B      192.168.100.0/24 [20/0] via 192.168.1.1, 00:25:20
SanJose2#
```

The next issue to consider is BGP policy routing between autonomous systems. The next-hop attribute of a route in a different AS is set to the IP address of the border router in the next AS toward the destination, and this attribute is not modified by default when advertising this route through IBGP. Therefore, for all IBGP peers, it is either necessary to know the route to that border router (in a different neighboring AS), or our own border router needs to advertise the foreign routes using the next-hop-self feature, overriding the next-hop address with its own IP address. The SanJose2 router is passing a policy to SanJose1 and vice versa. The policy for routing from AS 64512 to AS 200 is to forward packets to the 192.168.1.1 interface. SanJose1 has a similar yet opposite policy: It forwards requests to the 192.168.1.5 interface. If either WAN link fails, it is critical that the opposite router become a valid gateway. This is achieved if the **next-hop-self** command is configured on SanJose1 and SanJose2.

d. To better understand the **next-hop-self** command we will remove ISP advertising its two WAN links and shut down the WAN link between ISP and SanJose2. The only possible path from SanJose2 to ISP's 192.168.100.0/24 is through SanJose1.

```
ISP(config)# router bgp 200
ISP(config-router)# no network 192.168.1.0 mask 255.255.255.252
ISP(config-router)# no network 192.168.1.4 mask 255.255.255.252
ISP(config-router)# exit
ISP(config)# interface serial 0/0/1
ISP(config-if)# shutdown
ISP(config-if)#
```

e. Display SanJose2's BGP table using the **show ip bgp** command and the IPv4 routing table with **show ip route**.

```
SanJose2# show ip bgp
BGP table version is 1, local router ID is 172.16.32.1
Status codes: s suppressed, d damped, h history, * valid, > best, i - internal,
              r RIB-failure, S Stale, m multipath, b backup-path, f RT-Filter,
              x best-external, a additional-path, c RIB-compressed,
Origin codes: i - IGP, e - EGP, ? - incomplete
RPKI validation codes: V valid, I invalid, N Not found

     Network          Next Hop            Metric LocPrf Weight Path
 * i 172.16.0.0       172.16.64.1              0    100      0 i
 * i 192.168.100.0    192.168.1.5              0    100      0 200 i
SanJose2#


SanJose2# show ip route
Codes: L - local, C - connected, S - static, R - RIP, M - mobile, B - BGP
```

```
        D - EIGRP, EX - EIGRP external, O - OSPF, IA - OSPF inter area
        N1 - OSPF NSSA external type 1, N2 - OSPF NSSA external type 2
        E1 - OSPF external type 1, E2 - OSPF external type 2
        i - IS-IS, su - IS-IS summary, L1 - IS-IS level-1, L2 - IS-IS level-2
        ia - IS-IS inter area, * - candidate default, U - per-user static route
        o - ODR, P - periodic downloaded static route, H - NHRP, l - LISP
        a - application route
        + - replicated route, % - next hop override

Gateway of last resort is not set

        172.16.0.0/16 is variably subnetted, 6 subnets, 3 masks
S          172.16.0.0/16 is directly connected, Null0
C          172.16.1.0/24 is directly connected, Serial0/0/1
L          172.16.1.2/32 is directly connected, Serial0/0/1
C          172.16.32.0/24 is directly connected, Loopback0
L          172.16.32.1/32 is directly connected, Loopback0
D          172.16.64.0/24 [90/2297856] via 172.16.1.1, 02:41:46, Serial0/0/1
SanJose2#
```

Notice that SanJose2 has 192.168.100.0 in its BGP table but not in its routing table. The BGP table shows the next hop to 192.168.100.0 as 192.168.1.5. Because SanJose2 does not have a route to this next hop address of 192.168.1.5 in its routing table, it will not install the 192.168.100.0 network into the routing table. It won't install a route if it doesn't know how to get to the next hop.

EBGP next hop addresses are carried into IBGP unchanged. As we saw previously, we could advertise the WAN link using BGP, but this is not always desirable. It means advertising additional routes when we are usually trying to minimize the size of the routing table. Another option is to have the routers within the IGP domain advertise themselves as the next hop router using the **next-hop-self** command.

f. Issue the **next-hop-self** command on SanJose1 and SanJose2 to advertise themselves as the next hop to their IBGP peer.

```
SanJose1(config)# router bgp 64512
SanJose1(config-router)# neighbor 172.16.32.1 next-hop-self

SanJose2(config)# router bgp 64512
SanJose2(config-router)# neighbor 172.16.64.1 next-hop-self
```

g. Reset BGP operation on either router with the **clear ip bgp *** command.

```
SanJose1# clear ip bgp *
SanJose1#

SanJose2# clear ip bgp *
SanJose2#
```

h. After the routers have returned to established BGP speakers, issue the **show ip bgp** command on SanJose2 and notice that the next hop is now SanJose1 instead of ISP.

```
SanJose2# show ip bgp
BGP table version is 5, local router ID is 172.16.32.1
Status codes: s suppressed, d damped, h history, * valid, > best, i - internal,
              r RIB-failure, S Stale, m multipath, b backup-path, f RT-Filter,
              x best-external, a additional-path, c RIB-compressed,
Origin codes: i - IGP, e - EGP, ? - incomplete
RPKI validation codes: V valid, I invalid, N Not found

     Network          Next Hop            Metric LocPrf Weight Path
 *>  172.16.0.0       0.0.0.0                  0          32768 i
```

```
    * i                      172.16.64.1          0    100     0 i
    *>i 192.168.100.0    172.16.64.1          0    100     0 200 i
SanJose2#
```

i. The **show ip route** command on SanJose2 now displays the 192.168.100.0/24 network because SanJose1 is the next hop, 172.16.64.1, which is reachable from SanJose2.

```
SanJose2# show ip route
Codes: L - local, C - connected, S - static, R - RIP, M - mobile, B - BGP
       D - EIGRP, EX - EIGRP external, O - OSPF, IA - OSPF inter area
       N1 - OSPF NSSA external type 1, N2 - OSPF NSSA external type 2
       E1 - OSPF external type 1, E2 - OSPF external type 2
       i - IS-IS, su - IS-IS summary, L1 - IS-IS level-1, L2 - IS-IS level-2
       ia - IS-IS inter area, * - candidate default, U - per-user static
       route
       o - ODR, P - periodic downloaded static route, H - NHRP, l - LISP
       a - application route
       + - replicated route, % - next hop override

Gateway of last resort is not set

      172.16.0.0/16 is variably subnetted, 6 subnets, 3 masks
S        172.16.0.0/16 is directly connected, Null0
C        172.16.1.0/24 is directly connected, Serial0/0/1
L        172.16.1.2/32 is directly connected, Serial0/0/1
C        172.16.32.0/24 is directly connected, Loopback0
L        172.16.32.1/32 is directly connected, Loopback0
D        172.16.64.0/24 [90/2297856] via 172.16.1.1, 04:27:19, Serial0/0/1
B     192.168.100.0/24 [200/0] via 172.16.64.1, 00:00:46
SanJose2#
```

j. Before configuring the next BGP attribute, restore the WAN link between ISP and SanJose3. This will change the BGP table and routing table on both routers. For example, SanJose2's routing table shows 192.168.100.0/24 will now have a better path through ISP.

```
ISP(config)# interface serial 0/0/1
ISP(config-if)# no shutdown
ISP(config-if)#
```

```
SanJose2# show ip route
Codes: L - local, C - connected, S - static, R - RIP, M - mobile, B - BGP
       D - EIGRP, EX - EIGRP external, O - OSPF, IA - OSPF inter area
       N1 - OSPF NSSA external type 1, N2 - OSPF NSSA external type 2
       E1 - OSPF external type 1, E2 - OSPF external type 2
       i - IS-IS, su - IS-IS summary, L1 - IS-IS level-1, L2 - IS-IS level-2
       ia - IS-IS inter area, * - candidate default, U - per-user static
       route
       o - ODR, P - periodic downloaded static route, H - NHRP, l - LISP
       a - application route
       + - replicated route, % - next hop override

Gateway of last resort is not set

      172.16.0.0/16 is variably subnetted, 6 subnets, 3 masks
S        172.16.0.0/16 is directly connected, Null0
```

```
C         172.16.1.0/24 is directly connected, Serial0/0/1
L         172.16.1.2/32 is directly connected, Serial0/0/1
C         172.16.32.0/24 is directly connected, Loopback0
L         172.16.32.1/32 is directly connected, Loopback0
D         172.16.64.0/24 [90/2297856] via 172.16.1.1, 04:37:34, Serial0/0/1
      192.168.1.0/24 is variably subnetted, 2 subnets, 2 masks
C         192.168.1.0/30 is directly connected, Serial0/0/0
L         192.168.1.2/32 is directly connected, Serial0/0/0
B      192.168.100.0/24 [20/0] via 192.168.1.1, 00:01:35
SanJose2#
```

Step 8: Set BGP local preference.

At this point, everything looks good, with the exception of default routes, the outbound flow of data, and inbound packet flow.

a. Because the local preference value is shared between IBGP neighbors, configure a simple route map that references the local preference value on SanJose1 and SanJose2. This policy adjusts outbound traffic to prefer the link off the SanJose1 router instead of the metered T1 off SanJose2.

```
SanJose1(config)# route-map PRIMARY_T1_IN permit 10
SanJose1(config-route-map)# set local-preference 150
SanJose1(config-route-map)# exit
SanJose1(config)# router bgp 64512
SanJose1(config-router)# neighbor 192.168.1.5 route-map PRIMARY_T1_IN in

SanJose2(config)# route-map SECONDARY_T1_IN permit 10
SanJose2(config-route-map)# set local-preference 125
SanJose1(config-route-map)# exit
SanJose2(config)# router bgp 64512
SanJose2(config-router)# neighbor 192.168.1.1 route-map SECONDARY_T1_IN in
```

b. Use the **clear ip bgp * soft** command after configuring this new policy. When the conversations have been reestablished, issue the **show ip bgp** command on SanJose1 and SanJose2.

```
SanJose1# clear ip bgp * soft
SanJose2# clear ip bgp * soft

SanJose1# show ip bgp
BGP table version is 3, local router ID is 172.16.64.1
Status codes: s suppressed, d damped, h history, * valid, > best, i - internal,
              r RIB-failure, S Stale, m multipath, b backup-path, f RT-Filter,
              x best-external, a additional-path, c RIB-compressed,
Origin codes: i - IGP, e - EGP, ? - incomplete
RPKI validation codes: V valid, I invalid, N Not found

     Network          Next Hop            Metric LocPrf Weight Path
 *  i 172.16.0.0       172.16.32.1              0    100      0 i
 *>                    0.0.0.0                  0           32768 i
 *>   192.168.100.0    192.168.1.5              0    150      0 200 i
SanJose1#

SanJose2# show ip bgp
BGP table version is 7, local router ID is 172.16.32.1
Status codes: s suppressed, d damped, h history, * valid, > best, i - internal,
              r RIB-failure, S Stale, m multipath, b backup-path, f RT-Filter,
              x best-external, a additional-path, c RIB-compressed,
Origin codes: i - IGP, e - EGP, ? - incomplete
RPKI validation codes: V valid, I invalid, N Not found

     Network          Next Hop            Metric LocPrf Weight Path
```

```
  * i 172.16.0.0          172.16.64.1              0    100      0 i
  *>                      0.0.0.0                  0           32768 i
  *>i 192.168.100.0       172.16.64.1              0    150      0 200 i
  *                       192.168.1.1              0    125      0 200 i
SanJose2#
```

This now indicates that routing to the loopback segment for ISP 192.168.100.0 /24 can be reached only through the link common to SanJose1 and ISP. SanJose2's next hop to 192.168.100.0/24 is SanJose1 because both routers have been configured using the **next-hop-self** command.

Step 9: Set BGP MED.

a. In the previous step we saw that SanJose1 and SanJose2 will route traffic for 192.168.100.0/24 using the link between SanJose1 and ISP. Examine the return path ISP takes to reach AS 64512. Notice that the return path is different from the original path. This is known as asymmetric routing and is not necessarily an unwanted trait.

```
ISP# show ip bgp
BGP table version is 22, local router ID is 192.168.100.1
Status codes: s suppressed, d damped, h history, * valid, > best, i - internal,
              r RIB-failure, S Stale, m multipath, b backup-path, f RT-Filter,
              x best-external, a additional-path, c RIB-compressed,
Origin codes: i - IGP, e - EGP, ? - incomplete
RPKI validation codes: V valid, I invalid, N Not found

     Network          Next Hop          Metric LocPrf Weight Path
  *  172.16.0.0       192.168.1.6            0           0 64512 i
  *>                  192.168.1.2            0           0 64512 i
  *> 192.168.100.0    0.0.0.0               0         32768 i
ISP# show ip route
Codes: L - local, C - connected, S - static, R - RIP, M - mobile, B - BGP
       D - EIGRP, EX - EIGRP external, O - OSPF, IA - OSPF inter area
       N1 - OSPF NSSA external type 1, N2 - OSPF NSSA external type 2
       E1 - OSPF external type 1, E2 - OSPF external type 2
       i - IS-IS, su - IS-IS summary, L1 - IS-IS level-1, L2 - IS-IS level-2
       ia - IS-IS inter area, * - candidate default, U - per-user static route
       o - ODR, P - periodic downloaded static route, H - NHRP, l - LISP
       a - application route
       + - replicated route, % - next hop override

Gateway of last resort is not set

B     172.16.0.0/16 [20/0] via 192.168.1.2, 00:12:45
      192.168.1.0/24 is variably subnetted, 4 subnets, 2 masks
C        192.168.1.0/30 is directly connected, Serial0/0/1
L        192.168.1.1/32 is directly connected, Serial0/0/1
C        192.168.1.4/30 is directly connected, Serial0/0/0
L        192.168.1.5/32 is directly connected, Serial0/0/0
      192.168.100.0/24 is variably subnetted, 2 subnets, 2 masks
C        192.168.100.0/24 is directly connected, Loopback0
L        192.168.100.1/32 is directly connected, Loopback0
ISP#
```

How will traffic from network 192.168.100.0 /24 on ISP return to SanJose1 or SanJose2? Will it be routed through SanJose1 or SanJose2?

_____

_____

_____

To verify this, the simplest solution is to issue the **show ip bgp** command on the ISP router as was done earlier. What if access was not given to the ISP router? Traffic returning from the Internet should not be passed across the metered T1. Is there a simple way to verify before receiving the monthly bill? How can it be checked instantly?

_____

_____

_____

b. Use an extended **ping** command to verify this situation. Specify the **record** option and compare your output to the following. Notice the return path using the exit interface 192.168.1.1 to SanJose2.

```
SanJose2# ping
Protocol [ip]:
Target IP address: 192.168.100.1
Repeat count [5]:
Datagram size [100]:
Timeout in seconds [2]:
Extended commands [n]: y
Source address or interface: 172.16.32.1
Type of service [0]:
Set DF bit in IP header? [no]:
Validate reply data? [no]:
Data pattern [0xABCD]:
Loose, Strict, Record, Timestamp, Verbose[none]: record
Number of hops [ 9 ]:
Loose, Strict, Record, Timestamp, Verbose[RV]:
Sweep range of sizes [n]:
Type escape sequence to abort.
Sending 5, 100-byte ICMP Echos to 192.168.100.1, timeout is 2 seconds:
Packet sent with a source address of 172.16.32.1
Packet has IP options:  Total option bytes= 39, padded length=40
 Record route: <*>
    (0.0.0.0)
    (0.0.0.0)
    (0.0.0.0)
    (0.0.0.0)
    (0.0.0.0)
    (0.0.0.0)
    (0.0.0.0)
    (0.0.0.0)
    (0.0.0.0)

 Reply to request 0 (20 ms).  Received packet has options
  Total option bytes= 40, padded length=40
  Record route:
    (172.16.1.2)
    (192.168.1.6)
```

```
   (192.168.100.1)
   (192.168.1.1)
   (172.16.32.1) <*>
   (0.0.0.0)
   (0.0.0.0)
   (0.0.0.0)
   (0.0.0.0)
End of list

Reply to request 1 (20 ms).  Received packet has options
 Total option bytes= 40, padded length=40
 Record route:
   (172.16.1.2)
   (192.168.1.6)
   (192.168.100.1)
   (192.168.1.1)
   (172.16.32.1) <*>
   (0.0.0.0)
   (0.0.0.0)
   (0.0.0.0)
   (0.0.0.0)
End of list

Reply to request 2 (20 ms).  Received packet has options
 Total option bytes= 40, padded length=40
 Record route:
   (172.16.1.2)
   (192.168.1.6)
   (192.168.100.1)
   (192.168.1.1)
   (172.16.32.1) <*>
   (0.0.0.0)
   (0.0.0.0)
   (0.0.0.0)
   (0.0.0.0)
End of list

Reply to request 3 (24 ms).  Received packet has options
 Total option bytes= 40, padded length=40
 Record route:
   (172.16.1.2)
   (192.168.1.6)
   (192.168.100.1)
   (192.168.1.1)
   (172.16.32.1) <*>
   (0.0.0.0)
   (0.0.0.0)
   (0.0.0.0)
   (0.0.0.0)
End of list

Reply to request 4 (20 ms).  Received packet has options
 Total option bytes= 40, padded length=40
 Record route:
   (172.16.1.2)
   (192.168.1.6)
   (192.168.100.1)
```

```
     (192.168.1.1)
     (172.16.32.1) <*>
     (0.0.0.0)
     (0.0.0.0)
     (0.0.0.0)
     (0.0.0.0)
  End of list

Success rate is 100 percent (5/5), round-trip min/avg/max = 20/20/24 ms
SanJose2#
```

If you are unfamiliar with the **record** option, the important thing to note is that each IP address in brackets is an outgoing interface. The output can be interpreted as follows:

1. A ping that is sourced from 172.16.32.1 exits SanJose2 through s0/0/1, 172.16.1.2. It then arrives at the s0/0/1 interface for SanJose1.

2. SanJose1 S0/0/0, 192.168.1.6, routes the packet out to arrive at the S0/0/0 interface of ISP.

3. The target of 192.168.100.1 is reached: 192.168.100.1.

4. The packet is next forwarded out the S0/0/1, 192.168.1.1 interface for ISP and arrives at the S0/0/0 interface for SanJose2.

5. SanJose2 then forwards the packet out the last interface, loopback 0, 172.16.32.1.

Although the unlimited use of the T1 from SanJose1 is preferred here, ISP currently takes the link from SanJose2 for all return traffic.

c. Create a new policy to force the ISP router to return all traffic via SanJose1. Create a second route map utilizing the MED (metric) that is shared between EBGP neighbors.

```
SanJose1(config)#route-map PRIMARY_T1_MED_OUT permit 10
SanJose1(config-route-map)#set Metric 50
SanJose1(config-route-map)#exit
SanJose1(config)#router bgp 64512
SanJose1(config-router)#neighbor 192.168.1.5 route-map PRIMARY_T1_MED_OUT out

SanJose2(config)#route-map SECONDARY_T1_MED_OUT permit 10
SanJose2(config-route-map)#set Metric 75
SanJose2(config-route-map)#exit
SanJose2(config)#router bgp 64512
SanJose2(config-router)#neighbor 192.168.1.1 route-map SECONDARY_T1_MED_OUT
out
```

d. Use the **clear ip bgp * soft** command after issuing this new policy. Issuing the **show ip bgp** command as follows on SanJose1 or SanJose2 does not indicate anything about this newly defined policy.

```
SanJose1# clear ip bgp * soft
SanJose2# clear ip bgp * soft

SanJose1# show ip bgp
BGP table version is 4, local router ID is 172.16.64.1
Status codes: s suppressed, d damped, h history, * valid, > best, i - internal,
              r RIB-failure, S Stale, m multipath, b backup-path, f RT-Filter,
              x best-external, a additional-path, c RIB-compressed,
Origin codes: i - IGP, e - EGP, ? - incomplete
RPKI validation codes: V valid, I invalid, N Not found

     Network          Next Hop            Metric LocPrf Weight Path
```

```
   * i 172.16.0.0        172.16.32.1              0     100      0 i
   *>                    0.0.0.0                  0             32768 i
   *>  192.168.100.0     192.168.1.5              0     150      0 200 i
SanJose1#


SanJose2# show ip bgp
BGP table version is 8, local router ID is 172.16.32.1
Status codes: s suppressed, d damped, h history, * valid, > best, i - internal,
              r RIB-failure, S Stale, m multipath, b backup-path, f RT-Filter,
              x best-external, a additional-path, c RIB-compressed,
Origin codes: i - IGP, e - EGP, ? - incomplete
RPKI validation codes: V valid, I invalid, N Not found

      Network           Next Hop         Metric LocPrf Weight Path
   * i 172.16.0.0        172.16.64.1           0    100      0 i
   *>                    0.0.0.0               0           32768 i
   *>i 192.168.100.0     172.16.64.1           0    150      0 200 i
   *                     192.168.1.1           0    125      0 200 i
SanJose2#
```

e. Reissue an extended **ping** command with the **record** command. Notice the change in return path using the exit interface 192.168.1.5 to SanJose1.

```
SanJose2# ping
Protocol [ip]:
Target IP address: 192.168.100.1
Repeat count [5]:
Datagram size [100]:
Timeout in seconds [2]:
Extended commands [n]: y
Source address or interface: 172.16.32.1
Type of service [0]:
Set DF bit in IP header? [no]:
Validate reply data? [no]:
Data pattern [0xABCD]:
Loose, Strict, Record, Timestamp, Verbose[none]: record
Number of hops [ 9 ]:
Loose, Strict, Record, Timestamp, Verbose[RV]:
Sweep range of sizes [n]:
Type escape sequence to abort.
Sending 5, 100-byte ICMP Echos to 192.168.100.1, timeout is 2 seconds:
Packet sent with a source address of 172.16.32.1
Packet has IP options:  Total option bytes= 39, padded length=40
 Record route: <*>
    (0.0.0.0)
    (0.0.0.0)
    (0.0.0.0)
    (0.0.0.0)
    (0.0.0.0)
    (0.0.0.0)
    (0.0.0.0)
    (0.0.0.0)
    (0.0.0.0)

Reply to request 0 (28 ms).  Received packet has options
 Total option bytes= 40, padded length=40
 Record route:
    (172.16.1.2)
    (192.168.1.6)
```

```
    (192.168.100.1)
    (192.168.1.5)
    (172.16.1.1)
    (172.16.32.1) <*>
    (0.0.0.0)
    (0.0.0.0)
    (0.0.0.0)
 End of list

Reply to request 1 (28 ms).  Received packet has options
 Total option bytes= 40, padded length=40
 Record route:
    (172.16.1.2)
    (192.168.1.6)
    (192.168.100.1)
    (192.168.1.5)
    (172.16.1.1)
    (172.16.32.1) <*>
    (0.0.0.0)
    (0.0.0.0)
    (0.0.0.0)
 End of list

Reply to request 2 (28 ms).  Received packet has options
 Total option bytes= 40, padded length=40
 Record route:
    (172.16.1.2)
    (192.168.1.6)
    (192.168.100.1)
    (192.168.1.5)
    (172.16.1.1)
    (172.16.32.1) <*>
    (0.0.0.0)
    (0.0.0.0)
    (0.0.0.0)
 End of list

Reply to request 3 (28 ms).  Received packet has options
 Total option bytes= 40, padded length=40
 Record route:
    (172.16.1.2)
    (192.168.1.6)
    (192.168.100.1)
    (192.168.1.5)
    (172.16.1.1)
    (172.16.32.1) <*>
    (0.0.0.0)
    (0.0.0.0)
    (0.0.0.0)
 End of list

Reply to request 4 (28 ms).  Received packet has options
 Total option bytes= 40, padded length=40
 Record route:
    (172.16.1.2)
    (192.168.1.6)
    (192.168.100.1)
```

```
            (192.168.1.5)
            (172.16.1.1)
            (172.16.32.1) <*>
            (0.0.0.0)
            (0.0.0.0)
            (0.0.0.0)
        End of list

    Success rate is 100 percent (5/5), round-trip min/avg/max = 28/28/28 ms
    SanJose2#
```

Does the output look correct? Does the preceding 192.168.1.5 mean that the ISP now prefers SanJose1 for return traffic?

_____

_____

The newly configured policy MED shows that the lower MED value is considered best. The ISP now prefers the route with the lower MED value of 50 to AS 64512. This is just opposite from the **local-preference** command configured earlier.

```
ISP# show ip bgp
BGP table version is 24, local router ID is 192.168.100.1
Status codes: s suppressed, d damped, h history, * valid, > best, i - internal,
              r RIB-failure, S Stale, m multipath, b backup-path, f RT-Filter,
              x best-external, a additional-path, c RIB-compressed,
Origin codes: i - IGP, e - EGP, ? - incomplete
RPKI validation codes: V valid, I invalid, N Not found

     Network          Next Hop         Metric LocPrf Weight Path
 *>  172.16.0.0       192.168.1.6         50            0 64512 i
 *                    192.168.1.2         75            0 64512 i
 *>  192.168.100.0    0.0.0.0              0        32768 i
ISP#
```

Step 10: Establish a default route.

The final step is to establish a default route that uses a policy statement that adjusts to changes in the network.

a. Configure ISP to inject a default route to both SanJose1 and SanJose2 using BGP using the **default-originate** command. This command does not require the presence of 0.0.0.0 in the ISP router. Configure the 10.0.0.0/8 network, which will not be advertised using BGP. This network will be used to test the default route on SanJose1 and SanJose2.

```
ISP(config)# router bgp 200
ISP(config-router)# neighbor 192.168.1.6 default-originate
ISP(config-router)# neighbor 192.168.1.2 default-originate
ISP(config-router)# exit
ISP(config)# interface loopback 10
ISP(config-if)# ip address 10.0.0.1 255.255.255.0
ISP(config-if)#
```

b. Verify that both routers have received the default route by examining the routing tables on SanJose1 and SanJose2. Notice that both routers prefer the route between SanJose1 and ISP.

```
SanJose1# show ip route
Codes: L - local, C - connected, S - static, R - RIP, M - mobile, B - BGP
       D - EIGRP, EX - EIGRP external, O - OSPF, IA - OSPF inter area
```

```
              N1 - OSPF NSSA external type 1, N2 - OSPF NSSA external type 2
              E1 - OSPF external type 1, E2 - OSPF external type 2
              i - IS-IS, su - IS-IS summary, L1 - IS-IS level-1, L2 - IS-IS level-2
              ia - IS-IS inter area, * - candidate default, U - per-user static
              route
              o - ODR, P - periodic downloaded static route, H - NHRP, l - LISP
              a - application route
              + - replicated route, % - next hop override

Gateway of last resort is 192.168.1.5 to network 0.0.0.0

B*    0.0.0.0/0 [20/0] via 192.168.1.5, 00:00:36
      172.16.0.0/16 is variably subnetted, 6 subnets, 3 masks
S        172.16.0.0/16 is directly connected, Null0
C        172.16.1.0/24 is directly connected, Serial0/0/1
L        172.16.1.1/32 is directly connected, Serial0/0/1
D        172.16.32.0/24 [90/2297856] via 172.16.1.2, 05:47:24, Serial0/0/1
C        172.16.64.0/24 is directly connected, Loopback0
L        172.16.64.1/32 is directly connected, Loopback0
      192.168.1.0/24 is variably subnetted, 2 subnets, 2 masks
C        192.168.1.4/30 is directly connected, Serial0/0/0
L        192.168.1.6/32 is directly connected, Serial0/0/0
SanJose1#


SanJose2# show ip route
Codes: L - local, C - connected, S - static, R - RIP, M - mobile, B - BGP
       D - EIGRP, EX - EIGRP external, O - OSPF, IA - OSPF inter area
       N1 - OSPF NSSA external type 1, N2 - OSPF NSSA external type 2
       E1 - OSPF external type 1, E2 - OSPF external type 2
       i - IS-IS, su - IS-IS summary, L1 - IS-IS level-1, L2 - IS-IS level-2
       ia - IS-IS inter area, * - candidate default, U - per-user static
       route
       o - ODR, P - periodic downloaded static route, H - NHRP, l - LISP
       a - application route
       + - replicated route, % - next hop override

Gateway of last resort is 172.16.64.1 to network 0.0.0.0

B*    0.0.0.0/0 [200/0] via 172.16.64.1, 00:00:45
      172.16.0.0/16 is variably subnetted, 6 subnets, 3 masks
S        172.16.0.0/16 is directly connected, Null0
C        172.16.1.0/24 is directly connected, Serial0/0/1
L        172.16.1.2/32 is directly connected, Serial0/0/1
C        172.16.32.0/24 is directly connected, Loopback0
L        172.16.32.1/32 is directly connected, Loopback0
D        172.16.64.0/24 [90/2297856] via 172.16.1.1, 05:47:33, Serial0/0/1
      192.168.1.0/24 is variably subnetted, 2 subnets, 2 masks
C        192.168.1.0/30 is directly connected, Serial0/0/0
L        192.168.1.2/32 is directly connected, Serial0/0/0
SanJose2#
```

c. The preferred default route is by way of SanJose1 because of the higher local preference attribute configured on SanJose1 earlier.

```
SanJose2# show ip bgp
BGP table version is 38, local router ID is 172.16.32.1
Status codes: s suppressed, d damped, h history, * valid, > best, i - internal,
```

```
           r RIB-failure, S Stale, m multipath, b backup-path, f RT-Filter,
           x best-external, a additional-path, c RIB-compressed,
Origin codes: i - IGP, e - EGP, ? - incomplete
RPKI validation codes: V valid, I invalid, N Not found

      Network            Next Hop          Metric LocPrf Weight Path
 *>i 0.0.0.0             172.16.64.1            0    150      0 200 i
 *                       192.168.1.1                125      0 200 i
 *  i 172.16.0.0         172.16.64.1            0    100      0 i
 *>                      0.0.0.0                0          32768 i
 *>i 192.168.100.0       172.16.64.1            0    150      0 200 i
 *                       192.168.1.1            0    125      0 200 i
SanJose2#
```

d. Using the **traceroute** command verify that packets to 10.0.0.1 are using the default route through SanJose1.

```
SanJose2# traceroute 10.0.0.1
Type escape sequence to abort.
Tracing the route to 10.0.0.1
VRF info: (vrf in name/id, vrf out name/id)
  1 172.16.1.1 8 msec 4 msec 8 msec
  2 192.168.1.5 [AS 200] 12 msec *  12 msec
SanJose2#
```

e. Next, test how BGP adapts to using a different default route when the path between SanJose1 and ISP goes down.

```
ISP(config)# interface serial 0/0/0
ISP(config-if)# shutdown
ISP(config-if)#
```

f. Verify that both routers have modified their routing tables with the default route using the path between SanJose2 and ISP.

```
SanJose1# show ip route
Codes: L - local, C - connected, S - static, R - RIP, M - mobile, B - BGP
       D - EIGRP, EX - EIGRP external, O - OSPF, IA - OSPF inter area
       N1 - OSPF NSSA external type 1, N2 - OSPF NSSA external type 2
       E1 - OSPF external type 1, E2 - OSPF external type 2
       i - IS-IS, su - IS-IS summary, L1 - IS-IS level-1, L2 - IS-IS level-2
       ia - IS-IS inter area, * - candidate default, U - per-user static
       route
       o - ODR, P - periodic downloaded static route, H - NHRP, l - LISP
       a - application route
       + - replicated route, % - next hop override

Gateway of last resort is 172.16.32.1 to network 0.0.0.0

B*    0.0.0.0/0 [200/0] via 172.16.32.1, 00:00:06
      172.16.0.0/16 is variably subnetted, 6 subnets, 3 masks
S        172.16.0.0/16 is directly connected, Null0
C        172.16.1.0/24 is directly connected, Serial0/0/1
L        172.16.1.1/32 is directly connected, Serial0/0/1
D        172.16.32.0/24 [90/2297856] via 172.16.1.2, 05:49:25, Serial0/0/1
C        172.16.64.0/24 is directly connected, Loopback0
L        172.16.64.1/32 is directly connected, Loopback0
B     192.168.100.0/24 [200/0] via 172.16.32.1, 00:00:06
SanJose1#
```

```
SanJose2# show ip route
Codes: L - local, C - connected, S - static, R - RIP, M - mobile, B - BGP
       D - EIGRP, EX - EIGRP external, O - OSPF, IA - OSPF inter area
       N1 - OSPF NSSA external type 1, N2 - OSPF NSSA external type 2
       E1 - OSPF external type 1, E2 - OSPF external type 2
       i - IS-IS, su - IS-IS summary, L1 - IS-IS level-1, L2 - IS-IS level-2
       ia - IS-IS inter area, * - candidate default, U - per-user static
       route
       o - ODR, P - periodic downloaded static route, H - NHRP, l - LISP
       a - application route
       + - replicated route, % - next hop override

Gateway of last resort is 192.168.1.1 to network 0.0.0.0

B*      0.0.0.0/0 [20/0] via 192.168.1.1, 00:00:30
        172.16.0.0/16 is variably subnetted, 6 subnets, 3 masks
S          172.16.0.0/16 is directly connected, Null0
C          172.16.1.0/24 is directly connected, Serial0/0/1
L          172.16.1.2/32 is directly connected, Serial0/0/1
C          172.16.32.0/24 is directly connected, Loopback0
L          172.16.32.1/32 is directly connected, Loopback0
D          172.16.64.0/24 [90/2297856] via 172.16.1.1, 05:49:49, Serial0/0/1
        192.168.1.0/24 is variably subnetted, 2 subnets, 2 masks
C          192.168.1.0/30 is directly connected, Serial0/0/0
L          192.168.1.2/32 is directly connected, Serial0/0/0
B       192.168.100.0/24 [20/0] via 192.168.1.1, 00:00:30
SanJose2#
```

g. Verify the new path using the **traceroute** command to 10.0.0.1 from SanJose1. Notice the default route is now through SanJose2.

```
SanJose1# trace 10.0.0.1
Type escape sequence to abort.
Tracing the route to 10.0.0.1
VRF info: (vrf in name/id, vrf out name/id)
  1 172.16.1.2 8 msec 8 msec 8 msec
  2 192.168.1.1 [AS 200] 12 msec * 12 msec
SanJose1#
```

Lab 7-4 IBGP, Next Hop, and Synchronization

Topology

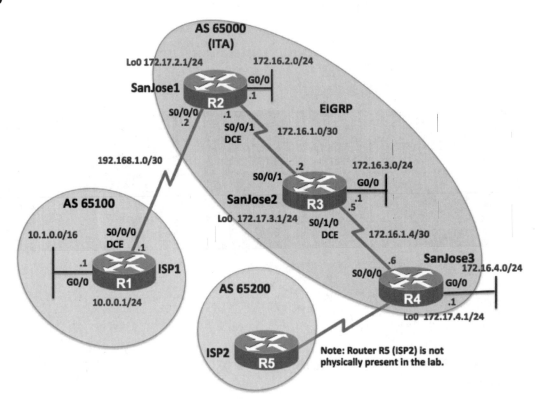

Objectives

- Configure EBGP and IBGP.
- Configure EIGRP in the ITA domain.
- Troubleshoot and resolve next hop issues in IBGP.
- Configure full-mesh IBGP to resolve routing issue within ITA domain.
- Configure ITA so it is not a transit AS.
- Verify connectivity.

Background

The International Travel Agency (ITA) runs BGP on its SanJose1 and SanJose3 routers in AS 65000. SanJose1 in AS 65000 is running EBGP with the ISP1 router in AS 65100. SanJose3 in AS 65000 is running EBGP with the ISP2 router in AS 65200. ITA routers need to receive IPv4 networks from both ISPs. To ensure AS 65000 is not a transit AS, SanJose1 and SanJose3 will only include ITA networks 172.16.2.0/24 and 172.16.4.0/24 in its BGP updates to the ISP routers. Your job is to configure EIGRP BGP for this internetwork.

Note: The topology shows SanJose3 in AS 65000 is running EBGP with the ISP2 router in AS 65200. ISP2 (router R5) does not actually exist in the physical lab topology. This is done due to the limitations of four routers in our CCNP NetLab topologies.

Note: This lab uses Cisco 1941 routers with Cisco IOS Release 15.4 with IP Base. The switches are Cisco WS-C2960-24TT-L with Fast Ethernet interfaces; therefore, the router will use routing metrics associated with a 100 Mb/s interface. Depending on the router or switch model and Cisco IOS Software version, the commands available and output produced might vary from what is shown in this lab.

Required Resources

- 4 routers (Cisco IOS Release 15.2 or comparable)
- 4 switches (LAN interfaces)
- Serial and Ethernet cables

Step 0: Suggested starting configurations.

a. Apply the following configuration to each router along with the appropriate **hostname**. The **exec-timeout 0 0** command should only be used in a lab environment.

```
Router(config)# no ip domain-lookup
Router(config)# line con 0
Router(config-line)# logging synchronous
Router(config-line)# exec-timeout 0 0
```

Step 1: Configure interface addresses on all routers and EBGP on ISP1.

a. Using the addressing scheme in the diagram, create the loopback interfaces and apply IPv4 addresses to these and the serial interfaces on ISP (R1), SanJose1 (R2), and SanJose2 (R3).

Router R1 (hostname ISP1)

```
ISP(config)# interface Loopback0
ISP(config-if)# ip address 10.0.0.1 255.255.255.0
ISP(config-if)# exit
ISP(config)# interface GigabitEthernet0/0
ISP(config-if)# ip address 10.1.0.1 255.255.0.0
ISP(config-if)# no shutdown
ISP(config-if)# exit
ISP(config)# interface Serial0/0/0
ISP(config-if)# ip address 192.168.1.1 255.255.255.252
ISP(config-if)# clock rate 64000
ISP(config-if)# no shutdown
ISP(config-if)# exit
ISP(config)# router bgp 65100
ISP(config-router)# bgp router-id 1.0.0.1
ISP(config-router)# neighbor 192.168.1.2 remote-as 65000
ISP(config-router)# network 10.1.0.0 mask 255.255.0.0
ISP(config-router)#
```

ISP1 has an EBGP peering session with SanJose1. ISP1 is advertising the 10.1.0.0/16 network. A similar BGP configuration is assumed on ISP2, which does not physically exist in this lab topology.

Router R2 (hostname SanJose1)

```
SanJose1(config)# interface Loopback0
SanJose1(config-if)# ip address 172.17.2.1 255.255.255.0
SanJose1(config-if)# exit
SanJose1(config)# interface GigabitEthernet0/0
```

```
SanJose1(config-if)# ip address 172.16.2.1 255.255.255.0
SanJose1(config-if)# no shutdown
SanJose1(config-if)# exit
SanJose1(config)# interface Serial0/0/0
SanJose1(config-if)# ip address 192.168.1.2 255.255.255.252
SanJose1(config-if)# no shutdown
SanJose1(config-if)# exit
SanJose1(config)# interface Serial0/0/1
SanJose1(config-if)# ip address 172.16.1.1 255.255.255.252
SanJose1(config-if)# clock rate 64000
SanJose1(config-if)# no shutdown
SanJose1(config-if)#
```

Router R3 (hostname SanJose2)

```
SanJose2(config)# interface Loopback0
SanJose2(config-if)# ip address 172.17.3.1 255.255.255.0
SanJose2(config-if)# exit
SanJose2(config)# interface GigabitEthernet0/0
SanJose2(config-if)# ip address 172.16.3.1 255.255.255.0
SanJose2(config-if)# no shutdown
SanJose2(config-if)# exit
SanJose2(config)# interface Serial0/0/1
SanJose2(config-if)# ip address 172.16.1.2 255.255.255.252
SanJose2(config-if)# no shutdown
SanJose2(config-if)# exit
SanJose2(config)# interface Serial0/1/0
SanJose2(config-if)# ip address 172.16.1.5 255.255.255.252
SanJose2(config-if)# clock rate 64000
SanJose2(config-if)# no shutdown
SanJose2(config-if)#
```

Router R4 (hostname SanJose3)

```
SanJose3(config)# interface Loopback0
SanJose3(config-if)# ip address 172.17.4.1 255.255.255.0
SanJose3(config-if)# no shutdown
SanJose3(config-if)# exit
SanJose3(config)# interface Serial0/0/0
SanJose3(config-if)# ip address 172.16.1.6 255.255.255.252
SanJose3(config-if)# no shutdown
SanJose3(config-if)# exit
SanJose3(config)# interface GigabitEthernet0/0
SanJose3(config-if)# ip address 172.16.4.1 255.255.255.0
SanJose3(config-if)# no shutdown
SanJose3(config-if)#
```

b. Use **ping** to test the connectivity between the directly connected routers.

Step 2: Configure EIGRP on ITA routers.

Configure EIGRP on the SanJose1, SanJose2, and SanJose3 routers. Both routers should be able to ping the other router's LAN and loopback interfaces. (Note: If using an IOS prior to 15.0, use the no auto-summary router configuration command to disable automatic summarization. This command is the default beginning with IOS 15.)

Configure EIGRP for IPv4 and IPv6 on SanJose1.

```
SanJose1(config)# router eigrp 1
SanJose1(config-router)# eigrp router-id 1.1.1.1
SanJose1(config-router)# network 172.16.0.0
SanJose1(config-router)# network 172.17.0.0

SanJose2(config)# router eigrp 1
SanJose2(config-router)# eigrp router-id 2.2.2.2
SanJose2(config-router)# network 172.16.0.0
SanJose2(config-router)# network 172.17.0.0

SanJose3(config)# router eigrp 1
SanJose3(config-router)# eigrp router-id 3.3.3.3
SanJose3(config-router)# network 172.16.0.0
SanJose3(config-router)# network 172.17.0.0
```

a. Use **ping** to test the reachability between the ITA routers. For example, SanJose3's G0/0 interface should be able to ping SanJose1's G0/0 interface.

```
SanJose3# ping 172.16.2.0 source gig 0/0
Type escape sequence to abort.
Sending 5, 100-byte ICMP Echos to 172.16.2.0, timeout is 2 seconds:
Packet sent with a source address of 172.16.4.1
!!!!!
Success rate is 100 percent (5/5), round-trip min/avg/max = 52/55/56 ms
SanJose3#
```

Step 3: Configure BGP on SanJose1 and SanJose3.

a. On SanJose1, configure EBGP to peer with ISP1. ISP1 has already been configured to peer with SanJose1. Configure SanJose1 to IBGP peer with SanJose3 using its loopback0 address. SanJose1 will be advertising the 172.16.2.0/24 network in BGP.

```
SanJose1(config)# router bgp 65000
SanJose1(config-router)# bgp router-id 1.1.1.1
SanJose1(config-router)# neighbor 192.168.1.1 remote-as 65100
SanJose1(config-router)# neighbor 172.17.4.1 remote-as 65000
SanJose1(config-router)# neighbor 172.17.4.1 update-source Loopback0
SanJose1(config-router)# network 172.16.2.0 mask 255.255.255.0
SanJose1(config-router)#
```

b. Configure SanJose3 to IBGP peer with SanJose1 using its loopback0 address. SanJose3 will be advertising the 172.16.4.0/24 network in BGP.

```
SanJose3(config)# router bgp 65000
SanJose3(config-router)# bgp router-id 3.3.3.3
SanJose3(config-router)# neighbor 172.17.2.1 remote-as 65000
SanJose3(config-router)# neighbor 172.17.2.1 update-source Loopback0
SanJose3(config-router)# network 172.16.4.0 mask 255.255.255.0
SanJose3(config-router)#
```

Step 4: Verify BGP on SanJose1.

a. Examine SanJose1's BGP table using the **show ip bgp** command.

```
SanJose1# show ip bgp
BGP table version is 7, local router ID is 1.1.1.1
Status codes: s suppressed, d damped, h history, * valid, > best, i - internal,
              r RIB-failure, S Stale, m multipath, b backup-path, f RT-Filter,
              x best-external, a additional-path, c RIB-compressed,
Origin codes: i - IGP, e - EGP, ? - incomplete
RPKI validation codes: V valid, I invalid, N Not found

     Network          Next Hop            Metric LocPrf Weight Path
 *>  10.1.0.0/16      192.168.1.1              0             0 65100 i
 *>  172.16.2.0/24    0.0.0.0                  0         32768 i
 r>i 172.16.4.0/24    172.17.4.1               0    100      0 i
SanJose1#
```

Notice that there are three entries in SanJose1's BGP table.

- 10.1.0.0/16—The status codes "*>" indicate that this network is reachable using the next hop IPaddress 192.168.1.1.

- 172.16.2.0/24—The status codes "*>" indicate that this network is reachable. The next hop address 0.0.0.0 indicates that this router is originating the network.

- 172.16.4.0/24—The status "r>i" indicate that this network is reachable. The "r" indicates a RIB failure and the "i" means this entry was learned via IBGP.

Why is there a RIB failure for the 172.16.4.0/24 network? What command would help you determine the cause?

_____

_____

b. Use the **show ip bgp rib-failure** command to examine the cause of the RIB failure.

```
SanJose1# show ip bgp rib-failure
   Network            Next Hop                       RIB-failure    RIB-NH
Matches
172.16.4.0/24         172.17.4.1             Higher admin distance            n/a
SanJose1#
```

As you might have answer in the previous question, the RIB failure is due to SanJose1 having a better routing source to this destination. SanJose routers are using EIGRP to share internal ITA networks. IBGP has a higher administrative distance (200) than EIGRP (90), so the EIGRP router is preferred.

c. Verify SanJose1's routing table using the **show ip route** command.

```
SanJose1# show ip route
Codes: L - local, C - connected, S - static, R - RIP, M - mobile, B - BGP
       D - EIGRP, EX - EIGRP external, O - OSPF, IA - OSPF inter area
       N1 - OSPF NSSA external type 1, N2 - OSPF NSSA external type 2
       E1 - OSPF external type 1, E2 - OSPF external type 2
```

```
        i - IS-IS, su - IS-IS summary, L1 - IS-IS level-1, L2 - IS-IS level-2
        ia - IS-IS inter area, * - candidate default, U - per-user static
        route
        o - ODR, P - periodic downloaded static route, H - NHRP, l - LISP
        a - application route
        + - replicated route, % - next hop override

Gateway of last resort is not set

        10.0.0.0/16 is subnetted, 1 subnets
B          10.1.0.0 [20/0] via 192.168.1.1, 00:14:14
        172.16.0.0/16 is variably subnetted, 7 subnets, 3 masks
C          172.16.1.0/30 is directly connected, Serial0/0/1
L          172.16.1.1/32 is directly connected, Serial0/0/1
D          172.16.1.4/30 [90/2681856] via 172.16.1.2, 00:30:41, Serial0/0/1
C          172.16.2.0/24 is directly connected, GigabitEthernet0/0
L          172.16.2.1/32 is directly connected, GigabitEthernet0/0
D          172.16.3.0/24 [90/2172416] via 172.16.1.2, 00:30:41, Serial0/0/1
D          172.16.4.0/24 [90/2684416] via 172.16.1.2, 00:29:42, Serial0/0/1
        172.17.0.0/16 is variably subnetted, 4 subnets, 2 masks
C          172.17.2.0/24 is directly connected, Loopback0
L          172.17.2.1/32 is directly connected, Loopback0
D          172.17.3.0/24 [90/2297856] via 172.16.1.2, 00:30:41, Serial0/0/1
D          172.17.4.0/24 [90/2809856] via 172.16.1.2, 00:29:42, Serial0/0/1
        192.168.1.0/24 is variably subnetted, 2 subnets, 2 masks
C          192.168.1.0/30 is directly connected, Serial0/0/0
L          192.168.1.2/32 is directly connected, Serial0/0/0
SanJose1#
```

Notice that SanJose1 has a BGP route to 10.1.0.0/16 on ISP1 and an EIGRP route to the 172.16.4.0/24 network on SanJose3.

d. Verify SanJose1's reachability to 10.1.0.0/16 on ISP1.

```
SanJose1# ping 10.1.0.1
Type escape sequence to abort.
Sending 5, 100-byte ICMP Echos to 10.1.0.1, timeout is 2 seconds:
!!!!!
Success rate is 100 percent (5/5), round-trip min/avg/max = 24/27/28 ms
SanJose1#
```

Step 5: Examine and troubleshoot IBGP next hop reachability on SanJose3.

a. Examine the routing table on SanJose3 using the **show ip route** command.

```
SanJose3# show ip route
Codes: L - local, C - connected, S - static, R - RIP, M - mobile, B - BGP
        D - EIGRP, EX - EIGRP external, O - OSPF, IA - OSPF inter area
        N1 - OSPF NSSA external type 1, N2 - OSPF NSSA external type 2
        E1 - OSPF external type 1, E2 - OSPF external type 2
        i - IS-IS, su - IS-IS summary, L1 - IS-IS level-1, L2 - IS-IS level-2
```

```
            ia - IS-IS inter area, * - candidate default, U - per-user static
            route
            o - ODR, P - periodic downloaded static route, H - NHRP, l - LISP
            a - application route
            + - replicated route, % - next hop override

Gateway of last resort is not set

        172.16.0.0/16 is variably subnetted, 7 subnets, 3 masks
D          172.16.1.0/30 [90/2681856] via 172.16.1.5, 01:00:03, Serial0/0/0
C          172.16.1.4/30 is directly connected, Serial0/0/0
L          172.16.1.6/32 is directly connected, Serial0/0/0
D          172.16.2.0/24 [90/2684416] via 172.16.1.5, 01:00:03, Serial0/0/0
D          172.16.3.0/24 [90/2172416] via 172.16.1.5, 01:00:03, Serial0/0/0
C          172.16.4.0/24 is directly connected, GigabitEthernet0/0
L          172.16.4.1/32 is directly connected, GigabitEthernet0/0
        172.17.0.0/16 is variably subnetted, 4 subnets, 2 masks
D          172.17.2.0/24 [90/2809856] via 172.16.1.5, 01:00:03, Serial0/0/0
D          172.17.3.0/24 [90/2297856] via 172.16.1.5, 01:00:03, Serial0/0/0
C          172.17.4.0/24 is directly connected, Loopback0
L          172.17.4.1/32 is directly connected, Loopback0
SanJose3#
```

Notice that SanJose3 does not include a route to the 10.1.0.0/16 network on ISP1.

b. Examine the BGP table on SanJose3 using the **show ip bgp** command to try to determine the reason why the 10.1.0.0/16 network is not in its routing table.

```
SanJose3# show ip bgp
BGP table version is 3, local router ID is 3.3.3.3
Status codes: s suppressed, d damped, h history, * valid, > best, i - internal,
              r RIB-failure, S Stale, m multipath, b backup-path, f RT-Filter,
              x best-external, a additional-path, c RIB-compressed,
Origin codes: i - IGP, e - EGP, ? - incomplete
RPKI validation codes: V valid, I invalid, N Not found

     Network          Next Hop            Metric LocPrf Weight Path
 * i 10.1.0.0/16      192.168.1.1              0    100      0 65100 i
 r>i 172.16.2.0/24    172.17.2.1               0    100      0 i
 *>  172.16.4.0/24    0.0.0.0                  0           32768 i
SanJose3#
```

The output shows that the 10.1.0.0/16 network is in the BGP table but is missing the ">" status code indicating that it is not being offered to the IP routing table. The next hop address used for this route is 192.168.1.1. SanJose3's routing table in Step 3a shows that SanJose3 does not have a route to this next hop address. If the router does not have a route to the next hop address then the route will not be included in the IP routing table.

In routing, the term "next hop" does not always mean the next hop is a physically adjacent interface. The next hop, as in this case, can be more than one router away.

BGP specifies that routes learned through IBGP are never propagated to other IBGP peers. SanJose1 has learned via EBGP about the 10.1.0.0/16 network from ISP1 with a next hop address of 192.168.1.1, the IP address of ISP1. SanJose1 uses this same next hop address of 192.168.1.1 in its IBGP update to SanJose3.

What are two solutions to this problem?

_____

_____

c. The decision is made to modify the behavior on SanJose1 so that it uses its loopback0 interface as the next hop address in its IBGP updates.

```
SanJose1(config)# router bgp 65000
SanJose1(config-router)# neighbor 172.17.4.1 next-hop-self
SanJose1(config-router)#
```

Note: For consistency, a similar configuration for SanJose3 is shown. You do **not** need to configure this. This would need to be done if ISP2 router actually existed in our lab topology.

```
SanJose3(config)# router bgp 65000
SanJose3(config-router)# neighbor 172.17.2.1 next-hop-self
SanJose3(config-router)#
```

d. Re-examine the BGP table on SanJose3 using the **show ip bgp** command to see if SanJose3 now has a valid next hop to the 10.1.0.0/16 network.

```
SanJose3# show ip bgp
BGP table version is 5, local router ID is 3.3.3.3
Status codes: s suppressed, d damped, h history, * valid, > best, i - internal,
              r RIB-failure, S Stale, m multipath, b backup-path, f RT-Filter,
              x best-external, a additional-path, c RIB-compressed,
Origin codes: i - IGP, e - EGP, ? - incomplete
RPKI validation codes: V valid, I invalid, N Not found

     Network          Next Hop            Metric LocPrf Weight Path
 *>i 10.1.0.0/16      172.17.2.1               0    100      0 65100 i
 r>i 172.16.2.0/24    172.17.2.1               0    100      0 i
 *>  172.16.4.0/24    0.0.0.0                  0           32768 i
SanJose3#
```

Notice that the next hope address has been changed to SanJose1's loopback0 address 172.17.2.1, which is reachable because it is being advertised in EIGRP updates from SanJose1.

e. Re-examine the routing table on SanJose3 using the **show ip route** command to see if SanJose3 now has a route to the 10.1.0.0/16 network.

```
SanJose3# show ip route
Codes: L - local, C - connected, S - static, R - RIP, M - mobile, B - BGP
       D - EIGRP, EX - EIGRP external, O - OSPF, IA - OSPF inter area
       N1 - OSPF NSSA external type 1, N2 - OSPF NSSA external type 2
       E1 - OSPF external type 1, E2 - OSPF external type 2
       i - IS-IS, su - IS-IS summary, L1 - IS-IS level-1, L2 - IS-IS level-2
       ia - IS-IS inter area, * - candidate default, U - per-user static
       route
       o - ODR, P - periodic downloaded static route, H - NHRP, l - LISP
```

```
            a - application route
            + - replicated route, % - next hop override

Gateway of last resort is not set

        10.0.0.0/16 is subnetted, 1 subnets
B          10.1.0.0 [200/0] via 172.17.2.1, 00:03:17
        172.16.0.0/16 is variably subnetted, 7 subnets, 3 masks
D          172.16.1.0/30 [90/2681856] via 172.16.1.5, 01:26:06, Serial0/0/0
C          172.16.1.4/30 is directly connected, Serial0/0/0
L          172.16.1.6/32 is directly connected, Serial0/0/0
D          172.16.2.0/24 [90/2684416] via 172.16.1.5, 01:26:06, Serial0/0/0
D          172.16.3.0/24 [90/2172416] via 172.16.1.5, 01:26:06, Serial0/0/0
C          172.16.4.0/24 is directly connected, GigabitEthernet0/0
L          172.16.4.1/32 is directly connected, GigabitEthernet0/0
        172.17.0.0/16 is variably subnetted, 4 subnets, 2 masks
D          172.17.2.0/24 [90/2809856] via 172.16.1.5, 01:26:06, Serial0/0/0
D          172.17.3.0/24 [90/2297856] via 172.16.1.5, 01:26:06, Serial0/0/0
C          172.17.4.0/24 is directly connected, Loopback0
L          172.17.4.1/32 is directly connected, Loopback0
SanJose3#
```

f. In the previous output, SanJose3 shows a route to the 10.1.0.0/16 network. Verify reachability to this network by pinging ISP1's G0/0 interface.

```
SanJose3# ping 10.1.0.1
Type escape sequence to abort.
Sending 5, 100-byte ICMP Echos to 10.1.0.1, timeout is 2 seconds:
U.U.U
Success rate is 0 percent (0/5)
SanJose3#
```

Notice that the ping was **not** successful. One reason is because SanJose3 is not advertising the network used as the source IP address in the ping, the 172.16.1.4/30 network.

SanJose3 is advertising its 172.16.4.0/24 network in its BGP updates using the **network** command in its initial BGP configuration. Use the ping command, changing the source IP address for the ping to use SanJose3's G0/0 IP address 172.16.4.1.

```
SanJose3# ping 10.1.0.1 source gig 0/0
Type escape sequence to abort.
Sending 5, 100-byte ICMP Echos to 10.1.0.1, timeout is 2 seconds:
Packet sent with a source address of 172.16.4.1
U.U.U
Success rate is 0 percent (0/5)
SanJose3#
```

Even with the correct source IP address the ping does not succeed.

Even though SanJose3 has a route to ISP1's 10.1.0.0/16 network, why do the pings from SanJose3 fail to 10.1.0.1?

_____

_____

Step 6: Examine the behavior of BGP synchronization being disabled.

a. The following output reminds us that SanJose3 has an entry in its BGP table and a route in its IP routing table for 10.1.0.0/16.

```
SanJose3# show ip bgp
BGP table version is 5, local router ID is 3.3.3.3
Status codes: s suppressed, d damped, h history, * valid, > best, i - internal,
              r RIB-failure, S Stale, m multipath, b backup-path, f RT-Filter,
              x best-external, a additional-path, c RIB-compressed,
Origin codes: i - IGP, e - EGP, ? - incomplete
RPKI validation codes: V valid, I invalid, N Not found

     Network          Next Hop          Metric LocPrf Weight Path
 *>i 10.1.0.0/16      172.17.2.1             0    100      0 65100 i
 r>i 172.16.2.0/24    172.17.2.1             0    100      0 i
 *>  172.16.4.0/24    0.0.0.0                0         32768 i
SanJose3#


SanJose3# show ip route bgp
Codes: L - local, C - connected, S - static, R - RIP, M - mobile, B - BGP
       D - EIGRP, EX - EIGRP external, O - OSPF, IA - OSPF inter area
       N1 - OSPF NSSA external type 1, N2 - OSPF NSSA external type 2
       E1 - OSPF external type 1, E2 - OSPF external type 2
       i - IS-IS, su - IS-IS summary, L1 - IS-IS level-1, L2 - IS-IS level-2
       ia - IS-IS inter area, * - candidate default, U - per-user static route
       o - ODR, P - periodic downloaded static route, H - NHRP, l - LISP
       a - application route
       + - replicated route, % - next hop override

Gateway of last resort is not set

      10.0.0.0/16 is subnetted, 1 subnets
B        10.1.0.0 [200/0] via 172.17.2.1, 00:26:43
SanJose3#
```

b. Use the ping command to see if SanJose3 can ping the 10.1.0.1 address on ISP1. Notice that the ping fails.

```
SanJose3# ping 10.1.0.1 source gig 0/0
Type escape sequence to abort.
Sending 5, 100-byte ICMP Echos to 10.1.0.1, timeout is 2 seconds:
Packet sent with a source address of 172.16.4.1
U.U.U
```

c. The problem is on SanJose2. SanJose2 does not have a route for 10.1.0.0/16 network as shown using the **show ip route** command.

```
SanJose2# show ip route
<output omitted>

      172.16.0.0/16 is variably subnetted, 8 subnets, 3 masks
C        172.16.1.0/30 is directly connected, Serial0/0/1
L        172.16.1.2/32 is directly connected, Serial0/0/1
C        172.16.1.4/30 is directly connected, Serial0/1/0
L        172.16.1.5/32 is directly connected, Serial0/1/0
D        172.16.2.0/24 [90/2172416] via 172.16.1.1, 01:56:50, Serial0/0/1
C        172.16.3.0/24 is directly connected, GigabitEthernet0/0
```

```
L          172.16.3.1/32 is directly connected, GigabitEthernet0/0
D          172.16.4.0/24 [90/2172416] via 172.16.1.6, 01:55:52, Serial0/1/0
       172.17.0.0/16 is variably subnetted, 4 subnets, 2 masks
D          172.17.2.0/24 [90/2297856] via 172.16.1.1, 01:56:50, Serial0/0/1
C          172.17.3.0/24 is directly connected, Loopback0
L          172.17.3.1/32 is directly connected, Loopback0
D          172.17.4.0/24 [90/2297856] via 172.16.1.6, 01:55:52, Serial0/1/0
SanJose2#
```

Even though SanJose2 does not have any knowledge of the 10.1.0.0/16 network, SanJose3 has the network in its IP routing table because it learned the route via IBGP from SanJose1 and has a valid next hop address to SanJose1 for the route. Even though there is not complete reachability in the ITA for 10.1.0.0/16, SanJose3 still has an IBGP route for this network because the default BGP behavior is **no synchronization**. Beginning with IOS 12.2(8)T, the default BGP behavior is **no synchronization**.

What is the BGP synchronization rule? The BGP synchronization rule states that a router will not include in its routing table nor advertise routes learned by IBGP unless that route is directly connected or learned from an IGP. In other words, with synchronization enabled, SanJose3 will not include the BGP route to 10.1.0.0/16 in its routing table unless it already knows about it via EIGRP. SanJose3 having the 10.1.0.0/16 network in its IP routing table as an EIGRP route would mean other routers in the domain, SanJose2, most likely have this route also.

Prior to IOS 12.2(8)T **synchronization** was the default behavior.

d. The affect of this behavior can be examined by enabling synchronization on SanJose3 using the BGP **synchronization** command. The **clear ip bgp *** command is used to test the neighbor adjacencies.

```
SanJose3(config)# router bgp 65000
SanJose3(config-router)# synchronization
SanJose3(config-router)# end
SanJose3#clear ip bgp *
*Sep 28 18:13:53.007: %BGP-5-ADJCHANGE: neighbor 172.17.2.1 Down User reset
*Sep 28 18:13:53.007: %BGP_SESSION-5-ADJCHANGE: neighbor 172.17.2.1 IPv4
Unicast topology base removed from session  User reset
*Sep 28 18:13:53.335: %BGP-5-ADJCHANGE: neighbor 172.17.2.1 Up
SanJose3#
```

e. Using the **show ip bgp** command to verify that SanJose3 is still receiving the IBGP update for 10.1.0.0/16 from SanJose1 but no longer is valid.

```
SanJose3# show ip bgp
BGP table version is 3, local router ID is 3.3.3.3
Status codes: s suppressed, d damped, h history, * valid, > best, i - internal,
              r RIB-failure, S Stale, m multipath, b backup-path, f RT-Filter,
              x best-external, a additional-path, c RIB-compressed,
Origin codes: i - IGP, e - EGP, ? - incomplete
RPKI validation codes: V valid, I invalid, N Not found

     Network          Next Hop          Metric LocPrf Weight Path
 * i 10.1.0.0/16      172.17.2.1             0    100      0 65100 i
 r>i 172.16.2.0/24    172.17.2.1             0    100      0 i
 *>  172.16.4.0/24    0.0.0.0                0          32768 i
SanJose3#
```

f. With synchronization enabled, using the **show ip route** command verify that SanJose3 no longer includes the 10.1.0.0/16 network in its routing table. SanJose3 does not include the 10.1.0.0/16 network in its IP routing table because it does not have this network as an IGP (EIGRP) route in its routing table.

```
SanJose3# show ip route
<output omitted>

      172.16.0.0/16 is variably subnetted, 7 subnets, 3 masks
D        172.16.1.0/30 [90/2681856] via 172.16.1.5, 02:09:59, Serial0/0/0
C        172.16.1.4/30 is directly connected, Serial0/0/0
L        172.16.1.6/32 is directly connected, Serial0/0/0
D        172.16.2.0/24 [90/2684416] via 172.16.1.5, 02:09:59, Serial0/0/0
D        172.16.3.0/24 [90/2172416] via 172.16.1.5, 02:09:59, Serial0/0/0
C        172.16.4.0/24 is directly connected, GigabitEthernet0/0
L        172.16.4.1/32 is directly connected, GigabitEthernet0/0
      172.17.0.0/16 is variably subnetted, 4 subnets, 2 masks
D        172.17.2.0/24 [90/2809856] via 172.16.1.5, 02:09:59, Serial0/0/0
D        172.17.3.0/24 [90/2297856] via 172.16.1.5, 02:09:59, Serial0/0/0
C        172.17.4.0/24 is directly connected, Loopback0
L        172.17.4.1/32 is directly connected, Loopback0
SanJose3#
```

With synchronization enabled, routes learned via EBGP would need to redistributed into the IGP (EIGRP). SanJose2 would then include the 10.1.0.0/16 network in its IP routing table. Because of the size of Internet routing tables and the potential for this to consume a lot of memory and CPU resources, this is no longer considered best practice.

The better solution is to configure full-mesh IBGP on the transit BGP routers. This is done in the next step.

g. To return to the default configuration, disable synchronization on SanJose3 using the **no synchronization** command and reset the BGP peering. Verify that SanJose3 has returned to this behavior using the **show ip bgp** and **show ip route bgp** commands.

```
SanJose3(config)# router bgp 65000
SanJose3(config-router)# no synchronization
SanJose3(config-router)# end
SanJose3# clear ip bgp *
SanJose3#
*Sep 28 18:25:39.415: %BGP-5-ADJCHANGE: neighbor 172.17.2.1 Down User reset
*Sep 28 18:25:39.415: %BGP_SESSION-5-ADJCHANGE: neighbor 172.17.2.1 IPv4
Unicast topology base removed from session  User reset
*Sep 28 18:25:40.155: %BGP-5-ADJCHANGE: neighbor 172.17.2.1 Up
SanJose3#
SanJose3# show ip bgp
BGP table version is 4, local router ID is 3.3.3.3
Status codes: s suppressed, d damped, h history, * valid, > best, i -
internal,
              r RIB-failure, S Stale, m multipath, b backup-path, f RT-
Filter,
              x best-external, a additional-path, c RIB-compressed,
```

```
Origin codes: i - IGP, e - EGP, ? - incomplete
RPKI validation codes: V valid, I invalid, N Not found

      Network             Next Hop            Metric LocPrf Weight Path
 *>i 10.1.0.0/16          172.17.2.1               0    100      0 65100 i
 r>i 172.16.2.0/24        172.17.2.1               0    100      0 i
 *>  172.16.4.0/24        0.0.0.0                  0           32768 i
SanJose3# show ip route bgp
Codes: L - local, C - connected, S - static, R - RIP, M - mobile, B - BGP
       D - EIGRP, EX - EIGRP external, O - OSPF, IA - OSPF inter area
       N1 - OSPF NSSA external type 1, N2 - OSPF NSSA external type 2
       E1 - OSPF external type 1, E2 - OSPF external type 2
       i - IS-IS, su - IS-IS summary, L1 - IS-IS level-1, L2 - IS-IS level-2
       ia - IS-IS inter area, * - candidate default, U - per-user static
       route
       o - ODR, P - periodic downloaded static route, H - NHRP, l - LISP
       a - application route
       + - replicated route, % - next hop override

Gateway of last resort is not set

      10.0.0.0/16 is subnetted, 1 subnets
B        10.1.0.0 [200/0] via 172.17.2.1, 00:09:43
SanJose3#
```

Step 7: Configure and verify full-mesh IBGP on all ITA transit routers.

a. With **no synchronization** being the default behavior with IOS, it is important that network administrators ensure IBGP reachability amongst all routers in the transit path. Looking at the topology, notice that SanJose3 has an EBGP peering relationship with ISP2. (This only exists in the topology but was not configured.) Without any further configuration to filter the 10.1.0.0/16 network, SanJose3 would advertise this network to ISP2. The routing policy on ISP2 could mean that it would forward packets for 10.1.0.0/16 to SanJose3. SanJose2 would then forward them to SanJose2, where they would be dropped because it does not have a route to this network.

The solution is to configure fully meshed IBGP among all routers in the transit path: SanJose1, SanJose2, and SanJose3.

Configure BGP on SanJose2 to have peering relationships with both SanJose1 and SanJose3. Configure SanJose1 and SanJose3 to have a peering relationship with SanJose2. Configure the peering to use the loopback0 addresses.

```
SanJose2(config)# router bgp 65000
SanJose2(config-router)# bgp router-id 2.2.2.2
SanJose2(config-router)# neighbor 172.17.2.1 remote-as 65000
SanJose2(config-router)# neighbor 172.17.2.1 update-source Loopback0
SanJose2(config-router)# neighbor 172.17.4.1 remote-as 65000
SanJose2(config-router)# neighbor 172.17.4.1 update-source Loopback0
SanJose2(config-router)#

SanJose1(config)# router bgp 65000
SanJose1(config-router)# neighbor 172.17.3.1 remote-as 65000
SanJose1(config-router)# neighbor 172.17.3.1 update-source Loopback0
SanJose1(config-router)# neighbor 172.17.3.1 next-hop-self
SanJose1(config-router)#
```

```
SanJose3(config)# router bgp 65000
SanJose3(config-router)# neighbor 172.17.3.1 remote-as 65000
SanJose3(config-router)# neighbor 172.17.3.1 update-source Loopback0
SanJose3(config-router)#
```

Note: Notice that SanJose1 is configured as the next hop for IBGP routes advertised to SanJose2. For consistency, a similar configuration for SanJose3 is shown. Once again, you do **not** need to configure this because the ISP2 router does not actually exist in our lab topology.

```
SanJose3(config)# router bgp 65000
SanJose3(config-router)# neighbor 172.17.3.1 next-hop-self
SanJose3(config-router)#
```

b. Use the **show bgp summary** command on each router to verify the neighbor adjacencies.

```
ISP1# show bgp summary
BGP router identifier 1.0.0.0, local AS number 65100
BGP table version is 18, main routing table version 18
3 network entries using 432 bytes of memory
3 path entries using 240 bytes of memory
3/3 BGP path/bestpath attribute entries using 480 bytes of memory
1 BGP AS-PATH entries using 24 bytes of memory
0 BGP route-map cache entries using 0 bytes of memory
0 BGP filter-list cache entries using 0 bytes of memory
BGP using 1176 total bytes of memory
BGP activity 6/3 prefixes, 8/5 paths, scan interval 60 secs

Neighbor        V          AS MsgRcvd MsgSent   TblVer  InQ OutQ Up/Down
State/PfxRcd
192.168.1.2     4       65000      20      21       18    0    0 00:14:25  2
ISP1#
```

```
SanJose1# show bgp summary
BGP router identifier 1.1.1.1, local AS number 65000
BGP table version is 4, main routing table version 4
3 network entries using 432 bytes of memory
3 path entries using 240 bytes of memory
3/3 BGP path/bestpath attribute entries using 480 bytes of memory
1 BGP AS-PATH entries using 24 bytes of memory
0 BGP route-map cache entries using 0 bytes of memory
0 BGP filter-list cache entries using 0 bytes of memory
BGP using 1176 total bytes of memory
BGP activity 7/4 prefixes, 8/5 paths, scan interval 60 secs

Neighbor        V          AS MsgRcvd MsgSent   TblVer  InQ OutQ Up/Down
State/PfxRcd
172.17.3.1      4       65000      18      18        4    0    0 00:12:12  0
172.17.4.1      4       65000      19      18        4    0    0 00:12:12  1
192.168.1.1     4       65100      18      18        4    0    0 00:12:12  1
SanJose1#
```

```
SanJose2# show bgp summary
BGP router identifier 2.2.2.2, local AS number 65000
BGP table version is 9, main routing table version 9
```

```
3 network entries using 432 bytes of memory
3 path entries using 240 bytes of memory
2/2 BGP path/bestpath attribute entries using 320 bytes of memory
1 BGP AS-PATH entries using 24 bytes of memory
0 BGP route-map cache entries using 0 bytes of memory
0 BGP filter-list cache entries using 0 bytes of memory
BGP using 1016 total bytes of memory
BGP activity 5/2 prefixes, 5/2 paths, scan interval 60 secs

Neighbor        V           AS MsgRcvd MsgSent   TblVer  InQ OutQ Up/Down
State/PfxRcd
172.17.2.1      4        65000      20      20        9    0    0 00:14:30  2
172.17.4.1      4        65000      68      66        9    0    0 00:53:14  1
SanJose2#


SanJose3# show bgp summary
BGP router identifier 3.3.3.3, local AS number 65000
BGP table version is 10, main routing table version 10
3 network entries using 432 bytes of memory
3 path entries using 240 bytes of memory
3/3 BGP path/bestpath attribute entries using 480 bytes of memory
1 BGP AS-PATH entries using 24 bytes of memory
0 BGP route-map cache entries using 0 bytes of memory
0 BGP filter-list cache entries using 0 bytes of memory
BGP using 1176 total bytes of memory
BGP activity 11/8 prefixes, 11/8 paths, scan interval 60 secs

Neighbor        V           AS MsgRcvd MsgSent   TblVer  InQ OutQ Up/Down
State/PfxRcd
172.17.2.1      4        65000      20      22       10    0    0 00:14:35  2
172.17.3.1      4        65000      66      68       10    0    0 00:53:19  0
SanJose3#
```

c. Verify that SanJose2 now has the 10.1.0.0/16 network in its BGP table and in its IP routing table, using the **show ip bgp** and **show ip route bgp** commands.

```
SanJose2# show ip bgp
BGP table version is 5, local router ID is 2.2.2.2
Status codes: s suppressed, d damped, h history, * valid, > best, i - internal,
              r RIB-failure, S Stale, m multipath, b backup-path, f RT-Filter,
              x best-external, a additional-path, c RIB-compressed,
Origin codes: i - IGP, e - EGP, ? - incomplete
RPKI validation codes: V valid, I invalid, N Not found

     Network          Next Hop          Metric LocPrf Weight Path
*>i 10.1.0.0/16       172.17.2.1             0    100      0 65100 i
r>i 172.16.2.0/24     172.17.2.1             0    100      0 i
r>i 172.16.4.0/24     172.17.4.1             0    100      0 i
SanJose2#


SanJose2# show ip route bgp
Codes: L - local, C - connected, S - static, R - RIP, M - mobile, B - BGP
       D - EIGRP, EX - EIGRP external, O - OSPF, IA - OSPF inter area
       N1 - OSPF NSSA external type 1, N2 - OSPF NSSA external type 2
       E1 - OSPF external type 1, E2 - OSPF external type 2
       i - IS-IS, su - IS-IS summary, L1 - IS-IS level-1, L2 - IS-IS level-2
       ia - IS-IS inter area, * - candidate default, U - per-user static route
       o - ODR, P - periodic downloaded static route, H - NHRP, l - LISP
```

```
          a - application route
          + - replicated route, % - next hop override

Gateway of last resort is not set

      10.0.0.0/16 is subnetted, 1 subnets
B         10.1.0.0 [200/0] via 172.17.2.1, 00:06:53
SanJose2#
```

d. Verify that SanJose3 still has the 10.1.0.0/16 network in its BGP table and in its IP routing table, using the **show ip bgp** and **show ip route bgp** commands.

```
SanJose3# show ip bgp
BGP table version is 5, local router ID is 3.3.3.3
Status codes: s suppressed, d damped, h history, * valid, > best, i - internal,
              r RIB-failure, S Stale, m multipath, b backup-path, f RT-Filter,
              x best-external, a additional-path, c RIB-compressed,
Origin codes: i - IGP, e - EGP, ? - incomplete
RPKI validation codes: V valid, I invalid, N Not found

       Network          Next Hop        Metric LocPrf Weight Path
 *>i 10.1.0.0/16        172.17.2.1          0    100      0 65100 i
 r>i 172.16.2.0/24      172.17.2.1          0    100      0 i
 *>  172.16.4.0/24      0.0.0.0             0          32768 i
SanJose3#
```

```
SanJose3# show ip route bgp
Codes: L - local, C - connected, S - static, R - RIP, M - mobile, B - BGP
       D - EIGRP, EX - EIGRP external, O - OSPF, IA - OSPF inter area
       N1 - OSPF NSSA external type 1, N2 - OSPF NSSA external type 2
       E1 - OSPF external type 1, E2 - OSPF external type 2
       i - IS-IS, su - IS-IS summary, L1 - IS-IS level-1, L2 - IS-IS level-2
       ia - IS-IS inter area, * - candidate default, U - per-user static route
       o - ODR, P - periodic downloaded static route, H - NHRP, l - LISP
       a - application route
       + - replicated route, % - next hop override

Gateway of last resort is not set

      10.0.0.0/16 is subnetted, 1 subnets
B         10.1.0.0 [200/0] via 172.17.2.1, 00:54:55
SanJose3#
```

e. Verify that SanJose3 and ISP1 can now ping their BGP advertised networks from their G0/0 interfaces.

```
SanJose3# ping 10.1.0.1 source gig 0/0
Type escape sequence to abort.
Sending 5, 100-byte ICMP Echos to 10.1.0.1, timeout is 2 seconds:
Packet sent with a source address of 172.16.4.1
!!!!!
Success rate is 100 percent (5/5), round-trip min/avg/max = 80/82/84 ms
SanJose3#
```

```
ISP1# ping 172.16.4.1 source gig 0/0
Type escape sequence to abort.
Sending 5, 100-byte ICMP Echos to 172.16.4.1, timeout is 2 seconds:
Packet sent with a source address of 10.1.0.1
!!!!!
Success rate is 100 percent (5/5), round-trip min/avg/max = 80/83/84 ms
ISP1#
```

We now have complete reachability!

Would the pings have succeeded if they were not sourced from their G0/0 interfaces? Why or why not?

_____

_____

Step 8: Configure AS 65000 as a non-transit AS.

a. The configuration on SanJose1 and ISP1 allow both routers to exchange BGP learned routes. Although this router does not actually exist in our topology, ISP2 and SanJose3 could also be configured to exchange BGP learned routes. This would cause AS 65000 to be a transit AS. BGP routes learned from ISP1 would be advertised by SanJose3 to ISP2, and BGP routes learned from ISP2 would be advertised to by SanJose1 to ISP1.

To avoid being a transit AS, on SanJose1, configure an AS-path filter using an AS-path access list. The access list will only permit locally sourced routes to be sent to the provider, ISP1. Routes learned from another AS will be filtered and not included in its updates. This filter is applied to a set of routes announced to the ISP1 neighbor.

The regular expression "^$" matches only routes that are locally sourced, or do not contain an AS in its AS-path.

```
SanJose1(config)# router bgp 65000
SanJose1(config-router)# neighbor 192.168.1.1 filter-list 1 out
SanJose1(config-router)# exit
SanJose1(config)# ip as-path access-list 1 permit ^$
SanJose1(config)#
```

Note: A similar configuration would be done on SanJose3 with its neighbor ISP2.

b. Because our topology is not actually include the ISP2 network, we won't see any difference in our outputs. If ISP2 did actually exist, ISP1 and ISP2 would only receive BGP updates from SanJose1 and SanJose3, respectively, for the 172.16.2.0/24 and 172.16.4.0/24 networks. For example, ISP2 would not receive a BGP update for the 10.1.0.0/16 from SanJose3.

To verify that we have not removed any reachability between AS 65100 and AS 65000, once again use the ping command between ISP1 and SanJose3.

```
ISP1# ping 172.16.4.1 source gig 0/0
Type escape sequence to abort.
Sending 5, 100-byte ICMP Echos to 172.16.4.1, timeout is 2 seconds:
Packet sent with a source address of 10.1.0.1
!!!!!
Success rate is 100 percent (5/5), round-trip min/avg/max = 80/83/84 ms
ISP1#

SanJose3# ping 10.1.0.1 source gig 0/0
Type escape sequence to abort.
Sending 5, 100-byte ICMP Echos to 10.1.0.1, timeout is 2 seconds:
Packet sent with a source address of 172.16.4.1
!!!!!
Success rate is 100 percent (5/5), round-trip min/avg/max = 80/83/84 ms
SanJose3#
```

Lab 7-5 Configuring MP-BGP

Topology

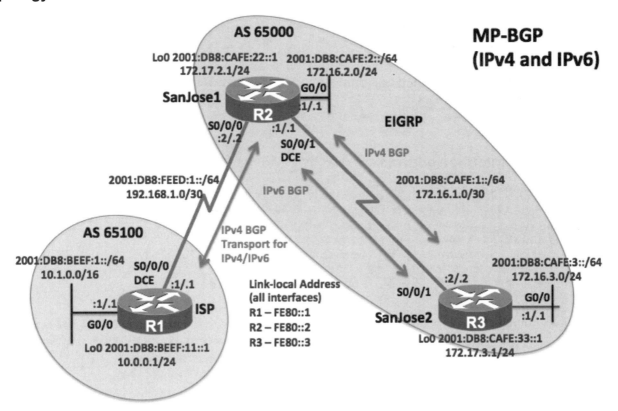

Objectives

- Configure EIGRP on an ITA network.
- Using MP-BGP, configure EBGP for IPv4 and IPv6 between ISP and SanJose1, using IPv4 BGP transport for both protocols.
- Configure MP-BGP IBGP between SanJose1 and SanJose2.
- Verify BGP neighbors, BGP tables, and routing tables for IPv4 and IPv6.

Background

SanJose1 in AS 65000 is running MP-BGP with the ISP router in AS 65100. The International Travel Agency runs MP-BGP on its SanJose1 and SanJose2 routers in AS 65000. The International Travel Agency and the ISP need to share both IPv4 and IPv6 prefixes. Your job is to configure MP-BGP for this internetwork. You will need to configure internal and external BGP sessions and advertise IPv6 network prefixes via BGP. You will deploy IPv4 and IPv6 transport. You will use route-maps to set the next-hop attribute to an IPv6 address when exchanging the IPv6 networks over an IPv4 transport session between ISP and SanJose1.

Note: This lab uses Cisco 1941 routers with Cisco IOS Release 15.4 with IP Base. The switches are Cisco WS-C2960-24TT-L with Fast Ethernet interfaces; therefore, the router will use routing metrics associated with a 100 Mb/s interface. Depending on the router or switch model and Cisco IOS Software version, the commands available and output produced might vary from what is shown in this lab.

Required Resources

- 3 routers (Cisco IOS Release 15.2 or comparable)
- 3 switches (LAN interfaces)
- Serial and Ethernet cables

Step 0: Suggested starting configurations.

a. Apply the following configuration to each router along with the appropriate **hostname**. The **exec-timeout 0 0** command should only be used in a lab environment.

```
Router(config)# no ip domain-lookup
Router(config)# line con 0
Router(config-line)# logging synchronous
Router(config-line)# exec-timeout 0 0
```

Step 1: Configure interface addresses.

a. Using the addressing scheme in the diagram, create the loopback interfaces and apply IPv4 addresses to these and the serial interfaces on ISP (R1), SanJose1 (R2), and SanJose2 (R3).

Router R1 (hostname ISP)

```
ISP(config)# interface gigabitethernet 0/0
ISP(config-if)# ip address 10.1.0.1 255.255.0.0
ISP(config-if)# ipv6 address 2001:db8:beef:1::1/64
ISP(config-if)# ipv6 address fe80::1 link-local
ISP(config-if)# no shutdown
ISP(config-if)# exit
ISP(config)# interface loopback 0
ISP(config-if)# ip address 10.0.0.1 255.255.255.0
ISP(config-if)# ipv6 address 2001:db8:beef:11::1/64
ISP(config-if)# no shutdown
ISP(config-if)# exit
ISP(config)# interface serial 0/0/0
ISP(config-if)# ip address 192.168.1.1 255.255.255.252
ISP(config-if)# ipv6 address 2001:db8:feed:1::1/64
ISP(config-if)# ipv6 address fe80::1 link-local
ISP(config-if)# clock rate 64000
ISP(config-if)# no shutdown
```

Router R2 (hostname SanJose1)

```
SanJose1(config)# interface gigabitethernet 0/0
SanJose1(config-if)# ip address 172.16.2.1 255.255.255.0
SanJose1(config-if)# ipv6 address 2001:db8:cafe:2::1/64
SanJose1(config-if)# ipv6 address fe80::2 link-local
SanJose1(config-if)# no shutdown
SanJose1(config-if)# exit
SanJose1(config)# interface serial 0/0/0
SanJose1(config-if)# ip address 192.168.1.2 255.255.255.252
SanJose1(config-if)# ipv6 address 2001:db8:feed:1::2/64
SanJose1(config-if)# ipv6 address fe80::2 link-local
SanJose1(config-if)# no shutdown
SanJose1(config-if)# exit
SanJose1(config)# interface serial 0/0/1
SanJose1(config-if)# ip address 172.16.1.1 255.255.255.252
```

```
SanJose1(config-if)# ipv6 address 2001:db8:cafe:1::1/64
SanJose1(config-if)# ipv6 address fe80::2 link-local
SanJose1(config-if)# clock rate 64000
SanJose1(config-if)# no shutdown
SanJose1(config-if)# exit
SanJose1(config)# interface loopback 0
SanJose1(config-if)# ip address 172.17.2.1 255.255.255.0
SanJose1(config-if)# ipv6 address 2001:db8:cafe:22::1/64
SanJose1(config-if)# no shutdown
```

Router R3 (hostname SanJose2)

```
SanJose2(config)# interface gigabitethernet 0/0
SanJose2(config-if)# ip address 172.16.3.1 255.255.255.0
SanJose2(config-if)# ipv6 address 2001:db8:cafe:3::1/64
SanJose2(config-if)# ipv6 address fe80::3 link-local
SanJose2(config-if)# no shutdown
SanJose2(config-if)# exit
SanJose2(config)# interface serial 0/0/1
SanJose2(config-if)# ip address 172.16.1.2 255.255.255.252
SanJose2(config-if)# ipv6 address 2001:db8:cafe:1::2/64
SanJose2(config-if)# ipv6 address fe80::3 link-local
SanJose2(config-if)# no shutdown
SanJose2(config)# interface loopback 0
SanJose2(config-if)# ip address 172.17.3.1 255.255.255.0
SanJose2(config-if)# ipv6 address 2001:db8:cafe:33::1/64
```

b. Use **ping** to test the connectivity between the directly connected routers for both IPv4 and IPv6. Both SanJose routers should be able to ping each other and SanJose1 should be able to ping the ISP on the serial link IP addresses. The ISP router cannot reach the segment between SanJose1 and SanJose2, or their LAN interfaces.

Step 2: Configure EIGRP.

a. Configure EIGRP between the SanJose1 and SanJose2 routers. Both routers should be able to ping the other router's LAN and loopback interfaces. (Note: If using an IOS prior to 15.0, use the **no auto-summary** router configuration command to disable automatic summarization. This command is the default beginning with IOS 15.)

b. Configure EIGRP for IPv4 and IPv6 on SanJose1.

```
SanJose1(config)# ipv6 unicast-routing
SanJose1(config)# router eigrp 1
SanJose1(config-router)# eigrp router-id 2.2.2.2
SanJose1(config-router)# network 172.16.0.0
SanJose1(config-router)# network 172.17.0.0

SanJose1(config)# ipv6 router eigrp 2
SanJose1(config-rtr)# eigrp router-id 2.2.2.2
```

```
SanJose1(config)# interface gigabitethernet 0/0
SanJose1(config-if)# ipv6 eigrp 2
SanJose1(config-if)# exit
SanJose1(config)# interface serial 0/0/1
SanJose1(config-if)# ipv6 eigrp 2
SanJose1(config-if)# exit
SanJose1(config)# interface loopback 0
SanJose1(config-if)# ipv6 eigrp 2
```

c.   Configure EIGRP for IPv4 and IPv6 on SanJose2.

```
SanJose2(config)# ipv6 unicast-routing
SanJose2(config)# router eigrp 1
SanJose2(config-router)# eigrp router-id 3.3.3.3
SanJose2(config-router)# network 172.16.0.0
SanJose2(config-router)# network 172.17.0.0


SanJose2(config)# ipv6 router eigrp 2
SanJose2(config-rtr)# eigrp router-id 3.3.3.3

SanJose2(config)# interface gigabitethernet 0/0
SanJose2(config-if)# ipv6 eigrp 2
SanJose2(config-if)# exit
SanJose2(config)# interface serial 0/0/1
SanJose2(config-if)# ipv6 eigrp 2
SanJose2(config-if)# exit
SanJose2(config)# interface loopback 0
SanJose2(config-if)# ipv6 eigrp 2
```

Step 3: Configure MP-BGP on ISP—EBGP.

a.   Configure EBGP between the ISP and SanJose1. ISP and SanJose1 will be using IPv4 as the BGP transport for both IPv4 and IPv6 sessions. After enabling IPv6 routing on ISP, configure BGP for AS 65100 with a router ID of 1.1.1.1. In its peering with SanJose1, the IPv4 address of SanJose1 will be used for the IPv4 BGP transport session.

```
ISP(config)# ipv6 unicast-routing
ISP(config)# router bgp 65100
ISP(config-router)# bgp router-id 1.1.1.1
ISP(config-router)# neighbor 192.168.1.2 remote-as 65000
```

b.   Enter the router configuration mode for the IPv4 address family. Enter the commands to advertise the 10.1.0.0/16 network and activate the IPv4 neighbor 192.1681.2 within the IPv4 AF.

```
ISP(config-router)# address-family ipv4 unicast
ISP(config-router-af)# network 10.1.0.0 mask 255.255.0.0
ISP(config-router-af)# neighbor 192.168.1.2 activate
ISP(config-router-af)# exit-address-family
```

c.   Enter the router configuration mode for the IPv6 address family and enter the command to advertise the 2001:DB8:BEEF:1::/64 prefix. Since you are using IPv4 as the BGP transport, you must also activate the IPv4 neighbor 192.168.1.2 within the IPv6 AF. Configure the route-map NEXT-HOP-IPV6 to attach to the

BGP neighbor in the outbound direction. Outbound direction means that this information in the route-map will be applied to IPv6 BGP updates as they are sent to SanJose1.

```
ISP(config-router)# address-family ipv6 unicast
ISP(config-router-af)# network 2001:DB8:BEEF:1::/64
ISP(config-router-af)# neighbor 192.168.1.2 activate
ISP(config-router-af)# neighbor 192.168.1.2 route-map NEXT-HOP-IPV6 out
ISP(config-router-af)# exit-address-family
```

The route-map is applied in the outbound direction. What will this do?

_____

_____

d. The route-map NEXT-HOP-IPV6 is configured to overwrite the next-hop parameter with the appropriate IPv6 next-hop address. Notice that the next-hop address is the local IPv6 address of this router, ISP. The neighbor, SanJose1, will use this IPv6 address as its next-hop address in its IPv6 BGP table.

```
ISP(config)# route-map NEXT-HOP-IPV6 permit 10
ISP(config-route-map)# set ipv6 next-hop 2001:DB8:FEED:1::1
```


Step 4: Configure MP-BGP on SanJose1—EBGP and IBGP.

a. Enable IPv6 routing on SanJose1 and then configure BGP for AS 65000 with a router ID of 2.2.2.2. The IPv4 address of ISP will be used for the IPv4 BGP transport session with ISP.

```
SanJose1(config)# router bgp 65000
SanJose1(config-router)# bgp router-id 2.2.2.2
SanJose1(config-router)# neighbor 192.168.1.1 remote-as 65100
```

b. Configure IBGP on SanJose1 to peer with SanJose2 for both IPv4 and IPv6. The **update-source loopback 0** command instructs the router to use the IP address of the interface loopback 0 as the source IP address for all BGP messages sent to that neighbor. The IP address of the loopback interface is used in the **neighbor** command.

```
SanJose1(config-router)# neighbor 2001:DB8:CAFE:33::1 remote-as 65000
SanJose1(config-router)# neighbor 2001:DB8:CAFE:33::1 update-source Loopback0
SanJose1(config-router)# neighbor 172.17.3.1 remote-as 65000
SanJose1(config-router)# neighbor 172.17.3.1 update-source Loopback0
```

c. Enter the router configuration mode for the IPv4 address family for SanJose1. Enter the command to advertise the 172.16.2.0/24 network. Activate the IPv4 neighbor within the IPv4 AF for the EBGP peering session with ISP.

```
SanJose1(config-router)# address-family ipv4 unicast
SanJose1(config-router-af)# network 172.16.2.0 mask 255.255.255.0
SanJose1(config-router-af)# neighbor 192.168.1.1 activate
```

d. Activate the IPv4 neighbor within the IPv4 AF for the IBGP peering session with SanJose2. Configure the **next-hop-self** parameter so SanJose1 uses its own IPv4 address as the next-hop address in its IBGP updates to SanJose2. By default, SanJose1 would include the next-hop address from the ISP in its IBGP updates to SanJose2. This would be for any routes learned from ISP using EBGP.

```
SanJose1(config-router-af)# neighbor 172.17.3.1 activate
SanJose1(config-router-af)# neighbor 172.17.3.1 next-hop-self
SanJose1(config-router-af)# exit-address-family
```

e. Enter the router configuration mode for the IPv6 address family and enter the command to advertise the 2001:DB8:CAFE:2::/64 prefix. Similarly to ISP, since you are using IPv4 as your BGP transport, you must also activate the IPv4 neighbor within the IPv6 AF. Configure the route-map NEXT-HOP-IPV6 to attach to the BGP neighbor in the outbound direction. Outbound direction means that this information in the route-map will be applied to IPv6 BGP updates as they are sent to ISP.

```
SanJose1(config-router)# address-family ipv6 unicast
SanJose1(config-router-af)# network 2001:DB8:CAFE:2::/64
SanJose1(config-router-af)# neighbor 192.168.1.1 activate
SanJose1(config-router-af)# neighbor 192.168.1.1 route-map NEXT-HOP-IPV6 out
```

f. Activate the IPv6 neighbor within the IPv6 AF for the IBGP peering session with SanJose2. Similarly to BGP for IPv4, configure the **next-hop-self** parameter so SanJose1 uses its own IPv6 address as the next-hop address in its IBGP updates to SanJose2.

```
SanJose1(config-router-af)# neighbor 2001:DB8:CAFE:33::1 activate
SanJose1(config-router-af)# neighbor 2001:DB8:CAFE:33::1 next-hop-self
SanJose1(config-router-af)# exit-address-family
```

If the **next-hop-self** parameter is not used, what needs to be done to ensure reachability to routes advertised by the ISP router?

_____

_____

g. Because SanJose1 is using IPv4 transport in its peering with ISP, the route-map NEXT-HOP-IPV6 is configured to overwrite the next-hop parameter with the appropriate IPv6 next-hop address. Notice that the next-hop address is the IPv6 address of SanJose1. Using its local IPv6 address in the route-map, neighbor ISP will use this IPv6 address as it's next-hop address in its IPv6 BGP table.

```
SanJose1(config)# route-map NEXT-HOP-IPV6 permit 10
SanJose1(config-route-map)# set ipv6 next-hop 2001:DB8:FEED:1::2
```

Step 5: Configure MP-BGP on SanJose2—IBGP.

a. Enable IPv6 routing on SanJose2 and then configure BGP for AS 65000 with a router ID of 3.3.3.3.

```
SanJose2(config)# router bgp 65000
SanJose2(config-router)# bgp router-id 3.3.3.3
```

b. Configure IBGP on SanJose2 to peer with SanJose1 for both IPv4 and IPv6. SanJose2's loopback 0 interface will be used in the peering for both IPv4 and IPv6.

```
SanJose2(config-router)# neighbor 2001:DB8:CAFE:22::1 remote-as 65000
SanJose2(config-router)# neighbor 2001:DB8:CAFE:22::1 update-source Loopback0
SanJose2(config-router)# neighbor 172.17.2.1 remote-as 65000
SanJose2(config-router)# neighbor 172.17.2.1 update-source Loopback0
```

c. Enter the router configuration mode for the IPv4 address family for SanJose2. Enter the command to advertise the 172.16.3.0/24 network. Activate the IPv4 neighbor within the IPv4 AF for the IBGP peering session with SanJose1.

```
SanJose2(config-router)# address-family ipv4 unicast
SanJose2(config-router-af)# network 172.16.3.0 mask 255.255.255.0
SanJose2(config-router-af)# neighbor 172.17.2.1 activate
SanJose2(config-router-af)# exit-address-family
```

d. Enter the router configuration mode for the IPv6 address family and enter the command to advertise the 2001:DB8:CAFE:3::/64 prefix. Activate the IPv6 neighbor within the IPv6 AF for the IBGP peering session with SanJose1.

```
SanJose2(config-router)# address-family ipv6 unicast
SanJose2(config-router-af)# network 2001:DB8:CAFE:3::/64
SanJose2(config-router-af)# neighbor 2001:DB8:CAFE:22::1 activate
SanJose2(config-router-af)# exit-address-family
```

Step 6: Verifying BGP neighbor peering relationships for IPv4 and IPv6.

a. Use the **show bgp all neighbors** command on SanJose1 to display information about BGP connections to neighbors for all (IPv4 and IPv6) address families. Each neighbor shows that it is in the "Established" state indicating the router can send and receive BGP messages.

SanJose1 has two neighbor addresses, ISP and SanJose2, for each address family, IPv4 and IPv6. The internal link is the IBGP neighbor relationship with SanJose2 whereas the external link is the EBGP neighbor relationship with ISP. Notice for the IPv6 address family, there are SanJose2's IPv6 address and ISP's IPv4 address. SanJose1 employs IPv6 as the IBGP transport with SanJose2, using the IPv6 address with 2001:DB8:CAFE:33::1. IPv4 is used as the EBGP transport with ISP, so the IPv4 address 192.168.1.1 is shown for the IPv6 address family.

```
SanJose1# show bgp all neighbors
For address family: IPv4 Unicast
BGP neighbor is 172.17.3.1,  remote AS 65000, internal link
  BGP version 4, remote router ID 3.3.3.3
  BGP state = Established, up for 03:47:09
  Last read 00:00:33, last write 00:00:53, hold time is 180, keepalive
interval is 60 seconds
  <output omitted>

BGP neighbor is 192.168.1.1,  remote AS 65100, external link
```

```
   BGP version 4, remote router ID 1.1.1.1
   BGP state = Established, up for 03:47:17
   Last read 00:00:19, last write 00:00:53, hold time is 180, keepalive
interval is 60 seconds
   <output omitted>


For address family: IPv6 Unicast
BGP neighbor is 2001:DB8:CAFE:33::1,  remote AS 65000, internal link
   BGP version 4, remote router ID 3.3.3.3
   BGP state = Established, up for 03:47:25
   Last read 00:00:38, last write 00:00:04, hold time is 180, keepalive
interval is 60 seconds
   <output omitted>

BGP neighbor is 192.168.1.1,  remote AS 65100, external link
   BGP version 4, remote router ID 1.1.1.1
   BGP state = Established, up for 03:47:43
   Last read 00:00:46, last write 00:00:19, hold time is 180, keepalive
interval is 60 seconds
   <output omitted>

SanJose1#
```

What is the relationship between the "remote AS" and whether it is an internal or external link?

_____

_____

b. Other options to the **show bgp all neighbors** command, are the **show ip bgp neighbors** and **show bgp ipv6 unicast neighbors** commands, which can be used for their respective address families. An excerpt from the **show ip bgp neighbors** command is displayed next. In this command, the IPv6 address family information not only displays the IPv4 address used as the transport, but the name of the route map that was used on the SanJose1 end of the connection.

```
SanJose1# show ip bgp neighbors
<output omitted>

   For address family: IPv6 Unicast
   Session: 192.168.1.1
   BGP table version 12, neighbor version 12/0
   Output queue size : 0
   Index 11, Advertise bit 0
   11 update-group member
   Outbound path policy configured
   Route map for outgoing advertisements is NEXT-HOP-IPV6
   Slow-peer detection is disabled
   Slow-peer split-update-group dynamic is disabled
   Interface associated: Serial0/0/0
   <output omitted>

SanJose1#
```

c. Use the **show bgp ipv4 unicast summary** and **show bgp ipv6 unicast summary** commands on ISP to display a summary of IPv4/IPv6 peering information with SanJose1. The **show bgp ipv4 unicast summary** is the equivalent of **show ip bgp** and either command can be used. Notice that BGP connectivity for both IPv4 and IPv6 is over an IPv4 BGP transport session, using the neighbor address of 192.168.1.2.

```
ISP# show bgp ipv4 unicast summary
BGP router identifier 1.1.1.1, local AS number 65100
BGP table version is 21, main routing table version 21
3 network entries using 432 bytes of memory
3 path entries using 240 bytes of memory
3/3 BGP path/bestpath attribute entries using 480 bytes of memory
1 BGP AS-PATH entries using 24 bytes of memory
0 BGP route-map cache entries using 0 bytes of memory
0 BGP filter-list cache entries using 0 bytes of memory
BGP using 1176 total bytes of memory
BGP activity 9/3 prefixes, 18/12 paths, scan interval 60 secs

Neighbor        V        AS MsgRcvd MsgSent   TblVer  InQ OutQ Up/Down
State/PfxRcd
192.168.1.2     4     65000      80      78       21    0    0 01:03:46      2
ISP#
```

```
ISP# show bgp ipv6 unicast summary
BGP router identifier 1.1.1.1, local AS number 65100
BGP table version is 23, main routing table version 23
3 network entries using 504 bytes of memory
3 path entries using 312 bytes of memory
3/3 BGP path/bestpath attribute entries using 480 bytes of memory
1 BGP AS-PATH entries using 24 bytes of memory
0 BGP route-map cache entries using 0 bytes of memory
0 BGP filter-list cache entries using 0 bytes of memory
BGP using 1320 total bytes of memory
BGP activity 9/3 prefixes, 18/12 paths, scan interval 60 secs

Neighbor        V        AS MsgRcvd MsgSent   TblVer  InQ OutQ Up/Down
State/PfxRcd
192.168.1.2     4     65000      86      85       23    0    0 01:09:28      2
ISP#
```

d. Use the **show bgp ipv4 unicast summary** command on SanJose1 to display a summary of IPv4 peering information with ISP and SanJose2. Notice that SanJose1 has two IPv4 peers, one in each AS. Also notice, that the IBGP peering relationship with SanJose2 uses SanJose2's loopback address 172.17.3.1. This is why this network was included in the EIGRP configuration on SanJose1 and SanJose2.

```
SanJose1# show bgp ipv4 unicast summary
BGP router identifier 2.2.2.2, local AS number 65000
BGP table version is 6, main routing table version 6
3 network entries using 432 bytes of memory
3 path entries using 240 bytes of memory
3/3 BGP path/bestpath attribute entries using 480 bytes of memory
1 BGP AS-PATH entries using 24 bytes of memory
0 BGP route-map cache entries using 0 bytes of memory
```

```
0 BGP filter-list cache entries using 0 bytes of memory
BGP using 1176 total bytes of memory
BGP activity 23/17 prefixes, 25/19 paths, scan interval 60 secs

Neighbor          V           AS MsgRcvd MsgSent   TblVer  InQ OutQ Up/Down
State/PfxRcd
172.17.3.1        4        65000       93      93        6    0    0 01:19:50   1
192.168.1.1       4        65100       98      98        6    0    0 01:19:50   1
SanJose1#
```

e. Use the **show bgp ipv6 unicast summary** command on SanJose1 to display a summary of IPv6 peering information with ISP and SanJose2. Similarly to IPv4, notice that SanJose1 has two peers, one in each AS. However, the IPv6 peering session with ISP in AS 65100 uses IPv4 as its transport, so the IPv4 neighbor address 192.168.1.1 is displayed.

```
SanJose1# show bgp ipv6 unicast summary
BGP router identifier 2.2.2.2, local AS number 65000
BGP table version is 8, main routing table version 8
3 network entries using 504 bytes of memory
3 path entries using 312 bytes of memory
3/3 BGP path/bestpath attribute entries using 480 bytes of memory
1 BGP AS-PATH entries using 24 bytes of memory
0 BGP route-map cache entries using 0 bytes of memory
0 BGP filter-list cache entries using 0 bytes of memory
BGP using 1320 total bytes of memory
BGP activity 23/17 prefixes, 25/19 paths, scan interval 60 secs

Neighbor          V           AS MsgRcvd MsgSent   TblVer  InQ OutQ Up/Down
State/PfxRcd
2001:DB8:CAFE:33::1
                  4        65000       93      97        8    0    0 01:19:59   1
192.168.1.1       4        65100       98      98        8    0    0 01:19:59   1
SanJose1#
```

Step 7: Verifying the BGP tables for IPv4 and IPv6.

a. Use the **show bgp ipv4 unicast** command on ISP to display its IPv4 BGP table. This command is equivalent to the **show ip bgp** command and either command can be used. Notice that ISP shows three IPv4 networks in its IPv4 BGP table. Each network is valid "*" and has one path that is the best path ">." Among other information, the next hop IPv4 address and the AS path are included.

```
ISP# show bgp ipv4 unicast
BGP table version is 22, local router ID is 1.1.1.1
Status codes: s suppressed, d damped, h history, * valid, > best, i -
internal,
              r RIB-failure, S Stale, m multipath, b backup-path, f RT-
Filter,
              x best-external, a additional-path, c RIB-compressed,
Origin codes: i - IGP, e - EGP, ? - incomplete
RPKI validation codes: V valid, I invalid, N Not found

     Network          Next Hop            Metric LocPrf Weight Path
```

```
*>  10.1.0.0/16       0.0.0.0                   0         32768 i
*>  172.16.2.0/24     192.168.1.2               0             0 65000 i
*>  172.16.3.0/24     192.168.1.2                             0 65000 i
ISP#
```

b. Use the **show bgp ipv6 unicast** command on ISP to display its IPv6 BGP table. As with the BGP table for IPv4, notice that ISP shows three IPv6 prefixes in its IPv6 BGP table. Each network is a valid "*" and has one path that is the best path ">." The next hop IPv6 address and AS path are also included.

Notice that the next-hop address for the prefixes 2001:DB8:CAFE:2::/64 and 2001:DB8:CAFE:3::/64, advertised by SanJose1, is using the address from SanJose1's NEXT-HOP-IPV6 route-map, 2001:DB8:FEED:1::2.

```
ISP# show bgp ipv6 unicast
BGP table version is 26, local router ID is 1.1.1.1
Status codes: s suppressed, d damped, h history, * valid, > best, i - internal,
              r RIB-failure, S Stale, m multipath, b backup-path, f RT-Filter,
              x best-external, a additional-path, c RIB-compressed,
Origin codes: i - IGP, e - EGP, ? - incomplete
RPKI validation codes: V valid, I invalid, N Not found

     Network          Next Hop            Metric LocPrf Weight Path
*>  2001:DB8:BEEF:1::/64
                      ::                       0         32768 i
*>  2001:DB8:CAFE:2::/64
                      2001:DB8:FEED:1::2
                                               0             0 65000 i
*>  2001:DB8:CAFE:3::/64
                      2001:DB8:FEED:1::2
                                                             0 65000 i
ISP#
```

c. Using the **show bgp ipv4 unicast** command on SanJose1 displays information for its IPv4 BGP table. Both the 10.1.0.0/24 network learned via EBGP from the ISP, and its own advertised network of 172.16.2.0/24 are included.

Notice that the 172.16.3.0/24 and 2001:DB8:CAFE:3::/64 prefixes do not include the "*" indicating best path, but rather the "r" signifying an RIB (routing information base) failure. Although these prefixes are being advertised by IBGP with an administrative distance of 200, the router is preferring the EIGRP source with a lower administrative distance of 90. Therefore, the EIGRP route is the preferred source and will be the one added to the IPv4 routing table.

```
SanJose1# show bgp ipv4 unicast
BGP table version is 6, local router ID is 2.2.2.2
Status codes: s suppressed, d damped, h history, * valid, > best, i - internal,
              r RIB-failure, S Stale, m multipath, b backup-path, f RT-Filter,
              x best-external, a additional-path, c RIB-compressed,
Origin codes: i - IGP, e - EGP, ? - incomplete
RPKI validation codes: V valid, I invalid, N Not found

     Network          Next Hop            Metric LocPrf Weight Path
*>  10.1.0.0/16       192.168.1.1              0             0 65100 i
*>  172.16.2.0/24     0.0.0.0                  0         32768 i
r>i 172.16.3.0/24     172.17.3.1              0    100        0 i
SanJose1#
```

d. Similarly, the **show bgp ipv6 unicast** command on SanJose1 displays its IPv6 BGP table. ISP shows three IPv6 prefixes in its IPv6 BGP table. Each network is a valid "*" and has one path that is the best path ">." Among other information, the next hop IPv6 address and AS path are included.

As with its IPv4 BGP table, notice that the next-hop address for the prefix 2001:DB8:BEEF:1::/64, advertised by SanJose1, is using the address from ISP's NEXT-HOP-IPV6 route-map, 2001:DB8:FEED:1::1.

```
SanJose1# show bgp ipv6 unicast
BGP table version is 8, local router ID is 2.2.2.2
Status codes: s suppressed, d damped, h history, * valid, > best, i - internal,
              r RIB-failure, S Stale, m multipath, b backup-path, f RT-Filter,
              x best-external, a additional-path, c RIB-compressed,
Origin codes: i - IGP, e - EGP, ? - incomplete
RPKI validation codes: V valid, I invalid, N Not found

     Network          Next Hop            Metric LocPrf Weight Path
 *>  2001:DB8:BEEF:1::/64
                      2001:DB8:FEED:1::1
                                               0          0 65100 i
 *>  2001:DB8:CAFE:2::/64
                      ::                       0              32768 i
 r>i 2001:DB8:CAFE:3::/64
                      2001:DB8:CAFE:33::1
                                               0    100    0 i
SanJose1#
```

e. Similar BGP table output is shown for SanJose2. Notice that the next hop address is the loopback interface of SanJose1. In SanJose1's peering configuration with SanJose2, SanJose1 uses the **next-hop-self** option and its loopback address 172.17.2.1. Remember, without this option IBGP carries EBGP routes into the domain with the next hop address unchanged—the next hop address of the ISP in this case.

```
SanJose2# show bgp ipv4 unicast
BGP table version is 22, local router ID is 3.3.3.3
Status codes: s suppressed, d damped, h history, * valid, > best, i - internal,
              r RIB-failure, S Stale, m multipath, b backup-path, f RT-Filter,
              x best-external, a additional-path, c RIB-compressed,
Origin codes: i - IGP, e - EGP, ? - incomplete
RPKI validation codes: V valid, I invalid, N Not found

     Network          Next Hop            Metric LocPrf Weight Path
 *>i 10.1.0.0/16      172.17.2.1               0    100    0 65100 i
 r>i 172.16.2.0/24    172.17.2.1               0    100    0 i
 *>  172.16.3.0/24    0.0.0.0                  0          32768 i
SanJose2#

SanJose2# show bgp ipv6 unicast
BGP table version is 24, local router ID is 3.3.3.3
Status codes: s suppressed, d damped, h history, * valid, > best, i - internal,
              r RIB-failure, S Stale, m multipath, b backup-path, f RT-Filter,
              x best-external, a additional-path, c RIB-compressed,
Origin codes: i - IGP, e - EGP, ? - incomplete
RPKI validation codes: V valid, I invalid, N Not found

     Network          Next Hop            Metric LocPrf Weight Path
 *>i 2001:DB8:BEEF:1::/64
                      2001:DB8:CAFE:22::1
```

```
                                              0    100      0 65100 i
    r>i 2001:DB8:CAFE:2::/64
                        2001:DB8:CAFE:22::1
                                              0    100      0 i
    *>  2001:DB8:CAFE:3::/64
                        ::                    0           32768 i
SanJose2#
```

Step 8: Verifying the IP routing tables for IPv4 and IPv6.

a. By examining the IPv4 and IPv6 routing tables on ISP you can verify that BGP is receiving the IPv4 and IPv6 prefixes from SanJose1.

```
ISP# show ip route
Codes: L - local, C - connected, S - static, R - RIP, M - mobile, B - BGP
       D - EIGRP, EX - EIGRP external, O - OSPF, IA - OSPF inter area
       N1 - OSPF NSSA external type 1, N2 - OSPF NSSA external type 2
       E1 - OSPF external type 1, E2 - OSPF external type 2
       i - IS-IS, su - IS-IS summary, L1 - IS-IS level-1, L2 - IS-IS level-2
       ia - IS-IS inter area, * - candidate default, U - per-user static
       route
       o - ODR, P - periodic downloaded static route, H - NHRP, l - LISP
       a - application route
       + - replicated route, % - next hop override

Gateway of last resort is not set

      10.0.0.0/8 is variably subnetted, 4 subnets, 3 masks
C        10.0.0.0/24 is directly connected, Loopback0
L        10.0.0.1/32 is directly connected, Loopback0
C        10.1.0.0/16 is directly connected, GigabitEthernet0/0
L        10.1.0.1/32 is directly connected, GigabitEthernet0/0
      172.16.0.0/24 is subnetted, 2 subnets
B        172.16.2.0 [20/0] via 192.168.1.2, 02:59:37
B        172.16.3.0 [20/0] via 192.168.1.2, 03:00:10
      192.168.1.0/24 is variably subnetted, 2 subnets, 2 masks
C        192.168.1.0/30 is directly connected, Serial0/0/0
L        192.168.1.1/32 is directly connected, Serial0/0/0
ISP#


ISP# show ipv6 route
IPv6 Routing Table - default - 9 entries
Codes: C - Connected, L - Local, S - Static, U - Per-user Static route
       B - BGP, R - RIP, H - NHRP, I1 - ISIS L1
       I2 - ISIS L2, IA - ISIS interarea, IS - ISIS summary, D - EIGRP
       EX - EIGRP external, ND - ND Default, NDp - ND Prefix, DCE -
       Destination
       NDr - Redirect, O - OSPF Intra, OI - OSPF Inter, OE1 - OSPF ext 1
       OE2 - OSPF ext 2, ON1 - OSPF NSSA ext 1, ON2 - OSPF NSSA ext 2
       a - Application
C   2001:DB8:BEEF:1::/64 [0/0]
     via GigabitEthernet0/0, directly connected
L   2001:DB8:BEEF:1::1/128 [0/0]
     via GigabitEthernet0/0, receive
C   2001:DB8:BEEF:11::/64 [0/0]
```

```
          via Loopback0, directly connected
L    2001:DB8:BEEF:11::1/128 [0/0]
          via Loopback0, receive
B    2001:DB8:CAFE:2::/64 [20/0]
       via FE80::2, Serial0/0/0
B    2001:DB8:CAFE:3::/64 [20/0]
       via FE80::2, Serial0/0/0
C    2001:DB8:FEED:1::/64 [0/0]
          via Serial0/0/0, directly connected
L    2001:DB8:FEED:1::1/128 [0/0]
          via Serial0/0/0, receive
L    FF00::/8 [0/0]
          via Null0, receive
ISP#
```

Are the BGP routes learned via EBGP or EBGP? How can you tell by just the information in the routing table?

_____

_____

b. Examine the IPv4 and IPv6 routing tables on SanJose1. SanJose1 is EIGRP receiving routes from SanJose2 for SanJose2's LAN and networks. Using EBGP, SanJose1 is receiving IPv4 and IPv6 prefixes from the ISP.

```
SanJose1# show ip route
Codes: L - local, C - connected, S - static, R - RIP, M - mobile, B - BGP
       D - EIGRP, EX - EIGRP external, O - OSPF, IA - OSPF inter area
       N1 - OSPF NSSA external type 1, N2 - OSPF NSSA external type 2
       E1 - OSPF external type 1, E2 - OSPF external type 2
       i - IS-IS, su - IS-IS summary, L1 - IS-IS level-1, L2 - IS-IS level-2
       ia - IS-IS inter area, * - candidate default, U - per-user static
       route
       o - ODR, P - periodic downloaded static route, H - NHRP, l - LISP
       a - application route
       + - replicated route, % - next hop override

Gateway of last resort is not set

      10.0.0.0/16 is subnetted, 1 subnets
B        10.1.0.0 [20/0] via 192.168.1.1, 03:01:19
      172.16.0.0/16 is variably subnetted, 5 subnets, 3 masks
C        172.16.1.0/30 is directly connected, Serial0/0/1
L        172.16.1.1/32 is directly connected, Serial0/0/1
C        172.16.2.0/24 is directly connected, GigabitEthernet0/0
L        172.16.2.1/32 is directly connected, GigabitEthernet0/0
D        172.16.3.0/24 [90/2172416] via 172.16.1.2, 04:17:47, Serial0/0/1
      172.17.0.0/16 is variably subnetted, 3 subnets, 2 masks
C        172.17.2.0/24 is directly connected, Loopback0
L        172.17.2.1/32 is directly connected, Loopback0
D        172.17.3.0/24 [90/2297856] via 172.16.1.2, 04:17:47, Serial0/0/1
      192.168.1.0/24 is variably subnetted, 2 subnets, 2 masks
C        192.168.1.0/30 is directly connected, Serial0/0/0
L        192.168.1.2/32 is directly connected, Serial0/0/0
```

```
SanJose1#

SanJose1# show ipv6 route
IPv6 Routing Table - default - 12 entries
Codes: C - Connected, L - Local, S - Static, U - Per-user Static route
       B - BGP, R - RIP, H - NHRP, I1 - ISIS L1
       I2 - ISIS L2, IA - ISIS interarea, IS - ISIS summary, D - EIGRP
       EX - EIGRP external, ND - ND Default, NDp - ND Prefix, DCE -
       Destination
       NDr - Redirect, O - OSPF Intra, OI - OSPF Inter, OE1 - OSPF ext 1
       OE2 - OSPF ext 2, ON1 - OSPF NSSA ext 1, ON2 - OSPF NSSA ext 2
       a - Application
B   2001:DB8:BEEF:1::/64 [20/0]
     via FE80::1, Serial0/0/0
C   2001:DB8:CAFE:1::/64 [0/0]
     via Serial0/0/1, directly connected
L   2001:DB8:CAFE:1::1/128 [0/0]
     via Serial0/0/1, receive
C   2001:DB8:CAFE:2::/64 [0/0]
     via GigabitEthernet0/0, directly connected
L   2001:DB8:CAFE:2::1/128 [0/0]
     via GigabitEthernet0/0, receive
D   2001:DB8:CAFE:3::/64 [90/2172416]
     via FE80::3, Serial0/0/1
C   2001:DB8:CAFE:22::/64 [0/0]
     via Loopback0, directly connected
L   2001:DB8:CAFE:22::1/128 [0/0]
     via Loopback0, receive
D   2001:DB8:CAFE:33::/64 [90/2297856]
     via FE80::3, Serial0/0/1
C   2001:DB8:FEED:1::/64 [0/0]
     via Serial0/0/0, directly connected
L   2001:DB8:FEED:1::2/128 [0/0]
     via Serial0/0/0, receive
L   FF00::/8 [0/0]
     via Null0, receive
SanJose1#
```

c. Looking at the IPv4 and IPv6 routing tables on SanJose2 shows that SanJose2 is receiving EIGRP and BGP routes from SanJose1. SanJose1's LAN and loopback interfaces are being advertised to SanJose2 using EIGRP, and for ISP's IPv4/IPv6 prefixes, SanJose1 is advertising them using IBGP.

```
SanJose2# show ip route
Codes: L - local, C - connected, S - static, R - RIP, M - mobile, B - BGP
       D - EIGRP, EX - EIGRP external, O - OSPF, IA - OSPF inter area
       N1 - OSPF NSSA external type 1, N2 - OSPF NSSA external type 2
       E1 - OSPF external type 1, E2 - OSPF external type 2
       i - IS-IS, su - IS-IS summary, L1 - IS-IS level-1, L2 - IS-IS level-2
       ia - IS-IS inter area, * - candidate default, U - per-user static
       route
       o - ODR, P - periodic downloaded static route, H - NHRP, l - LISP
       a - application route
       + - replicated route, % - next hop override

Gateway of last resort is not set
```

```
          10.0.0.0/16 is subnetted, 1 subnets
B         10.1.0.0 [200/0] via 172.17.2.1, 03:02:16
          172.16.0.0/16 is variably subnetted, 5 subnets, 3 masks
C         172.16.1.0/30 is directly connected, Serial0/0/1
L         172.16.1.2/32 is directly connected, Serial0/0/1
D         172.16.2.0/24 [90/2172416] via 172.16.1.1, 04:18:45, Serial0/0/1
C         172.16.3.0/24 is directly connected, GigabitEthernet0/0
L         172.16.3.1/32 is directly connected, GigabitEthernet0/0
          172.17.0.0/16 is variably subnetted, 3 subnets, 2 masks
D         172.17.2.0/24 [90/2297856] via 172.16.1.1, 04:18:45, Serial0/0/1
C         172.17.3.0/24 is directly connected, Loopback0
L         172.17.3.1/32 is directly connected, Loopback0
SanJose2#


SanJose2# show ipv6 route
IPv6 Routing Table - default - 10 entries
Codes: C - Connected, L - Local, S - Static, U - Per-user Static route
       B - BGP, R - RIP, H - NHRP, I1 - ISIS L1
       I2 - ISIS L2, IA - ISIS interarea, IS - ISIS summary, D - EIGRP
       EX - EIGRP external, ND - ND Default, NDp - ND Prefix, DCE -
       Destination
       NDr - Redirect, O - OSPF Intra, OI - OSPF Inter, OE1 - OSPF ext 1
       OE2 - OSPF ext 2, ON1 - OSPF NSSA ext 1, ON2 - OSPF NSSA ext 2
       a - Application
B   2001:DB8:BEEF:1::/64 [200/0]
     via 2001:DB8:CAFE:22::1
C   2001:DB8:CAFE:1::/64 [0/0]
     via Serial0/0/1, directly connected
L   2001:DB8:CAFE:1::2/128 [0/0]
     via Serial0/0/1, receive
D   2001:DB8:CAFE:2::/64 [90/2172416]
     via FE80::2, Serial0/0/1
C   2001:DB8:CAFE:3::/64 [0/0]
     via GigabitEthernet0/0, directly connected
L   2001:DB8:CAFE:3::1/128 [0/0]
     via GigabitEthernet0/0, receive
D   2001:DB8:CAFE:22::/64 [90/2297856]
     via FE80::2, Serial0/0/1
C   2001:DB8:CAFE:33::/64 [0/0]
     via Loopback0, directly connected
L   2001:DB8:CAFE:33::1/128 [0/0]
     via Loopback0, receive
L   FF00::/8 [0/0]
     via Null0, receive
SanJose2#
```

Are the BGP routes learned via EBGP or IBGP? How can you tell by just the information in the routing table?

_____

_____

d. Verify IPv4 and IPv6 reachability pinging ISP's LAN interface from the LAN interface on SanJose2.

```
SanJose2# ping 10.1.0.1 source 172.16.3.1
Type escape sequence to abort.
Sending 5, 100-byte ICMP Echos to 10.1.0.1, timeout is 2 seconds:
Packet sent with a source address of 172.16.3.1
!!!!!
Success rate is 100 percent (5/5), round-trip min/avg/max = 56/56/60 ms
SanJose2#


SanJose2# ping 2001:db8:beef:1::1 source gig 0/0
Type escape sequence to abort.
Sending 5, 100-byte ICMP Echos to 2001:DB8:BEEF:1::1, timeout is 2 seconds:
Packet sent with a source address of 2001:DB8:CAFE:3::1
!!!!!
Success rate is 100 percent (5/5), round-trip min/avg/max = 52/55/56 ms
SanJose2#
```

Chapter 8: Routers and Routing Protocol Hardening

Lab 8-1 Secure the Management Plane

Topology

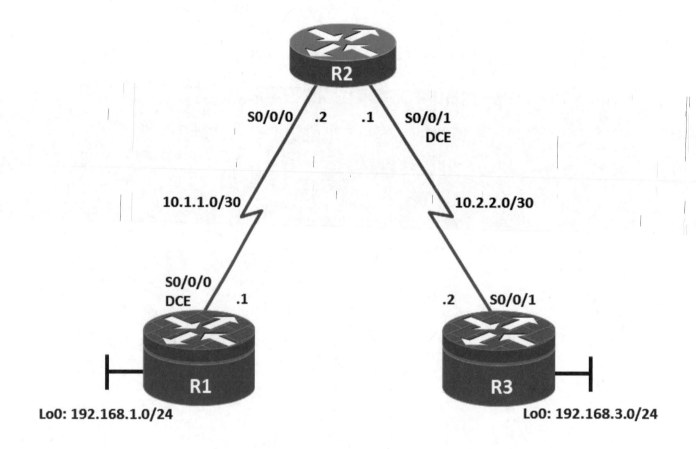

Objectives

- Secure management access.
- Configure enhanced username password security.
- Enable AAA RADIUS authentication.
- Enable secure remote management.

Background

The management plane of any infrastructure device should be protected as much as possible. Controlling access to routers and enabling reporting on routers are critical to network security and should be part of a comprehensive security policy.

In this lab, you build a multi-router network and secure the management plane of routers R1 and R3.

Note: This lab uses Cisco 1941 routers with Cisco IOS Release 15.2 with IP Base. Depending on the router or switch model and Cisco IOS Software version, the commands available and output produced might vary from what is shown in this lab.

Required Resources

- 3 routers (Cisco IOS Release 15.2 or comparable)
- Serial and Ethernet cables

Step 1: Configure loopbacks and assign addresses.

Cable the network as shown in the topology diagram. Erase the startup configuration and reload each router to clear previous configurations. Using the addressing scheme in the diagram, apply the IP addresses to the interfaces on the R1, R2, and R3 routers.

You can copy and paste the following configurations into your routers to begin.

Note: Depending on the router model, interfaces might be numbered differently than those listed. You might need to alter the designations accordingly.

R1

```
hostname R1

interface Loopback 0
 description R1 LAN
 ip address 192.168.1.1 255.255.255.0
exit
!
interface Serial0/0/0
 description R1 --> R2
 ip address 10.1.1.1 255.255.255.252
 clock rate 128000
 no shutdown
exit
!
end
```

R2

```
hostname R2
!
interface Serial0/0/0
 description R2 --> R1
 ip address 10.1.1.2 255.255.255.252
 no shutdown
exit
```

```
interface Serial0/0/1
 description R2 --> R3
 ip address 10.2.2.1 255.255.255.252
 clock rate 128000
 no shutdown
exit
!
end
```

R3

```
hostname R3
!
interface Loopback0
 description R3 LAN
 ip address 192.168.3.1 255.255.255.0
exit


interface Serial0/0/1
 description R3 --> R2
 ip address 10.2.2.2 255.255.255.252
 no shutdown
exit
!
end
```

Step 2: Configure static routes.

a. On R1, configure a default static route to ISP.

    R1(config)# **ip route 0.0.0.0 0.0.0.0 10.1.1.2**

b. On R3, configure a default static route to ISP.

    R3(config)# **ip route 0.0.0.0 0.0.0.0 10.2.2.1**

c. On R2, configure two static routes.

    R2(config)# **ip route 192.168.1.0 255.255.255.0 10.1.1.1**
    R2(config)# **ip route 192.168.3.0 255.255.255.0 10.2.2.2**

d. From the R1 router, run the following Tcl script to verify connectivity.

    foreach address {
    192.168.1.1
    10.1.1.1
    10.1.1.2
    10.2.2.1
    10.2.2.2
    192.168.3.1
    } { ping $address }

    R1# **tclsh**

    R1(tcl)#foreach address {
    +>(tcl)#192.168.1.1
    +>(tcl)#10.1.1.1
    +>(tcl)#10.1.1.2
    +>(tcl)#10.2.2.1

```
+>(tcl)#10.2.2.2
+>(tcl)#192.168.3.1
+>(tcl)#} { ping $address }
Type escape sequence to abort.
Sending 5, 100-byte ICMP Echos to 192.168.1.1, timeout is 2 seconds:
!!!!!
Success rate is 100 percent (5/5), round-trip min/avg/max = 1/1/1 ms
Type escape sequence to abort.
Sending 5, 100-byte ICMP Echos to 10.1.1.1, timeout is 2 seconds:
!!!!!
Success rate is 100 percent (5/5), round-trip min/avg/max = 1/2/4 ms
Type escape sequence to abort.
Sending 5, 100-byte ICMP Echos to 10.1.1.2, timeout is 2 seconds:
!!!!!
Success rate is 100 percent (5/5), round-trip min/avg/max = 1/1/4 ms
Type escape sequence to abort.
Sending 5, 100-byte ICMP Echos to 10.2.2.1, timeout is 2 seconds:
!!!!!
Success rate is 100 percent (5/5), round-trip min/avg/max = 1/1/4 ms
Type escape sequence to abort.
Sending 5, 100-byte ICMP Echos to 10.2.2.2, timeout is 2 seconds:
!!!!!
Success rate is 100 percent (5/5), round-trip min/avg/max = 12/14/16 ms
Type escape sequence to abort.
Sending 5, 100-byte ICMP Echos to 192.168.3.1, timeout is 2 seconds:
!!!!!
Success rate is 100 percent (5/5), round-trip min/avg/max = 12/15/16 ms
R1(tcl)#
```

Are the pings now successful?

_____

_____

Step 3: Secure management access.

a. On R1, use the **security passwords** command to set a minimum password length of 10 characters.

```
R1(config)# security passwords min-length 10
```

b. Configure the enable secret encrypted password on both routers.

```
R1(config)# enable secret class12345
```

How does configuring an enable secret password help protect a router from being compromised by an attack?

_____

_____

_____

Note: Passwords in this task are set to a minimum of 10 characters but are relatively simple for the benefit of performing the lab. More complex passwords are recommended in a production network.

c. Configure a console password and enable login for routers. For additional security, the **exec-timeout** command causes the line to log out after 5 minutes of inactivity. The **logging synchronous** command prevents console messages from interrupting command entry.

Note: To avoid repetitive logins during this lab, the **exec-timeout** command can be set to 0 0, which prevents it from expiring. However, this is not considered a good security practice.

```
R1(config)# line console 0
R1(config-line)# password ciscoconpass
R1(config-line)# exec-timeout 5 0
R1(config-line)# login
R1(config-line)# logging synchronous
R1(config-line)# exit
R1(config)#
```

d. Configure the password on the vty lines for router R1.

```
R1(config)# line vty 0 4
R1(config-line)# password ciscovtypass
R1(config-line)# exec-timeout 5 0
R1(config-line)# login
R1(config-line)# exit
R1(config)#
```

e. The aux port is a legacy port used to manage a router remotely using a modem and is hardly ever used. Therefore, disable the aux port.

```
R1(config)# line aux 0
R1(config-line)# no exec
R1(config-line)# end
R1#
```

f. Enter privileged EXEC mode and issue the **show run** command. Can you read the enable secret password? Why or why not?

_____

_____

Note: If the **enable secret** password command is lost or forgotten, it must be replaced using the Cisco router password recovery procedure. Refer to cisco.com for more information.

Can you read the console, aux, and vty passwords? Why or why not?

_____

_____

g. Use the **service password-encryption** command to encrypt the line console and vty passwords.

```
R1(config)# service password-encryption
R1(config)#
```

Note: Password encryption is applied to all the passwords, including the **username** passwords, the authentication key passwords, the privileged command password, the console and the virtual terminal line access passwords, and the BGP neighbor passwords.

h. Issue the **show run** command. Can you read the console, aux, and vty passwords? Why or why not?

_____

_____

Note: Type 7 passwords are encrypted using a Vigenère cipher, which can be easily reversed. Therefore this command primarily protects from shoulder surfing attacks.

i. Configure a warning to unauthorized users with a message-of-the-day (MOTD) banner using the **banner motd** command. When a user connects to one of the routers, the MOTD banner appears before the login prompt. In this example, the dollar sign ($) is used to start and end the message.

```
R1(config)# banner motd $Unauthorized access strictly prohibited!$
R1(config)# exit
```

j. Issue the **show run** command. What does the $ convert to in the output?

_____

_____

k. Exit privileged EXEC mode using the **disable** or **exit** command and press **Enter** to get started. Does the MOTD banner look like what you created with the **banner motd** command? If the MOTD banner is not as you wanted it, recreate it using the **banner motd** command.

l. Repeat the configuration portion of steps 3a through 3k on router R3.

Step 4: Configure enhanced username password security.

To increase the encryption level of console and VTY lines, it is recommended to enable authentication using the local database. The local database consists of usernames and password combinations that are created locally on each device. The local and VTY lines are configured to refer to the local database when authenticating a user.

a. To create local database entry encrypted to level 4 (SHA256), use the **username** *name* **secret** *password* global configuration command. In global configuration mode, enter the following command:

```
R1(config)# username JR-ADMIN secret class12345
R1(config)# username ADMIN secret class54321
```

Note: An older method for creating local database entries is to use the **username** *name* **password** *password* command.

b. Set the console line to use the locally defined login accounts.

```
R1(config)# line console 0
R1(config-line)# login local
R1(config-line)# exit
R1(config)#
```

c. Set the vty lines to use the locally defined login accounts.

```
R1(config)# line vty 0 4
R1(config-line)# login local
R1(config-line)# end
R1(config)#
```

d. Repeat the steps 4a to 4c on R3.

e. To verify the configuration, telnet to R3 from R1 and log in using the ADMIN local database account.

```
R1# telnet 10.2.2.2
Trying 10.2.2.2 ... Open
Unauthorized access strictly prohibited!
User Access Verification

Username: ADMIN
Password:
R3>
```

Step 5: Enable AAA RADIUS Authentication with Local User for Backup.

Authentication, authorization, and accounting (AAA) is a standards-based framework that can be implemented to control who is permitted to access a network (authenticate), what they can do on that network (authorize), and audit what they did while accessing the network (accounting).

Users must authenticate against an authentication database that can be stored:

- **Locally:** Users are authenticated against the local device database, which is created using the username secret command. Sometimes referred to as self-contained AAA.

- **Centrally:** A client-server model where users are authenticated against AAA servers. This provides improved scalability, manageability, and control. Communication between the device and AAA servers is secured using either the RADIUS or TACACS+ protocols.

In this step, you will configure AAA authentication to use a RADIUS server and the local database as a backup. Specifically, the authentication will be validated against one of two RADIUS servers. If the servers are not available, then authentication will be validated against the local database.

a. Always have local database accounts created before enabling AAA. Since you created two local database accounts in the previous step, then you can proceed and enable AAA on R1.

```
R1(config)# aaa new-model
```

Note: Although the following configuration refers to two RADIUS servers, the actual RADIUS server implementation is beyond the scope. Therefore, the goal of this step is to provide an example of how to configure a router to access the servers.

b. Configure the specifics for the first RADIUS server located at 192.168.1.101. Use **RADIUS-1-pa55w0rd** as the server password.

```
R1(config)# radius server RADIUS-1
R1(config-radius-server)# address ipv4 192.168.1.101
R1(config-radius-server)# key RADIUS-1-pa55w0rd
R1(config-radius-server)# exit
R1(config)#
```

c. Configure the specifics for the second RADIUS server located at 192.168.1.102. Use **RADIUS-2-pa55w0rd** as the server password.

```
R1(config)# radius server RADIUS-2
```

```
R1(config-radius-server)# address ipv4 192.168.1.102
R1(config-radius-server)# key RADIUS-2-pa55w0rd
R1(config-radius-server)# exit
R1(config)#
```

d. Assign both RADIUS servers to a server group.

```
R1(config)# aaa group server radius RADIUS-GROUP
R1(config-sg-radius)# server name RADIUS-1
R1(config-sg-radius)# server name RADIUS-2
R1(config-sg-radius)# exit
R1(config)#
```

e. Enable the default AAA authentication login to attempt to validate against the server group. If they are not available, then authentication should be validated against the local database.

```
R1(config)# aaa authentication login default group RADIUS-GROUP local
R1(config)#
```

Note: Once this command is configured, all line access methods default to the default authentication method. The **local** option enables AAA to refer to the local database. Only the password is case sensitive.

f. Enable the default AAA authentication Telnet login to attempt to validate against the server group. If they are not available, then authentication should be validated against a case-sensitive local database.

```
R1(config)# aaa authentication login TELNET-LOGIN group RADIUS-GROUP local-
case
R1(config)#
```

Note: Unlike the **local** option that makes the password is case sensitive, local-case makes the username and password case sensitive.

g. Alter the VTY lines to use the TELNET-LOGIN AAA authentication method.

```
R1(config)# line vty 0 4
R1(config-line)# login authentication TELNET-LOGIN
R1(config-line)# exit
R1(config)#
```

h. Repeat the steps 5a to 5g on R3.

i. To verify the configuration, telnet to R3 from R1 and log in using the ADMIN local database account.

```
R1# telnet 10.2.2.2
Trying 10.2.2.2 ... Open
Unauthorized access strictly prohibited!
```

```
User Access Verification

Username: admin
Password:

% Authentication failed

Username: ADMIN
Password:

R3>
```

Note: The first login attempt did not use the correct username (that is, ADMIN), which is why it failed.

Note: The actual login time is longer since the RADIUS servers are not available.

Step 6: Enable secure remote management using SSH.

Traditionally, remote access on routers was configured using Telnet on TCP port 23. However, Telnet was developed in the days when security was not an issue; therefore, all Telnet traffic is forwarded in plaintext.

Secure Shell (SSH) is a network protocol that establishes a secure terminal emulation connection to a router or other networking device. SSH encrypts all information that passes over the network link and provides authentication of the remote computer. SSH is rapidly replacing Telnet as the remote login tool of choice for network professionals.

Note: For a router to support SSH, it must be configured with local authentication, (AAA services, or username) or password authentication. In this task, you configure an SSH username and local authentication.

In this step, you will enable R1 and R3 to support SSH instead of Telnet.

a. SSH requires that a device name and a domain name be configured. Since the router already has a name assigned, configure the domain name.

```
R1(config)# ip domain-name ccnasecurity.com
```

b. The router uses the RSA key pair for authentication and encryption of transmitted SSH data. Although optional it may be wise to erase any existing key pairs on the router.

```
R1(config)# crypto key zeroize rsa
```

Note: If no keys exist, you might receive this message: `% No Signature RSA Keys found in configuration.`

c. Generate the RSA encryption key pair for the router. Configure the RSA keys with **1024** for the number of modulus bits. The default is 512, and the range is from 360 to 2048.

```
R1(config)# crypto key generate rsa general-keys modulus 1024
The name for the keys will be: R1.ccnasecurity.com
```

```
% The key modulus size is 1024 bits
% Generating 1024 bit RSA keys, keys will be non-exportable...[OK]

R1(config)#
Jan 10 13:44:44.711: %SSH-5-ENABLED: SSH 1.99 has been enabled
R1(config)#
```

d. Cisco routers support two versions of SSH:

   - **SSH version 1 (SSHv1):** Original version but has known vulnerabilities.

   - **SSH version 2 (SSHv2):** Provides better security using the Diffie-Hellman key exchange and the strong integrity-checking message authentication code (MAC).

The default setting for SSH is SSH version 1.99. This is also known as compatibility mode and is merely an indication that the server supports both SSH version 2 and SSH version 1. However, best practices are to enable version 2 only.

Configure SSH version 2 on R1.

```
R1(config)# ip ssh version 2
R1(config)#
```

e. Configure the vty lines to use only SSH connections.

```
R1(config)# line vty 0 4
R1(config-line)# transport input ssh
R1(config-line)# end
```

Note: SSH requires that the **login local** command be configured. However, in the previous step we enabled AAA authentication using the TELNET-LOGIN authentication method, therefore **login local** is not necessary.

Note: If you add the keyword **telnet** to the **transport input** command, users can log in using Telnet as well as SSH. However, the router will be less secure. If only SSH is specified, the connecting host must have an SSH client installed.

f. Verify the SSH configuration using the **show ip ssh** command.

```
R1# show ip ssh
SSH Enabled - version 2.0
Authentication timeout: 120 secs; Authentication retries: 3
Minimum expected Diffie Hellman key size : 1024 bits
IOS Keys in SECSH format(ssh-rsa, base64 encoded):
ssh-rsa
AAAAB3NzaC1yc2EAAAADAQABAAAAgQC3Lehh7ReYlgyDzls6wq+mFzxqzoaZFr9XGx+Q/yio
dFYw00hQo80tZy1W1Ff3Pz6q7Qi0y00urwddHZ0kBZceZK9EzJ6wZ+9a87KKDETCWrGSLi6c81E/y
4K+
Z/oVrMMZk7bpTM1MFdP41YgkTf35utYv+TcqbsYo++KJiYk+xw==
R1#
```

g. Repeat the steps 6a to 6f on R3.

h. Although a user can SSH from a host using the SSH option of TeraTerm of PuTTY, a router can also SSH to another SSH-enabled device. SSH to R3 from R1.

```
R1# ssh -l ADMIN 10.2.2.2
Password:
Unauthorized access strictly prohibited!
R3>
R3> en
Password:
R3#
```

Lab 8-2 Routing Protocol Authentication

Topology

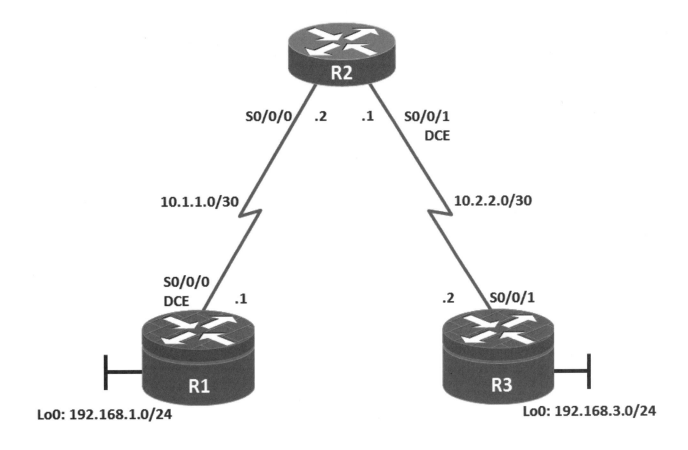

Objectives

- Secure EIGRP routing protocol using named EIGRP and SHA-256 authentication.
- Secure OSPF routing protocol using the OSPFv2 Cryptographic Authentication feature and SHA-256 authentication.

Background

In this lab, you build a multi-router network and secure the EIGRP and OSPFv2 routing protocols using SHA-256 between R1, R2, and R3.

Note: This lab uses Cisco 1941 routers with Cisco IOS Release 15.4 with IP Base. Depending on the router or switch model and Cisco IOS Software version, the commands available and output produced might vary from what is shown in this lab.

Required Resources

- 3 routers (Cisco IOS Release 15.4 or comparable)
- Serial and Ethernet cables

Step 1: Configure loopbacks and assign addresses.

Cable the network as shown in the topology diagram. Erase the startup configuration and reload each router to clear previous configurations. Using the addressing scheme in the diagram, apply the IP addresses to the interfaces on the R1, R2, and R3 routers.

You can copy and paste the following configurations into your routers to begin.

Note: Depending on the router model, interfaces might be numbered differently than those listed. You might need to alter the designations accordingly.

R1

```
hostname R1

interface Loopback 0
 description R1 LAN
 ip address 192.168.1.1 255.255.255.0
exit
!
interface Serial0/0/0
 description R1 --> R2
 ip address 10.1.1.1 255.255.255.252
 clock rate 128000
 no shutdown
exit
!
end
```

R2

```
hostname R2
!
interface Serial0/0/0
 description R2 --> R1
 ip address 10.1.1.2 255.255.255.252
 no shutdown
exit

interface Serial0/0/1
```

```
 description R2 --> R3
 ip address 10.2.2.1 255.255.255.252
 clock rate 128000
 no shutdown
exit
!
end
```

R3

```
hostname R3
!
interface Loopback0
 description R3 LAN
 ip address 192.168.3.1 255.255.255.0
exit


interface Serial0/0/1
 description R3 --> R2
 ip address 10.2.2.2 255.255.255.252
 no shutdown
exit
!
end
```

Step 2: Configure named EIGRP routing.

In this step, you will configure named EIGRP.

Note: EIGRP SHA authentication can only be configured when using the named EIGRP method.

a. On R1, configure named EIGRP.

```
R1(config)# router eigrp ROUTE
R1(config-router)# address-family ipv4 autonomous-system 1
R1(config-router-af)# network 10.1.1.0 0.0.0.3
R1(config-router-af)# network 192.168.1.0 0.0.0.255
R1(config-router-af)#
```

b. On R2, configure named EIGRP.

```
R2(config)# router eigrp ROUTE
R2(config-router)# address-family ipv4 autonomous-system 1
R2(config-router-af)# network 10.1.1.0 0.0.0.3
R2(config-router-af)#
*Jan 10 13:57:33.727: %DUAL-5-NBRCHANGE: EIGRP-IPv4 1: Neighbor 10.1.1.1
(Serial0/0/0) is up: new adjacency
R2(config-router-af)# network 10.2.2.0 0.0.0.3
R2(config-router-af)#
```

c. On R3, configure named EIGRP.

```
R3(config)# router eigrp ROUTE
R3(config-router)# address-family ipv4 autonomous-system 1
R3(config-router-af)# network 10.2.2.0 0.0.0.3
R3(config-router-af)#
*Jan 10 06:27:57.423: %DUAL-5-NBRCHANGE: EIGRP-IPv4 1: Neighbor 10.2.2.1
(Serial0/0/1) is up: new adjacency
```

```
R3(config-router-af)# network 192.168.3.0 0.0.0.255
R3(config-router-af)#
```

d. Verify the routing table of R1.

```
R1# show ip route eigrp | begin Gateway
Gateway of last resort is not set

        10.0.0.0/8 is variably subnetted, 3 subnets, 2 masks
D          10.2.2.0/30 [90/23796062] via 10.1.1.2, 00:05:56, Serial0/0/0
D       192.168.3.0/24 [90/23796702] via 10.1.1.2, 00:05:44, Serial0/0/0
R1#
```

e. From the R1 router, run the following Tcl script to verify connectivity.

```
foreach address {
192.168.1.1
10.1.1.1
10.1.1.2
10.2.2.1
10.2.2.2
192.168.3.1
} { ping $address }

R1(tcl)#foreach address {
+>(tcl)#192.168.1.1
+>(tcl)#10.1.1.1
+>(tcl)#10.1.1.2
+>(tcl)#10.2.2.1
+>(tcl)#10.2.2.2
+>(tcl)#192.168.3.1
+>(tcl)#} { ping $address }
Type escape sequence to abort.
Sending 5, 100-byte ICMP Echos to 192.168.1.1, timeout is 2 seconds:
!!!!!
Success rate is 100 percent (5/5), round-trip min/avg/max = 1/1/1 ms
Type escape sequence to abort.
Sending 5, 100-byte ICMP Echos to 10.1.1.1, timeout is 2 seconds:
!!!!!
Success rate is 100 percent (5/5), round-trip min/avg/max = 28/28/28 ms
Type escape sequence to abort.
Sending 5, 100-byte ICMP Echos to 10.1.1.2, timeout is 2 seconds:
!!!!!
Success rate is 100 percent (5/5), round-trip min/avg/max = 12/14/16 ms
Type escape sequence to abort.
Sending 5, 100-byte ICMP Echos to 10.2.2.1, timeout is 2 seconds:
!!!!!
Success rate is 100 percent (5/5), round-trip min/avg/max = 12/13/16 ms
Type escape sequence to abort.
Sending 5, 100-byte ICMP Echos to 10.2.2.2, timeout is 2 seconds:
!!!!!
Success rate is 100 percent (5/5), round-trip min/avg/max = 28/28/28 ms
Type escape sequence to abort.
Sending 5, 100-byte ICMP Echos to 192.168.3.1, timeout is 2 seconds:
!!!!!
Success rate is 100 percent (5/5), round-trip min/avg/max = 28/28/28 ms
```

```
R1(tcl)#
```

Are the pings now successful?

_____

_____

Step 3: Secure the named EIGRP routing process.

a. Enable SHA-256 authentication on the serial 0/0/0 interface of R1.

```
R1(config)# router eigrp ROUTE
R1(config-router)# address-family ipv4 autonomous-system 1
R1(config-router-af)# af-interface S0/0/0
R1(config-router-af-interface)# authentication mode hmac-sha-256 secret-2
R1(config-router-af-interface)#
Jan 10 10:19:35.035: %DUAL-5-NBRCHANGE: EIGRP-IPv4 1: Neighbor 10.1.1.2
(Serial0/0/0) is down: authentication HMAC-SHA-256 configured
R1(config-router-af-interface)#
```

Notice how the adjacency with R2 has changed to down. This is because R1 no longer accepts the updates from R2 because they are not authenticated.

b. Next, enable SHA-256 authentication on the serial 0/0/0 and serial 0/0/1 interfaces of R2.

```
R2(config)# router eigrp ROUTE
R2(config-router)# address-family ipv4 autonomous-system 1
R2(config-router-af)# af-interface S0/0/0
R2(config-router-af-interface)# authentication mode hmac-sha-256 secret-2
R2(config-router-af-interface)# exit
R2(config-router-af)# af-interface S0/0/1
R2(config-router-af-interface)# authentication mode hmac-sha-256 secret-2
R2(config-router-af-interface)#
Jan 10 10:22:03.299: %DUAL-5-NBRCHANGE: EIGRP-IPv4 1: Neighbor 10.2.2.2
(Serial0/0/1) is down: authentication HMAC-SHA-256 configured
R2(config-router-af-interface)#
Jan 10 10:22:05.503: %DUAL-5-NBRCHANGE: EIGRP-IPv4 1: Neighbor 10.1.1.1
(Serial0/0/0) is up: new adjacency
R2(config-router-af-interface)#
```

Notice how the first informational message is saying that the adjacency with R3 has changed to down. This is because R2 no longer accepts the updates from R3 because they are not authenticated.

However, the second information message is saying that the adjacency with R1 has been restored because they are now authenticating each other's routing updates.

c. Next, enable SHA-256 authentication on the serial 0/0/1 interface of R3.

```
R3(config)# router eigrp ROUTE
R3(config-router)# address-family ipv4 autonomous-system 1
```

```
R3(config-router-af)# af-interface S0/0/1
R3(config-router-af-interface)# authentication mode hmac-sha-256 secret-2
R3(config-router-af-interface)#
Jan 10 10:28:17.455: %DUAL-5-NBRCHANGE: EIGRP-IPv4 1: Neighbor 10.2.2.1
(Serial0/0/1) is up: new adjacency
R3#
```

d. Verify the routing table of R1.

```
R1# show ip route eigrp | begin Gateway
Gateway of last resort is not set

      10.0.0.0/8 is variably subnetted, 3 subnets, 2 masks
D        10.2.2.0/30 [90/23796062] via 10.1.1.2, 00:08:18, Serial0/0/0
D     192.168.3.0/24 [90/23796702] via 10.1.1.2, 00:01:56, Serial0/0/0
R1#
```

e. From the R1 router, run the following Tcl script to verify connectivity.

```
foreach address {
192.168.1.1
10.1.1.1
10.1.1.2
10.2.2.1
10.2.2.2
192.168.3.1
} { ping $address }

R1(tcl)#foreach address {
+>(tcl)#192.168.1.1
+>(tcl)#10.1.1.1
+>(tcl)#10.1.1.2
+>(tcl)#10.2.2.1
+>(tcl)#10.2.2.2
+>(tcl)#192.168.3.1
+>(tcl)#} { ping $address }
Type escape sequence to abort.
Sending 5, 100-byte ICMP Echos to 192.168.1.1, timeout is 2 seconds:
!!!!!
Success rate is 100 percent (5/5), round-trip min/avg/max = 1/1/1 ms
Type escape sequence to abort.
Sending 5, 100-byte ICMP Echos to 10.1.1.1, timeout is 2 seconds:
!!!!!
Success rate is 100 percent (5/5), round-trip min/avg/max = 28/28/28 ms
Type escape sequence to abort.
Sending 5, 100-byte ICMP Echos to 10.1.1.2, timeout is 2 seconds:
!!!!!
Success rate is 100 percent (5/5), round-trip min/avg/max = 12/14/16 ms
Type escape sequence to abort.
Sending 5, 100-byte ICMP Echos to 10.2.2.1, timeout is 2 seconds:
!!!!!
Success rate is 100 percent (5/5), round-trip min/avg/max = 12/14/16 ms
Type escape sequence to abort.
Sending 5, 100-byte ICMP Echos to 10.2.2.2, timeout is 2 seconds:
```

```
!!!!!
Success rate is 100 percent (5/5), round-trip min/avg/max = 28/28/28 ms
Type escape sequence to abort.
Sending 5, 100-byte ICMP Echos to 192.168.3.1, timeout is 2 seconds:
!!!!!
Success rate is 100 percent (5/5), round-trip min/avg/max = 28/28/28 ms
R1(tcl)#
```

Are the pings now successful?

_____

_____

f. Next we will configure OSPF routing protocol authentication. Therefore, remove EIGRP from R1, R2, and R3 using the **no router eigrp ROUTE** command on all three routers.

```
R1(config)# no router eigrp ROUTE
R1(config)
```

Step 4: Configure OSPF routing.

Since Cisco IOS Software Release 15.4(1)T, OSPFv2 supports SHA hashing authentication using key chains. Cisco refers to this as the OSPFv2 Cryptographic Authentication feature. The feature prevents unauthorized or invalid routing updates in a network by authenticating OSPFv2 protocol packets using HMAC-SHA algorithms.

a. On R1, configure OSPF.

```
R1(config)# router ospf 1
R1(config-router)# network 192.168.1.0 0.0.0.255 area 0
R1(config-router)# network 10.1.1.0 0.0.0.3 area 0
R1(config-router)#
```

b. On R2, configure OSPF.

```
R2(config)# router ospf 1
R2(config-router)# network 10.1.1.0 0.0.0.3 area 0
R2(config-router)# network 10.2.2.0 0.0.0.3 area 0
R2(config-router)#
```

c. On R3, configure OSPF.

```
R1(config)# router ospf 1
R1(config-router)# network 192.168.3.0 0.0.0.255 area 0
R1(config-router)# network 10.2.2.0 0.0.0.3 area 0
R1(config-router)#
```

d. From the R1 router, run the following Tcl script to verify connectivity.

```
foreach address {
192.168.1.1
10.1.1.1
10.1.1.2
10.2.2.1
10.2.2.2
192.168.3.1
} { ping $address }
```

```
R1(tcl)#foreach address {
+>(tcl)#192.168.1.1
+>(tcl)#10.1.1.1
+>(tcl)#10.1.1.2
+>(tcl)#10.2.2.1
+>(tcl)#10.2.2.2
+>(tcl)#192.168.3.1
+>(tcl)#} { ping $address }
Type escape sequence to abort.
Sending 5, 100-byte ICMP Echos to 192.168.1.1, timeout is 2 seconds:
!!!!!
Success rate is 100 percent (5/5), round-trip min/avg/max = 1/1/1 ms
Type escape sequence to abort.
Sending 5, 100-byte ICMP Echos to 10.1.1.1, timeout is 2 seconds:
!!!!!
Success rate is 100 percent (5/5), round-trip min/avg/max = 24/27/28 ms
Type escape sequence to abort.
Sending 5, 100-byte ICMP Echos to 10.1.1.2, timeout is 2 seconds:
!!!!!
Success rate is 100 percent (5/5), round-trip min/avg/max = 12/14/16 ms
Type escape sequence to abort.
Sending 5, 100-byte ICMP Echos to 10.2.2.1, timeout is 2 seconds:
!!!!!
Success rate is 100 percent (5/5), round-trip min/avg/max = 12/14/16 ms
Type escape sequence to abort.
Sending 5, 100-byte ICMP Echos to 10.2.2.2, timeout is 2 seconds:
!!!!!
Success rate is 100 percent (5/5), round-trip min/avg/max = 28/28/28 ms
Type escape sequence to abort.
Sending 5, 100-byte ICMP Echos to 192.168.3.1, timeout is 2 seconds:
!!!!!
Success rate is 100 percent (5/5), round-trip min/avg/max = 28/28/28 ms
R1(tcl)#
```

Are the pings now successful?

_____

_____

Step 5: Secure the OSPF routing protocol.

OSPF will authenticate its peer routers using the OSPFv2 Cryptographic Authentication method and SHA-256.

a. On R1, create the key chain to be used for OSPF authentication.

```
R1(config)# key chain SHA-CHAIN
R1(config-keychain)# key 1
R1(config-keychain-key)# key-string secret-1
R1(config-keychain-key)# cryptographic-algorithm hmac-sha-256
R1(config-keychain-key)# exit
R1(config-keychain)# exit
R1(config)#
```

b. Next, enable authentication on the serial 0/0/0 interface of R1.

```
R1(config)# interface s0/0/0
R1(config-if)# ip ospf authentication key-chain SHA-CHAIN
R1(config-if)#
Jan 10 11:08:34.075: %OSPF-5-ADJCHG: Process 1, Nbr 10.2.2.1 on Serial0/0/0
from FULL to DOWN, Neighbor Down: Dead timer expired
```

Notice how the adjacency with R2 has changed to down. This is because R1 no longer accepts the updates from R2 because they are not authenticated.

c. On R2, create the key chain to be used for authentication.

```
R2(config)# key chain SHA-CHAIN
R2(config-keychain)# key 1
R2(config-keychain-key)# key-string secret-1
R2(config-keychain-key)# cryptographic-algorithm hmac-sha-256
R2(config-keychain-key)# exit
R2(config-keychain)# exit
R2(config)#
```

d. Next, enable authentication on the serial 0/0/0 and serial 0/0/1 interfaces of R2.

```
R2(config)# interface s0/0/0
R2(config-if)# ip ospf authentication key-chain SHA-CHAIN
R2(config-if)# exit
R2(config)#
R2(config)# interface s0/0/1
R2(config-if)# ip ospf authentication key-chain SHA-CHAIN
R2(config-if)#
Jan 10 11:08:42.523: %OSPF-5-ADJCHG: Process 1, Nbr 192.168.1.1 on
Serial0/0/0 from LOADING to FULL, Loading Done
R2(config-if)#
Jan 10 11:09:14.487: %OSPF-5-ADJCHG: Process 1, Nbr 192.168.3.1 on
Serial0/0/1 from FULL to DOWN, Neighbor Down: Dead timer expired
```

Notice how the first informational message is saying that the adjacency with R1 has been restored because they are now authenticating each other's routing updates.

However, the second information message is saying that the adjacency with R3 has changed to down. This is because R2 no longer accepts the updates from R3 because they are not authenticated.

e. On R3, create the key chain to be used for authentication.

```
R3(config-router)# key chain SHA-CHAIN
R3(config-keychain)# key 1
R3(config-keychain-key)# key-string secret-1
R3(config-keychain-key)# cryptographic-algorithm hmac-sha-256
R3(config-keychain-key)# exit
```

```
R3(config-keychain)# exit
R3(config)#
```

f. Next, enable authentication on the serial 0/0/1 interface of R3.

```
R3(config)# interface s0/0/1
R3(config-if)# ip ospf authentication key-chain SHA-CHAIN
R3(config-if)#
Jan 10 11:09:20.223: %OSPF-5-ADJCHG: Process 1, Nbr 10.2.2.1 on Serial0/0/1
from LOADING to FULL, Loading Done
R3#
```

g. Verify the routing table of R1.

```
R1# show ip route ospf | begin Gateway
Gateway of last resort is not set

      10.0.0.0/8 is variably subnetted, 3 subnets, 2 masks
O        10.2.2.0/30 [110/128] via 10.1.1.2, 00:05:23, Serial0/0/0
      192.168.3.0/32 is subnetted, 1 subnets
O        192.168.3.1 [110/129] via 10.1.1.2, 00:04:23, Serial0/0/0
R1#
```

h. Verify the S0/0/0 OSPF interface configuration of R1.

```
R1# show ip ospf interface s0/0/0 | section Crypto
  Cryptographic authentication enabled
    Sending SA: Key 1, Algorithm HMAC-SHA-256 - key chain SHA-CHAIN
R1#
```

i. From the R1 router, run the following Tcl script to verify connectivity.

```
foreach address {
192.168.1.1
10.1.1.1
10.1.1.2
10.2.2.1
10.2.2.2
192.168.3.1
} { ping $address }

R1(tcl)#foreach address {
+>(tcl)#192.168.1.1
+>(tcl)#10.1.1.1
+>(tcl)#10.1.1.2
+>(tcl)#10.2.2.1
+>(tcl)#10.2.2.2
+>(tcl)#192.168.3.1
+>(tcl)#} { ping $address }
Type escape sequence to abort.
Sending 5, 100-byte ICMP Echos to 192.168.1.1, timeout is 2 seconds:
!!!!!
```

```
Success rate is 100 percent (5/5), round-trip min/avg/max = 1/1/1 ms
Type escape sequence to abort.
Sending 5, 100-byte ICMP Echos to 10.1.1.1, timeout is 2 seconds:
!!!!!
Success rate is 100 percent (5/5), round-trip min/avg/max = 28/28/28 ms
Type escape sequence to abort.
Sending 5, 100-byte ICMP Echos to 10.1.1.2, timeout is 2 seconds:
!!!!!
Success rate is 100 percent (5/5), round-trip min/avg/max = 12/14/16 ms
Type escape sequence to abort.
Sending 5, 100-byte ICMP Echos to 10.2.2.1, timeout is 2 seconds:
!!!!!
Success rate is 100 percent (5/5), round-trip min/avg/max = 12/14/16 ms
Type escape sequence to abort.
Sending 5, 100-byte ICMP Echos to 10.2.2.2, timeout is 2 seconds:
!!!!!
Success rate is 100 percent (5/5), round-trip min/avg/max = 28/28/28 ms
Type escape sequence to abort.
Sending 5, 100-byte ICMP Echos to 192.168.3.1, timeout is 2 seconds:
!!!!!
Success rate is 100 percent (5/5), round-trip min/avg/max = 28/28/28 ms
R1(tcl)#
```

Are the pings now successful?

_____

_____

CISCO™

ciscopress.com: Your Cisco Certification and Networking Learning Resource

Subscribe to the monthly Cisco Press newsletter to be the first to learn about new releases and special promotions.

Visit **ciscopress.com/newsletters**.

While you are visiting, check out the offerings available at your finger tips.

–Free Podcasts from experts:
 · OnNetworking
 · OnCertification
 · OnSecurity

Podcasts

View them at **ciscopress.com/podcasts**.

–Read the latest author **articles** and **sample chapters** at **ciscopress.com/articles**.

–Bookmark the Certification Reference Guide available through our partner site at **informit.com/certguide**.

Connect with Cisco Press authors and editors via Facebook and Twitter, visit **informit.com/socialconnect**.

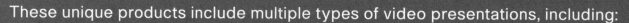

CISCO. **Cisco Press**

NEW Complete Video Courses for CCNP Routing & Switching 300 Series Exams

These unique products include multiple types of video presentations, including:

- Live instructor whiteboarding
- Real-world demonstrations
- Animations of network activity
- Dynamic KeyNote presentations
- Doodle videos
- Hands-on command-line interface (CLI) demonstrations
- Review quizzes

Complete Video Course
CCNP Routing and Switching v2.0
Kevin Wallace
livelessons
9780789754493

CCNP Routing and Switching v2.0 — Complete Video Course Library
Specially priced library including ALL THREE Complete Video Courses: *CCNP Routing and Switching ROUTE 300-101, CCNP Routing and Switching SWITCH 300-115, and CCNP Routing and Switching TSHOOT 300-135.*

Complete Video Course
CCNP Routing and Switching ROUTE 300-101
Kevin Wallace
livelessons
9780789753731

CCNP Routing and Switching ROUTE 300-101 — Complete Video Course
149 VIDEOS with 12+ HOURS of video instruction from best-selling author, expert instructor, and double CCIE **Kevin Wallace** walk you through the full range of topics on the CCNP Routing and Switching ROUTE 300-101 exam, including fundamental routing concepts; IGP routing protocols including RIPng, EIGRP, and OSPF; route distribution and selection; BGP; IPv6 Internet connectivity; router security; and routing protocol authentication.

Complete Video Course
CCNP Routing and Switching SWITCH 300-115
Wayne Lewis
livelessons
9780789754073

CCNP Routing and Switching SWITCH 300-115 — Complete Video Course
10+ HOURS of unique video training walks you through the full range of topics on the CCNP SWITCH 300-115 exam. This complete video course takes you from the design and architecture of switched networks through the key technologies vital to implementing a robust campus network. You will learn, step-by-step, configuration commands for configuring Cisco switches to control and scale complex switched networks.

Complete Video Course
CCNP Routing and Switching TSHOOT 300-135
Elan Beer and Chris Avants
livelessons
9780789754295

CCNP Routing and Switching TSHOOT 300-135 — Complete Video Course
10+ HOURS of unique video instruction from expert instructors and consultants **Elan Beer** and **Chris Avants** walks you through the full range of topics on the CCNP TSHOOT 300-135 exam. This complete video course teaches you the skills you need to plan and perform regular maintenance on complex enterprise routed and switched networks and how to use technology-based practices and a systematic ITIL-compliant approach to perform network troubleshooting commands for configuring Cisco switches to control and scale complex switched networks.

SAVE ON ALL NEW
CCNP R&S 300 Series Products
www.CiscoPress.com/CCNP

CISCO **Cisco Press**

NEW Learning Materials for CCNP Routing & Switching 300 Series Exams

Increase learning, comprehension, and certification readiness with these Cisco Press products!

Complete Exam Preparation

Late Stage Preparation and Reference

Official Certification Guides

Each Official Cert Guide includes a test preparation routine proven to help you pass the exams, two practice tests with thorough exam topic reviews, hundreds of questions, a study plan template, unique review exercises like mind maps and memory tables, and much more.

Official Certification Guide Premium Editions

Digital-only products combining an Official Cert Guide eBook with additional exams in the Pearson IT Certification Practice Test engine.

Complete Video Courses

Real-world demonstrations, animations, configuration walkthroughs, whiteboard instruction, dynamic presentations, and live instruction bring Cisco CCNP ROUTE, SWITCH, and TSHOOT exam topics to life.

Foundation Learning Guides

Provide early and comprehensive foundation learning for the new CCNP exams. These revisions to the popular Authorized Self-Study Guide format are fully updated to include complete coverage.

Quick References

As a final preparation tool, these provide you with detailed, graphical-based information, highlighting only the key topics on the latest CCNP exams in cram-style format.

Cert Flash Cards Online

This online exam preparation tool consists of a custom flash card application loaded with 300 questions that test your skills and enhance retention of exam topics.

Portable Command Guide

Summarizes all CCNP certification-level Cisco IOS Software commands, keywords, command arguments, and associated prompts.

SAVE ON ALL NEW
CCNP R&S 300 Series Products

Plus **FREE SHIPPING** in the U.S. at **www.CiscoPress.com/CCNP**

PEARSON

ALWAYS LEARNING

PEARSON IT CERTIFICATION

Browse by Exams ▼   Browse by Technology ▼   Browse by Format   Explore ▼   I'm New Here – Help!

Store   Forums   Safari Books Online

Pearson IT Certification
THE LEADER IN IT CERTIFICATION LEARNING TOOLS

Visit **pearsonITcertification.com** today to find:

- IT CERTIFICATION EXAM information and guidance for

Pearson is the official publisher of Cisco Press, IBM Press, VMware Press and is a Platinum CompTIA Publishing Partner— CompTIA's highest partnership accreditation

- EXAM TIPS AND TRICKS from Pearson IT Certification's expert authors and industry experts, such as

  - *Mark Edward Soper* – CompTIA
  - *David Prowse* – CompTIA
  - *Wendell Odom* – Cisco
  - *Kevin Wallace* – Cisco and CompTIA
  - *Shon Harris* – Security
  - *Thomas Erl* – SOACP

- SPECIAL OFFERS – pearsonITcertification.com/promotions

- REGISTER your Pearson IT Certification products to access additional online material and receive a coupon to be used on your next purchase

Articles & Chapters

Blogs

Books

Cert Flash Cards Online

eBooks

Mobile Apps

Newsletters

Podcasts

Question of the Day

Rough Cuts

Short Cuts

Software Downloads

Videos

CONNECT WITH PEARSON IT CERTIFICATION

Be sure to create an account on **pearsonITcertification.com** and receive members-only offers and benefits